Ma, I've Got Meself Locked Up in the Mad House

Also by Martha Long

Ma, He Sold Me for a Few Cigarettes
Ma, I'm Getting Meself a New Mammy
Ma, It's a Cold Aul Night an I'm Lookin for a Bed
Ma, Now I'm Goin Up in the World

Ma, I've Got Meself Locked Up in the Mad House

MARTHA LONG

MAINSTREAM
PUBLISHING

EDINBURGH AND LONDON

This edition, 2012

First published in Great Britain in 2011 by
MAINSTREAM PUBLISHING COMPANY
(EDINBURGH) LTD
7 Albany Street
Edinburgh EH1 3UG

ISBN 9781780575414

This book is a work of non-fiction based on the life, experiences and recollections of
the author. In some cases, names of people and places, dates, sequences or the detail
of events have been changed to protect the privacy of others. The author has stated
to the publishers that, except in such respects, not affecting the substantial accuracy
of the work, the contents of this book are true

A catalogue record for this book is available
from the British Library

Printed and bound by
CPI Group (UK) Ltd, Croydon, CR0 4YY

3 5 7 9 10 8 6 4 2

ACKNOWLEDGEMENTS

To the memory of my brother, who died tragically.

Oh! If only you were here now, there are so many things I would like to share with you, but all I can do now is remember you.

You were the quiet, shy one. The gentle one. You were content to stand in the shadows and let others take the limelight. But it was you who took centre stage, when devilment ended in trouble!

When you were little, they called you 'The Lamp', with your halo of gold-red hair. It couldn't be missed, as it gloriously stood out among the crowd.

'Yeah! It was him! "The Lamp" tha got us caught! Wit tha bleedin roarin head a hair of his!'

You would stand thinking about this, then your little face would light up, getting a fit of the giggles. It amused you, seeing them act so tragically.

Oh! But you were deep! When you were only little, I once asked you, 'Why do you never say much?'

You said, 'Cos I like hearin people talkin. How can ye listen if ye talk?'

You were seven years old, then our fate took us apart. You were a man of twenty-eight when we spoke again.

I see the exquisite tenderness in your eyes, as you proudly showed me your new baby daughter, cradled so lovingly in the palm of your open hands. I see the compassion in your eyes as you dip into your pockets to help out a poor unfortunate down on his luck. I see an ocean of pain and despair swimming in those velvet blue eyes as you look at me with unshed tears.

I tried to reach across the chasm, and pull you back from that despair, but it was too late. I was not there when you plunged out into the great unknown, heading away from this world, making for eternity.

Why? Why did the birds still sing and the world keep turning, when you, my little brother, had left us for ever?

You were only twenty-eight.

This world is a poorer place without you. I will not forget you. My last thoughts are of you, at night, when I whisper, 'Sleep in peace, little brother, sleep in peace.'

To Bill, my friend; indeed he is! He is so very caring. But a word of caution, dear reader. I am only the author of this book, so don't come looking to me for your money back. He is the publisher.

To Ailsa, my long-suffering editor. What a master! Only a genius such as her could make sense of someone who writes like me!

AUTHOR'S NOTE

Dear readers,

I suspect some of you may be confused why this book does not immediately pick up and continue the journey into the future. The answer is, quite honestly, I was now a young adult. Those years of my life became too personal and private. So, what I have done here is to pick up once again during a very dark time in my life. From then on, I must go back, searching the long and dark lonely roads of my past, trying to find where I lost my way.

Believe me, I am both privileged and warmed to know you may take that journey with me.

My very best wishes to you.

Martha Long

I

I rattled into the kitchen, feeling like a nomad in search of leafy bushes. My eyes peeled around, searching, then stopped, lighting on the kettle. Tea! My heart lurched with excitement. Have a cup of tea! I reached out to fill it.

No! Ye're not getting any. No tea for you! Ye gave that up.

My heart dropped down into my thick woolly socks. I turned around, digging my hands deeper into the pockets of my red, romper-suit dressing gown. It was my day and evening wear, and, of course, I sleep in it. It was buttoned up to my neck. I bought it for a bargain in Dunnes Stores. Well, the sale sign said it was a bargain, so I bought it, believing them. Gobshite! I rambled down the road and discovered it sitting in another shop at half the price. Bleedin robbers! I'm not going back there again. Anyway, with my thermal granny nightdress underneath, I'm always ready for bed.

I gave a big sigh, snorting air out through my nose, and my chest complained, wheezing like bagpipes. Aah! I'm smoking too many cigarettes.

Good idea, have a smoke. Oh, yes! I felt myself lifting. Happiness is in a packet of roll-ups, I thought, reaching for the packet.

No! Forget it. Ye're not having a smoke!

Jesus! What then? Something to eat? I asked meself timidly. Yeah! Toast and a boiled egg. Lovely. I cheered up immediately.

No! You gave that up, too. It was gradual, mind! Very gradual, like everything else you have done to yourself. But no! You have stopped eating. Another big sigh.

I wandered out to the hall and into the dining room, feeling like a displaced person. My body is trapped in the wrong mind. It's dying for pleasure. But the mind is brutally perverse, utterly determined to stick with the mission of giving myself a slow and painful death. I stood in the middle of the grey, cold, lifeless room. Everything is spic and span. The fire is set, ready for lighting. I stared at it for a minute. No! I couldn't be bothered lighting that. It would most definitely be too much trouble. I would only have to clean it out in the morning. So bloody freeze yourself.

I stood very still, listening to the emptiness of the room. There's no life in it; no one lives here. The greyness of the evening, now turning even as I watch, is creeping into the darkness of the February night. A sudden gust of wind blew up, tearing and keening through the trees, shaking them in a fury. It looks like a storm is blowing up, I thought, staring out into the garden. I should do something . . . put on the light.

My eyes settled on the television in the corner. I could switch that on . . . but I made no move. Just continued to stare at the little grey box sitting in the corner. It's been a long time since that came to life. When is this going to end? I felt as empty as the house; there was nothing left I could punish myself with. I had deprived myself of all pleasure, even the basics for survival. This was indeed a slow death I was giving myself.

The doorbell rang. Jaysus! Who could that be? I leapt with excitement. I hadn't spoken to anyone in a long time. They all got fed up with me, because I wouldn't accept their invites to do anything or go anywhere. I even stopped inviting friends here for dinner. So the passage of time has dimmed their memory of me. Now I'm forgotten. I could call myself Martha Who? Hmm, I really am perverse.

I dashed to open the front door. It could be Jack the Ripper for all I care. I'm not choosy; I'd yank him off his feet and drag him in. Yeah! I'm desperate. When you're as desperate as me, anything is better than talking to yourself.

I whipped the door open. Sister Eleanor!

'Ah, hello, Martha. How are you, pet?' she crooned, flying in the door and reaching out to give me a tight hug.

I held on for dear life. She's just what the doctor ordered, I thought, grabbing her by the arm and rushing her into the sitting room. I was delirious with excitement, wanting anything to get rid of the painful, deep loneliness snaking its way around this barren house and coiling itself up through my body, leaving me with a terrible sense of desolation.

'How are you, darling? Oh, I've been meaning to get up to see you. But we've been so busy in the convent,' she said, giving me the mother-of-all-sorrows look. Then she leaned into me, readying herself to pump me with sympathy, empathy and any amount of understanding a body could want. I stared, slowly taking in a deep breath. She did the same, then held it, letting her nostrils flare.

'Eh, not too bad,' I rasped. That's all I could get out! I'm still waiting for me voice box to heal after the operation a year ago to remove a rotten and diseased thyroid that was poisoning me.

'Yes, it took us longer than we thought!' the big beefy surgeon informed me. 'It was twice the size of my hands,' he said, holding out his fists in the air. I looked: they were like shovels. 'It was wrapped around everything, completely diffused.

'Your trachea was nearly cut off!' he continued, reminding me of the day I nearly choked on me hamburger. 'Yes,' he said, shaking his head, a faraway look in his eyes, thinking about it. 'Must have been growing for years. I never saw the like of it.'

'So what have you been doing with yourself?' Sister Eleanor breathed at me, making it sound like she was praying.

'What?' I blinked, trying to shake off the mist wafting over my eyes. 'Oh, eh . . .'

I was dying to talk about myself – there's nothing more fascinating – but nothing came out. I was blank. All my thoughts, all the anxieties, everything, just fell into a hole somewhere and a tight lid clamped shut over them. I was left feeling empty, confused. We stared at each other. I wanted to tell her . . . but tell her what?

'Have you eaten? God, Martha! You are skin and bone! You're not feeding yourself!'

I didn't argue with that.

'Look,' she said, rushing over to the fireplace. 'I'll just put a match to this fire. It's freezing in here!' she said, shaking her shoulders, hoping I'd get the message.

'No! Leave it, Sister Eleanor. I don't want it lit!'

I felt suffocated by her fussing, and she was stampeding all over my newly cleaned room. I instantly felt very territorial; she was threatening the order I had imposed. It must remain exactly as I had it. Nothing can be touched, or I will fall into chaos! End up back where I started . . . I don't know! Something dreadful will happen. I feel safe as long as I have order. Yeah, I know where I stand with order.

This is not order! the voice of sanity complained. This is nuts!

Fuck off! the winning perverse, broken-down side of me said.

I started to get agitated. 'Sit down, Sister. Leave everything.'

'But, Martha, you must have heat. Look, let me get you something to eat.'

'No!' I croaked, as loudly as I could wheeze out, sounding like a cat being strangled. 'Leave me alone!' I whined, filling up with despair and a sense of hopelessness.

'What am I going to do? I can't leave you like this!'

I stared into her face, afraid of the chaos she was creating and terrified of seeing her go out the door. She was the only person left in the world I wanted to talk to and trusted.

'Martha,' she started to say slowly, thinking. 'Will you come down to the convent and stay overnight?'

'The children's part?' I asked, ready to give a flat no.

'Well, you would be staying in one of the children's houses. It's empty at the moment; they're all away. But I'll be there, and we could take you to see the doctor in the morning. Will you do that? You really need to see a doctor, pet.'

I hesitated, thinking about it. 'I don't know, Sister Eleanor. What can doctors do? They just fill you full of pills that don't solve anything. The bloody pills just poison you, and they are very addictive. No, I don't like pills, especially tranquillisers. I would be going around like a zombie! No, the only pills I'm taking are the ones I have to take daily, because I got rid of the thyroid, and I'm only taking those because they keep me alive. So that's it. There's no cure, Sister, for what's wrong with me.'

'What is wrong with you, Martha?' she suddenly said, leaning down, staring at me, ready to hear my answer and produce the cure, probably from her big black leather handbag. I wonder what she carries around in that? I know she keeps a bottle of holy water, with the picture of Our Lady of Lourdes on it, and gives you a good sprinkle when she meets you. It's her cure for everything.

'Tell me, Martha!' she said, giving me a poke in the arm.

I looked at her, not knowing what to say.

'I want to know what's wrong with you? Why are you hurting yourself?'

'I wish I knew,' I said, dropping my shoulders and looking around me, seeing only a prison.

We stared at each other, the air heavy with our wants. Her wanting me to see a doctor; me wanting her to wave a magic wand so the world will suddenly be lifted off my shoulders and we can jump up singing like Julie Andrews in *The Sound of Music*. 'The hills are alive, with the sound of music' – Sob, lovely!

The silence dragged on. I felt the hope vanishing down from my chest and out through my belly like greased lightning, leaving only a wisp of warmth. That too evaporated.

'Look, Martha. You can't stay here. Come on, we'll go down to the convent. Things always look better in the morning.' She grabbed my arm and propelled me out the door.

'OK . . . but wait, I need to get dressed,' I said, looking down at me romper-suit dressing gown.

'No! You are fine as you are. Come on, let's go.'

2

We drove in through the gates of the children's house.
'Right! Now, Martha. We're here!'

I hesitated, not wanting to move. The security light beamed on, showing the convent across the fields. I shuddered, remembering the old days when I was locked up here.

But that was the old building. That's now gone and replaced by a purpose-built, state-of-the-art modern convent, well away from the homes for the children.

What the hell am I doing here? Jesus! I left this place behind years ago. I'm getting out of here! I reached for the door handle, then stopped. She's not going to give me a lift back. She'll start bloody fussing, and I'm not in the mood to argue with her.

The hall door was open, then she was back.

'Come along, Martha, quickly!'

I sat there, unsure what I wanted to do.

'Are you all right?' she asked, bending into the driver's side. 'Ah! Come along now,' she said, rushing around to grab my arm and get me moving, steering me in the direction of the hall door. 'You'll be right as rain after a good night's sleep,' she clucked, banging the door shut behind her and locking it.

She rushed past me, heading for the stairs. I stopped, looking at the children's boots and bags and coats hanging in the hall. I was feeling uneasy, like I'd trapped myself. The clock was turning backwards. It should be going forward.

'Ah, Martha! For God's sake! Will you come on out of that and go to bed like a good girl.'

A what? Jesus Christ! Now she's treating me like one of the children. I'm a grown woman in my thirties with a whole life behind me. But now I've put myself in her hands, and I feel more helpless than I did as a child.

I dragged myself up the stairs and followed her along the passage.

'In here, Martha! This is the staff bedroom.' She whipped down the bedcovers. 'Now! In you get,' she said, giving the pillows a hearty thump. 'Now goodnight, God bless. Sleep well,' and she was gone, out the door, leaving a draught behind her.

The room was still echoing, with dust flying and floorboards creaking as it tried to settle itself after a whirlwind had hit it.

Jaysus! I thought. That woman meets herself coming backwards, she moves so fast! I sniffed, staring at the door rocking on its hinges after she slammed it shut.

I sat up on the bed, propping the pillows against the headboard, and lay back, stretching out my legs. I suddenly felt the weariness and futility of hanging on like a pain of hot then cold air sweeping down from my chest and flying all around my body, then settling like a dead weight, paralysing me. Jesus! What happened to me? Why am I like this? Your woman is fussing around me like I'm a helpless child. And that's what you're letting her do! When did this start? How?

I closed my eyes, trying to think. Images flew across my brain.

I stopped. The doctor! That gobshite I went to see about the pain I'm always in. It has been crippling me for years. No one could explain it. But he could. 'Left Limb Syndrome!' he screeched to his audience of reluctant onlookers. Doctors he had dragged away from the other rooms in the clinic, trying to mind their own business and get on and see to the unfortunate patients waiting stoically for their turn.

'Look at this!' and he grabbed my left arm, squeezing the artery.

The whole side of my face, right down my body, went blue, then black. Right down to my foot. I couldn't breathe! It felt like a ton weight on my chest, and the pain was unbearable.

They stared, with one foot out the door, wanting to get back to work.

'Look at that!' he roared maniacally, watching my face turn black, and me gasping to get a breath. He let go and raced to the phone. The others flew out the door, making their escape.

'I'm convinced I've discovered a new condition! We'll be in the medical books!' he puffed, getting himself out of breath with all his excitement. 'Oh, yes!' he told himself, pointing his finger at the air. 'But first things first! I must inform someone,' he gasped, spluttering at me as he tore himself over to grab up the phone.

'Hello! Yes, I'm hanging on!' he shouted, bending himself in two, rocking backwards and forwards as he leaned his head into the phone.

Then he straightened himself, stretching his neck to the ceiling, giving out a big snort of impatience. 'Stupid girl,' he muttered, drumming his fingers on the desk, nearly crying with the impatience on him. 'Come on! Come on!' he moaned, snapping his teeth together. Then he discovered something interesting – his tongue – and started sucking like mad, trying to lick the tip of his nose. He got fed up and whipped himself around, staring at me. Suddenly his eyes lit up, as if he just remembered something interesting.

'I have three other patients with the same condition!' he babbled, seeing me still trying to get my shoes on and recover from near death.

'How are they doing?' I gasped, still fighting to get a breath.

'Oh! One is in a wheelchair, the other one is doing fine. Now! The third one?' He thought about this, scratching his head. 'I don't know. She hasn't come back.'

I hobbled out the door.

'Wait! Where are you going?' he shouted. 'Come back! No, wait! I'm not finished with you yet!'

I heard the phone dropping as he came tearing out after me. I hurried off, hearing his heels hammering down the passage, then felt his hot breath down me neck as he reached out to grab me.

Fuck! Help! This aul fella is a raving lunatic. I gasped as he grabbed hold of my left arm, cutting off the circulation. It was making it hard for me to breathe. 'Let go!' I roared, dragging meself away from him.

'You can't leave now!' he shrieked. 'We've only just started!'

'What?' I said, not able to take anything in, me brain was all muddled. Jesus! I don't know where I am. This pain is killing me. Me heart feels like a sledgehammer crushing me chest, and the pain is twisting itself around my body, crippling me muscles. That's because of all his fucking mauling!

I glared at him, snorting air in and out with the rage.

'Where do you think you are going?' he barked, pinning me to the spot with his huge bloodshot eyes. I couldn't see much of them.

His glasses were too thick. I stared closer, seeing his bull's eyes were nearly boring holes in me.

'That's it! I'm getting out of here!' I roared. It came out in a rasp. 'Listen! Who the hell do you think you are? Out of my way!' I pushed past him.

'No! Wait!' He rushed after me, putting his hand on my arm again.

'Let go!' I growled, gritting me teeth and slapping his hand away.

'You have "Left Limb Syndrome!"' he boomed. 'It could CRIPPLE you without my intervention!' He beamed at this thought, rubbing his hands together.

'Oh!' I said, feeling the rage seep outa me and me stomach fill with heat as hope flared up through me chest.

'Can you cure me?' I asked hopefully. 'Take away the pain?' I asked quietly, looking into his massive goitre eyes.

'Hmm,' he said, thinking about this. Letting his mind wander. I waited, holding me breath. Then it looked to me like he was only thinking about himself. Getting the picture of himself being famous in the medical world.

There will be wonderful write-ups about myself in The Lancet. *There will be accolades, applause. I will have invitations to tour across the world, giving lectures! Money no object. Women! They will throw themselves at my feet.*

'Well?' I said, getting impatient to hear the news. 'Can you help me?'

He blinked, then settled his eyeballs on me. 'Well, eh, nooo,' he said slowly, beginning to look very shifty. 'There is no cure. It's not even in the textbooks. It would be trial and error. I would have to experiment with various drugs,' he said, looking at me, seeing me shaking my head with disappointment.

His head shook with me, agreeing. Then his face creased with sudden worry. He could see everything was fast going down the swanney, seeing another 'Left Limb Syndrome' vanish from his clutches.

'Let's go back to my clinic,' he said, wringing his hands. Then his head flew back to the phone. It was sitting on the desk with a voice shouting, 'Hello? Hello? Anyone there?'

'Someone on the phone,' I said, throwing me head over at it.

He flew to the phone, snatching it up, saying, 'Oh yes! Sorry! This is . . .'

Then it hit me. 'Drugs!' I squeaked. 'You want to fill me full of drugs!' The rage hit me again. The cheek! 'How dare you? Get stuffed! Find another guinea pig,' I rasped, making me way out the door again.

'No! No, wait!' he choked, dropping the phone to make another go after me. 'You could end up in a wheelchair without treatment!' he gasped, landing himself right in front of me.

I watched as he stretched his arms, holding them rigid down by his side. Only letting the fingers curl like mad.

'Nutter!' I muttered to meself, then walked around him, making me escape, then hurrying, desperate to make me way out of the hospital.

So! That's that then. There's no cure for whatever is causing this godforsaken never-ending pain. Right! But that's the last time I ever expose myself to them fool doctors. They just mess me around with no idea of what they are doing. I will just have to find a way of living with it. Christ! What a madman! I seem to spend my life attracting madness. Bloody hell! Am I glad just to be out of there!

3

I opened my eyes slowly, staring out the window, seeing the trees
shaking their branches, fighting to stay upright, determined not
to be beaten by a howling wind. They had stood their ground for
centuries, and no February storm was going to get the better of them.
No. The gobshite yelling I might end up in a wheelchair didn't bother
me. What would he know?

The heavy weight sitting inside me sank deeper into me, and I
felt cold, numb. I stared at my hands sitting in my lap, waiting. For
what? Morning to come, then the day to pass, and another night to
get through without even the pleasure of a bit of sleep. I can't bloody
sleep! I just doze fitfully.

I closed my eyes, and the images started flying across my brain
again. Months! But it could only be yesterday. It is so painfully etched
in my mind, it haunts me day and night. I am still there, locked in
that time. Harry! My poor Harry. Is this what you felt, Harry?

I had been happily sitting down to a pot of tea and a smoke. Feeling
all delighted with myself to get the pile of ironing out of the way. You
would have thought I was ironing for the Salvation Army, there was
so much of it! Sheets, pillowcases and nearly every stitch of clothes
in the house. I had let it all pile up. Jaysus, I hate ironing!

Then the phone rang. I hope that's Charlie. Yeah, it probably is
Charlie. My poor little long-suffering brother. He'll be ringing now
to give me fifteen verses of the 'Tinker's Litany'. Ah! Poor thing. He
called earlier as usual. But I wouldn't let him cook himself something
to eat. Jaysus! He messes up me kitchen! 'Wait, love,' I'd said. 'Leave it
to me. I will cook you something nice when I've finished this ironing.'

'Ah, Jaysus, no, Martha! I'm starvin wit the hunger!' he gasped, staring at me with the big blue eyes lifting outa his head.

'No, Charlie!' I was ruthless, determined to carry on with my 'Little Susie Homemaker' chores.

'But I brought me own stuff, Martha!' he snorted, flinging open his palm, showing me the two little Oxo cubes sitting snugly in the palm of his hand. 'All I need now wit these is a bit a bread,' he puffed.

I stared at them. 'No! We don't need them. I have a lovely bit of fish I got in Moore Street today. We can fry that with a lovely fluffy omelette.' I was planning something else for our dinner.

'Ah, come on outa tha, Martha! Ye're goin te kill me! I'm droppin outa me standin, Martha. Jaysus! I don't know what's come over you. Ye never used te be like this, Martha,' he whispered, looking very worried. Then he whipped his head around, letting his eyes bulge at the amount of stuff all waiting for my ministrations with the iron.

I was stone deaf to his moans, pleas, nearly crying, about, 'I'm droppin dead wit the hunger.'

'No!' I ploughed on, determined to get the ironing done.

So that was that. Charlie left in a sulk. Not understanding where the new brutal Martha came from. Not since Sarah, my daughter, left home, leaving me with one arm longer than the other. Not knowing what hit me! I had nothing to mother. Now I put all my mothering and nurturing into the house. Except now it's gone too far. I'm now gone a little bit funny. Sort of peculiar! Yeah. No one can upset the cushions. You can't lean against them! Oh no! Or I'll rush to grab them up, giving them a smack to get the stuffing fluffed up again. Or even walk on me fireside rug. Definitely not! It ruins the pile! Jaysus! No wonder poor Charlie is the only one left willing to put up with me madness!

I picked up the phone.

'Hello, Martha! Is tha you, Martha?'

My antenna went up. I was instantly on alert. 'Is that you, Dinah?'

'Yeah! It is me, Martha.'

Ah, Jaysus! What do they want now? It's a pity that Charlie fella gave the ma me phone number. Or did I give it to her in one of me magnanimous moods? It's the only way she has of contacting me, and that's under strict instructions. For emergencies only, please. Otherwise the ma would eat me alive with her wants! Jaysus, she's insatiable. She would have the life sucked outa me and the home from over me head. Not to mention run ragged trying to dig her outa the latest 'Big Troubles'. No, she knows very little about me, certainly not to come to where I live. Oh no. My life is my own. I've had enough to do, paddling up the creek without a paddle!

So I dash over to their world, pick them up, dust them down, then rush back to me own bright and airy, very civilised world. Well, it's peaceful now. Too peaceful! Pity poor Charlie and me had that row. We could have been sitting here having a lovely dinner. I was going to forget the fish and omelette, and cook instead his favourite – 'Martha's Pie'! Invented it meself. A mixture between shepherd's pie and the Greek moussaka one! I put thick white sauce in mine, with loads of grated cheese. Lovely! Then we could have sat and talked and laughed ourselves stupid, remembering who it was that caused that particular trouble as we wandered back down through all the days of our life together. We are very close. Charlie has always depended on me. 'Now these days I need him,' I sighed.

Tut! That's a pity. Now I'm stuck with me own company and only the silence to listen to, or maybe Bonzo me dog might come rambling home tonight. He better! Or next time he decides to come home from his gallivanting – with his wandering the streets from one day till the next. Well! That fella won't see the light of day outside this door for at least a week! Yes, that should put a stop to his gallop!

Jaysus! I never get anything right! But the less I see of me ma, the better for me. I hear, though, what's going on through Charlie. He meets some of them around the town and gets the news from them. No! We live lives apart. I've now become terribly respectable. You'd nearly need an appointment to see me! I live in the middle of others who think they are terribly respectable too.

We were all doing grand until they built that bloody awful fancy estate up the road. Some gobshite architect came rolling back from America with the plans under his arm. We never saw the like of it! Huge houses on the outside, with open gardens. But you have to go in sideways to get into the house. They're dog boxes! And the price of them! We said they would never sell. Sure, who'd have that kind of money?

But they did. To a shower of yuppies! They tear around in dark sunglasses in the pitch-black evenings. I see them. They pass my window, humped over the steering wheel, leaning themselves out through the windscreens, trying to see where they're going. Blind as bats they are. But not a bother on them as they sit up there in their new Jags and show-off Mercedes, waving at us. The cheek!

We stare at them, saying, 'Ah! They're very vulgar. No class at all.' 'Thank God they are well away from us!' we sniff. But we're really only jealous because we don't have Mercedes and fur coats like them. None of us can figure out where they got the money. Then we lift ourselves with the comforting thought, Ah, sure, our houses are better than theirs! We have lovely, cosy old family houses.

'The state of that awful, modern American-looking rubbish! It actually brings down the tone of our quiet, select neighbourhood!' my old dear of a neighbour whispered to me.

'Agreed!' I sniffed, shaking me head in disgust. 'Shocking! Shocking the lack of taste of these people,' I snorted.

Everyone standing around agreed with me. We all shook our heads, agreeing with each other, then wandered off to mind our own business, feeling self-satisfied, knowing we have good taste and breeding!

Mind you! But the real truth is, come to think about it, our bleedin houses are 'Jerry Built'! Yeah. They were knocked up just as the war ended. I only realised that when I tried to put up wallpaper and it kept falling down, taking the fingernail, inch-thick plaster with it. The bloody walls are so thin I'm expecting the neighbours any day now to put their hands through the walls and dip into my gravy!

Course I don't admit that. No! It looks very classy from the outside. Neighbours rush in, wanting to know where I bought me 'French doors' from. That's what I call them. They cover in the porch. Now they've all copied me! The road is a line of French doors. So now I have an apple tree growing right in my front garden. I'm to be seen picking them off the tree come September, telling the jealous, sour-faced neighbours, 'They're organic, you know! It's simply marvellous having one's own orchard!' They don't have one. I robbed mine, when it was newly planted, from the convent grounds across the road.

Anyway! The yuppies go mad trying to outdo each other. The latest is the facelifts. They got that idea from watching *Dallas*. Mind you, they need it! Because of all the worrying about bank drafts and loans, and that sort of thing. You'd get a pain in yer face listening to them.

'Darling!' they say, purring at each other. Bloody awful people. 'Bank manager's sooo boring, my dear. Always going on about sorting out one's finances! Really! I ask you!' they breathe at each other, squinting behind the dark glasses to see if the newly dyed blonde clone of themselves has her black roots showing.

That's what I had to listen to down at the private school my daughter Sarah attended. Now there's a financial crash and the facelifts are drooping. They can't give their houses away! No one wants a big house. They're too expensive to run. And it's the same with the big cars. Everyone is standing at the bus stop. I'm enjoying myself no end, driving slowly past them standing at the bus stop. Watching the miserable faces staring gloomily after me. Seeing the sopping umbrellas dripping down the backs of their neck. They're left waiting for a bus that's never going to come. It's broken down! CIE can't afford new ones, not with the depression. It fills me to the brim with emotion. I sigh all the way into town, feeling nice and cosy. I keep the heater going full blast and snort in me contentment, listening to Bach playing on the radio. It's soothing me into a false sense of security, of course.

I worry now all the time about money. Not having enough to pay the bills. One of these days I'm going to be dragging me belly around with the hunger. I worry about what's going to be on the dinner menu. Soon, I'll be shovelling inta bread an dripping. What with the way the recession is digging even deeper!

They don't call it that any more. It's now a world depression. Money is becoming a rarity. The EEC have huge mountains of food. All taken off the farmers to give them a few bob. Our government get their hands on the stuff and give it out to us. One year it can be the butter mountain. Then we're all living on good butter for a while. The next year it might be cans of meat. Some people open the can and sniff at it suspiciously, saying it reminds them of the stuff their grandads used to get in the trenches in the First World War – 'Bully Beef'! It might still be the same stuff, so they won't eat it. Or then again, another time we might even get the best of rump steak. Some people manage to get their hands on so much of it they even sell it to the rest of us! Them with the few bob.

Very few people have cars now. The few who do only have them because they're handy with fixing them up. It's mostly clapped-out bangers, all held together with bits of other junked cars. Rust buckets that gave up staggering around the roads.

We have to drive with our headlights on because we can't see through the black fumes coming outa the exhausts and the engines! The latest hint from the government is we should turn off our engines when waiting at the traffic lights. Saves petrol! I mostly walk and only take 'Daisy' out for emergencies.

At this rate of going . . .

'Hello! Hello! Are ye gone, Martha?!'

'What! Oh, sorry, Dinah. No! No, I'm listening. Go on!' Jaysus! My mind is always bloody wandering these days.

'Martha, I'm at the hospital! They phoned me te come in! Me ma is here. It's Harry! He's dead, Martha!'

'Whadyemean "dead"?'

'He is, Martha! He threw himself offa the top of the balcony!'

Silence. I'm trying to take this in.

'Did ye hear me, Martha?'

'Where are you, Dinah?'

'Over at the new hospital. Are ye comin in now?'

'I'm on my way!'

'Hurry, Martha! Me ma is in an awful state! An Gerry went mad! They asked him te identify Harry, cos me ma couldn't look at Harry, an Gerry kept shakin Harry, screamin at him te wake up. Come in, Martha! I'm on me own. I don't know wha te do!'

'Take it easy, Dinah love. I'm on me way.'

I dropped the phone and ran to get my car keys. No! No! Harry! Why didn't you wait? Why couldn't you have phoned me? I tore through the hall, grabbing coat, keys, tobacco and papers. Jesus! I need a smoke! Can't. Just keep going!

I slammed out the front door and raced for the car, me little Fiat 127. I reversed out of the garage by ear, stopped by the hedge opposite. It was put up to protect the wall and stop people climbing it and getting demolished. Right, Daisy! Move!

4

I tore up through the gears and was already locking the steering to the right before I hit the turn, taking it on two wheels. Gerry! Left to identify poor Harry? Jesus Christ! What's going on? Poor Gerry is retarded! He has the mind of a child. Oh, sweet divine Jesus! The poor kid! He was born after I was sent away to the convent. He is the youngest, and they never cut the umbilical cord. He and the ma are still attached.

The lights turned to amber. I hesitated for a split second – put the foot down or . . .? Right! Go!

I gunned across the road just as the lights turned red, a car caught in my peripheral vision coasting to a slow-down. He suddenly gets the green light. His engine gunned up, and the driver came barrelling across me, straight from the right.

Jesus! Help! I clamped my feet down on the brake and the clutch simultaneously, tearing down through the gears, landing in first. Then nursed the steering to the left, locking hard again to the right, managing to avoid the footpath. Then spun the wheel furiously, straightening up again.

I could see the terror in the whites of the other driver's eyes as he came thundering towards me. He, too, suddenly woke up to the fact we are not sitting at home in armchairs. I could almost hear his prayer as he screamed.

Help, Mammy. Help! We're going to get killed. No, no, no! Please God! I prayed as our eyes locked.

He wrestled the steering wheel, tearing up onto the footpath, barely missing the high granite wall bordering someone's property. I continued to slide on the black inky road shining with oily rain. My heart sat in my mouth as the road slid from under me. I gripped the steering wheel, holding on for me life. Hoping and praying a car wouldn't come out of the left turn.

The brakes screamed in agony. Smoke belched into the car, filling my nostrils through the open window. Then there was silence. My heart belted out a tango. I slowly released the grim death lock on the steering wheel, peeling my hands off, seeing my knuckles are snow-white.

I looked back slowly. The other driver was still slumped over the steering wheel. I hesitated, about to get out on me shaking legs and see if he was OK. It was then he lifted his head, looking in my direction. He's OK! Oh, thank God! But he looks badly shocked.

I drove on. Oh, Jesus! Let that be a lesson. Cars are lethal weapons, and they need to be treated with respect.

Then it hit me like a punch to the stomach. Me head saw stars. Harry is dead? Really dead? Gone? But he can't be! I felt suddenly like I was falling. I don't want to see that. No! I can't face any more! Too much has been happening to me, I can't even look after myself right now. No! I don't want to go back down that road. Jackser? Christ, no! And the ma? Fucking never! They will drag me right back. Wanting me to get involved in their problems, ringing me in the middle of the night. Particularly the girls. 'Wha did ye mean it's one a clock in the mornin? We only rang ye te say hello!' Then Charlie! When he's drunk, he'll ring at bloody four o'clock in the morning! Crying, 'I'm feelin very depressed, Martha! I'm goin te kill meself.' Jaysus! Then the ma! 'Listen, Martha. Cough. Can ye help me?'

NO! I don't believe a word of this. There's no such thing as Harry being dead!

I spent most of my early life helping them, and all through my adult life. But they won't help themselves, and now I can hardly look after myself with all that's been happening. But I've no one to turn to. So I get on with it like everyone else and paddle my own bloody canoe. I've tried to put distance between me and them. They only turn against me in the end anyway.

Oh, Jesus, Jesus! Why do these two bastards keep coming back to haunt my life? I sat staring down the road, seeing Jackser's face menacing over me. A giant, ready at the drop of a hat to beat me to death! I could feel the dirty black grease on the stinking floorboards as I lay crouched, my hands out in front of my face, jerking with every twitch he made. Getting ready to protect whatever part of my little body . . .

Stop! That's enough! Open your eyes. It's over! Hundreds of years ago, Martha. I put me hands on me forehead. Oh, dear God, what is happening to me lately? I'm disappearing fast down the plughole. NO! Stop! Get a grip, Martha.

I lifted my head up slowly from my arms, sitting up straight and letting air out through my nose, then inhaled deeply and slowly. He's only a little old man now. Pathetic! I could fuck him under the wheels of my car if it came down to it. But that will never happen. He would have to have a death wish if he even looked crooked at me! No, the problem is I don't want to resurrect old memories left dead and buried. I'm not able for anything or anyone these days. My health needs looking after.

On the other hand. If poor Harry really does need your help, you can't turn your back on him. No! Not for a minute do I believe he is dead. Bleedin drama merchants! No! But you can't turn your back on him. I never could, it's not in me nature. Right! At least go over to the hospital and see what's really going on. It may only be the usual 'Abbey Acting'. Fuck! The drama outa that lot! 'Martha! Ye have te come over quick! It's me ma! She's after takin a heart attack! Hurry!' I break the sound barrier getting there only to see the ma sitting up, large as life, with not a bother on her.

'MA! What's going on? They said ye were havin a heart attack!' I snort, waving me hand at the lot of them all sitting around drinking tea. 'I thought ye were at bleedin death's door, Ma!'

'Wha?' she says, looking at me, then looking at them for hints on what to do next. 'Well, eh! Oh, Jesus! I've a pain in me chest! I'm not well, Martha!'

'But ye were OK a minute ago, Ma. When I walked through that door there!'

'Yeah, well, ye see, cough! It's the pain. It does come an go. But I'm all right at the minute. Eh, cough! I was wonderin, Martha, if ye could lend us a couple a bob?'

Hmm, yeah. Always making a fool outa me. Still, you never know. Supposing it's true?

It's not! I shook me head. But go anyway. Right, you silly cow! Drive slowly this time. Take it easy.

I drove on, gently putting the car into fourth gear, letting it coast at thirty miles an hour. I'm definitely very much chastised. I took in a deep breath, feeling very glad to be still in one piece. Thank God the other fellow came to no harm either!

I looked up at the clock perched on top of the library. Twenty past eleven. It's late! There's not even a soul to be seen walking through the village; everything is locked up. I suppose everyone is getting an early night after wasting themselves on the weekend. Monday night. Yeah, start of another week ahead, with everyone facing into another day's grind. That's for the lucky ones – those that still have the jobs. They're mostly the civil servants. A lot of the shops are lying empty now. There's no money about. So no one is doing any business. Nowadays, the shops won't even let you away with a penny if you are short.

'That's the equivalent of three whole old pennies! Come back when ye have the right money!' they screech, snatching back the packet of Lyons tea.

But I'm a lot luckier than most, so I'm not going to complain. There's young ones with law degrees and medical degrees all down queuing at the dole office, hoping for a start. They end up sitting for days outside the American Embassy, praying for one of the Donnelly visas.

I headed into town, passing very few cars as I drove down O'Connell Street. A few taxi drivers stood huddled together outside the Carlton Cinema. They threw the odd word to each other, blowing on their hands and stamping their feet, trying to keep out the cold, damp night air. Then they shot their heads up and down the street, hopeful of getting a few stragglers coming out of the pubs. The ones, anyway, with a few quid still left in their pockets, getting ready to take a taxi home. Very few people do that. I watched as they dropped their shoulders and glanced back to each other, carrying on their inane conversation. I could see the look of disgust and disappointment. It was the thought at losing all hope of making a few bob tonight.

5

Right! Here we are. I turned the car in through the entrance and straight into the car park, manoeuvring around broken glass, rubble and an old bicycle wheel. I headed over to a high wall with a bit of light thrown in from the avenue. Jesus! The state of the place. It looks like a bombsite!

I switched off the engine and reached for a smoke, taking my time rolling the tobacco. Then I stuck it in my mouth and lit up, taking a deep drag into my lungs. They immediately started protesting, and I spluttered, coughed and wheezed, trying to get a breath. These things are going to kill me.

Enough! Get yourself moving. You've got to face it. Come on! You know it's not too bad.

I heaved myself out of the car, slamming the door shut behind me, locking it. Then sucked greedily on the cigarette as I dragged myself forward, moving out of the darkness. I steadily got closer, moving in to the bright lights of the hospital entrance. I stopped to look up at the neon light flashing over the hospital entrance: 'Casualty'. Me heart gave a kick. I took in a deep breath and threw down the cigarette, crushing it under me shoe. Then I took in another deep breath, feeling the cold night air sting my chest.

For Jesus' sake, get going!

I pushed the door in and immediately saw the Accident & Emergency sign and headed straight for it. 'Excuse me,' I said, moving towards a nurse writing at a desk.

She ignored me and continued writing.

'I'm looking for my brother, Harry,' I said, shaking her arm. 'I was told he was taken in here.' I could see cubicles all around me, and I wondered which one he was in. 'Can you show me where he is, please?' I said, looking at her and ready to move off and look for myself. 'I need to see him! Where's the ma?' I looked around the room, but there was no sign of any of them.

'Who are you?' the nurse asked, peering at me closely.

'Martha Long. I'm his sister. His big sister. Where is he?' My eyes flew around the room.

'Oh! Would you please come with me,' she said, heading off to a room.

I followed quickly behind, anxious to see Harry. Maybe it was a mistake. He's OK after all. He's probably badly injured, but he'll recover. That lot panic over nothing. My heart was going like the clappers as I pushed in behind the nurse.

The room was empty. I looked around. There's nobody here! It's just a waiting room. 'Where's my mother? And Dinah? And where's Gerry?' I stared at the nurse, wondering what is going on. Knowing, but not wanting to hear.

Her mouth opened. I stared, then she closed it again and gave a little cough in the back of her throat. Her eyes flicked away from me and trailed the ground, settling on a seat, and she slowly lowered herself down onto it, indicating with her arm that I should do the same. 'Sit down for a minute,' she said.

I did as she asked. Never taking my eyes off her.

'Harry is dead,' she said quietly, staring at me with a look of infinite sadness. 'He was already dead when he arrived in here. There was nothing we could do for him.'

She stopped, searching my face to see how I was taking this information.

I didn't! It's only a conversation. Something terrible has happened, but it's not real.

'Did he die instantly? Would he have suffered? Was he conscious after he hit the ground?' I was talking about someone else.

'No, he would have died instantly,' she said, shaking her head. 'He would not have been aware of any pain. He fell from a great height.'

I listened, taking in every word, seeing him hit the ground. But not in real life. But it was over instantly. He would not have felt the pain. It was too quick!

'Your mother . . .'

I lifted my head, pulling myself back to listen to what else she had to tell me. She gave another little cough, clearing her throat. 'Was, ahem, not able to identify Harry, and we asked Gerry,' she said slowly, watching me closely.

I stared, horrified, dreading what was coming next.

'He, ahem, became distraught, and started shaking Harry, screaming at him to wake up. We did not realise . . .'

'I know,' I said, interrupting her. 'Gerry has subnormal intelligence. He would not have been able to cope with that. He wouldn't understand, and my mother – how was she?'

'Your mother . . .' The nurse sighed, thinking about this. 'She kept saying it was a mistake. Nobody told her. She was put into the police car when she came running down to find out what happened. She thought it was one of her other children. The police drove her here. They came in behind the ambulance. But she didn't know what was happening.'

I stared at her blonde curly hair under the white cap, her blue eyes filled with such compassion, willing me to understand she sympathised. Seeing her, but not seeing. The haze around her hypnotising me. My vision filled with the pain and brutal torment my mother must have felt sitting here being told her lovely Harry was dead.

'Where is he? I would like to go and see him now, Nurse.' I stood up and moved myself towards the door.

She didn't move, just looked at me like she wanted to say something but didn't know how to say it. 'Are you sure you are up to it?' she asked me, looking worried.

Ah! She thinks I am going to react badly because of the ma and poor Gerry. 'Yes, yes. I am fine, thank you. But I really would like to see him now, please.'

'OK. He has been taken down to the morgue. I'll take you down there,' she said reluctantly, standing up slowly, still not convinced I wouldn't be trouble.

I whipped open the door and stood back, indicating I would brook no further discussion. That got her moving. I can't stand it. I have to see him for myself! I thought, feeling numb inside.

We walked through Casualty, passing the cubicles. They probably had him in one of them, but they're only for the living. I glanced through the open curtain at a doctor asking a man how often he got the pain. You have to be alive to feel pain. Harry didn't get a chance to lie there and tell them he was in pain. He's no more! I thought, looking around at the patients waiting to be seen.

One fellow was sitting on a chair, the leg of his trousers rolled up and his foot stuck up in the air, his big toe looking very prominent. It was black and blue, and quite swollen, and your man was looking very worried. He was staring at the toe like it was about to explode, and looking around to see if anyone was going to take pity on him and rush over and start fussing around him. A fat little woman with a red face and a red coat to match – it was much too tight for her, and she had to leave some of the buttons open so she could breathe – sat next to him.

'Are ye all right, son?' she said, leaning in to get a better look at the toe. 'Is it painin ye much?' she asked, looking very worried up at his face.

'Yeah, Ma! The pain is somethin brutal!' he gasped out, with his face screwing up to make sure she got the message.

'Right! Wait there,' she whispered, glancing down at her bag of messages sitting next to her chair. Then, catching my eye, she rolled her eyes to heaven, meaning *It's terrible bein a mother! An he's a fella, they can't take pain!*

I lowered my eyes to her, barely acknowledging her plight. My heart felt dead.

'I'll just run over an ask tha nurse how much longer we'll have te wait before we get te see a doctor,' she grunted, trying to lift herself out of the plastic chair.

I moved on, trailing the nurse out of Casualty, envying that woman her place next to her son. Harry never lay here, bruised but alive. No, my head told me. I had been fooling myself.

6

I left behind the last sense of hope as I lengthened my stride to catch up with the nurse now taking off down a corridor. I matched pace with her, neither of us speaking as we walked the long silent corridor. The air was cooler down here, and the light was dim.

We reached the end of the corridor, turned right, then left. Another long corridor, white – everything white. White shiny doors, white walls, white-tiled floor, white ceiling. Everything clinically white. The silence thickened as we rounded another corner, heading deeper into the bowels of the hospital. I could see the faint wisps of air coming out of my mouth as we breathed in the heavy cold air, the only sound coming from the squeak of the nurse's rubber-soled shoes and the smacking of my leather-shod feet on the tiles. The rhythm of them sounding like the death march.

The dead house! Everyone down here is dead. Waiting for the last act to be performed by the living. Then they will be no more. Claimed by the earth, and another newborn takes their place. I felt a shiver as something stirred deep inside me – another hope gone. We don't last for ever. A faint cloud settled deep inside me as I felt another loss. We walked on – an endless labyrinth of corridors. Then the nurse moved forward and gently pushed open a door.

She quickly whispered something to a man; he looks like a porter. He nodded to the nurse and stepped quietly out of the room, keeping his head down, not wanting to make eye contact.

I paused at the entrance, peering in at the semi-darkened room, the only light being thrown in from the hall.

'He's in here, Martha,' the nurse whispered, standing beside a slab with my Harry lying on it.

I hesitated, then slowly crept closer. He was lying so rigid. I followed the long shape of him, covered by a white sheet, stopping at his hands, crossed under the sheet. Then my eyes flew to his face, the only part of him not covered. His eyes were half open! I rushed to touch his face, maybe get a last glimpse of him before he left us for ever. No. He's gone.

I stared at his half-closed eyes, searching, seeing only eternity. Then I bent down close to him, kissing his forehead, my lips lingering, hoping for some sense of him.

'He is so cold,' I whispered, stroking his face, wanting him to know he is so precious. But it's too late! I can't tell him. He won't know. I whispered a little prayer into his ear, imploring he would find peace and maybe get his reward. He didn't get much in this life. But as the words came out of my mouth, I knew now there was no God. There was no reward, there was nothing. Just life. It doesn't discriminate. Good, bad and indifferent, it is all the same. You are born, you live and you die. That's it! It only matters if you find love.

You didn't, Harry. You loved, and for a short while you too were loved. Then the love stopped. But you, poor Harry, never stopped loving, even after losing your wife and children. She was too young. She wanted more than you, Harry, could give her, and the abandonment was too much for you. You spent your days searching for her and, in the end, your nights drinking. Looking for comfort in a bottle. Life is a bitch, Harry! It's like a painted whore. Full of promise but delivers only emptiness.

Oh, Harry! My lovely, darling Harry. I felt warm tears softly and slowly stream down my face and stop at the corner of my mouth. I could taste the salt. I bent down again, kissing him, leaving my tears wetting his lips. Oh, Harry! You have left me with a hole in my heart. I will miss you until the end of my days. Rest in peace, little brother.

I turned away, walking slowly the few paces to the door, my hands still wrapped around each other as if in prayer, but it was now only a primitive gesture. I will hold my own hand; I am not alone, it said. But I am alone. I have lost not only you, Harry, but God, my father. My childish belief we are not alone. That there was something higher to aim for.

I stopped and took one last look at Harry. No! There is no God. I'm so sorry, Harry, I failed you. I should have tried harder to help you, and you promised you would call me. I made you promise. You just went, and you didn't even warn me!

I turned my head towards the door.

'Are you ready?'

I looked up to see the face of the nurse leaning towards me.

'Are you OK?' she whispered, her eyes very kind, and she put her arm lightly around my shoulder and led me out, very gently closing the door behind her, as if Harry was just sleeping.

I walked out into the cold night air feeling dazed. My eyes drifted towards the heavy, dark sky. It was pitch black, and the mist floating in the air had settled itself on the car, promising to freeze the marrow in me if I hung around here. It's time to go and see the poor ma. Or is it? I could feel the life ebbing out of me. Nothing matters, nothing was really worth the effort. See the ma? Go home. Drive somewhere. Anywhere! It's all the same. Just drive, keep on the move.

7

I drove out of the hospital, meeting no traffic. Everyone is wrapped up in their beds, everything is so quiet and peaceful. I drove through the dark, silent streets, then down the hill, past the convent on my right, and my heart suddenly jerked! The ghost of little Martha flitted across my vision, and I saw her tearing in through the convent gates, swinging the pillowcase over her shoulder, running to get her two loaves of stale bread. Dreaming and planning and praying and worrying.

'*One day! One day this'll all end, an I'm goin te be free!*' she kept muttering.

Oh, there's no such thing, you poor innocent! Yes, I got what I wanted. The ascent was slow, slipping and sliding on the way. There were a lot of laughs, a lot of tears, gnashing of teeth and losing my foothold. But I continued to climb, and, yeah, I made it. I escaped. But it's cold up here, little one, and lonely, and the price was heavy. It cost me my health. But I'm still alive! Yeah, I'm grateful for that. Or am I?

I drove on, not knowing where I'm heading. I turned left, passing the Rotunda Hospital on my right, and pulled over, switching off the engine. I need a cigarette. I opened the packet of tobacco and started filling the paper, rolling it into a cigarette, and lit it up.

The streets were empty in the dead of night. Even the doors into the hospital were shut. I'll just sit here for a while; somehow, I feel a sense of belonging here. These are the streets of my childhood. The faces of the people are familiar to me. Much more than where I live now. Even though I have spent most of my adult life there, I still don't feel I belong.

I looked up at the hospital building, seeing lights in some of the windows. Right now, there is a woman, or maybe even more, struggling to bring a new life into the world. Oh, Harry! How could you do it? For fuck sake! You still had your life ahead of you! Why, for God's sake?

The tears burst down my cheeks and I wiped them away with the snots, giving a look around. No, not a soul in sight. Or anyone who cares. I know it's fuckin lonely, Harry! I know what it feels to lose someone. I know the pain of being lost in a crowd. I know the emptiness of a house that can be quieter and colder than the grave. But still an all.

No! Let go, Martha. It's no good. He's gone. Stop. You'll destroy what's left of your health. You're still trying to get that back. Now take it easy. It's bad, very bad, but things could always get worse. How? I don't know. Think straight. Look at the hospital. It's a lovely old building. Just think, if that building could talk, think of the stories it could tell! Yeah, I better not let myself go. Keep a grip of the mind. I looked up at the building again, thinking that's the oldest maternity hospital in Europe.

Then I remembered something. I thought of the women trying to make their way there, some completely alone. Stopping to hang on to the railings of the old houses, gripping, with their knuckles turning white to stop themselves sliding, while caught in the middle of a red-hot pain.

I came across one such woman one night long ago when Jackser sent me out in the pitch-black night to beg for money. It was close to Halloween, and I might have a chance of getting something. I saw her, slumped against the railings of Marlborough Street Church. She had her head between the railings and was moaning. I looked for a minute.

'Are ye all righ, Missus?' I asked her quietly, movin closer te her.

'I'm not goin te make it!' she gasped. 'Jesus! Help me!' She turned her face to the sky.

I looked aroun. No one was out on the streets. It was damp, an ye could see the mist in the air, reflected by the street lamps.

'Little one!' she said, looking at me sideways. 'See if there's anyone aroun te help me. I'm tryin te get over te the Rotunda. This child's in a hurry! It won't wait till I get there! Ohhhh!!!!' She started again, gripped by another pain.

I took off, turnin right. Me matchstick legs hammerin along the ground. Flyin across O'Connell Street, turnin left, me legs pumpin across the road, an bangin wit me clenched fists on the big doors of the hospidal. Then I spotted the big roundy bell in the wall an hung out of it.

A little weasel aul fella wit the hair standin up an the eyes rollin in his head whipped open the big door, not knowin where he was cos he was still asleep, dozy bastard! Sleepin on the job.

'Gerraway from tha bell, ye little bastard! I'll cut the ground from under ye!' he screamed, walkin backwards, then comin towards me wit his ham fists clenched. Ragin at me, he was!

'Send someone, Mister! Quick! Te Marlborough Street Church. There's a woman wantin help! She says the child won't wait!' I gasped. 'So it won't,' I muttered, starin at him, waitin te see wha he does.

'Where did ye say?'

'Marlborough Street Church, Mister!' I roared, takin only a bit a breath.

'Hang on! I'll get the stretcher,' he said. 'No, wait!' Then he started scratchin his head, thinkin. 'She's further back! She's goin te be needin the ambulance!'

I shook me head, agreein wit him. 'Will I wait, Mister?' I hopped from my right foot, ready to take off, and back to him on me left foot. 'Can I come back wit ye's in the ambulance? Te show ye's?'

'No! Go on! Get outa there!'

I took off, headin back te the woman.

I was puffin me way across O'Connell Street when I heard the alarm bells of the ambulance come tearin outa the side a the hospidal. Ah! It's comin! I'm gettin meself there first! I threw me head back, pushin out me chest, then took in more wind. Me chest is gaspin for the want a breath. But I'm not goin te miss anythin.

It flew around the corner on two wheels, rockin then steadyin, an took off again, flyin past me wit the alarm bells ringin an janglin like mad. I could see people runnin from the end of the road as the ambulance slowed, turnin the corner. Ah! Me chest bones is crackin an me wind is heavin out through me mouth, makin a keenin sound wit every slap on the pavement. Even me bare feet is gettin an unmerciful bangin. But I don't care! I'm goin te keep goin. Cos I'm wantin everyone te know it was me tha got tha ambulance out! An anyways! Be rights! It's only me tha can be the one te lead them te tha poor woman. I was the one te find her first. She might even be dead be now! Cos she was all ailin! Ye never know.

I rounded the corner, seein the ambulance was stopped. The men jumped out wit the doors thrown open. A crowd a women was surroundin the woman, an the aul fellas got pushed out. They mooched off, pretendin not te be lookin, an just let themselves drop against the railins. Then they lit up their Woodbine butts an started mutterin te each other, sayin, 'Ah, God love her! Isn't it terrible all the same?' But at the one time, listenin an watchin outa the corner a their eye in case they missed anythin.

'Make way! Get back! Give the woman air!' I could hear the ambulance men shout in the middle of them.

'Get back! Leave her room!' an aul one wrapped in a black shawl was shoutin, puttin out her arms an wavin the people away.

I came gaspin up an tried te push me way in.

'Here! Get the hell outa there, you!'

I was dragged back be another aul one wearin a hat wit a pin in it. An a long coat. It was too big fer her!

'Outa there, you! This is no place fer a child,' she roared.

I was yanked back offa me feet an thrown against the railins, landin smack in against the aul fellas.

'Hey, Missus! It was me tha got the ambulance, ye know, fer tha woman!' I screamed, runnin over and pushin me way back in again.

'Did ye?' asked the woman in the shawl.

'Yeah!' I gasped. 'She was sprawled against them railins there! An I was the one tha got here first!' I heaved, runnin outa wind.

'Gawd! Aren't ye very good altogether?' she said, lookin down at me, not able te get over wha I just did.

'Yeah!' I agreed, shakin me head up an down, then throwin me eye te the ailin woman in the middle a the crowd. 'She could be dead an buried now, only I came along.' Then it hit me.

'An, Missus, lookit!' I roared. 'I'm supposed te be collectin fer the Halloween party, so I am!' I said, shakin Jackser's dirty smelly sock at her, hopin she'd put money in it. I had blackened me face with the soot from the chimney. Jackser couldn't lend me his trousers, cos he was wearin them. So this was the best I could do.

'Help the Halloween party!' I shouted, shakin the sock in the middle a the crowd.

'Here! Here's a penny fer ye, love!'

Me head shot aroun. The aul one put in a penny, sayin, 'Ye're a very nice young one! An ye should be rewarded fer tha, so ye should.'

'Wat she do?' an aul one asked, squintin at the old woman, then down at me.

'Ohh, she did a very good turn fer tha poor woman, there, so she did.'

I stood beside the old woman, listenin an noddin me head. Then she pulled herself up an straightened her shawl, wrappin it tight aroun her head and chest. 'Yes!' she hummed, tightenin her chin, darin anyone te contradict her.

'Isn't tha very good!' they all started sayin te each other. 'Here! Come over here, love, till I see wha I have fer ye.'

They all started rootin in their purses, an I made a collection. When I emptied out the sock, I had one shillin an ninepence halfpenny! I had enough te buy Jackser five Woodbines an bring home change te me ma te make her happy!

8

I shook my head, remembering. The present coming back into view. Even with the recession, and everyone out of work, they are still better off today. Life was raw back then. Yeah! The eldest child was left to mind the rest of the kids. Their mothers, some of them barely making it in the Rotunda door before they lay down in a place of sanctuary to gave birth. Some of those mothers I knew very well. Struggling from around the city. That woman outside that church was familiar to me. I had seen her face around many a time. That's why the hospital was started in the first place. Before that, long ago, mothers would come crawling out of their rat-infested hovels to seek help on the streets, only to die there along with their babies who never saw the light of day. Yeah. That's life. You sure knew that, Harry.

I lit up another cigarette and sat quiet in myself, just content to sit staring around me, feeling all the memories of long ago wash over me. Somehow, it brings me close to you, Harry. We were children together on these streets. I stared out at the quiet, cold, dark, empty streets. 'Martha! Martha!' I heard the faint, quiet whisper of a little voice coming from deep within me. I held me breath, waiting. It was the little Martha from these streets. I let her rise.

'Martha! I want ye te be able te tell me something. Will ye listen te me? Harry is not supposed te be dead. But he wasn't supposed te die, at all, Martha. If ye work hard an do yer best, then ye get te be happy, don't ye? Cos ye have te!'

A pinched little scruffy thin white face suddenly appeared in my mind's eye. 'Ye do get te be happy, don't ye, Martha?' she whispered, already knowing the answer. Her eyes looked haunted with the weight of the world showing through them. They were the eyes of an old woman that has seen too much, yet still held all the trust and innocence of a young child.

I shook my head. 'Yes,' I whispered. I did believe that. Even running from you was a waste of time. Now I don't know who I am or why I bothered.

'*Why do ye never want me, Martha? Ye can't do without me, ye know! I belong te ye!*' she roared, bringing her face in closer, daring me.

I searched her blue-grey eyes, seeing them spitting fire. A fire flared up in me own belly. Because? I wanted to blaze at her! So many thoughts flew through my mind at the same time. Then the fire died down. And I felt the truth.

'You were nobody. I was ashamed of you, so I buried you. Oh, yes, little one. I did what I said I would do. First, I educated myself. I read big books; they call them "Classics". It's what all the big important people who are "Somebody" read when they go to the university. So I did the same.

'Most of the stuff, I couldn't make head nor tail out of any of them. But I gradually got to understand what they were talking about. I discovered I could understand a lot of things. I started to speak and sound quite knowledgeable, educated. Like I had been to the university. I spoke properly. My tastes grew. I learned the difference between "Classic" and "Cheap". Quality and rubbish. I could pass myself off as "One of the Quality". I became "Somebody". People accepted me. The more "Quality" I became, the deeper I had to bury you. I always feared some day somebody would find out about you. The more distance I put between you and me, little one, the more I could forget you and the ma and Jackser ever existed. All the pain they inflicted! Well, it never happened to me. I could leave it all behind with you. We had to live in different worlds. I needed to be beyond the reach of my old life. That is what drove me, little one.

'I fooled everyone. The decision makers, the professionals, the middle-class respectable. I moved among them all, accepted as one of them. But inside me, my little one, I am empty. I am nobody,' I whispered. 'Everything about me is a lie. The more I moved away from you, the emptier I was. The person my world knows and accepts does not, and never did, exist. I have no real friends, because they do not know the real me. To do that, I would have to let them see you. I can't do that, because I am afraid they will turn their back on me. The way they did on you.

'I never found love, little one. Because the one person who knew me, loved me and accepted you, well, he went away. I gave my heart to Sarah. I never stopped loving him. He never stopped loving me. I know that, because . . . You know, don't you, little one?'

'*Yeah, I do, Martha,*' she whispered, shaking her head slowly. Then she leaned into me. '*Cos he's waitin on you, an ye're waitin on him! An none of ye's want te be the first te say it! An he's not goin te come te you. An you won't go te him. Cos ye're afraid a wha might happen. Ye think he might turn ye away. He won't. You know tha, but ye won't chance it. So now you've walked away.*'

'How do you know all that, little one?'

'*Cos I'm always wit ye! I'm listenin! I know it all! An like you are over him, an all the painin he gave ye. Well, I'm always cryin meself.*'

'Why, little one?' I said.

She said nothing.

'Tell me!' I said, leaning into her, seeing her little face lift as she grabbed hold of a lock of matted hair landing in her eyes.

She took in a deep breath. I watched her bony little chest heave, then she whispered, shaking her head, '*Because ye don't want me, Martha. I'm all on me own, just waitin. Waitin for you te want me,*' she said, watching me, hoping I might have the answer.

I said nothing. Just sat feeling empty. 'Nothing really matters to me any more. I gave up hoping one day he and I might . . . That's over. Well over! Sarah doesn't need me any more. Sure, what's left to bother about?' I muttered, staring beyond her into the darkness, then letting my eyes rest on her, feeling myself sink even lower.

She stared at me, listening very intently. I could see the loss and pain in her bright, intelligent eyes. The light was going out of them, dulled by the loss of hope.

I sighed, feeling her pain and loss. Just as she felt mine. 'Little one!' I reached into her, staring into her thin, bony little face, streaked with the dirt. And the hollow cheeks, caused by lack of nourishment – that's malnutrition. Her poor face was drawn and pinched, showing the marks of too much pain and suffering. 'I want to say this to you, my little Martha. If I get through this – and I'm not sure if I'm going to be able to pick myself up and dust meself down again. This time it's a heavy fall. But! I make you this promise – one day I will come back for you. I will claim you, make you my own. I don't know when, but some day. When I get the strength and the will. Because I know now you will haunt me to my grave if I don't. We both need to find peace, little one,' I sighed, feeling very weary.

I switched on the engine and took off. I continued following the road, keeping the hospital on my right, up Parnell Square, with the old Georgian houses on my left. The odd house here and there still had lights on. Most of them are now used as offices. Especially by the culchies, the Teachers' Union. Shower of moaners. They spend their time sitting around discussing how hard they have to work. 'It's not on, lads! We have to work from nine o'clock in the morning until three o'clock in the day. With only the three months' holiday the country does begrudge us!

'Sure we don't get paid half enough! Think of all the work we're supposed te do. All that preparation! Having to mark papers in our own free time after school! Sure, we get no rest at all!'

'Hear! Hear! Let's go on strike!'

Yeah! The cute culchies own Dublin now. All the city people got themselves pushed out to the middle of nowhere. They walk miles to the shops and wait hours for a bus. There's not enough Dubliners left to argue. They spilled out in droves across the water to the four corners of England. They're settled down now, with grown-up families, living out dreams of returning to the 'Aul Sod' one day. Sadly, not for all. Some of them are tragically, even after forty years, 'still waitin on a start'. They are keeping out the cold, sleeping in doorways on the streets of London with a drop of 'Red Biddy' methylated spirits for company. Trying to ward off the pain of failure.

I drove up the hill, taking it easy, and stopped for the red light. I glanced across the road, letting my eyes settle on the waste ground. There's nothing left there now but decay and death. Lovely old houses used to stand there, built by the British. Then, when the old tenements started leaning dangerously close to the passers-by, in rolled the corporation with their wrecking ball. They demolished the lot and rolled off satisfied with themselves. They left a bombsite for everyone to step around and shout to each other. 'Mind yerself there,

Missus! Don't fall over dem aul bricks or ye'll kill yerself!'

Dublin is ravaged by the dereliction. Now it's crumbling around our ears. Let go, by the lack of interest from the city fathers.

I turned right, heading down to Dorset Street, seeing it showing nothing but boarded-up shops. Some are even bricked up. I sighed: more decay and neglect. It would put years on ye! I drove up Drumcondra, taking in the lovely red-brick houses built by Irish craftsmen. Not one real Dubliner lives here. They're occupied by the crafty culchies who let out rooms. That money paid for their sons to become doctors, lawyers, 'An I've one a priest! and dhe other one, dhe daughter, she is a nun in South Africa. Yeah! Yu're right dhere, Mammy! We did do well for ourselves up here! How are dhe hens layin? Send us up a few auld eggs!'

I drove on, meeting very little traffic, seeing the streets are almost deserted. Then I spotted the policeman scratching his arse. He lowered his back, bending in close to a window, letting his arse stick out. I slowed down to twenty-five miles an hour. I don't want him stopping me, then whipping out his little notebook, getting all excited about me not having a bulb in me little sidelight.

I crept past him, looking very intent on my driving, A model citizen. But he was giving all his attention with his nose pressed to the window of a jewellery shop.

It's a cold and damp aul night for them to be on the prowl. They're usually inside the station roasting their arse against the heaters and supping cups of tea. You could be mugged, robbed and raped for the want of one of them!

I'm up now onto the road heading for the ma. I must be nearly there. Jesus! I didn't really know where I was heading tonight. I only know now, it seems, in the ma's direction.

My heart started fluttering in my chest as I got closer to the ma's. I could feel the lid threatening to blow off my tightly controlled nerves. The stillness in me is starting to slip away. I could feel myself now beginning to harden. I'm getting gripped by a cold anger. I know what it is. It's the thought at having to face back into Jackser and the ma's life. It's bringing closer the realisation I'll never see Harry again. Jesus! It's really beginning to hit me. That Harry! Poor Harry! He really is gone! How can that be? Yeah, but I saw him with me own eyes!

It's that thundering little snot rag's fault. That fucking Jackser! Ohh, the scumbag! He has a lot to answer for. Now, he still lives and my little brother is dead. Yeah, we can leave it all down to you, fucking bandy bastard Jackser! If I had me way, I would fuck him under the wheels of this car! But that would be too easy for him.

Right, Martha. But there's no need for any trouble. So keep your thoughts to yourself. You have to think about Harry. Anyway, everyone is going to have their own troubles now. Especially the poor ma.

9

Right! Here we are. That didn't take long. I slowed down, searching along the balconies of the flats. Which one is the ma's? They all look the same to me.

I continued driving down to the end of the flats, then I looked up, seeing the ma leaning over the balcony. There she is! All my anger suddenly melted away at the sight of the lonely little figure just standing there all alone. She was huddled inside an old grey overcoat, staring into the freezing-cold, pitch-black night. Ah! God love her! She must have been out there all this time, for hours on end probably, maybe even waiting for me. 'God! Ma, I'm sorry. I wasn't thinking straight,' I muttered to myself.

I pulled over and parked quickly, jumping out of the car.

'Did ye see him! Did ye go te the hospidal, Martha?' she shouted down.

I stopped and looked up at her, nodding my head slowly, and said, 'Yeah, Ma. I went to the hospital.'

I stopped to pull out my packet of tobacco and rolled a cigarette, heading up to the ma. But then she appeared in front of me and stopped. Her head dropped, and her eyes stared at the ground, seeing nothing. Then suddenly her head swung on her shoulders, with her eyes searching up and down the road. I watched her. She thinks if she looks hard enough Harry will suddenly arrive.

'Ma! Come here to me,' I said, walking over to her and taking her in my arms. She rested her head on my shoulder, saying nothing.

I held her, stroking her head, and she stayed passive, letting us have that bit of comfort. For the few seconds, time stood still. We blocked out the world. Then she stirred.

'I didn't know!' she said, staring at me, her face twisted in pain and confusion. 'They didn't tell me. Why wouldn't they tell me anythin, Martha?'

'Who, Ma?'

'The police! The hospidal! They put me an Gerry in the back a the police car, but they wouldn't say wha happened! I sat in tha hospital not knowin wha was happenin. Nobody would tell me anythin!' she sobbed, wiping her nose with the sleeve of her jumper as she pulled it out of the arm of her coat.

I listened, staring into her face. She's in terrible shock. 'Come on, Ma. Let's go up.' I put my arm around her, guiding her up the stairs.

Jackser appeared out as we arrived on the balcony. 'Ye're here! Yer poor mammy has been waitin on ye! Haven't ye, Sally?' he said, waving his arm towards me ma. 'Come on! Come in. Youse will catch yer death a cold, standin out here.'

I pushed past him standing in the hall. 'Come on, Ma! Let's get you a hot cup of tea. Where's Dinah? Is she here?'

'She's in the sittin room,' Jackser said, slamming the front door shut.

Dinah was slumped on the couch, staring at the wall, seeing nothing. 'Dinah,' I whispered, sitting down beside her and putting my hand on her shoulder. 'Are you all right? How did you get home?' I asked, looking at her swollen eyes and red puffy face.

'Wha? Oh, it's you, Martha. I didn't hear ye come in. Did ye just come from the hospital?' Her eyes lit up, looking hopeful.

'Yeah,' I said, lowering my head, seeing the hope vanish as quickly as it came. We sat quietly, me examining my hands folded in my lap, her staring around the room with her mouth half open, looking very confused. She was trying to make sense of what happened.

'Martha!' I looked up to see Gerry rushing in from the kitchen. 'He's dead, Martha! Harry is dead!'

'I know, Gerry love,' I said, reaching out to bring him down beside me.

'He threw himself offa the balcony!' he roared, getting very agitated and swinging his arms through the air to show me what happened. 'I tried te wake him up! But he wouldn't wake up fer me! I kept shakin him!' and he waved his fists furiously in the air, needing to show me the effort he made. 'But it was no good. Me ma says he's dead!' Then he rushed around the room, pressing his hands over his ears.

'I can hear him, Martha! He's callin me!'

'Yeah! Can ye hear him, Martha?' Dinah suddenly said, leaning towards me. 'I can hear him too! Listen!'

'It's like he's whispering te me, Dinah!' Gerry said, looking over at the window.

I stopped for a minute, hearing nothing of course. 'No! He's not calling you. Don't be upsetting yourself. You're all in shock.' I looked over at me ma, staring out the window. 'Ma, do you want a cup of tea?' I asked, getting up and going over to put my arms around her.

'No! I don't want anythin,' she muttered, shaking her head and turning away from me.

'Me ma doesn't like seeing anyone dead,' Dinah whispered to me, nodding her head towards me ma.

'No!' me ma muttered, shaking her head and closing her eyes, trying to block out the thought. 'I saw enough of it when me own poor mother died. I was only young, an we were all fast asleep in bed when all of a sudden we heard a bang on the winda. Me big sister jumped outa the bed an looked out. It was our aunt. She threw a stone up at the winda, then she shouted up, "She's gone! Yer poor mammy is dead! I've just come back from the hospidal. Yeah! They sent for me. So youse all better get te bed, an I'll be up te see ye's in the mornin." Then she was gone!' me ma said, looking like she was back in that time, in that place.

Her head was hanging down to the floor with her body suspended, like she was frozen in time. Then she lifted her head and said, with her eyes staring into the distance, 'We all stood there, lookin at each other, an lookin at the winda, shiverin wit the fright, watchin me aunt hurryin back home. It was dark out, an we didn't know wha te think or wha te do. Then suddenly, without any warnin, the aul Victorian glass globe – it covered over the statue underneath, me mother always kept tha sittin in the middle of the table – it exploded wit an unmerciful bang, right on the table,' me ma said, lifting her arms, then throwing them away from her. 'We all started screamin. Jesus! I will never forget tha night as long as I live! I kept havin terrible nightmares. I was haunted be them fer years,' she said, staring at the floor, with her face creased in agony.

'The first night after we buried her, I woke up in the middle of the night an me mother was sittin on the chair beside the bed. The one she used te keep her clothes on when she went te bed. I could see her long hair, Martha!' me ma said, lifting her face to look at me.

I stared at me ma's face. She's white as a sheet, and her eyes are bulging out of her head. She's looking like she has the fear of God in them.

'She kept tellin me te pray for her, Martha! "Pray for me," she was whisperin.'

I watched me ma repeat the words over and over again as her lowered head stared at the floor, not seeing it. She was back in that time long ago, seeing her long dead mother imploring her to pray. My ma, her little Sally. All them long years ago, I thought.

Then me ma slowly lifted her head, gently shaking it from side to side, saying, 'Everyone in the family had kept dyin. One by one they went. Even me father, then we lost our mammy. All a them gone! All in a few months. Until in the end . . .' Then me ma's voice trailed off, holding her hands in the air, then she slumped against the window. 'I never got over it,' she whispered.

I lifted her into my arms and held her, stroking her hair. 'You're OK, Ma. I'm here. I'll look after you. Don't worry about anything. I'll take care of everything. I know life has been terrible for you, but you're not on your own. You know I have always looked after you,' I murmured into her ear. 'Hush, Ma. Take it easy. Do you want me to put you to bed?' I asked, lifting her face to look at me.

She stared at me, looking very lost, saying nothing. 'Come on, Ma. Let's get you to bed,' I said, leading her out of the room.

I took off her coat and shoes, then slipped her skirt off and put her under the blankets. Then I sat down beside her on the bed. She lay on her side, staring at nothing, gripping the blankets with her two hands.

'Close your eyes, Ma,' I whispered, putting my hands on her face and closing her eyelids. 'Shush, get a little sleep.' I stroked her head. It felt so small, and her hair was thin, and her skin was grey and beginning to wrinkle. She's old before her time. Barely in her fifties, but she could be seventy. Poor ma. She's like a helpless child. It's no wonder! It looks like now she never got over the shock of losing her mother and half of her family when she was still only a child.

I sat on, stroking her, until she finally dozed off. Then I tiptoed out of the room, closing the door quietly behind me.

'Dinah, where's Teddy? Does he know? And what about Charlie?' I asked her, sitting down on the sofa.

'I don't know, Martha. I haven't seen Teddy all day. Usually he calls over te see me da. An Charlie never comes over here. He doesn't get on wit me ma. An she wouldn't let him in anyway.'

'Right. OK, Dinah. I'll try and contact Charlie tomorrow. And what about young Sally?'

'No, she doesn't know either. It's just us. We came back here, an we've been waitin for you te come. We didn't know wha te do,' she said, looking very lost. 'You're the only one tha came.' Then she stared at me, wondering what was going to happen next.

'Listen, Dinah, you go into bed and get a bit of sleep, and get Gerry to bed. He's exhausted, and so are you. Come on,' I said, standing up and pulling Dinah to her feet.

'Gerry, it's time for bed,' I whispered over to him. He was still marching up and down, with his fingers stuck in his ears, talking to himself.

'Ah no, Martha. I'm talkin te Harry! He keeps whispering te me, but I can't understand wha he's sayin, Martha!' Then he turned away from me and started marching up and down again.

'No, Gerry! Come on,' I said, grabbing his arm and steering him out the door. 'Come on, Dinah.' She was standing where I left her, staring into space.

I pushed Gerry down the hall and into his bedroom. 'Now, get into that bed and go to sleep. Will you do that for me?'

'Yeah, OK, Martha. But wha about Harry? He wants te talk te me. But I don't like it, Martha. He won't stop! Will ye make him stop it, Martha!' he said, leaning over to stare into my face, hoping I would make his pain go away.

I looked into his eyes, seeing absolute trust and the pure innocence of a very young child. 'Yes, Gerry. He's going to stop. He just wants you to go to bed and get a good night's sleep. Now, come on, into bed.'

'Yeah! I'm goin te bed, Martha. Yeah! Yeah! Thanks, Martha! I think he'll stop now,' Gerry said, shaking his head slowly, content at that thought. Then he lifted his head, trying to give me a smile. But it couldn't reach his eyes. They stared out at me, confused. Showing terrible pain and loss.

His eyes swam in tears, waiting to burst, but he was too shell shocked. Not able to make sense of this dark night of horror. It has cruelly grabbed him up in its snare, holding him fast. Leaving him trapped in its never-ending nightmare and a world of pain.

'Goodnight, Martha,' he whispered as he pulled his jumper over his head, getting the buttons in the neck caught in his hair. 'Ah! I'm stuck! Me hair's caught! Will ye get me outa this, Martha!'

I rushed to grab the jumper and peel his hair loose from the buttons. I pulled it over his head and threw it on the chair beside his bed. 'Now you're grand,' I said, grabbing him to me and wrapping me arms around him.

'Listen to me, Gerry,' I whispered into him. 'Harry is safe now. He's all smiling and happy because he's gone up to Holy God in heaven. Holy God couldn't wait for him to get old, because, you see, Harry was very special. He was Holy God's favourite person. So that's why he had to go. Now, they know it's going to pain you and the ma and Dinah and everyone, because he belonged to you, and you all wanted to keep him for yourselves. But you couldn't, because Harry decided he wanted to go and live in heaven. Now he's really, really happy, and he even has a new job. Do you know what that is, Gerry?' I asked him, lifting his face to me.

His eyes stared intently with his mouth half open, not saying a word, just taking everything in, waiting to hear.

'He has to watch out for you and me ma, and all the rest of the family. He's up there now, living with Holy God. So you see, Harry will be watching the lot of you like a hawk. If one of you needs a hand or is worried about something, well, you just tell Harry about it. And Harry will be straight away telling Holy God and making sure Holy God doesn't take his eye off any of you. OK?' I said, bending me face into him.

He shook his head, letting his eyes wander to the floor, thinking about this.

'Now, Gerry. Into bed, love, and I'll see you tomorrow,' I said, walking out of the room and closing the door quietly behind me. Yes, Gerry, I thought. If I still only had your innocence, I too would have Holy God to watch over me. 'Oh, Harry, wherever you are. If by any chance you are listening to me, if you come across God, tell him I am lost without him. I need him back,' I muttered, feeling cold as the grave.

'Dinah, you go on off to bed. I'm going home, and I'll be back tomorrow as soon as I can. There's a lot to do. We have to arrange the funeral, Dinah.'

'But there's no money te bury him! Wha are we going te do?' she whispered, beginning to panic.

'No! Don't worry yourself about that now. I will work that out. Go on! Get to bed. I'll see you tomorrow.'

'OK, Martha. What time will ye be over at?'

'I don't know, Dinah love. I have to make a few phone calls first. But I'll get here as soon as I can.'

I headed off down the hall and turned the handle on the front door. It's locked. I suppose Jackser has the key. I put my head in the kitchen. 'Goodnight, Jackser. I'm off home,' I said. 'Will you let me out? The door's locked.'

He was sitting at the kitchen table, puffing on his Woodbine and sipping on a mug of tea. 'Oh! Are ye off so? Right!' and he shook his head, trying to bring himself out of a trance, and stood up, looking at me, then dropped his eyes down to the floor and lifted his head, swinging it over to the window, and gave a little laugh down in his throat and started snufflin.

I watched him. He's looking very shifty. Then he looked at me with a glint in his eye. Fucking hell! I could feel myself getting very irritated.

'Will you open the door, Jackser? I want to get home. It's late,' I said coldly.

'Listen! Come over here, there's somethin I want te tell ye,' he said. Then he rushed past me, putting his head out the door and peering around to make sure no one could hear him, looking like a seedy little conman who wanted to sell me something he'd robbed. Then he closed the door quietly, and I watched him creeping over towards me, still throwing his head back to the door to make sure no one could hear him.

'Listen!' he said, with his eyes dancing in his head, snufflin and laughing like he was embarrassed and excited all at the same time. 'Yer mammy thinks I'm in love wit you!' He paused, watching my reaction, staring into my face. Then he rushed on. 'She thinks I want te go te bed wit ye! Can ye believe tha? Isn't tha a good one?' he said, throwing his head back laughing. Then he stared at me, with his red bulging eyes swimming with lust. His head cocked down at me, and the silence that hung between us was pregnant with his anticipation.

I swept my eyes from his brown wrinkled face with the big nose down to his short bandy legs covered with filthy greasy trousers that must have lost their colour not too long after the First World War. They probably belonged to Kaiser Wilhelm. The state of him, the little runt! My stomach turned over with disgust. Yeah, it's clear to me now. This man has always been insane.

'Is that right now?' I said, moving towards the door and opening it.

'She fuckin does!' he said, laughing.

I stood at the entrance of the door, feeling an icy coldness sweep through me, and stared at him. 'Listen, Jackser,' I whispered, wriggling my fingers at him. 'Come over here. I want to tell you something.'

'Shush! Don't say anythin. Yer mammy will hear. She gets very jealous,' he said, rushing over to hear what I had to say and trying to close the door, hoping I would step back in.

I put my hand on the door, pushing it open, and he stopped to listen, cocking his ear close to my face, like he was going to be privy to some big dirty secret.

'Your son is lying dead on a cold slab in the morgue up in that hospital,' I said, with ice dripping between me clenched teeth. 'Are you aware of that?'

His head snapped straight up, and he stared at me with hard, cold eyes. Then they began to narrow, and I watched his hands drop down by his side and curl up into fists.

The coldness, the icy calm suddenly vanished, leaving me with a rapidly growing red-hot fire. It swept down into my belly, and I tensed, feeling myself like a tightened coil. 'Listen,' I said, leaning my head into his face. 'Say one more word to me about what is in your filthy, diseased mind, and I will rip your balls off, Jackser, with one of your very own Silver Gillette blades, then ram them down your throat.'

I stared at him, and he blinked. Then his mouth curled. 'Don't fuckin threaten me!' Jackser snarled, moving closer to me, looking like he would rip me head off.

I looked around the kitchen, ready to pick up something and land it on his head if he pushed me. 'Jackser! I am mad enough to do just that!' I said slowly, leaning even closer to his face. 'Remember! You taught me well, and you better pray I don't come after you some dark night and carry out my threat!'

'Ah! I'm sorry! I wasn't thinkin!' he started to say, lowering his eyes and shifting away from me, like a vicious dog that has met its match and now slinks off feeling very chastised.

I turned around, heading down the hall, while Jackser stood back, holding the door open for me. I swept out, listening as Jackser quietly shut the front door behind me, turning the key and locking it. I could feel me breathing coming very heavy.

Jesus! For one minute, I was willing to do time for killing that bastard. I shook me head. No! He's not worth it, Martha. He could never beat me. I can walk away, leaving him to stew in his own hell.

I walked along the piss-ridden balcony, with the rubbish tumbled out of the overflowing chute, and headed down the stone stairs, stepping over dirty needles left behind by the junkies. I eyed the filthy mattress on the landing with what looked like a poor wasted human lying on it. He was curled up in a ball, trying to get the bit of comfort of a few hours' fitful sleep.

I leapt out the last few steps onto the street, feeling the noose around my neck loosen and fall away after my run-in with Jackser. I took in a deep lungful of pissy, rotten-vegetable air, looked up at the early-morning grey sky and felt glad to be free. Yeah! Where there's life, there's always the hope that one day I will see Jackser planted. I can stand on his grave and do a morris dance. I will even hire the full regalia! I sat into the car and rolled myself a cigarette, then switched the engine on and turned the car for home.

IO

I woke up slowly, then felt the rush of cold blood flying around my body. I paused. What is it? Then my brain rapidly engaged. Harry! Oh, sweet Jesus! That wasn't a nightmare. I could feel a heavy weight sinking down into me chest and working its way into me belly. No! None of that! I better get moving. There's a lot to get done. I lifted my head slowly off the pillow and squinted over to the clock sitting on the dressing table. I can't read that clock. Which is the big hand? I opened both eyes, staring hard. Half past eight. Two hours' sleep probably. 'Well, that's enough,' I sighed, feeling my body ache.

I swung my feet out of the big old Victorian bed, landing a long way down on the rug. I'm always forgetting how high that bloody bed is! One of these days I'm going to break me neck. Where's that dressing gown? My eyes swept around the room, landing on a big fisherman's jumper. That will do. I pulled it over my head, heading down the stairs, when I heard the barking. Ah! The big black hairy mutt is back. I wonder where he was off gallivanting to? I unlocked the front door, and a blur of black hair shot across my vision. It streaked past me, banging my legs. I slammed the front door shut, whirling on him.

'Sit! Where were you?'

He finished doing his cartwheels and thumped his arse on the floor, bringing himself instantly to attention, with his two front paws straight out in front of him. He stared up at me, knowing he was in trouble.

'Bonzo! You are a very bold boy,' I said slowly, pointing my finger into his face.

His paws started drumming out a tap dance, and his mouth curled into a grimace. It looked like he was laughing.

'Right! Get into that kitchen!' I roared, pointing my finger at the kitchen door.

The gobshite sprang for the handle of the kitchen door before I was even finished getting the last word out and threw his weight on the handle. I watched as he thumped the door wide open, smacking it against the wall with an almighty bang. Then he was in. He was in such a hurry, he slid across the tiles on his arse, straight into the kitchen sink.

'Take it easy!' I roared down at him as he picked himself up from the floor.

He ignored me, and I jumped out of the way as he crashed over to the press low down on the floor and gripped the handle with his teeth. He started pulling it backwards and nosed his way into the press. He grabbed his big bag of dry 'Everything Your Dog Needs for a Healthy Diet', then clenched it tightly between his teeth and dragged it across the floor, letting it sit at me feet.

I picked up the bag and emptied some into his bowl, while he went back to the press and pawed out a can of Pedigree Chum and gently rolled it over to me. Then he dropped down on his belly, letting out a big sigh. His head leaned to one side, watching me spoon his meat into his bowl. I scraped every last bit of meat out of the can or he would go after it in the rubbish bin. It would only end up getting dragged around the floor, making a mess of me kitchen. Jaysus! He's an awful savage, this dog.

'Now! There's your dinner!' I said, stepping out of his way as he launched a flying tackle at it. Jaysus! One of these days, that dog will be the death of me! He weighs a ton and demolishes everything and everybody that happens to be in his way. No wonder he was dumped with the vet when he was only a little pup.

'He's a bit wild,' the vet puffed, dragging him in by the scruff of the neck, saying, 'I had a job trying to catch him.'

We both stared down at the little ball of fluff whirling around the room, growling and chewing on everything in sight. 'He's half bearded collie, very nervous!' the vet muttered.

'I'll take him!' I said, sweeping him up in my arms, and he immediately started to attack my long hair, chewing it.

'Now look at the size of you! You're actually five years old, but you still haven't got a blade of sense!' I snorted at him, seeing the dinner vanish as he put his paw on the bowl to steady it for a good lick. He stopped to look up at me and made to rub his dirty chin all over me. It was covered in dinner! 'No! Eat your dinner! I don't want your mess,' I said, rushing to get the kettle on and get moving.

I sat munching on a bit of toast, dipping it into a soft-boiled egg, wondering where I should start first. Better ring the hospital, I suppose. Yes, that's the first thing.

I rinsed out the dishes and dashed up to shower, then dressed quickly and came hurrying down the stairs, whipping open the front door. 'Bonzo!'

He came flying out of the kitchen, straight out the front door, heading for the gate. 'Here, boy!' I roared, opening the side gate. 'Come on! Go and get your ball!'

The mention of 'ball' sent him flying at breakneck speed out to the back garden, and I slammed the gate shut, locking him in.

He came rushing back, heading the ball, and stopped dead, staring up at me. He knew he was not going to get a game out of me, and he'd been fooled! 'Now! Be a good boy and don't jump over the wall.' I looked up at the ten-foot-high wall, knowing it would not keep him in. I suddenly knelt down, giving him a big hug through the bars of the gate. I don't know what I'd do without him, I thought, as I rushed in to sit down and ring the hospital.

'You have to ring the coroner's office, to see when they will be ready to release the body,' they told me.

I dialled the coroner's office. 'Hello, I would like to enquire, please, when you are ready to release my brother Harry's body?'

'He will be ready for removal this afternoon, from two-thirty.'

'But we are not ready to make the funeral arrangements yet.'

'Well, you have to claim him by tomorrow at the latest,' a grumpy, bored aul man's voice informed me.

'But what do we do? There's no money to bury him.'

'Well, he has to be buried by Thursday at the latest. You can't leave a body lying around, ye know!' he barked down the phone at me.

'Yes, I know that. But you have to give us time to organise the money!'

'Well!' he roared back. 'If you don't collect him by Thursday, we'll bury him for you!'

'You will?' I asked. 'How?'

I could hear him sucking on his false teeth. Then he sucked in his breath, and I pressed the phone closer to my ear, holding my breath, not wanting to miss what he had to say.

'We will bury him in a pauper's grave!' he roared.

'A what?' Me heart leapt. 'You will do no such thing! My brother is going into no pauper's grave!' I roared down the phone. My heart was beating like the clappers, and a white-hot rage was erupting in my chest.

'If you don't collect him by tomorrow, Wednesday,' and he paused for another suck on his false teeth, then he spat out, 'the council will bury him in a pauper's grave on Thursday. Your choice.'

'No, you bloody will not!' I hissed through me clenched teeth. 'If you bury him in a pauper's grave.' I stopped to get a breath. 'We will DIG HIM UP!' I screeched, slamming down the phone.

Jesus Christ almighty! The little bastard! I rushed into the kitchen to make myself a cup of tea and roll a cigarette, trying to think. I could see me hands shaking. He thinks he is the voice of authority. The bastards always get you when you are down and out. There is no respect for the poor. Who the fuck does that little aul fella think he is? I bet he still lives with his mammy! There has to be a way around this. What would get through to a little aul fella like that?

I sat sipping and puffing, getting a picture of a skinny little aul fella with false teeth. A white face hanging down in soft folds. Probably wears brown trousers with turn-ups at the bottom. They're too short for him after twenty-six years of washing. Now they've settled just above his ankles. He doesn't need to go to the barber's. He sweeps the six hairs from the side of his head over his bald dome. He wears 1960s prescription glasses. Yeah! He probably got them from the dispensary!

Hmm! So what does he do for excitement? Ah! The highlight! He takes himself out on a Sunday, leaving his aul ma sitting in the armchair beside the fire. But he's good to her. He leaves her with a shawl wrapped around her bony shoulders. Then leaves her behind, complaining she might as well be dead for the want of a drop of tea, and she knew she was 'cursed' the day she gave birth te him! Meanwhile, he rushes out the door wearing a trench coat he bought in 1932 with his first week's wages.

He gallops off, heading in the direction of the Phoenix Park, clutching a shopping bag under his arm. When he gets there, he waits for some unfortunate middle-aged woman walking her dog. Then he whips open his trench coat, reaches in to his shopping bag and drags out a bell, ringing it to get her attention. When she stops to fix her gaze on him, that's it! He exposes himself! Dangling his little worm at her. While the poor woman stands there frozen in shock, yer man gallops off home te get the mammy's tea. He's now satisfied for another week, and that's the nearest he gets to a woman!

No, Martha. When you're poor and down and out, the authorities walk all over you. They don't care about all the suffering the ma and the family are going through. So, no point in expecting any help or sympathy. You're going to have to be ruthless. Show no fucking mercy. Do what you have to do. It's the last thing you can ever do for Harry. The last thing he will ever need. Let him rest side by side with all the other people who came into the world and had a normal decent life. You didn't, Harry. You came in a pauper. Now they want to send you out a pauper. To lie for ever in an unknown grave with all the other lost souls who didn't even get a quiet resting place they could call their own! No, if you can hear me, Harry, don't fear! This aul fella needs, and is going to get, a red-hot poker shoved right up his arse. So here goes, just watch the 'Abbey Acting' of your big sister, Martha. I swear I can hear, or sense, that little giggle of yours when you were a little boy.

Right! Plan B. I headed out into the hall and picked up the phone then dialled.

'Hello! Coroner's office.'

'Hello! Yes! I have just been speaking to you a moment ago, regarding the arrangements for the removal of my brother Harry.'

'Oh, it's you again! I've nothin further to say to you.'

'Well, Mr . . . What did you say your name was?'

'I didn't,' he muttered.

'I really would like your name, please!'

'Joe Hammond! Mr Hammond to you!'

'Ah! Thank you, Mr Hammond. Now! I do think it fair to warn you I intend making my next phone call to the *Times* newspaper. I think it will be of considerable interest to the general public to know an elderly couple, whose only son committed suicide, and he was insolvent . . .'

'He was wha?' your man interrupted.

'Insolvent! No money! And his elderly parents, "faded gentry" you might call them . . .'

'They're wha?' he roared, interrupting me again.

'Very dignified! Genteel! They have fallen on hard times, and they are forced to live on a very small stipend. Income, Mr Hammond!'

I got the picture of Jackser and the ma and lost me flow. I took in a deep breath, snorting it in slowly, and took off again. 'And now in the twilight of their years,' I continued, 'they are being threatened with a pauper's grave for their tragic son! Hmm! Oh, no, Mr Hammond. It is not enough they have suffered this tragic loss. But the bureaucrats have to put the boot in and cause them the ultimate indignity of a pauper's grave for our beloved Harry!

'I intend taking this matter to the Dail, Mr Hammond. This is grotesquely inhuman, and I shall be quoting you, Mr Hammond. Every single word of our conversation!'

'Hang on now! Just hang on a minute. There's no need to be hasty!' yer man whined, interrupting. 'Look! If you get on to the department, they have a grant. It's a death grant for them that hasn't got the means.'

'Oh, thank you, Mr Hammond! Pity you bloody well didn't say that in the beginning! We could have saved ourselves a lot of argument!'

'Well, I'm sayin it now!' he growled.

'OK, thank you,' and I hung up. Bureaucratic bastards! They are always trying to save money on the backs of the poor! You would think it was coming out of his own pocket!

I dialled the number he gave me, then waited. It started ringing.

'Hello,' a male voice answered.

'Hello, I'm ringing about the death grant. My brother has just died, and we have no money to bury him.' I held my breath, waiting for a response.

'Ahem, yes, you're on to the right department. But are you in receipt of any social welfare payment?'

'Oh, yes!' I breathed. 'His father is getting the dole.'

'Right,' the voice answered. Then a pause.

I waited, holding another breath. Wanting to break the pregnant silence between us.

'Was the deceased working?'

I hesitated, thinking.

'The deceased working when he was alive,' the voice prompted, trying to be helpful.

'Oh! No! He nev . . . No! He was on the dole,' I said firmly.

'Right,' your man said. 'You can go in to Dinny's Funeral Undertakers. Do you know where they are? They're over before you get to the Liffey.'

'Oh, yes. I know where you are talking about,' I squeaked, getting very hopeful.

'Well, if you take yourself over to them, and tell them the department sent you – and we don't deal with anyone else mind, only them – they will sort you out.'

Silence while I digested this. 'So, they will arrange the funeral, and we won't have to pay a penny. Is that right?' I asked him.

'Yes. But only up to a certain amount. The grant is for a fixed sum.'

'Right. Thank you,' I said. 'Oh! But I can't go anywhere else, is that right?'

'No. They have the contract.'

'OK. Thank you very much,' I said, hanging up.

Now! One more phone call before I go. Where's that phone book? I picked up the directory, and my eyes flew over the listings for churches. Where does Charlie live? I don't know the exact address; he's always on the move. But the area should be enough. I'll get a local priest to call and give him the message about Harry. It's too far to drive down there. I won't have the time.

This sounds like a presbytery near to his house. I dialled the number. It's ringing! I waited, letting it ring. There's no answer. I dialled again, there's still no answer. I looked for another presbytery in the book. This should do. I dialled the number. It's ringing. My heart leapt when a voice said, 'Hello.'

'Eh, hello! Whom am I speaking to, please?' I breathed down the phone.

'This is Father Noel Harris. Can I help you?'

'Oh, yes, Father. I am trying to contact my brother, Charlie Long.

We have had a death in the family. It's our brother Harry. I am trying to get a message to Charlie. He doesn't have a phone in the house. Could you possibly call on him, Father, and tell him to come as soon as possible to my mother's house?'

'Yes. Yes, certainly I will do that. What is his address?'

'Father, I don't know the exact address. But he is living two doors down from Ryan's sweet shop. Do you know where that is?'

'Ah, yes. That's no problem. I will go up there now myself. And I am very sorry to hear of your tragic loss. You have my deepest condolences.'

'Thank you, Father. Thank you very much for your help. I am grateful.'

'Not at all. I am only too happy to help. Goodbye now.'

'Goodbye, Father,' and I gently put down the phone with my heart filling with pain. Harry! Why did you have to go before your time? I sat without moving, seeing his face lying on that cold . . .

No! It's better to keep moving. I jumped up, grabbing my warm duffle coat from the coat rack. It's going to be very cold out. Then I grabbed my bag from the hall table and checked for my house and car keys. I need a notebook and pen. Where's me tobacco?

I rushed into the kitchen, grabbing them off the table. Are the windows locked? Cooker off? Then back out to the hall and put on my boots, pushing my jeans down inside them. I locked the doors behind me, making sure the French doors are locked, and headed out the front gate. There's no point in going around to the garage; I left the car out. Anyway, I don't want that bloody dog seeing me go out; he will only jump over the wall and tear after me.

II

I parked the car and headed in the door to the undertaker's. A loud bell clanged over the door as I opened it. Jesus! That nearly took the ears offa me, the size of it! I looked up at a huge big brass bell, then whipped my head around the room. It's only a cubbyhole. I've more room at home for a sweeping brush!

'Can I help you?'

My head shot around, wondering where the voice was coming from. An aul fella with a solid, round, bald head poked his nose through a door just behind the entrance.

'Eh, yes!' I said, getting ready to speak, then staring at the ham sandwich he shoved into his mouth while he examined me.

'Take a seat over there,' he said, waving what was left of the sandwich as he opened his mouth wide, showing me his big black horse's teeth and his jaws working up and down, making short work of the grub.

I looked to see where he was pointing. The only thing I could see was a three-legged stool and an aul Victorian desk that had seen better days. One of the legs was propped up with old books. The woodworm had eaten the life outa the leg, and it was now practically honeycombed! What a dump! It hasn't changed for years. This place is still limping through the 1800s.

I sat down, balancing myself on the stool, and opened my bag, taking out a packet of roll-ups, gasping for a cigarette.

'Now! What can I do for you?' he said, squeezing his huge belly past me.

I slammed my feet down on the floor, reaching my hands forward trying to balance myself as I tipped backwards from the force of him. I pushed the stool back against the wall and stood up, leaning against his desk, feeling very annoyed.

'I'm here to arrange my brother's funeral,' I announced crisply.

'Oh, yes,' he said, lowering his head and fixing his face into a very sorrowful look. Then he reached for a notebook and pen, and lifted his shoulders and arms, trying to stretch his nylon pink shirt with the two buttons missing in the middle. His belly button was straining through his vest. Then he stretched his chin sideways, jerking his neck, and tried to loosen the collar with his two fingers, rolling them inside. Satisfied that was sorted, he then bounced up and down on his old Victorian office chair, settling his arse and giving it a few rubs, like Bonzo does when he gets worms.

I waited.

'OK,' he said, finally satisfied he was comfortable and he could get down to business. Then he snapped his head up, finally paying me a bit of notice. 'Now! I am going to need some details of the deceased. Where is the body to be collected from?' He held the pen in mid air, waiting for my answer.

'Actually, before we begin, may I have some details from you first, please?' I said, looking at him.

'OK. What do you want to know? It depends on how much you want to spend . . .'

'Well, we have the death grant,' I said, interrupting him.

He paused, looking at his notebook, then threw down his pen and pushed himself back in the chair, wrapping his massive arms around his head.

'Ah! So it's a pauper's burial ye're talkin about,' he said, looking very disappointed and losing his 'Mother-of-Sorrows' look.

'No! Absolutely not! We want a decent burial. So what exactly are you offering?' I barked, glaring at him.

He snorted and flicked his eyes away from me, then looked back at me with sheer boredom.

'Have you opened the grave yet?'

'What do you mean? I thought it was your job to arrange the funeral,' I asked him, feeling very confused.

He suddenly leaned forward, spreading himself on the desk. 'The department will only pay for,' and he lifted his big hairy hand and started to tick off one by one what the grant will pay for, 'the coffin: plain pine; the shroud; and one car. That's it! If ye don't want him going into a pauper's grave, you have to come up with the money. And this you do yourself. You have to go over to Glasnevin Cemetery, and it will cost you two hundred and fifty pounds. And you can't make any arrangements until you have the grave opened. Now, I must warn you. Where is the body, by the way?'

'In the new hospital,' I said in shock.

'Was there a post-mortem?'

'Yes,' I said.

'Well,' he said, shaking his head, 'if you don't get your own grave opened within the time after the body is released, the coroner's office will bury him in a pauper's grave.'

I stared in shock as he shook his head. It was going round and round like he was having a fit. My eyes followed his every movement, trying to take in what he was saying.

I don't have two hundred and fifty pounds, I was thinking. If I hadn't bought the plane tickets for Sarah, hoping she would be able to come home to see me. God! She's due on Sunday! I blinked and straightened myself up. 'So! I can't make any arrangements with you until I have the grave opened. Is that what you are saying?'

'Yep! That's it in a nutshell,' he said, shaking his head with energy.

'Right! I will get back to you,' I said, turning for the door and heading for the car.

I sat at the steering wheel, taking a deep drag of smoke into my lungs, wondering how I was going to work this out. OK. Think! What resources do I have? Sister Eleanor? No! Don't beg. Friends? No! Don't borrow. What friends anyway? They've all faded away since I started hibernating. Jeff? Or maybe Trilby (because he wears a trilby hat)? No! They would be after my body! I'm saving that for the worms. What then? Bloody hell! Think.

I can't go out to the ma until I get this sorted out. Ah! The ma's! The very place. I have an idea. It just might work. I gunned the engine and swung the car out into oncoming traffic. I swung out my arm, waving them down, making it clear my intention to take the centre of the road. Then I swung the car around in the opposite direction and took off like a bullet, heading towards the ma's. Time will not be on my side. I need to act quick. Them bastards will not think twice about burying Harry in a pauper's grave. Shouting or no shouting. They can do what they like. They have the power with their fucking rules.

Right. Here we are, back again. I've arrived at the flats. I'll head over to the shops and park outside the pub.

12

'Where's the boss?' I asked a moody-looking barman who was dragging a dirty dishcloth across the counter.

'He's inside,' the fellow said, shaking his head towards the back of the pub.

'Could I have a word with him, please?' I asked, smiling at him, showing him me white pearls.

'Can I help you?' he asked, brightening up and dropping his dishcloth. 'I'm the manager here.'

'Well, eh, thanks. But it's probably better to speak to himself,' I whispered, waving my hand towards the back, leaning into the counter.

He hesitated, his eyes flickering with disappointment and annoyance because he wasn't good enough. An he the bloody manager! He continued slapping the cloth up and down the counter wearily, deciding to ignore me. I watched him, waiting. Boring holes in his bent head, letting him see I meant business. Finally, he lifted his head, throwing me a dirty look, then steamed off to find the boss.

No, sunshine! With that sullen, dozy attitude of yours, it's quite clear to me you couldn't organise a piss-up in a brewery! I thought, snorting out me disgust as I looked miserably around the huge barn of a place. This pub was obviously purpose built to squeeze in as many people from around here willing to cough up their dole money and anything else they can get their hands on for the money.

They live in an ocean of misery. But at night this place stands out like a beacon. The lure of its bright lights and the noise of its lonely foghorn sending out sad, haunting music, touching the hearts of the lonely, the abandoned and the forgotten, as they raise their voices singing lustily, 'If I Only Had My Time Again' or 'The Happy Days

Of My Childhood'. For a while, they belong among the laughter, the shared sorrows and the tears. They gulp, wanting more, as the drink warms their bellies and mellows their heart.

Then the light slowly fades, as the music stops and the laughter dies, leaving only a darkness. It's then they make their lonely way back to the squalor of a bare, empty flat. The only thing taking up room is the cold, hungry children lying on the dirty beds. They have been waiting listlessly for a good day that never came.

The carpet was manky, black from the dirt, and the smell of stale smoke, spilt drink and dusty air was giving me a headache. An aul codger sitting in the corner waved his pint of stout over at me. He kept grinning, showing me his gummy mouth. All his front teeth were missing. I stared impassively. On second thoughts, he's not that old after all, probably in his mid forties. He just looks ancient. Yeah, that's years of neglect and booze. Jaysus! What a waste of a life!

'Who is looking for me?'

I whirled around, seeing a freckled-face aul fella with red greying hair.

'Yes? Can I help you?' he snapped, looking very annoyed I had interrupted him.

'Oh, yeah,' I said, trying to think, feeling me heart sink. I'm not going to get very far with this fella, I thought, seeing the watery blue eyes take me in from head to toe, then narrowing, giving me a suspicious look. Fuck! Bet this aul fella thinks he owes himself money. He has that mean, hungry look about him. You'd need a can opener to get any money outa his pockets.

I watched him as he rounded the bar, coming over to me. He kept staring at me like I had done something wrong.

'I remember you!' he said, waving his finger at me. Then he suddenly bent his head, saying, 'Well! So, you didn't join them after all!' Then he stood with a laugh ready on his face, waiting to hear me answer.

'Join who?' I said, wondering what the hell he was talking about.

'The nuns! The Carmelites!' he roared.

'ME? Sorry, I have no idea what you are talking about. I never . . . Eh, no! I'm not a nun.'

'That's for sure!' he roared again, laughing his head off, looking me up and down. I stared at him with me mouth open. Not able to make head nor tail outa what the hell he's talking about.

'Do you not remember me?' he said, laughing with a mad glint in his eye.

'No! I never met you before in my life,' I said, getting outa breath from trying to work this out.

'Come over here,' he said, leading me to a table in a little alcove.

I followed him, taking in the dark pinstripe suit with the Italian black-leather shoes. Hmm! He's not short of a few bob. This place must sure pay its way. But how the bloody hell can he know me? He's obviously mixing me up with someone else.

'Well, now then!' he said, pulling out a chair for me to sit on, then planking himself down beside me. 'The last time I met you, you told me you were taking yourself off into a nunnery!'

'Ah, would you go on outa that!' I said, giving him a slap on the arm, feeling now on safer ground because, whoever he was, he was certainly being very friendly.

'Yes,' he said. 'You were with that bowzie, Georgie Peacock!'

'Oh, right,' I said slowly, getting a picture of Georgie. A fella I used to know with plenty of money and no sense. He threw it around like confetti! Dragging me all over the place. He even had his own box at the races. But that went nowhere. He was a bloody alcoholic! Anyway! I wasn't interested in getting serious. I think he just wanted me for the company more than anything else. For a while, I was glad to oblige.

'But how do you know him?' I said. 'Or, at least both of us together? I'm still not able to make the connection. Georgie had a lot of friends. I don't remember half of them,' I said, staring into his icy-blue eyes that seemed to be softer now, when he let go and smiled. Pity about the hair, though. It would never have matched the eyes before it turned nearly stone grey.

'Ahh! Georgie and I go way back,' he said, leaning himself back on the chair. Then he sat with his hand on his chin, resting his elbow on the table, watching me.

I kept shaking me head slowly. 'No, can't say I remember you.'

'No?' he said, shaking his head, agreeing with me. 'The yacht club. I do a bit of sailing.'

'No! Definitely not!' I said. 'You wouldn't catch me anywhere near a boat. I can't swim and I get seasick!' I said, getting more annoyed with meself and puzzled by the minute.

'Well! Obviously I didn't make much of an impression on you!' he said, laughing, then shaking his head, trying to look sad. He lifted his head, looking around, and sighed, 'Do you want a drink? What would you like? Martin!' he shouted, roaring over to the barman.

'No, no thanks, but I won't. I have a lot of work ahead of me. It's going to be a long day, and I certainly need a clear head,' I said, giving a little laugh but feeling nervous about wasting the time.

'Ahh, yeah! You told me you were in the wine business,' he said. 'Are you still flogging wine with that company? What was it called? Hang on. Martin! Bring me over . . . What do you want to drink?'

'Oh, God, no, thanks. I couldn't!'

'Ahh! Just have something. It will put a bit of colour into them cheeks. You look a bit peaky to me.'

'OK,' I said, not wanting to annoy him. 'I'll have . . .' I tried to think.

'Have a glass of wine,' he said.

'Yeah, OK. White, please. Do you have Chablis?'

'Ha, ha! Where do you think you are? St George's Yacht Club?'

'Eh, sorry! No, anything will do,' I said, feeling foolish.

'No,' he said, turning back to me, saying easily, 'we wouldn't have any call for that over here.' He laughed.

'Yeah, right,' I said, thinking, for a while there I was getting carried away with meself. It's all this talk of Georgie, reminding me of the old days, when I was living the high life.

'So, you seem to remember a lot about me,' I said. 'Even down to the job I was doing. I still can't place you.'

'Well, you and the bold rake Georgie arrived in the club one night. We got together after the party thinned out. I invited you both down to my house in Dalkey. Remember?'

'Ahhh!' Then it dawned on me. The aul chancer! 'Yeah, indeed I do remember you very well,' I said, thinking back. The wife was away and the Georgie fella collapsed in a heap on the sitting-room couch. Bleedin mouldie drunk he was. This gobshite invited me to look around his house and admire his 'etchings', as he called them.

When we arrived at the 'etchings', it turned out to be a guest bedroom. I stared nervously at the big double bed while he waxed lyrical about the magnificent sea view!

'Come over here, you beautiful creature,' he purred, grabbing me around the waist to fly me over to the window and look out while he tried to rush his hands and roam his fingers all over me chaste body! I was having none a tha! He wasn't a man to give up easily. After cranking up the heat to full blast, he thought I might take me ease, climbing into something more comfortable. Me birthday suit!

NO! I was definitely havin none a that! Then he propositioned me! He's an awful fuckin chancer. The little rat bag! Chased me all around the bleedin house. I had te keep going to save me virtue!

'I see you have your hair tied up,' he said, with a glint in his eye as he leaned over to take the drinks from the barman. He handed me the glass of white wine and sipped on a whiskey for himself. 'You have lovely hair,' he said, reaching up to touch it. I had it tied up in several knots and secured at the back with a big ivory slide. Then he dropped his hand and lifted his drink, taking a sip, saying, 'Ah, yes. A woman's crowning glory is her hair.'

Oh, fuck! Here we go again. Bored married men and a single woman!

'How long is that hair?' he said. 'You must have been growing it for years.'

'Oh, yeah. Years. I haven't cut it since I was a young one,' I said, thinking, it hasn't had a cut since the day I left the convent and escaped Sister Eleanor and her bloody shears, as she called that big scissors of hers. 'How long is it?' I repeated. 'Oh, I don't know. It goes down to me ankles,' I said. 'Like Mary Magdalene.'

He roared laughing, saying, 'Ah, well now! That certainly was not my experience of you! By the time you left, burning rubber in that taxi . . . Hell's bells! You left in an awful hurry. It was terrible. I nearly pole-vaulted out the window! Whatever put such a hurry on you?' he said, looking outraged.

'What do you mean, pole-vaulted?' I said, looking at him all confused.

He gave me a sideways look, saying, 'Tut, tut! Are you sure you haven't been living in that convent since I last saw you? Think about it! A young attractive woman, and a . . .'

'Oh! I get the picture,' I muttered, then said quietly, 'You really are incorrigible.'

'Really?' he said, grinning, then let it slide off his face when he saw I wasn't amused.

'No,' I muttered. 'The whole experience was not very nice.' I didn't care if he wasn't going to help me raise the money. He wasn't going to get away with thinking he could piss on me then think nothing of it.

He stared at me, then lowered his head, saying quietly, 'Mea culpa, mea culpa,' as he slowly thumped his chest. 'No, I behaved very badly. That was very wrong of me. I didn't realise.

'Look! This is no excuse,' he said, looking straight at me.

I shifted myself, dropping my head to one side, and folded my arms, taking in what he had to say.

'You see the women . . . girls Georgie usually hangs around with are what you might call "gold diggers". Out for what they can get. So, I assumed wrongly. Well, I was chancing my arm! I'm sorry, terribly sorry for putting you through that. I only realised later. You were a nice girl, not someone out to take advantage.'

I nodded my head, closing my eyes. Letting him know I certainly was not an easy mark.

'Am I forgiven?' he said, leaning into me, looking into my face and laughing.

'Oh, I suppose. You wouldn't be the first to try it on,' I said, sighing. 'But it's going to get less and less,' I said, feeling like letting out something inside meself. Not caring what he thought. 'I'm getting a bit fed up with men. I might just take meself off, after all, to that Carmelite nunnery.'

'Ah, Gawd no! Don't be so rash! There's an awful shortage of good-looking single women at the minute!' he said, laughing his head off. Then we just sat quietly. Him staring at his drink, thinking, and me wondering how the hell I was going to ask him now about money.

'Now! Tell me,' he suddenly said, lifting up his jacket sleeve to look at his watch. 'What brings you here? You didn't say. Are you still with that wine company? Are you going to try and sell me something? Is that it?' he laughed, looking around me to see if I was carrying something.

'No!' I laughed, looking at him, then pulled out my tobacco to roll meself a cigarette. I licked my way around the paper, thinking how I was going to approach this. Pity he knows people I know. I don't want him knowing my business.

I took a deep breath and plunged in. 'It really is lovely meeting you again,' I said, beaming at him. 'It certainly is a surprise meeting you here. I didn't know you owned a pub,' I said, looking around.

'Oh!' he said, throwing his eye, taking in the place. 'I have a lot of other interests. In fact, I'm only here because I have some staff problems to sort out. Martin is my new bar manager. I'm showing him the ropes. Then let him get on with it. I have another meeting in half an hour. I better get moving shortly. So, tell me, what brings you here?' and he mooched closer to me, leaving little space between us.

'Have you heard about the young fellow who went over the balcony last night?' I paused, waiting for his reaction.

'Oh, yes. That was a terrible business,' he said, shaking his head sadly. 'Why? Did you know him?'

I nodded, saying quietly, 'Yes, yes I did, very well,' looking him squarely in the face.

He studied me, wanting to know more. But I left it at that, leaving him to draw his own conclusions.

'That's why I'm here. His name is Harry. He's . . . was twenty-eight years old. Now he's lying in the morgue, up in the new hospital, waiting to be claimed. But there's no money to bury him. Just a grant of a few quid. It will only cover the coffin, a shroud and one car. That's it. Two hundred and fifty pounds is needed to open a grave. Today. If the money can't be found, then he will end up in a pauper's grave.' I looked at him, not wanting to show him how upset I really was.

He stared at me, thinking. He looked confused, then stared at me more intently. Then I saw his eyes soften with compassion and then curiosity, as he blinked, trying to work out what exactly was my connection.

'I was hoping you would be able to raise some money, maybe run a benefit or something. I know he is very well known and liked around here.' I hesitated, holding my breath. 'Is that possible?' I asked, staring into his face, seeing the concern in his eyes.

He said nothing. Just sat still, staring at the table, thinking. Then he very slowly started nodding his head, like he had made a decision. Without saying another word, he very gently put his hand over mine, covering it, still sitting on the table. 'Would you like another drink?'

'No, thanks. I really better get moving,' I said, feeling very anxious about the time, and worrying about the money.

'Yeah, I'll have to move too,' he said, sighing, looking worried himself about the time moving on.

Then I suddenly said, 'Listen, I'm sorry, but what's your name again? Mine is Martha.'

He reached back, laughing, then grabbed my hand, saying, 'I was afraid to ask! Martha! Lovely name for a lovely girl. Paul!'

'Ah, that's it!' I said. 'Now I remember. You and Georgie went to school together.'

'Yep, we did,' he said, laughing at the mention of Georgie's name. 'The Jesuits!' he grinned. Then he loped off, weaving in and out of the tables.

I lit up another cigarette and took a sip of the wine. It burned its way down my neck, making my head fuzzy. I hadn't eaten much today, or any day for that matter.

He came back, heading straight towards me with purpose in his step, looking very serious. My stomach started fluttering with nerves. God! I hope it's good news. I need to get that grave sorted out.

I looked up nervously as he bent down towards me. He put his hand in his pocket and took out a white envelope, then gave a glance around to see if anyone was watching. I held my breath. Afraid to hope.

'Here! Take this,' he said, sliding an envelope across the table, pressing my hand over it. It felt very bulky! 'Take this, it will see you through. One thing, though!'

I looked up at him, waiting for the catch, feeling a momentary sense of disappointment.

'I would prefer if you didn't mention this to anyone. Especially around here,' he laughed, looking around him. 'It wouldn't do to let them think I'm a soft touch!'

I laughed with relief. 'No! I'm absolutely discreet.' Then I stood up.

'Listen,' he said, looking at me. 'I will arrange with Martin the manager to organise a fund,' he said, putting his hand on my arm.

'Don't worry about that; everything will be looked after. You just go and do what you have to do.'

I stared at him, not knowing what to say, feeling overwhelmed by his kindness. Then he hesitated. 'Perhaps we might meet some time? Do you still live in the same area?'

I hesitated.

'I'm not married, you know.'

'You're not?' I said, sounding shocked. 'But I assumed . . .'

'What? I had a wife and six kids tucked away? No, no. Oh, I was married once, as a young fella with no sense and no money. She left me after a couple of years. So that was that,' he said, shaking his head, thinking mournfully about his mistake. 'We're well divorced. No kids. No ties!'

'Oh!' I said, looking at him in a different light. 'Listen, Paul,' I said, reaching to touch his arm. 'You have no idea what this means. I really am very grateful for your kindness,' thinking his lovely blue eyes go very well with his stony-grey hair! 'By the way, Paul, I'm still living in the same place. Close to Georgie's place. I might see you around when I'm passing the yacht club. Only passing, mind. I wouldn't have any business going in there,' I laughed.

'Great!' he beamed. 'Give me your telephone number, and I will ring you. Would you mind?'

'No, I'd be delighted,' I said, peeling off a page from my notebook and scribbling down my phone number, then handing it to him. 'Thanks again, Paul,' I said, taking his hand to shake it.

'It was nothing. Think nothing of it,' he said, waving away his generosity.

Then I turned and waved, saying, 'I hope to see you again, Paul. Take care.' Then I was out the door, heading for my car.

I leapt into the car, slamming the door shut, then whipped open the envelope. I could feel me heart hammering in my chest. Oh, what did he give me? I thought, clapping eyes on the money. Dear God! If only I could get enough to cover the cost of the grave! I counted out the twenty-pound notes. Five hundred pounds! I stared! Jesus Christ almighty! The man is a saint! I wanted to cry and laugh. Oh, Harry! You should have waited. There is still a lot of goodness in the world. Then I felt the hot tears stream down my face. Happiness at meeting goodness. There is still hope! And deep loss and sorrow at losing you, Harry. But you are going to have your own grave, and I will get you a headstone. You won't be forgotten as long as there is one of us left, especially the poor ma. At least she will have the consolation of being able to visit you, and your gravestone will let everyone know you existed.

I turned the engine on, wondering what time it is. I never carry a watch. I don't like to be dictated to by time unless it's necessary. I pulled the car around, heading off to Glasnevin Cemetery. I hope it's not too late. Maybe I'll make it there before they knock off for home. But I can always do it in the morning. I felt a quiet calm inside me, a stillness. That man will never know he gave me more than just money. It's true! Kindness goes a long way.

13

I threw the shopping bags in the back of the car and climbed in. Jaysus! I'm glad that's over. I hate shops! I always start to rattle and shake. I never got over the old days. I still expect someone to creep up behind me and land their hand on my shoulder, saying, 'Will you come with me, please!' and I'm caught. Oh! My stomach lurched again, and I felt myself shake all over just thinking about it.

Right! Stop yer carry-on! That was centuries ago. Now! Where's that tobacco? And I gave myself a shake to clear my head and pulled out my tobacco to have a well-earned smoke. I sat puffing and peeled my eyes down the list of things to do and marked them off one by one. Grave? Done. Removal from hospital to church? Five o'clock this evening. Right! That means I better give that gobshite in the funeral home a phone call just to check he will arrive at the house by four o'clock to collect everybody. Harry's wife? Social welfare found her. She's arriving this evening. She's living in London. Her sister will be collecting her from the airport. Burial? That's after the eleven o'clock Mass in the morning. So the priest is sorted. Flowers? Two wreaths. One from the ma saying 'Son', and the other from the family saying 'Brother'. Clothes? Black for the ma. I bought her a white blouse, black mohair cardigan, black skirt, black stockings and the bloody black headscarf! It took me hours searching for that. The ma had to have her scarf. Bleedin black hat wouldn't do her! Then I snorted, giving a big laugh. The sight of the ma in a black hat? Definitely not! She'd probably get herself arrested. They'd think she'd probably escaped from the nearest loony bin! Me? I got the same. Without the scarf! Food? Sister Eleanor is bringing the chickens I gave her to cook. She can leave them in the flat in the morning before we set off for the funeral. So there's plenty of grub, and she said she would get Sister Benedict in the convent kitchen to rustle up a bit of baking. Quiches, sandwiches and stuff. So, I think that's the lot.

Now! What's next? Now I get myself home for a shower, a quick bite of something to eat, then it's out the door and make haste to the ma's. I have got to get her ready, then speak to the priest about readings for the Mass. Who will be reading what? Dinah can give a reading. I will probably end up getting into a row with the priest; they like to control everything. Not this time, me boy! Oh no! Harry belonged to us, and I put plenty of rearing into him when he was only a baby. So, to hell with you, Father!

I slammed the front door shut behind me and tore out to the car. What happens to the time? Three o'clock! I better move fast. The car is arriving at quarter to four to collect everyone and take us to the hospital.

I raced down the hill, the lights still with me. Have I got the stuff for the ma? I glanced in the back of the car. The bags with the ma's clothes sat there. Good! And the grub. A bit of ham, tomatoes, bread, butter, milk, tea, biscuits and other stuff. It will keep them going until the morning, when Sister Eleanor brings over the cooked stuff.

The traffic was still light. It won't start getting heavy until around half past four. Good! It won't matter then.

I saw the flats just ahead of me in the distance; no one can miss them. I sighed in me breath, feeling everything was under control. Good, I'm nearly there!

I rounded the bend, passing the shops, then slowed down, taking care to watch out for the kids. They can come tearing up, shooting out from nowhere. Jaysus! They would put the heart crossways in ye. Then I braked suddenly as an ashen-faced, haggard-looking junkie stepped out in front of the car. He was covered in scabs, with red bloodshot eyes. He staggered straight out in front of me, then stopped in the middle of the road, noticing me for the first time. He stared, waiting for his face to twist in annoyance, then started to wave his arms at the car. 'Fuckin wait, will ye! Ye'll knock me down, ye bleedin cow!'

I sat there, staring at him calmly, waiting for him to get over his frustration of me driving and him walking. Satisfied he'd sorted me out, and I was well and truly in me place, left sitting here waiting for him to decide when he was going to get moving again, he swung his head, then shifted his body around to follow his head and stared across the road, judging the distance to the footpath.

I waited. A few seconds of him thinking how to manoeuvre this, and, yep! He's off! Straightening up. One leg first, quickly followed by the other. We have a stagger! Now he's moving and racing towards the footpath. He never takes his eyes off that path, mesmerised by it. Pause. Lift one leg high into the air. Slam it down on the footpath. Balance. Now lift the other one. And he's off! Heading straight into the shopping centre to organise his next fix. Jesus, help us! The Dubliners are being wiped out with the cursed drugs!

I drove into the flats and parked the car. It's safe here. They don't rob their own – honour among thieves.

'Martha!'

I looked around to see who was calling me. Ah! The bold Teddy. Me eyes narrowed, watching the carry-on of him.

'Dish is me sister. The one I was telling youse about!' He waved his arm like he was giving out benediction to a crowd of fellas standing around him. He was drunk as a skunk! I walked over to the stairs, and he tried to stand up.

The fellas moved to let me pass, and Teddy tried to grab me around the shoulders, and cried, 'Dish is Martha! She's me big sister!'

They all flicked their eyes up and down me, giving half-smiles. Then they nodded their heads, lowering their eyes, then moved away a little, giving me more room.

I looked at Teddy, seeing him the image of Jackser and getting more like him every day. He took a swig of a drink from a big cider bottle and wiped his mouth with the sleeve of his jacket.

'Right! Give me that, you!' and I lunged for the bottle, grabbing it out of his hand before he knew what happened. 'No more drink, Teddy!' I roared, pouring it onto the grass. 'This is what killed Harry in the first place!' I screamed, losing me rag with disgust. He should be up looking after everyone.

He was too gobsmacked to say anything. His eyes stared at the empty bottle as I raced to the chute and threw it down.

'Now, you! Up them stairs,' and I grabbed him by the arm and pulled him up the stairs.

'Ah, Martha! Wha did ye go an do tha for? I'm in bits over Harry.'

'Yes! So you are going to go up them stairs and put your head under that cold tap in the bathroom and sober up. You have fifteen minutes before that car arrives to take us to collect him. Teddy! You are not going to let Harry down! He would want you to be stone-cold sober and to give him a quiet and respectable send-off. He doesn't want any fucking blackguarding! Do you get that?'

I stopped on the stairs and lowered my face into his, staring into his eyes. He stared back, looking confused. 'Do it for him, Teddy,' I whispered. 'One last time. Stay sober, stay in the house, look after the ma. Make Harry proud of us. Will you do that, Teddy?'

I lowered my face even closer to his. He stared at me, showing his heart had been ripped outa him. Harry and him had been like Siamese twins. You see one, you see the other.

'Darling, do it for Harry,' I said, wrapping me hands on his face.

He closed his eyes and blinked, shaking his head at me. I took him into my arms, and he cried quietly. I said nothing. Just held him. 'OK, Teddy. Let's go up,' I said quietly.

Me ma was standing in her bare feet, staring at the black tights I bought her.

'Hurry up, Ma! You have to get ready!'

'Ah, no. I wouldn't wear them,' she said, chewing her lip, holding them away from her as if they were going to bite her.

I stared at her white blouse and black cardigan over the black skirt. She looked fine until you got down to her white hairy legs!

'Come on, Ma! Sit down,' and I pushed her sitting on the bed. 'Now try them on!' and I grabbed her foot, rolling up the tights. But they got caught in her toenails.

'Ah, Ma! For the luv a Jaysus! Look at the length of your toenails! Did you ever cut them in your life?' I said, trying to hold her foot and peel the tights back without laddering them.

'Ah! Don't be annoyin me! You an yer bleedin tights!' she whined, snatching her foot back.

'Holy Jaysus! Has anyone made me a sup a tea yet?' Jackser roared, his head appearing at the bedroom door.

I looked up at him standing there, glaring from me to the ma, his fists curled down by his sides.

'Jackser!'

'Wha?' he snorted, leaning over to hear what I was going to say.

'Make your own fucking tea!' I said quietly.

He paused, his head still leaning towards me. Then it hit him and he straightened his back.

'Righ! Tha's it! Youse can all go and fuck yerselves. I'm doin no more fer ye's! Tha bleedin car is goin te be here any minute now an none a youse is ready. So! They'll just turn tha fuckin car aroun an go off wit out the lot of ye's. So youse may WALK! So fuck ye's!' he roared, marching up the hall.

'God, Ma! How do you stand it?' I said, swinging my head back to look at the ma.

'Ah, don't be mindin tha fuckin eegit,' she said, looking down at the stockings.

'Ma! You are wearing these,' and I grabbed her foot again, curling the tights carefully over her steel nails.

'No! I'm not wearin them!' she laughed, trying to get her foot back. 'They'll only fall offa me!'

'No! Come on, they won't. Now stand up and pull them on.'

I lifted her to her feet, grabbing for her shoes.

'They're grand,' I said pulling them the rest of the way up and pulling down her skirt. 'Now sit down and put these shoes on. You are the same size as me. They're black, Ma. They will go with the skirt and jumper.'

I stood back to look at her. 'Yeah, you're fine,' I said, eyeing her hair. Pity I didn't get a chance to wash it. 'Right! Get your coat, and here's the black scarf I bought you,' I said, lifting it out of the bag.

'Maaa! Where's me navy-blue jumper?' young Sally roared, flying her head in the door, glaring at me ma. Then she swung back out again before me ma had a chance to open her mouth.

'Dinah! Did you take me new jumper? Cos if ye did . . .'

'I didn't see no jumper!' Dinah roared back.

'Ah, Ma! They have to be ready on time,' I said, looking at the ma, seeing her staring down at her legs.

'Do ye think I look all right, Martha?' me ma asked, looking down at herself and swinging herself from side to side.

'Of course you do, Ma. You look grand,' I said, sweeping past her and heading for the front door. 'But come on! Hurry, Ma! Will you get them out the door? We have to leave.'

I raced down the stairs and over to my car, grabbing my tobacco from the front seat. I'm dying for a cigarette. I put the tobacco in my bag and lit up, taking a deep puff into my lungs. I would love a cup of tea to go with this. Then I spotted the car cruising past the shops, heading down to the flats. I turned suddenly, about to make a run up to the flat to warn the others, when I spotted a familiar figure standing over by the wall, close to the stairs. Our eyes locked.

'Martha!' she whispered, looking very frightened.

'Nora!' I stared, not taking her in for a minute. She stood there next to another girl. The girl was trying to look like she'd protect Nora with her life. She was standing very stiff, with her lips clamped together. Then she threw her head back in defiance when she saw I spotted them. But I saw, too, the fear in her eyes. That must be Nora's big sister.

I rushed over, taking Nora's hands and squeezing them. 'You got here, then,' I whispered, looking into her huge grey eyes. They're all red and swollen from crying. She was white as a sheet, with deep purple circles under her eyes. She could have been twelve years old, she looked so young and frightened.

'Oh, Martha! Martha, I'm so sorry. I can't believe wha's happened. He's gone! Just like tha! Gone for ever,' she said, waving her hands at me, then looking at the ground. Not able to take any of it in.

She started to cry. I watched her face breaking up and huge tears started rolling down her cheeks.

'I'm so afraid,' she whispered, lifting her head to look at me. 'Will you tell the rest of them? I had te get away, Martha,' she said, looking down at her hands. 'We were supposed te make a new start, on our own.'

She stared into another time, another place, remembering. Then she slowly raised her eyes up to the ma's flat. 'I couldn't take any more, Martha,' she said, putting her arm lightly on mine.

I held it, listening to her. Seeing the terrible pain, the torture, the loss and the bewilderment – it all stared out through her eyes.

'So I left him,' she whispered. 'Even though we were married an had our own place. They were always after Harry, night an day.

They couldn't do anythin te help themselves, an Teddy couldn't give a damn. He was always missin. Ye very seldom find him up there, but Harry! My Harry. He was too soft, Martha.'

Then she collapsed crying. I wrapped my arms around her, hugging her very tight.

'You did the right thing, Nora! You got away! Harry couldn't. That's all. Don't blame yourself for having great courage. Because that's what it took for you to get away and do it on your own. You have to protect your children and yourself.

'Listen, Nora. I want you to listen very carefully. This is very important,' I said, taking her face in my hands and penetrating her eyes, looking for her awareness. 'Harry died here, trapped by them. Sally and Jackser. You and the children made him very happy, for the first time in his life. But you could never have saved him. Nobody could! The damage was done long before you met him. But remember, Nora, he is going to his grave knowing what it is to be loved. You gave him that, and you are the bravest woman I know. You got your children away from them, and now you can give them a better life.

'Be happy, Nora. You were only meant to have him for a short while, and always remember you fought like a tigress to save your family, but no one is a match for them. You can't fight madness! You just run for your life.

'Do you know the reason I escaped them, Nora? Because I didn't belong to Jackser, and the ma turned her back on me because he didn't want me. So I wasn't one of them, either.

'I was put away because of them. So, in the end, they did me a big favour. Because when I left the convent at sixteen, I had to make my own way in the world. It was bloody tough, Nora. Lonely, but it was worth it. You do survive! And life is what you make it. You're tough. You got this far, and I have to give it to you, you are here now, ready to stand up to them just so you can walk that last mile with Harry,' I said, smiling at her. 'Just keep your nerve, Nora. Don't let them get the better of you, and I won't be far away. Now! Wherever you are, don't ever let any of them here know. Don't look back! Keep moving forward.

'I am going to give you my telephone number, and if you ever need my help, I won't let you down.' I looked at her, seeing her shake her head up and down slowly. Then her eyes followed my hands reaching into the bag. I took out my notebook and scribbled down my name and phone number.

'Here! Take this, Nora,' I said, handing her the piece of paper.

She looked at it, then folded it carefully and put it in her pocket. Then she took out a tissue and sniffed, wiping her nose with the tissue. 'Thanks, Martha,' she whispered, trying to give me a smile. But it came out very weak. Her face was too stiff from all the tears.

'You will be fine, Nora darling,' I said, pulling her to me, giving her a tight hug, then holding her. 'I promise you,' I whispered, looking into her haunted eyes and stroking her face.

14

The car had stopped at the entrance to the stairs, and the driver was holding open the door, watching them all pile in. I stepped out from behind the stairs, holding Nora's hand. The ma appeared and stopped dead, staring at Nora. Everyone stared out of the car.

Suddenly, Aggie – she was born when I was in the convent – lunged out of the car and came rushing over to stand beside the ma, looking at Nora like she wanted to say something.

'Come on,' the ma said. 'Are ye getting in, love?' she whispered softly, talking to Nora very quietly. Then she grabbed hold of Aggie, pushing her towards the car, saying, 'Come on! Everyone get inta the car. We have te get goin!'

Me ma climbed in first, bending her head, then sat down. Aggie was next. Suddenly she stopped, leaving her arse hanging in the air. 'Here!' she screamed. 'Move over! Youse lot are not stickin me on tha little bleedin seat! Ma! Tell them. I'm not the youngest. He is!' she roared, making a grab for Gerry. He was sitting next to the aul fella.

'Sit down!' he roared.

'No! I'm not gettin in! Get up!' she huffed, trying to drag at Gerry.

'Leave him be!' little Sally heaved, pulling him back.

'Get in!' I roared.

'Fuck off, you! Who put her in charge?' she whipped, landing her vengeance on me.

'That's it!' I snorted, losing me rag and giving her a good push, trying to get her in. But she resisted, holding on to the outside of the door. All I could do was heave her arse in and out.

The driver waited patiently, saying nothing. He stood with his hat under his arm, just waiting to close the door.

'Ger in!' Teddy shouted, suddenly jumping up and pressing her neck down, pulling her into the car. Then the door was shut. I could hear the rumble of voices all arguing inside the car.

Jaysus! Am I glad not to be stuck inside that! I thought, breathing heavily, trying to get me breath back. I stood with my chest still heaving up and down, feeling very weak now, then looked at poor Nora standing at the wall.

'Listen,' I said, walking over to the driver. He eyed me warily, staring at me, wondering what was coming next. 'Put her,' and I rushed over, taking Nora gently by the waist, 'into the front seat with you. She's Harry's widow.'

He hesitated, trying to take in what's going on around him. I opened the front-seat passenger door, and he came to life and moved into action.

'Yes! Of course ye can sit in the front, love!' and he very gently helped her in and shut the door.

'I'm going to follow behind you,' I said, making for my own car. Enough is enough! I thought. I wonder why Charlie didn't turn up? Jesus! This is not the time to keep away, Charlie. You have your own troubles, I know. But! Ah, he'll probably go straight to the morgue at the hospital. I grabbed my bag, opening it, and tore out my tobacco pack, rolling a cigarette.

My hands were shaking. Jesus! I'm not able for this carry-on any more. I haven't got the health for it. I lit the cigarette, taking a deep drag, and started the engine. The funeral car was now taking off, and Aggie's face glared out at me from the back of the car. They were all still mouthing to each other, probably telling each other what to do. Yeah, better them than me. Thank God for small mercies. I like me bit of peace.

The car eased its way through the grounds of the hospital, stopping outside the chapel of rest. I pulled up behind it and parked closer to the wall, keeping well out of the way. I slammed the car door shut and stopped to take in a deep breath, then steady myself. I was beginning to feel a bit of weakness. It was running from me belly, making its way down to me legs. 'Right! I'm ready,' I muttered, taking another deep breath, then followed them in.

I stopped in surprise, taking in the huge size of the room. It's lovely, I thought, seeing the new deep-pile carpet and the walls lovely and bright. It was painted a snow-white. They have it well lit up, I thought, feeling the carpet sinking under me feet as I walked. I settled my eyes on the middle of the room, taking in where Harry lay. They had him on a long slab, covered with a white linen cloth, with the coffin open, resting on top. I slowly made my way over, walking past him, and stopped at his feet.

Jackser was staring down at him. Then he slowly lifted his arms, reaching down with his hands, and held Harry's face, stroking him with infinite gentleness. I stared, never seeing this side of him before. His face was grief-stricken. I watched as his head kept moving slowly towards Harry. It was like he was being pulled down, with his head getting slowly drawn into the coffin. His eyes looked like he was hypnotised.

When his face reached Harry's forehead, he pressed his lips down, leaving them lingering there. Then he lifted his head and stared into Harry's face, looking like someone had cut his heart out. Then he said, very quietly, barely above a whisper, 'Sleep. Sleep in peace, son. If only I could give ye back yer life, I wouldn't hesitate. No! Not for one hair's breadth, son, would I hesitate te take yer place. I'm goin te miss you now, wit every breath in me, for the rest of the days of me life. Yeah, Harry. Righ until the day I die.' Then his eyes and hands followed slowly down the length of Harry, gently stroking him. He stopped at Harry's joined hands and covered them with his own.

As I stared impassively at Jackser, I felt a momentary stirring of sympathy for him. He was suffering great pain. Even if it was of his own making. It was a glimpse of him I rarely saw.

'Jackser,' I whispered, moving up close beside him, taking the rosary beads out of my pocket. The Reverend Mother had given them to me the day I left the convent for the last time. 'Wrap these around his hands,' I whispered. 'He'll take something with him from us, to protect him on his way.'

Jackser stared down at the rosary beads. They were mother-of-pearl. I held them out to him. 'Oh, God! Yes! He'll need them,' Jackser said, taking them out of my hands. He leaned in and wrapped them through Harry's fingers, laying the cross over his hands.

Dinah came quietly over, standing beside me. She stared at Harry, letting her eyes travel the length of him. 'He was so tall,' she breathed.

'Look at the length of him, Martha! I never noticed tha about him before,' she said, shaking her head with a terrible sense of loss and bewilderment.

'Yeah, he really was tall,' I said, noticing he must have been nearly . . . I don't know, would he have been six foot? How did he ever get to be that tall? I wondered. When there had been no feeding put into him when he was a child. Maybe the dinners I brought home as a kid helped. Then I looked at Dinah. She's twice the size of meself, it's only Charlie and me are the smallest, even Gerry is taller. It must be on Jackser's side. But he's not tall, and the ma is the same size as me. I wonder where they all got the height from?

'Sally!'

I looked up, and Jackser was whispering over to the ma, who was standing well away, clinging to the wall.

'Come over, Sally, and see Harry!'

But the ma turned her head away in fear. 'No! No! I won't!' she muttered, shaking her head in panic and looking over towards the coffin. She couldn't see Harry, only the back of the coffin.

I went over to her and put my arm around her. 'Come on. Don't be afraid, Ma. It's Harry. If you don't say goodbye to him now, you will never get another chance,' I said, moving her over towards him.

'No!' She tried to pull away.

'Ma, if you don't see him, you will spend the rest of your life waiting for him to come home,' I said, staring into her face.

She looked unsure, so I eased her over, closer. Her eyes landed on her son, and she stared. 'Come over, Ma.' I pulled her closer. She was trying to resist me.

'Put your hands on him, Ma,' I whispered.

'He's gone! Harry!' she said, rubbing her hands in prayer and leaning down to look into his face.

'I warned ye! I kept tellin ye not te be takin tha drink!' and she put her hand on his forehead, then snatched it back, rubbing her hand like it had been burned. Then she hesitated, staring at him, looking like she wanted to wake him up.

I watched as she leaned in, then put her hand on his forehead again, rubbing it. 'Oh! Harry! Harry! Why wouldn't ye listen te me? Why did ye not listen te me, son?' she implored, leaning down and looking into his face. Then she lifted her head, looking around as if she was searching for someone.

She let her eyes fly, landing them on each of us in turn, looking as if she was thinking one of us could talk sense to Harry and bring him back. Then everything would be all right.

'Ma, it's all right,' I said, rushing to take her in my arms. 'Shush! Take it easy.'

'I don't know,' she kept muttering, shaking her head, sounding like she was in terrible torment.

'Come on, Ma,' I whispered. 'Let's go down here.'

I led her towards the back of the room, well away from the coffin. 'Here we are. Sit down here and rest yourself, Ma,' I said, putting her sitting down on the bench lined up against the wall.

'He wouldn't listen te me!' she said, to no one in particular. I held me arms around her, then caught Nora's eye. She was sitting just inside the door, terrified of making a move. I could see her glance up to the coffin, wanting to get up there, looking like she wanted to make her peace with her husband. No one took any notice of her.

Teddy came over and whispered to me, 'Is the ma all righ? Are ye all righ, Ma?' he said, sitting down beside her and wrapping his arm around her.

I pulled back and went to stand up, saying, 'Teddy, mind the ma. I want to go over to Nora.'

He stared over at Nora, seeing she was on her own. 'Yeah, you mind her. I'll look after me ma,' he said, nodding and smiling at me.

'Grand!' I whispered, making me way over to where she was sitting.

'Sweetheart,' I said, bending down and taking her arm, then helping her to her feet. 'Come over to Harry,' I whispered. 'It's quiet now, everyone is moving away,' I said, seeing them standing around the walls, lost in their own thoughts.

She looked around at everyone, looking like a frightened little deer. Then looked at me.

'Come on, Nora. You'll be all right. Take as much time as you want with Harry. There's no rush. Now's your time to say all you want to say to him. I pray, Nora, he'll give you peace,' I whispered into her ear, leading her over to the coffin.

Young Sally moved back, and Nora took her place, looking down into Harry's face. I moved away, taking young Sally with me. 'Come over to the ma, Sally. Look, she's taking it very badly!'

Dinah heard me as well and looked down to where the ma was sitting crying her heart out. We walked down to her, and the ma looked up at us, asking, 'What am I going to do now without Harry? How can he be gone just like tha? It doesn't make any sense te me!' she cried, looking at us all one by one.

'Come on, Ma. Let's get you outside,' I said, looking at the girls, seeing they were as confused as the ma. 'Bring her outside,' I said to them, helping the ma to her feet and nodding to the girls.

Jackser came up behind me, saying, 'They're goin te close the coffin now. Tha's the last time we'll ever see him, Martha,' he said, looking back. He had his right hand in a fist and the other one clamped over it, holding it tight to his chest as if in prayer. I looked back at the men preparing to put the lid on the coffin. Nora was standing alone. She stood back to let them seal up Harry for ever. But her face was locked on Harry, and she inched forward, wanting to get that last glimpse of him. I saw her hand fly up to her face as the men lowered the lid, and she shook her head slowly from side to side, mouthing, 'No! No!' Tears started to fall down her cheeks, and still she didn't make a sound. Her heart was breaking.

I went quickly up to her and took her wet face on my shoulder, holding her head tightly. 'I'm so sorry,' I murmured, rocking her as she heaved big silent screams. I felt her chest convulse and her body shake. But no sound came out. It was too deep down inside her. The terrible fear and pain and loss kept it locked up tight. But it would come. The poor child was still in shock.

'Come on, darling.' I started to walk her to the car, thinking she's never had it easy. The poor kid lost her mother when she was only a little girl.

Nora stopped, pulling herself away from me. 'Martha! Listen, wait,' she said.

'What? What is it, Nora?'

Her lips were moving, but nothing was coming out. I moved closer, looking into her face. She couldn't get out what she was trying to say.

'Come over here quickly,' I said, pulling her over to the corner. 'What's wrong?'

'It's Harry,' she whispered, letting her eyes stare into mine. Then she flicked them back to the coffin. We stared as the men made their way down towards us, then glided past as they carried him on the bier. I watched the coffin go slowly out the door and turned to Nora.

'He never knew he had a son! Last week I gave birth te a little baby boy, an he never even knew I was carryin his child!'

I was stunned, and couldn't open me mouth.

'He would have been delighted, Martha. He wanted a boy after havin two girls. But I didn't even know meself I was pregnant. Not until long after I left him. By then it was too late. I didn't want him te find me, so I kept it quiet. Martha, the baby is the image of Harry, the spitting image of his father,' she muttered, staring at me with the life gone out of her eyes. 'He has the same colour hair! I called him Harry, after his daddy. He never even knew!' she whispered, shaking her head, staring at the coffin being lifted into the funeral car.

'It's a miracle, Nora. You and Harry made that little baby! Now you will have a reminder, every day of your life, in little Harry. His dad was a good man, and little Harry will become the man one day his dad wanted to be. He will grow up to be confident, not afraid to take his place in life. Because he has you as his mother, Nora. I know you will move heaven and earth to make him happy, and his sisters. You can give them all the love Harry never got from his mother.

'Just do that much, Nora! As long as they know they can depend on you, and you'll never let them down, nothing else matters. Do you believe me?' I asked her, searching her eyes, wanting to see a little hope, something that will give her the courage to move on.

'Harry loved you, Nora, and you loved him, that's why you married and had your children. The baby was meant to be born. Harry was not meant to know, because Harry's time was up. None of this was anything to do with you. This was all coming long before you were born, Nora. Be happy you have the chance to carry on. Live life, enjoy the children. Poor Harry was never meant to get any older than twenty-eight years old. Don't have any regrets. You gave Harry love. That was a great gift. Some people never even get that! Now, come on! Wipe your snots and let's get moving. I'm gasping for a smoke!'

I took her hand, pulling her behind me out to the car. They were all sitting very quietly, with nobody saying a word. Everyone was lost in their own world of pain, just staring into space.

'Are you ready to go, ma'am?' the driver asked her, putting his hat back on his head.

Nora nodded as he opened the door. She gave me a little wave, then a slow sad smile, just before the door was slammed shut. The driver then walked around to the other side and climbed in, starting up the engine. He was getting himself ready to follow behind the funeral car. That car was now taking Harry to rest in the church overnight. It is close to his beloved flats. The very same flats that took his life away.

15

The funeral car carrying Harry pulled up outside the church, and the car carrying the family stopped a few feet back. I pulled up behind it, wanting another cigarette, but it was too late. Everyone was climbing out of the car, and people were lining up outside the church, waiting for Harry. I opened the door and climbed out just in time to see the priest arrive at the entrance from inside the church. He was wearing a purple vestment over his black cassock, with a purple stole around his neck. He stood waiting to receive Harry, holding holy vessels in each hand, ready to bless the coffin. Two little altar boys stood, one on each side of him.

The men started to place the coffin on the bier, ready to wheel it into the church, but Jackser leapt forward, saying, 'We don't want tha! We'll carry him in ourself.'

The undertakers hesitated, because most Dublin people didn't bother to carry the coffin any more. Only real Dubliners still do that. So Jackser pushed them out of the way and started to lift the coffin himself, telling Teddy and Gerry to help, and Charlie, who suddenly appeared out of the crowd and grabbed one end of the coffin.

Jackser then went down on one knee and said quietly, but letting his voice carry, 'Right! Get yer end up! Now! Put yer shoulders underneath!' and the boys went down on one knee. 'Ready?' Jackser shouted again. 'Lift!' And they all stood up together, straightening themselves up. They paused, raising their shoulders, then dropped their arms. The coffin settled on their shoulders, and they began the slow march into the church, putting their right leg forward, keeping in step, following behind the undertakers taking in the bier.

The church bell tolled, and Nora marched slowly behind the coffin, and the rest of us followed. The procession stopped at the altar rail, and the coffin was rested on the bier. Then the priest indicated to us to take our place, and we all filed into the bench at the top of the church, next to the coffin.

The priest went up onto the altar and started to chant the prayers for the dead. The people answered, in a slow quiet monotone, and I closed my eyes, covering my face with my hands. I suddenly felt weary, tired to my bones, aching all over. I didn't answer the prayers and started to lean back on the bench, quickly leaning forward again. Years of training in the convent wouldn't let me do that. The murmuring of the priest chanting the prayers brought back a familiar and old ritual. I let the memory wash over me.

I am sitting in the little convent chapel with the lights dimmed, gazing at the red glow from the Sacred Heart lamp that burns perpetually. I listen as the nuns answer the prayers in a sweet melodious cadence, being led by the Reverend Mother. The children are yawning. We are all tired as the night draws in and shout out the nightly ritual on a puff of breath, hoping to hurry along the last prayers so we can get to snuggle up in our warm beds.

I listen te the wind howlin outside an the trees screamin in rage on this dark wintry night. We sprawl in the benches, scratchin our heads under the blue berets. We all titter when Dilly Nugent turns aroun an mutters te Sister Eleanor, 'I have creepy crawlies in me head, Sister!'

'You will be creeping up to bed in a minute if you don't stop that nonsense!' Sister Eleanor growls, wavin her finger an tightenin her lips, then flickin her eyes back up te the altar again.

We lean back on the bench an get a poke in the back from Sister Eleanor, as she snarls, 'Sit up! Sit up straight.'

She is a very gentle nun, but now because all the other nuns are watchin from their prie-dieus at the back a the chapel – especially the Reverend Mother – Sister Eleanor knows they will be gossipin, sayin her group is terrible, an the Reverend Mother will be after the lot of us, her included!

The prayers are over. We give a sigh of relief an stand up, waitin our turn te make a quick genuflection – it's more a nod at the Blessed Sacrament – an then make a quick dive for the door. We are whipped back rapidly by the scruff a the neck. Sister Eleanor has eyes in the back a her head an moves wit lightnin speed. We are pushed down on our knees wit whispered promises of terrible punishments. 'You will get no marmalade for your breakfast in the morning!' Sister Eleanor spits through gritted teeth.

I hate marmalade! I'm thinkin, lookin down at the shiny polished floorboards as Sister Eleanor holds me down by the neck, makin me genuflect at the altar. Then we're out the door an make a stampede along the convent passage. The floor shakes as we all try te escape at the same time.

There are a hundred of us childre in the convent. Te keep order, we are supposed te walk in single file wit our heads bowed like the nuns. There's whispered screams of 'Quiet!' comin from behind me.

'Sweet Jesus! Who is making that noise?' roars from the back of Sister Eleanor's throat. She's exhausted, wit a roarin-red face, an she's grindin her teeth. 'The Reverend Mother is listening,' she gasps. 'All the nuns are listening!' Then she croaks out the threats: 'The whole house will be punished! You are not staying up to watch *The Virginian*.'

It's the only programme we are allowed te watch, once a week. I'm not bothered. I hate *The Virginian*!

A howl of screams starts from the big ones at the end a the passage. Sister Eleanor flies down the convent passage, rosary beads on her leather belt clankin, the massive bunch a keys rattlin. She locks up everythin wit them keys! Every door, every press, especially the sweet press. Oh! An the bread press, because we broke inta tha for a midnight feast. The big ones eat all the bread at teatime, so we are left still starvin.

Her long black habit is held up wit both hands, an the long black veil is flappin out behind her. We get a glimpse of a black-stockinged ankle – 'Oooh! Did ye see tha?' – as she flies past us in a blur. She's hell bent on her mission te catch the culprits.

'Severe repercussions will follow,' she screams, wavin her finger at us. We laugh at the big words. 'You are sent out of the group! The whole lot of you!'

'Ye can't do tha, Sister Eleanor! There won't be room for the lot a us on the passage!' I roar after her.

'Don't bother asking me for anything!' she shouts, wavin her finger at everyone, includin the wall. She's losin the run of herself, goin mad!

'Yeah! We know,' everyone mutters. 'You won't speak te us, an we'll have te eat our meals on the refectory passage! Ah, yak! Yakety yak! Who cares?' an Dilly Nugent stuck out her tongue an blew raspberries, spittin all over me!

'Fuck you!' I roared.

Sister Eleanor whirled aroun, screamin, 'Who said that?'

'She did, Sister Eleanor!' They all pointed their finger at me, dyin te get me inta trouble.

'I did not!' I roared. Sister Eleanor came flyin back an gave me an unmerciful slap on the gob. They roared laughin, an we were still on the chapel passage. I got such a shock an went inta an awful rage. I threw me head back, takin in an almighty breath, gettin ready te scream me lungs out.

The others suddenly went quiet, an I looked aroun, wonderin why, still holdin me breath, wit me face turnin red as a beetroot. The chapel door opened behind us, an the Reverend Mother stood lookin down at us, watchin without sayin a word.

Sister Eleanor's eyes bulged an her face turned bright purple. Then she stood still an pointed her arm at the lot of us te move fast, very fast, away from the convent passage. Then she gave me a slap on the back te hurry me along, knockin the wind outa me. 'Everyone is going to bed early!' she snorted, flappin out her arms again. I could feel her breath on the back a me neck an jumped te the side, lettin her miss me an give Dilly Nugent a slap across the ear.

'What was that for?' Dilly roared, rubbin her ear like mad.

The Reverend Mother called, 'Sister Eleanor. Sister! May I have a word with you, please!'

We looked back, seein Sister Eleanor turn white at the sight a the Reverend Mother. She was takin her hands out from under her alb an wrigglin her two fingers at Sister Eleanor, an starin daggers down at us from her milk-bottle eyeglasses.

We watched as Sister Eleanor rushed off down the passage te speak te the Reverend Mother an get a tongue lashin. I took off, flyin like the hammers a hell, an the others all started 'Oohhing!' an 'Gawding!', sayin, 'We're in big trouble now!'

I hid in the tilet just offa the passage an waited. Sure enough, Sister Eleanor came flyin back, leavin the door swingin out behind her, an it shut wit an almighty bang. She grabbed the first young one she got her hands on. 'Up to bed!'

'Whadidido?'

'Where are the rest of them?'

I could hear her rosary beads rattlin under her leather belt as she flew down the stairs. I was shakin, laughin an shiverin at the same time, knowin I was in fer big trouble.

'Where is that brazen madam? MARTHA LONG! Did any one of you see her?'

'No, Sister, she's probably hidin!' the licks said.

'I am not going to tolerate this outrageous behaviour,' I could hear her mutterin as she came back up the stairs. 'Wait until I get that one!' she muttered under her breath as she passed within inches a me, headin herself off up te the dormitory te find me.

'There will be no more sweets for a month! You won't be allowed out with your godparents on the orphans' outing!' she droned, listin all the punishments off one by one on her fingers as we lay in bed without gettin any tea.

Hmm, godparents. I don't care. I don't have any, I snorted te meself, hidin under the blankets, not wantin her te see me face again in case she remembered somethin else I did. I had enough punishments lined up for meself. Yeah! Godparents. Tha was the parade a kind-hearted people bringin ye te their home fer a taste a family life, the nuns called it. Nobody ever took me out. Sniff! Somethin always went wrong.

I nearly got te go out wit two aul spinster sisters in their green Morris Minor. I made it te the steps a the convent. I was millin around wit the other childre, waitin te see which of the happy laughin people I would get te go out wit. Some of them were havin te fly around te catch the kids they were given, because the childre were havin none of it! They all wanted the young ones wit the big fancy Rover. The 'orphans', as we were called, were very choosy! Nobody wanted the two spinsters. Sister Eleanor was mortified. The kids were makin a show a her. Then she turned te me.

'Martha, darling!' an she was smilin! 'You go now with the two lovely ladies,' she said, just about te hand me over.

I looked at them. One had a hairy chin, an she took a hankie outa her pocket an handed me a sweet wrapped up in it. I stared.

'Come along now, dear,' she said, reachin out fer me hand. 'My sister Maud and I shall take you for a lovely picnic under the trees in the Phoenix Park.'

'Oh, we are so looking forward to it,' Maud whispered, blowin stale air inta me face an smilin, showin me her yella false teeth an shakin her head up an down, makin her big maroon-felt hat wave at me, wit the feather stickin out the back.

I tried te pretend I didn't hear, an looked around fer someone else.

'Eeeek! Look wha tha aul one is givin tha eegit!' the kids roared, movin away fer a better look, watchin the two women tryin te grab me hand.

I looked at Sister Eleanor, wantin te go wit the woman in the fur coat an her husband wit the curly hair an the big smile, wearin the Crombie coat, tha just got outa tha big black motor car.

'I'm goin wit them!' Imelda MacDermot roared when she saw me lookin at them.

I turned te the nun. 'Eh, Sister Eleanor . . .'

'Good girl!' she roared, pushin me at the aul ones an smilin at me te encourage me.

I moved off wit me head hangin down te me belly button, an listenin te tha MacDermot one cacklin like a witch when Sister Eleanor said, 'Now, darling! You can go with these lovely people!'

Ah, fuck! She's a pet! Tha's why she gets te go wit them! I would do anythin fer Sister Eleanor. But she's makin a fool a me! Then I heard a familiar roar. Me head whipped around in shock.

'Are ye there, Martha? Where are ye?'

'Who's that?' the kids looked in shock. I tried te hide.

'Ah! There ye are, Martha! Ha, ha. I've come up te see ye!'

'Who is that mad woman?' one of the big young ones roared.

'Who are you callin mad?' me ma screamed. 'I'll be done fer you! I'll fuckin knife ye!'

The crowd scattered. I was left standin on me own on the steps. The nuns were grabbin the kids an whippin them down te the cars. I stared at the ma! The one an only time she decides te come te see me an it has te be this one! National Children's Day! Ah, fuck! An wit the whole convent listenin! I was ashamed a her an annoyed at the other kids fer laughin at me ma. I wanted te give them a box.

Tha was definitely very unlucky! She turnin up like tha.

Yeah! But I was safe there. Safe from men, safe from Jackser! Safe from Sally. No more trying to make her happy. I now spent my time trying to make Sister Eleanor happy. I got my first idea of love from her. It was watching her hugging the little ones.

But there was no hugs for me. I'd missed my opportunity; it was too late. I was too big. There were too many children looking for love from one person – Sister Eleanor. I had a terrible longing. It was painful. A deep, penetrating, obsessive desperation for just one hug! It must be a lovely feeling to be loved by her. To be special. I had wished with all my might she was my mother. I wanted a smile, to be called 'pet', 'darling'! It was a bit difficult, though. I was always in trouble! I was usually sent 'out of the group' because I fought with the other kids. I wasn't accepted by anyone, including the nuns. The children were very clannish. They had grown up together. I was the 'outsider', the 'street kid'. They had their rules and they were very competitive. No looking for attention! No sucking up to the enemy – the nuns! No, you can't suck up. This gets you praise. Jealousy would erupt! Everyone wanted love, affection. But this was only for the chosen few. I couldn't figure out the secret. But I never gave up!

I took meself te bed early, readin the *Bunty*, waitin fer the rustle of her black habit, the clankin a the rosary beads an the rattlin of keys. Listenin fer the squeakin of her leather shoes on the wooden staircase. Then I would shoot up in the bed an jam me *Bunty* inta the locker, whippin out the rosary beads, pretendin te be very holy! I would sit up straight, holdin me hands high up in the air so she would see me prayin. I would hang on te the last bead on the rosary, sayin the last prayer, lettin her think I said the whole thing. Tha takes hours! But, not too loud! It wouldn't look genuine! Then I would close me eyes, makin me lips move, then let me eyes fly open, pretendin I got a shock wit her appearin outa nowhere! I would watch her sweepin through the dormitory on her way te her room fer her Wednesday-night early bedtime.

'Oh! There's a good child! In bed early and getting the rosary. Goodnight, darling. If only the others would follow your example!'

'Yes, Sister Eleanor! I'm prayin fer yer special intentions!'

'Oh, thank you so much, darling! I have so many intentions!'

She continues inta the next dormitory, her mind on a million other tings. The dormitories are empty. All the childre are downstairs enjoyin themselves. I'm the only eegit up here! An I crane me neck, watching her vanish outa sight an hearin her footsteps fade away through another door an inta the convent, which is forbidden territory for us.

And for the bright warm seconds I basked in her affections, I *was* special. 'Darling, pet!' Then the light dimmed, and the warmth vanished, and I was cold again, empty, the familiar loneliness sweeping through me. I am bereft, feeling colder, more alone than before, the hunger for love gnawing at my centre. I know now there are worse things than fear, beatings, brutality. It is the hole in my heart I want to fill with love. A smile, a hug, a kiss; to feel the warmth of a mother's arms around me; to be accepted. So that is the love I want. There is such a thing as love! I've seen it in the smile of Sister Eleanor as she bends down and gently lifts a little one into her arms and looks into its eyes, smiling and crooning, her eyes shining with gentleness, and wraps her arms around the little one, burying her head and kissing it. Then she lifted her head and saw me staring very intently and gave me a look, knowing I would love that too. But I'm not a cuddly little one. I turned away, desperate because I'd missed my time and I hunger for the want of it. Desperation sweeps through me.

16

I get up early before the nuns wake us fer breakfast – it isn't even a mornin fer the children's Mass – an creep down te the chapel, joinin the nuns for Mass! Just me an one other suck-up. She had been at it for years! The nuns think she is goin te join them when she grows up.

'Oh, she's a beautiful child,' they cooed! Well, I'm here now te get me share. I crept inta the chapel wit me head bowed an me hands joined in the air. Then I saw the other eegit, kneelin wit her hands joined together pushed out in front a her, starin up at the priest, wearin the blue fer Our Lady Sunday mantilla, lookin like St Bernadette! Mantilla! The cheek a her! We're not supposed te be wearin them until Sunday! I look like a gobshite let outa Grangegorman fer the day in this bloody beret! Huh! So ye can get away wit murder when ye're a pet!

I pushed in beside her, thinkin she'd be happy wit the company. But she moved down the bench like she didn't want te know me, mutterin, 'Geshaway from me, ye notice box!' Then she glared at me from the other end a the bench.

She's not wantin te share the limelight. Tha's her trouble, I thought, flickin me eyes away from her an starin up at the altar, knowin the nuns from behind me were borin holes in me back.

She's not very 'holy', I thought, seein right through her game. She was one of Sister Eleanor's pets. I'm goin te become a pet as well, an as soon as possible. I yawned, wishin I was back in me bed, an thinkin this business a gettin inta the goodie club was hard work!

Me pinin fer love never lets up. I took meself down te the nursery an slobbered all over the babbies! Ahh! They were all lined up in a row, sittin on their little potties! But before I had a chance te even give one a them a kiss or even open me mouth, a big young one boxed me out the door.

'Gesh out of here, you!' she roared, pointin me out the door an draggin me wit her other hand.

I gave her a kick an she caught me foot an I lost me shoe. I kicked her again an lost the other shoe! I was gettin ready te lash at her when the nun in charge appeared back wit another load a babbies in from the tilets.

'No! You don't own the place, Abby Griffin! Now give me back me shoes, ye big overgrown ape, or I'll box ye!' I roared in a whisper, grittin me teeth.

She stood starin down at me wit her hands on her hips an laughed, 'Ye little scut. Gesh out! I'm in charge here!'

'What's that one doing here?' Sister Mary James suddenly roared an flew at me, grabbin me by the neck an landin me out the door. Then she banged it shut on me face. I was left lookin at the shut door, an me shoes still inside!

I was just about te put me head in the door again when it flew open an me shoes came flyin out, bangin me on the head. 'Ye mean cow!' I roared.

'Street kid!' she snorted at me.

'Culchie four eyes!' I roared back. Ah, let it go, I muttered te meself. It's not worth the bother. Then I had an idea. I never give up!

As soon as I heard the squeak a Sister Eleanor's leather shoes on the convent passage – I'd been waitin fer ages, just hangin aroun the landin, waitin. I knew her walk! – an the rattlin of her rosary beads, I leapt, havin her all te meself for about five seconds. Then the others came rushin out from different directions, swarmin aroun her like flies. They knew her walk as well. So it's me followin her along wit ten others. We're all like little shadows, she complains, lookin back at us, draggin outa her. All tellin each other we had special demands.

'I need te get me new sum copy! Tha's the only reason I'm followin her!'

'Yeah! An I want te know if she's givin out any sweets,' I say. 'I'm not lookin fer attention!'

'No! Neither am I!' we all tell each other.

'I don't even like her!' Dilly Nugent says in her squeaky voice, curlin up her nose an droppin her mouth, shakin her mop a red curly hair at us.

'No! Nor me!' we all agree. But she's not takin any notice a us. She's busy rushin along, talkin te herself an springin on people fer not doin their jobs. We crash inta her as she stops suddenly.

'Karen Bingley! Take that school uniform off at once!' she roars at yer woman. 'You are punished!'

'God, I hate you!'

'Don't you dare take the name of the Lord in vain. Get up those stairs!' an she grabs yer woman an pushes her up the stairs. 'You will go to bed early!' she roars, takin off again.

We rush after her. Then she stops suddenly at the door a the big young ones' playroom. 'Do you hear that disgraceful noise?' she asks us, squintin her eyes an curlin her mouth inta an 'O' shape. We squint an curl our mouths inta an 'O' shape, an suck in our breath, disgusted too! Then she whips open the door an runs at the big ones wit their legs sprawled on her sofa.

'Yeah! Suck-ups! Notice boxes!' they roar at us as we come chargin in behind Sister Eleanor. They're not bothered about lookin for attention, because they gave up long ago. They go aroun now wit sour faces, an give Sister Eleanor dirty looks an snarl at each other.

'Right! That is it!' she screams at them. 'I told you girls to keep that radio down.' Then she springs for it, takin out the plug an holdin it te her chest, cradlin it like a babby.

The big ones go mad. 'Give us back our radio! I hate you! Just because you can't have fun, you want the rest of us te live like nuns!'

'Well, really!' Sister Eleanor breathes, an bends herself in half, still holdin the radio, an squints at them, all red-faced an lookin very hurt an annoyed at the same time! 'I am going to punish the lot of you! You won't see this again for a month.'

Then the screams started up, an she flies out the door wit her radio, delighted she got the better a them until she trips over us, an the radio goes flyin, an Sister Eleanor lies splattered on the floor after hittin the back of her head. Then she starts cryin. An we laugh in shock.

The big ones grab the radio, but it's broken! An Sister Eleanor gets up an pushes us outa the way, roarin at us for annoyin her, an she can't get any peace wit the lot of us! So she flies back te the convent, an the big ones fly at us!

Then the wait would begin all over again. Waitin until the next time she came down. Probably teatime.

I volunteered meself for the next group up, from three te six year olds. Te sleep in their dormitory at night an take care a them. I was delighted wit meself! I got me own cubicle. It was very narrow. I had te walk in sideways te get te me bed. You'd have te wait years fer one a these down in me own dormitory. There is only four a them in the convent, an ye had te be nearly sixteen, ready te go out inta the world! I would be dead an buried waitin tha long! The best bit was Sister Eleanor had te come up every night te check I was in bed. So fer ten seconds I got her te meself!

We had a party every night, me an the little ones. I sang songs wit them, told them stories an combed their hair. They would all line up, takin their turn. I loved bein in charge. I practised the German hausfrau plait on their hair, curlin it up aroun their ears. I told them ghost stories, puttin the fear a God inta them! They shivered an whined, an came creepin inta me one by one, an climbed inta me bed, all piled on top a each other. I'm definitely not tellin them any more ghost stories, I snorted, tryin te get comfortable in the lumpy bed in the middle a the dormitory. I was havin it all te meself. They were all packed in my bed! So I had te sleep outside in the dormitory, te get some sleep for meself.

The singin got louder, an the little ones couldn't be dragged outa the bed in the mornins. They snoozed on the workroom table instead a sittin up an payin attention te their nun when she tried te teach them the hymns an prayers. 'They have circles under their eyes,' she complained te Sister Eleanor. So did I, because they wouldn't go te sleep fer me.

But they thought I was great, an so did I, until Sister Herod said, 'You are not suitable for the job. I have asked for someone else,' an sent me back te me own dormitory.

No! I'm not givin up. So it's back te Sister Eleanor! I make sure te get inta the bench in fronta her at chapel. She's sittin directly behind me. Lovely! I start te practise me new speakin voice. I open me mouth an start by sayin each word very carefully, makin sure all the nuns at the back can hear me, especially the Reverend Mother. She's promised te send me off te a reformatory school if me behaviour doesn't improve. She's been tryin te get rid a me from the first day she clapped eyes on me. But she's had no luck so far. The courts won't let her. Because they sent me here! So here I stay. Unless I get enough black marks against me.

She told me the day I arrived, 'We do not take the likes of you, and the court did not ask my permission to send you here!' They don't take robbers like me! Tha's wha she meant!

The prayers started, an I coughed, clearin me throat. 'Hail Mary, full a Grace.ze,' I roared, makin sure everyone could hear me.

The gobshites sittin next te me started sniggerin. They got a thump on the back from Sister Eleanor. Serves them right! I have a hard time, though, wit the dese, dose, dat an dem. Anita Cunningham told me te practise tha if I want te . . . to speak properly! She's very intelligent! She goes te . . . to a secondary school an . . . and knows loads a . . . of tings! She's very nice, too. Ye can talk te her. Not like the rest a the gobshites!

I opened my eyes slowly, feeling I was sinking lower. Those memories! That child is really beginning to haunt me lately. The past is catching up with me. It's growing stronger, taking me over. Nothing can be gained from allowing those memories to creep up on me. I opened my eyes, gazing up at the altar but not really seeing, just sensing the priest was coming to an end.

He came down from the altar to shake holy water over the coffin and murmur prayers for Harry's soul. That he may find eternal rest.

I wonder if I will find rest, peace, acceptance. I still have that deep ache inside me for love. It has settled down into a hollow feeling, an emptiness, and at the centre of it is the gnawing ache, like a chronic pain.

17

The priest leaned over the bench and whispered, 'Would you all like to come forward?' and he indicated with his outstretched arm the bench in front.

Everyone stood up and moved into the bench, sitting down. Immediately, people started filing past us, taking our hand and shaking it. They bent, looking into our eyes with sadness and shaking their heads, and murmuring to each of us in turn, 'I'm very sorry fer yer trouble. Harry was a lovely fella. May God rest him,' and the line moved on.

So many people! So many people knew Harry and wanted to pay their last respects to him and his family. The ma was finding it hard. She would glance up and try to smile, then drop her head down again into her lap. A lot of people gave me puzzled looks because they never clapped eyes on me before, and I didn't seem to match with the family. I looked like one a them social workers! But then, wha was I doin wearin the black? Ye only wear tha when ye're related! I could see it in their eyes and watch their brain turning over. They would probably work it out in the end and draw the right conclusions. *She was sent away! Probably fer robbin, an when she served her time, went off te England an never came back! Up till now!*

The line finally ended, and the ma stood up, everyone following her slowly down the aisle and out to the car for the short drive home. I turned to follow, saying to the priest, 'Thank you, Father,' and looked at the coffin. Harry would rest here for the night, I thought.

'Martha!'

I looked up to see the priest with the Mass book in his hand.

'Would you like to go over the reading you will give at Mass in the morning?'

'Is it the psalms, Father?'

'Yes,' he said, showing me the book.

I glanced at the reading, my eyes flicking down the page, and lifted my head and said, 'That is fine, Father. Thank you.'

He looked at me uncertainly, his eyes flickering over me. 'Are you sure? Would you not like to have a practice first? I could help you with some of the more difficult words.'

I stared at him, my eyes turning to flint. 'Oh, I think I can manage fine, Father. There's not too many big words.'

He stared at me, even more confused, wondering where my hostility was coming from. I stared at his well-fed, pale, anaemic face. Years of study! Poring over books. An academic, member of an elite order of priests. They moved themselves into the parish here to work with the poorest of the poor. A well-meaning snob who thought his years of study would prepare him to lift the poor out of their 'mire' and give hope and meaning to their lives. What a prat!

This afternoon in the sitting room, I had sat listening to him talk about the last moments of Harry's life.

'Harry and I were good friends,' he said. 'He used to come down to the oratory and sit in the corner and read the Bible. He was very active in the community. He ran discos for the children and did odd jobs for the elderly. All his own doing! It was not organised! We would talk,' he said, looking very far away, remembering. 'I was the last person to see him before he died.'

I sat up, my heart fluttering. I stared at him, waiting for him to continue.

'Yes!' he said, looking very intently at me. 'I was just passing. It was around nine o'clock, and I saw someone falling from the top balcony. I ran, reaching him just as he hit the ground. I lifted his head into my arms. He was dying, and I whispered the Last Rites into his ear. I did not know it was Harry. I held him in my arms and I did not know!'

He was shaking his head, trying to figure this out. I stared at him, my body leaning out of the chair, trying to catch everything he said. Trying to understand! 'Did he say anything?' I asked, holding my breath.

'No, he was dying. He did murmur, and I felt the last breath leave his body. But he was gone!'

My eyes dropped to the floor, picturing Harry's last moments dying in the priest's arms.

'Would ye like a sup a tea, Father?' the ma asked, handing him a mug with a chip on the rim and stains around the outside. 'An there's a few biscuits,' she said, smiling and handing him a plate full of Kimberley biscuits. She must have put the whole packet on that plate.

'No! No! I won't, thank you,' the priest said, looking at the mug and plate with horror. He waved his arm at her, dismissing her as if she was a nuisance.

Me ma looked at him, then at the plate, the smile fading from her face. 'Are ye sure?' she asked, shoving the plate at him and smiling, looking hopeful he might change his mind.

'No! No!' he said emphatically, waving both arms now and looking to the wall, waiting for her to go away.

I watched him, gobsmacked! Completely oblivious to the hurt he was causing her. Biscuits cost money! They didn't eat them every day of the week. And they were brought out specially for him. By refusing her, he was telling her she wasn't good enough. She's only dirt.

'Just take one, Father!' the ma said, leaning into him. She wasn't giving up!

I watched him recoil, holding his breath. When she moved back, staring at the plate, he sat up straight and leaned towards her, saying, 'Why don't you relax and take a bath?'

Me ma's eyes flickered, confused. Then she blinked at him and shook her head back, trying to smile, feeling very embarrassed, and rushed off to the kitchen. I could see she was very hurt. The bastard! Arrogant, patronising, self-righteous fool!

I took in a deep breath, sat back and said in a very crisp, clear, clipped cold voice, 'It must be a tremendous handicap for you, Father, having spent your life closeted in the dusty corridors of academia. I would say it's rather like being shut off in an ivory tower. Now, here you are, in the twilight years of your life, being thrown into the deep end of real life among real people.' I stared at him coldly, seeing his eyebrows knitting together, listening to the words resonate in his head.

Then he shook himself and said, 'No! No, absolutely not! I have chosen to come here myself. We are working with the community. Trying to get projects going, leadership, training the people to take control of their own lives.' Then he stared at me, too polite to ask how I fitted into the family. Why I was the odd one out, appearing to be educated.

I let him stare. Then broke the silence. 'I think you may get a real education now, Father. Listen and learn. These people have been through the university of life. They will teach you everything you need to know about real life. Any fool can learn to read. You can at least offer them that. Then I believe the Church will be redundant. It won't take them long to figure they've been had by "Old Mother Church".'

Yeah, so now I have no time for him. I wouldn't piss on him if he was on fire! I walked out of the church, saying, 'Goodbye, Father. I will see you in the morning. I have a lot to do now.'

I stepped out into the night; it was cold now and foggy. I shivered, feeling the damp go through me, and pulled up the collar of my coat. The funeral car was just about to pull off when I opened the door, leaned in and said to the ma, 'I won't come up to the house, Ma. I'm going home to get some sleep. You should do the same, all of you,' I said, looking at them. 'I'll get here first thing in the morning. Goodnight, everyone.'

'Goodnight,' they murmured, sounding very tired.

I slammed the door shut, watching the car take off slowly, heading for the flats and home. I rushed over to my own car, jumped in and rolled a cigarette, then started the engine, turning the car for home. It had been a very long day.

18

I knelt with my face in my hands, glancing up at the priest on the altar, his arms held out to the people, intoning the Mass for the dead. The church was packed, and the thick incense floated heavily around the coffin. I dropped my head again, feeling weak. I was beginning to feel the pressure taking its toll on my health.

'Martha!'

I looked up, seeing Dinah was pulling at the sleeve of my coat.

'Look!' she said, nodding to the priest.

I followed her eyes up to the priest. He was standing now, nodding down at me to come up and give the reading. 'Oh, sorry,' I muttered, shaking myself, trying to come back to my senses. I stood up, lifting up my long navy-blue army coat. It was wool, with silver buttons down both sides. The soldiers wore them during the First World War. They called it a 'great coat'. It certainly was. I was very glad of it, especially in this cold wintry weather, because it keeps me lovely and warm.

I walked up to the altar and stood in front of the lectern. The Bible was opened, and I glanced down, taking a deep breath, and straightened my shoulders. Then I swept my eyes around the church, taking in a huge sea of faces. Some people were staring up, looking very still, the strain showing on their faces. They all knew Harry. He was part of them. It pained them to lose one of their own. Especially a young one. Other people, older mothers and grannies, sat with their rosary beads, turning them and moving their lips in prayer. Everyone so quiet. I couldn't see Charlie. People were standing tightly packed together, filling the doorway and out to the yard. My breath caught in my throat. Jesus! So many people here just for Harry. Him alone!

My brain dimmed, and the book swam in front of my eyes. I put my hand on the lectern, steadied myself and took another deep breath, seeing Harry in my mind's eye, laughing at me. 'Go on,' he said. 'You can do it!'

I was happy to hear my voice ring out in a clear voice, projecting to the people outside.

'The Lord is my shepherd; I shall not want. He maketh me to lie down in green pastures. He leadeth me beside the still waters. He restoreth my soul. He leadeth me in the paths of righteousness for his name's sake. Yea . . .' My voice broke. I took a deep breath. 'Yea, though I walk through the valley of the shadow of death, I will fear no evil: for thou art with me, thy rod and staff they comfort me. Thou preparest a table before me in the presence of mine enemies. Thou anointed my head with oil. My cup runneth over. Surely goodness and mercy shall follow me all the days of my life; and I will dwell in the house of the Lord for ever.'

I did not look up again, feeling humbled my brother had such an impact on people. So many had turned up. They were willing to stand out in the cold and rain. Stand quiet, and with such respect. It was more than I will ever achieve if I live to be a hundred.

I walked to the middle of the altar, bowed to the blessed sacrament, then turned and headed back to my seat. I heard the ma give a little sob. 'Are you all right, Ma?' I whispered, putting my arm gently on her shoulder. She was staring at the coffin draped with the purple linen cloth, with a large black cross in the centre. She said nothing, just kept staring and wiping her nose with the corner of her scarf. Then everyone stood up, the priest giving his final blessing, and Jackser and Teddy took up the front of the coffin, and Gerry and Charlie – he appeared from behind somewhere – took the back. They steadied the coffin on their shoulders, giving it a little lift together, then started the slow march down the aisle, and we all fell in behind them. Taking Harry on his final journey, where we would lay him to rest for ever. In the hope he would find peace at last.

The churchyard was crowded with people; they spilled out onto the road. Behind, the crowd following slowly from the body of the church got stuck in a bottleneck. All stood still, silent, staring. Filled with sadness for one of their own. Lost before his time. I recognised a lot of the faces from my childhood. People who'd lived in the city centre, friends of Jackser.

I saw 'travelling people', outcasts to some. But they had been friends to Harry. A very noble people, with their own code of honour, loyalty and great respect for tradition. Nobody spoke; everyone was waiting for the funeral car to move off so they too could join the cortège for Harry's last journey on this earth.

The cortège moved off, very slowly winding its way around the area to the flats. All along the street, people stopped, with hands joined in prayer, and blessed themselves and lowered their heads as the cortège made its way to Harry's flat. It is an old tradition in Dublin, to bless yourself when a cortège passes in the street. But people stood waiting. Those who had not attended the Mass still wanted to show their last respects. I looked back and stared in astonishment. Every conceivable contraption on wheels was moving behind us. The cortège went back a long way; I couldn't see the end of it. Harry was really special, I thought. So many people respected him. The cortège stopped outside Harry's flat, and we all looked up.

'I keep expectin Harry te put his head over the balcony an shout, "Hang on! I'm comin down!"' Dinah whispered.

The flat was empty now. But I got a sense it was still filled with the ghosts of children's laughter and the haunting memory of Harry's last days of agonising pain.

The cortège moved off, heading slowly out of the flats, and picked up speed, but still slow enough to allow Harry time for his final journey.

We arrived in the gates of Glasnevin Cemetery and drove slowly along the high wall, past the lookout tower, where men stayed alert at night to catch the grave robbers in Victorian times. Past the high monuments erected by the nuns for the 'fallen women'. That's what the inscription read. Yes! Fallen into the grip of the religious gestapo. Past, now, the 'Angels' Plot'. Babies buried by the hospitals without a name because they were stillborn. The mothers didn't even get to see their babies.

Then the funeral car stopped under an old oak tree, where the grave was opened for Harry. I was happy about that. It would give him shelter, protect the gravestone when it's erected from the elements. Everyone climbed out, and the ma made straight for the tree. Jackser stood around the graveside with the boys grouped around him. The gravediggers placed the coffin on top of the green carpeting, holding it with ropes. Everyone stood well back, leaving the graveside free for the family and the priest. I went and stood beside the ma. She was very pale, and I put my arm around her. Dinah stood on the other side of her. Me ma never took her eyes off the coffin. Then the priest threw earth down on the coffin as the gravediggers lowered it down, intoning, 'From earth to earth, ashes to ashes, dust to dust, so shall you return.'

I went to throw earth down onto the coffin and suddenly the ma sprinted past me. I watched her go as if in slow motion. But she was heading for the grave, as she screamed, 'No! Don't.' She had her hands out. It was so quick, nobody had time to react. I was sprinting without knowing, with Dinah on my tail, and grabbed her coat, pulling her back without saying a word. I pulled her around, wrapping my arms firmly around her, and brought her back to stand beside the car.

'They're puttin him down there!' she wailed, looking terrified. She had her hands on her face, staring back at the grave in terror. 'Don't let them!' she screamed out on a long wail, throwing back her head with her eyes rolling in her head. Jesus! She's gone into shock. Everything is coming back to her! She's reliving her family's death. Her mother!

'Come on, Ma! Get into the car.' I opened the car door and put her sitting inside.

Dinah came over and sat in beside us. 'What's wrong, Ma?'

'She's in shock, Dinah. It's too much for her.'

The ma went very quiet and stared at her hands, opening them and closing them, and wrapping her arms around herself. But she didn't say another word. She was staring into another world, another time, another horror. One we could never enter.

Nobody spoke. We were all lost in our own world. Long ago. Another lifetime. We had all pushed the pram past this same cemetery in the dead of night with Baby Harry lying sleeping. On our way to start a new life, and the last leg of my journey before I would leave them mercifully for ever. To start my own journey alone, without them. Harry's journey had been a short one but a hard one, and he did not survive it. Now he would sleep in this place for ever. Rest in peace, Harry.

I drove home with my ears ringing and my head spinning. It was late when I left the ma. Five o'clock. I managed to get her into bed, and everyone sat around talking about Harry and their memories of him. They all had plenty to eat, and Jackser and Teddy stayed off the drink. Nobody was invited back to the house, and the people went to the nearest pub to have the wake, but without us. I think the message got through to them. Harry had lived on drink the last few months of his life.

I left the ma's flat and raced to the shops to buy food for the coming arrival of Sarah. I'll be collecting her from the airport on Sunday, so I better remember to get petrol. I shot through the village and raced up the hill, anxious to get home. I can't wait to get to bed. This week has been the longest week of my life.

I drove the car into the garage, locking it behind me, and walked through the garden wondering where Bonzo was, no sign of him! I pushed open the side gate, locking it, and walked along the side passage, finally locking the end gate, and looked around. Still no sign of the dog. Jaysus! That dog is the bane of my life.

I let myself in through the French doors, locking them. That bleedin dog can go and take a running jump for himself. I'm not getting up to let him in when he comes home barking to be let in at probably three o'clock in the morning. I slammed the front door shut, locking it. Serves him right! I could have done with his company!

I picked up the bags of shopping and dragged them into the kitchen, dropping them on the floor, and filled the kettle, dying for a cup of tea. I put the shopping away while the kettle was boiling, then sat down at the kitchen table and rolled a cigarette. The tea was lovely! Hot and sweet, as it slid down my neck. I took a deep drag of the cigarette and stared out the window, listening to the trees keening in the wind and watching the dark creep quickly around the house.

I gave a big sigh of relief, glad to be home. There's nothing like having your own little roof over your head and your own front door. Still! I listened to the silence inside the kitchen, and the only sound was the ticking of the clock on the wall and my breathing. It's been terribly lonely since Sarah left. God! I can't wait to see her. She's coming on Sunday. The day after tomorrow! I hope everything goes well. I only saw her once since she left me. How long ago was that? Ah! Last year. The first time since she left.

19

I remember now. I was in hospital waiting for that operation. The nurse had breezed over to me, sitting in the bed, and announced, 'Martha! Don't disappear! The priest is coming down to give you the Last Rites.'

'What! Why?'

'You might be going to theatre in the morning.'

'Yeah, like hell I will. They've been telling me that now for the last four months and I'm still waiting!'

The professor came in and told me the last time I lay here waiting and ready, bloody dehydrated – how many times did that happen? – anyway, he sat down on the side of my bed and told me mournfully, "My dear!" he said, taking my hand and wrapping it in his. "We cannot get an anaesthetist to work with the surgeon. You are too risky. Your thyroid, the Graves' disease, is so toxic that if an attempt were made to remove it, you would get a storming! That is, the thyroid would shoot huge amounts of thyroxine into your body, killing you!"'

He stared at me balefully; I stared back, me lip hanging down to me belly button, taking in every word he was saying to me. He continued, 'You see, the thyroid, as it is being removed, goes into emergency and starts to pump out an incredibly high dose of thyroxine. We call this a storming. It would be lethal. Your heart would start to race, trying to keep up. All your organs would shut down. You would be poisoned. We would lose you. That is why no anaesthetist is willing to take you on. Because you would die.'

I gasped.

He continued, 'Unfortunately, we cannot control it with drugs, to allow us to operate. We tried that and you got uremic poisoning. Your kidneys packed up. They could not cope with the amount of toxins flooding into you. Most extraordinary you survived! People don't usually. It's fatal! So! We need to operate as soon as possible. Anything could happen at any moment. You could go into cardiac failure! But I have been speaking with a top anaesthetist – he has worked on the liver-transplant operations with me. Remember we had one recently in this hospital?'

'Yeah, and it failed!' I croaked, looking into his face, being cruel. Then thinking it went on all night, teams of medics, booted and covered up from head to toe. A whole relay of them taking it in turn, staggering down exhausted – all to no avail. The patient died. No glory for the pioneering professor and his team. Ah, but he is a gorgeous little man, very kind.

'Yes!' the professor said, thinking about it sadly. 'However! I have asked him would he be willing to take you on, and he is examining your case. So, we may be lucky!' Then he smiled at me and gave me a big squeeze, saying, 'Whatever happens, we are not going to lose you!'

'Thank you very much, Professor!' I said, beaming at him. Delighted at the prospect of getting back on my feet instead of looking grey like cigarette ash and feeling ninety years old. Being able to walk with a stride again instead of gasping with palpitations on trying to make my way out to the toilet to have a smoke! What else is there?

I watched the nurse disappear out the door, feeling very contented. At last something may be happening, and I can start to live a normal life again after years of going downhill. Getting sick and feeling old before my time, and still trying to carry on. Working and looking after Sarah but never understanding why I was always tired.

The priest came rushing in through the door, heading straight for me. 'I'm not dying, and I don't need the Last Rites!' I said, watching him put his holy oils on my locker and pull the curtains around. 'This is the third time you've done this, and I'm still alive!'

'Yes! Of course you are not going to die! This is just a precaution,' he said, whipping the cloth off the oils.

'No! I am definitely going to live a long life. So I really mean it, Father. You are going to jinx me with this business of the Last Rites. So, don't argue with me Fat . . .'

The curtain was whipped back and a blonde head with long hair and huge blue eyes with a big smile on its face suddenly appeared and shouted, 'Mummy! You're here!'

I looked up, thinking, I was right! I really have died. That bloody priest and his Last Rites has killed me! I'm dead!

My vision cleared, and I screamed, 'SARAH!'

'Please wait outside, your mother won't be long,' the priest told her solemnly, whipping the curtain back and getting on with the business.

As soon as the priest uttered the last words, I was out of the bed. 'Thank you, Father!' I gasped, whipping back the curtain and peeling my eyes around the ward, looking around for Sarah. She must be down in the television room.

I grabbed my dressing gown off the bed. I keep it handy because I'm always on the mooch, visiting other patients, making new friends, helping out, rushing to help the bedridden. There are not enough nurses, and it keeps me busy but drives the consultant crazy. 'You have to get bed rest! Your condition is deteriorating! We have nothing else to treat you with.'

'Oh, yes, Doctor! You are absolutely right! I understand perfectly!'

'And no more smoking!' he barks, red in the face, fed up with me.

'No! Definitely not!' Then I vanish again. I never did have any sense. Besides! I don't believe it is possible for me to die. I have too many lives!

Where is she? I stopped at the entrance to the sitting room, looking around for her.

'Mummy!'

My head whirled around, following the voice. She came bounding over to me, giving me a hug.

'Let me see you!' I gasped, my heart going like the clappers, my skin coming out in a cold sweat.

She stood back, beaming down at me. She's grown, and her blonde hair is even lighter, and she's cut it to her shoulders. No more waist length. I grabbed her again, burying my face in her neck. 'Oh, Sarah! You've come home! I really have missed you! This last year has been hell on earth without you,' I said, looking into her face. 'God! You are all grown up. You are what? Seventeen now!' I had to sit down, dragging her down with me, and reached for my tobacco, taking it out of my pocket, starting to roll a cigarette.

'Tell me what's been happening? How was your new school? Pity you missed out the year at home! You could have been studying for your Leaving Cert instead of taking on A levels. It's a totally different subject, course, Sarah!'

'Mummy, the doctor wants to speak with you,' she said, pulling the sleeve of my dressing gown, interrupting my babble.

I whirled around to find myself staring at a man in a suit holding a chart in his hand.

'May I have a word with you, please?' he said, waving his hand at me.

I stood up, walking over to him.

'I'm the consultant anaesthetist who has done some work with the professor,' he said, giving me a piercing stare. 'He has asked me to be your anaesthetist. I have examined your case,' and he waved the thick volume of my chart towards me, then hesitated. 'But before I make my decision, I wanted to take a look at you.'

Then he hesitated and said, 'OK! We will go ahead with the operation on Wednesday.'

I stared at him. 'But that's my birthday!'

'Well, that will be your birthday present,' he said, beaming at me.

I stared, thinking. Then beamed back. 'The gift of my life,' I said. 'Thank you very much, Doctor. You are a gentleman and a scholar!'

He flipped the chart at me then marched off very smartly.

I looked around, and Sarah was enjoying herself talking to a young fella who was the colour of beetroot. He couldn't get over his good fortune at being noticed by a fine young one! He had spots and wore his long greasy locks down over the collar of his Blackrock College rugby shirt.

'Mummy!' she glanced up, noticing me, and bounced over. 'Listen, Mummy! I have to go. Grandad is waiting outside in the car park. He's driving me to the airport.'

'What? But, darling! What do you mean? You only just got here.'

'Oh, no, Mummy. I arrived over on Friday night. Our friend Jack phoned me and told me to come and see you. So Daddy bought my ticket, and I stayed the weekend with my cousins, at Daddy's sister's. So I called in to see you on the way back to the airport!'

I sat down heavily, with the wind knocked out of me. Everything was flying past me at the rate of knots. Not staying? I thought she was home for good! Ah, but she's going back to study. She has a new life now. I kept staring at her, seeing her laughing and joking with the young fella. Well, I can't complain. She's looking lovely, and she seems to have settled well over in England. Oh, well! We only have them for a short time.

'I better go, Mummy,' she said, wrapping her arms around me, giving me a tight hug. 'Grandad is waiting to take me to the airport. I better hurry. Goodbye, Mummy,' she said, waving as she took off. Then she was back, giving me another hug. But before I could really respond and give her a tight hug back, she was gone! Walking out the door, blowing me kisses and waving me goodbye.

I watched her disappear down the passage, and it was over! She's gone as quickly as she appeared. We never even got to talk. Why did she not come here first to see me? Why did she leave me until the last minute? It doesn't make any sense. I sighed. Kids! They never think. Then wandered back into the ward, thinking, Well! That was better than a kick up the arse. It was good of her father to send her over. Wonder does he know she blew his money having a good time for herself? Visiting the invalids was definitely not on her list of things to do! Jaysus! But still, I can't fault her. She is a good kid, she always was – one of the best, really.

I opened my eyes, staring out the window at the dark, still remembering. The operation was a success, though I did get a storming. It caused a cardiac arrest, with respiratory failure, just as the professor had feared. But, as they had said, the anaesthetist was the top man in the country, and the surgeon was the best. They kept me alive, filled with drugs and strapped to a machine. They knew exactly what they were doing, and I am grateful to them.

I woke up briefly for a few minutes in Intensive Care, propped up dead straight, to keep me from suffocating, and the priest was bending down beside me. When my eyes flickered open, I took in his presence and the fact I was surrounded by machines.

'You are in Intensive Care,' he whispered, leaning over me. 'You made it!' he breathed, letting his shoulders drop.

'Fuck off!' I wheezed, no sound coming out of my mouth. I wanted

Sarah! Where is she? My eyes darted around the room then peeled back to him. She didn't come. I stared at him, terrified of the pain.

My body was rigid. I was completely paralysed, unable to move, my head kept stable by a mountain of pillows that kept me dead upright. There was a jar hanging by the side filled with blood and a tube running up to my neck, draining away all the fluid.

'You are going to be fine,' he said with infinite tenderness. 'I stayed with you the entire night, praying for you.'

I understood he cared, but the pain was intense, and I glared at him, wanting him to stop talking and do something. Stop the pain.

'Do you want the nurse?'

I blinked.

'Nurse! She needs you more than me now,' he laughed, moving away and letting the nurse move in close.

'Yes!' the nurse said, looking straight at me. 'I'll get her the morphine injection.'

That was last year, I thought, dragging my eyes from the window. It was a long aul haul, getting back on my feet. But now, so long as I take the medication daily, to replace the job of the organ, well, I'm getting there slowly.

They say trouble comes in threes. Well, I have had the three now. First, Sarah taking wings. Then spending those months in the hospital. Now this year! It couldn't bloody end without something happening. But nothing could have been worse than losing Harry! Oh! God almighty. I pray now that things can only get better. Also, dear God, please look after the ma. She has suffered enough. More than enough in her lifetime.

But now, at last, Sarah's coming home. Well, for a short visit. She has to get back to school and concentrate on her A levels. I told her I would buy her a return plane ticket, and she's coming on Sunday! If only I had known we would be burying poor Harry the same week. Thank God I sent her that plane ticket. Now I have something to look forward to. God! I can't wait! Things can only get better from now on. I have the operation over, and next year will be a new start. I should have the full health back by then.

20

Right, I have a lot to do, I thought, looking around the kitchen. Clean the house from top to bottom! I'm feeling knackered even at the thought of all that cleaning. I'll cook her a nice meal. Her favourite. Spaghetti bolognese and garlic bread, and for dessert, banana fritter with golden syrup and ice cream. Lovely!

I had better get to bed. I stirred myself then stopped to listen. No sign of that dog yet! Bloody pest! I switched off the light in the kitchen and walked out to the hall, looking out through the French doors. No! Bonzo is still not back.

I dragged myself wearily up the stairs, feeling a bit lonely. The silence of the house telling me there should be a family here. It would be lovely to hear the sound of children's laughter again. Then I heard the haunting echo of Sarah's voice, tinkling with laughter. A little girl sharing secrets with her friends, full of the joys of life. I thought it would last for ever, but that sound is hollow now. Just ghosts from a long dead past.

Finished! At last, that's the end of the cleaning. I opened the press under the stairs and humped in the Hoover, then stood up, feeling dizzy. Right! Where am I? Bedrooms cleaned, Sarah's bed ready, everything done and dusted. Smashing! Now I can sit down in comfort and have a lovely cup of tea and a smoke. I headed into the kitchen, humming 'Life is a bowl of cherries!' and filled the kettle. Then I started on the dinner.

I can make the sauce now and leave it in the fridge overnight. Years of practice have me organised to great efficiency, I thought smugly as I whipped the packet of minced steak out of the fridge. Two tins of tomatoes, one tin of purée, three onions, mixed herbs, fresh thyme – it always brings out the flavour of the meat.

Ha! I laughed to myself, thinking about the time when I was only a young one and living in a bedsit. I couldn't boil water, never mind cook! I bought myself a packet of instant mash, hoping for a bit of dinner. I read the instructions, but I'm not very good with following instructions. 'Pour mash powder into saucepan,' it said. I did! 'Pour half pint of boiled water then stir.' I ended up with runny water! No dinner! Ha, ha! Those were the days when I was as thick as two short planks! I used to torment the other poor unfortunate tenants living in the house, knocking on their door, asking them where I went wrong. Showing them the burnt pot with the charred remains of a Lancashire hotpot. 'I followed the recipe to the last tee!' I would sniff. 'Look how it turned out!' Then shove the burnt pot under their nose. Jaysus! I was an awful torment!

Right! Concentrate. Eight cloves of garlic. Good for the lungs! Now, brown the mince, add the chopped onions, garlic, tomatoes and purée; whip it all together with wooden spoon and leave to simmer – the longer the better. Perfect!

I eyed the kettle. I'm well overdue for that cup of tea and a smoke. I poured a drop of boiling water into the teapot, emptied it, now add the tea and the boiled water – it has to be still on the boil! – and poured myself out a lovely cup of tea. I felt a bit weak. Hmm! I haven't had anything to eat! Ah, maybe later. I'm not hungry now.

I don't seem to bother much about eating any more. I don't like shopping. Supermarkets give me the creeps! But yesterday I trotted around quite happily. I had a purpose. Shopping for Sarah! My heart somersaulted. Sarah! I can't wait. Yeah! Definitely. It was incredibly lucky I sent her the tickets before poor Harry died. At least now I will have Sarah here.

I drank my tea and puffed on the cigarette, feeling a sense of peace. One door closes – I buried my poor Harry yesterday – but another door always opens. Sarah is coming.

I crushed out the cigarette butt in the ashtray and rinsed out the cup, emptying the teapot, and went in to set the dining-room table. White-linen tablecloth. Table mats with lovely Christmas scenes – horses and carriages racing through the snow. Victorian-looking. Lovely! Good cutlery, table napkins, wine glasses, and I got a bottle of Chablis. She's eighteen now. Probably drinks, and this is a special occasion.

Then I set the fire. Rolled-up newspapers, lots of firelighters broken up and placed strategically around the paper, then small lumps of coal placed on top. I stood back to admire the room. Yeah! The table looks lovely, and the sofa pushed against the far wall with the little antique table and the Tiffany lamp on top – lovely! It looks very cosy. I looked at the bookcases inside the alcoves each side of the fireplace and got a warm glow. Pick up one of those and you can shut out the world and travel into someone else's horror, drama – it doesn't matter what. You can enjoy yourself, experience whatever it is they are going through, and the beauty is it is not happening to you!

They keep me going these days – dogs and books. Well, one dog, and walking him in the woods. That's it. Jaysus! That's not much of a life. The sooner I get my strength back and get moving the better. I might rent the house out and take off to the States next year. I could get a job as a nanny for a while until I find my way around. Yeah! Good idea. I'm still young, only in my thirties. Yeah! Here I come, world.

I drove out to the airport, putting the boot down when I passed Whitehall. Bloody Sunday drivers! They get to drive the car once a week and forget how to drive. Ah! Slowed down again. The blue Toyota in front was driving me mad. Stop, start, the driver nattering to his wife in the passenger seat. Now she points to something, 'Ohh, lookit, George!' and gobshite George stops, no warning, nothing! Then starts again, just as I am about to overtake him. Then he suddenly makes a left turn without indicating.

I swerve, sitting on the horn, roaring. The wife gives me the V sign. 'Aul hag!' I scream, me heart thumping. Right! Control yourself. The flight comes in at ten past five. I'm nearly there now. I thought I had left enough time. Right! Forgot about the Sunday drivers heading home for their tea. Enjoy yourself.

I whizzed up the hill, stopping outside the entrance. Should I chance it and park the car here? I don't see anyone around. Still, I might get towed away. Sarah would have my guts for garters.

I drove over to the car park, collecting my ticket. Robbers, the price of it! I roared to meself, looking at the ticket man. I headed off into the entrance, and here she comes. I looked. One bag thrown over her shoulder and no duty free! Where's the tobacco? I said I would pay her the bloody money! She marched towards me, taking long strides. Men glanced at her from cars driving past. She knew this and flicked her lovely blonde hair back, straightening her back and pushing out her chest. She is extremely well developed. Huge breasts and a slim figure with long legs. Hmm! From the time she was only fourteen, I was screaming at aul fellas and young fellas in the street, 'Stop looking at the child! Filthy perverts!' I won't have to do that now, I thought, smiling. She's all grown up, a young woman of eighteen!

'Mummy!'

'Hi, darling!' I tried to wrap my arms around her shoulders. She had to lean down, then I was lifted off my feet.

'Ohhh! I missed you!' she squealed, kissing the face off me.

'Right! Lovely! Now put me down!' I roared, laughing me head off.

She put me standing back on me feet, and I grabbed her in a hug, saying, 'Oh, sweetheart! You will never have an idea just how much I missed you! How are you?' I asked, looking her up and down. 'At least they're feeding you!' I snorted, wondering if they were taking care of her. Hmm! She looks well. Then I eyed her shoulder bag. 'Did you bring me the tobacco I asked you to get?'

'No!' she said, sweeping past me. 'You shouldn't be smoking. I am certainly not helping you to kill yourself, Mummy!'

My heart dropped with disappointment. No smokes! 'But sure I'll have to buy them anyway!' I moaned, rushing to catch up with her.

'Where's the car?' she asked, stopping and looking around her.

'Oh! Daisy is over here.'

'What! You still have that banger?' she roared, laughing her head off.

'Of course!' I sniffed. 'Cheeky beggar! She's only . . . let me see! Hmm, yeah, well, she may be thirteen years old, but she still goes like a bomb and she's only got fifty thousand miles on the clock!'

'Great! Let's hope she doesn't decide to give up the ghost before we get home,' she laughed, looking the car up and down. Then she pointed her finger towards the windscreen. I followed where she was pointing.

'Ah, would you come on outa that, Sarah. It's only a bit of rust!' I said, taking a swipe at it, seeing a bigger hole appear.

'Come on, Mummy! Take it easy! This thing is ready to collapse in a heap, leaving us stranded.'

'Never!' I said. 'Come on! Get in!'

We climbed into the car, and Sarah threw her bag in the back, flicking her hair, and said, 'Daddy drives a Mercedes.'

'Yeah?' I said, wanting to say something sour after hearing that one. Don't be ridiculous, Martha. She might as well be talking about anybody. 'Ahh! Good for him, Sarah! That means you now manage to get driven around in style,' I said, grinning at her.

She watched me, twisting her mouth backwards and forwards, looking to see my reaction.

'Ah, yeah! That's great for him,' I said, turning to look at her.

'Oh, Mummy. Don't you worry. When I finish college and start earning, the first thing I'm going to do is buy you something you always wanted! Now! What would that be?'

'A mink fur coat!' we shouted together, looking at each other and laughing.

'Yes, Sarah. You are not getting outa my clutches until you pay me back every penny I ever spent on you!' I sniffed, flicking me eye over at her.

'Well, that won't take me long,' she snorted. 'Seeing as you . . .'

'WATCH OUT!' I suddenly said, instinctively flying my arm across to stop her banging her head, then slamming on the brakes at the same time.

The car came to a screeching stop. 'The dirty-looking little heap of shit!' I roared, as we both watched a mangy black-and-white mongrel shoot past, holding its tail between his arse, keeping one eye on us. Then it scarpered for the footpath, taking off again, chasing an aul one with a little dog on a lead. Then we happily watched as she turned around, giving the mongrel a smack of the stick, sending him flying back in the other direction.

'Jaysus! That dog is either the luckiest thing flying around on four legs or it's the unluckiest!' I said, laughing as it kept going without looking back, with its tail held tight under its back legs. I looked at Sarah, seeing her watching me and watching the dog with a laugh on her face.

'Oh, Mummy! You haven't changed a bit. I really miss all the fun we used to have.'

'Do you?' I said, feeling me heart turn over.

'Yeah, really,' she said quietly, nodding her head, letting her eyes go sad. Then she shifted closer to me, resting her head on me shoulder.

'It's so wonderful, real heaven, having you back home with me again, Sarah darling,' I murmured, kissing the side of her head. 'So tell me, Sarah! What's happening with your studies?'

'Well,' she sighed, thinking about it. 'I'm thinking of doing something in the sciences, Mummy,' she said, looking at me, wanting to see what I think.

'Yes! That's a good idea, Sarah! You got top marks in your intermediate exams,' I said, looking at her.

She turned away, looking moodily out the window. Oh! Bad mistake, I thought. That's when I let her go off to England to visit her father for a month, just after she finished her exams, during the summer. Two years ago, I thought, remembering. She stayed for good! Hmm, I better think before I open my mouth. She doesn't want to be reminded. It might not have been a good idea. Now she has to put in an extra year because of the different system with the English A levels. Right! Don't go saying something that will upset her. We only have this short time together.

I took a deep breath as we headed into the village, feeling relieved now we were nearly home.

'Oh, what a dreary place,' Sarah said, looking out the window. 'And awfully dreary people,' she said, curling up her lip and sniffing at the Sunday strollers. People minding their own business and wearily heading home for their tea, pushing tired children in buggies.

'But, darling! All your friends are here. People you have grown up with. This is where you grew up. I thought you were happy here.'

'Sorry, Mummy,' she said, turning around to look at me. 'I wasn't thinking. When I first moved over to stay with Daddy, I was really homesick. Then I kept telling myself it was really boring back home in Dublin. I kept trying to see everything here as dull and monotonous, whereas at Daddy's it was in fact great fun for the first few weeks. I was the new girl at school; everyone wanted to get to know me. I did a lot of partying!' she said, looking at me sideways, with a big grin on her face.

'Hmm! I bet you did,' I said. Not looking too impressed. 'I suppose your father let you away with murder!' I snorted, giving her an annoyed look.

'No, in fact, we had a lot of rows!'

'Did you?' I asked suddenly, snapping me head around to look at her, feeling delighted he got a dose of teenage temper tantrums. Good enough for him! I thought to meself. That would have been a shock to his system! Ha! The joys of being a father.

21

I turned the car in to the back of the house and drove into the garage. 'Home sweet home!' I said, switching off the engine, giving a big sigh of happiness. 'We're here, pet!' I said, smiling at her as I reached over to grab her in a hug.

'Oh, Mummy,' she said, lifting her head to look at me. 'It's just like I never left! Everything still looks the same. It feels like I'm a child again, and we've just arrived back home after a long day out,' she whispered, looking around in wonder at the bare concrete walls holding the shelves lined with old cans of paint, gardening tools, wellington boots and old garden shoes. 'Even the smell is the same!' she said, looking around, smiling.

'Right, darling! Let's get a move inside. Grab your bag,' I said, opening the car door and heaving myself out.

Jaysus! I'm feeling banjacksed! I thought, trying to stretch my neck and back as I made for the garage doors. I shut the two doors and slammed across the bolt, then made for the side door to head up the garden path.

'Where's Bonzo, Mummy?' Sarah said as she shut the car door, making to follow me.

I opened the side door, leaping back just as Bonzo came bounding in, taking a flying leap at Sarah. 'Down!' she screamed, getting the fright of her life as I staggered back, laughing the head off meself.

'I was expecting that! I knew bloody well he would be waiting to steamroll me!' I shouted, getting all excited because I was definitely wide awake this time.

'That dog is mad! Why do you keep him, Mummy?' she shouted, losing the rag because he knocked her flying. 'Mummy, he's definitely too wild for you!' she snorted, picking her stuff off the ground and throwing her hair back. It was all tangled, hanging right down the front of her face. She looked like she had been in a fight.

'He's stark, raving mad!' she puffed, stopping to stare at him as he stared back, with his back paws thrown behind him and his arse in the air, waiting and wondering if she wanted to have another go at this game.

'Out!' I roared, pointing me finger straight ahead. 'Come on, darling! Let's go!'

He took off, chasing his tail, flying ahead and tearing back to jump at Sarah.

'Stay!' she screamed.

'He's just excited at seeing you, love. See! He remembers you. Look, he's trying to lick your hand.'

She gave him a push on the snout, then grabbed him back, mangling him with hugs and slaps and shoving her face into his nose.

'Don't do that, Sarah! You never know where that fella has been putting his face!' I said, getting all worried she might catch disease.

'No, Mummy! Not our Bonzo!' she said, pulling the long ears offa him, then taking off, trying to fly ahead of him.

The pair of them nearly sent me flying flat on me back as they pummelled past. 'For the love a Jaysus! Would you watch where ye're going!' I screamed, getting the fright of me life, thinking I could have been killed stone dead with the knock I could have got!

I rounded the path, seeing the pair of them waiting for me to put the key in the door. Then Sarah turned her head, staring across the road to the high wall surrounded by beautiful old oak trees. They had been planted in the 1700s, when the aristocrats had lived in the old house. It's now a convent.

'What are you thinking, love?' I said, looking over to see what she was seeing.

'Oh!' she said slowly, letting out a big sigh. 'I'm just remembering all the happy years I spent playing in there with my friends, and of course Bonzo!'

His ears pricked up at the mention of his name, and she stroked his head without thinking, and continued to let her eyes rove up and down the forest.

'Yeah,' I whispered. 'Many happy years indeed.' I sighed, feeling very contented with all my memories. 'Yeah! It really was a child's paradise, wasn't it, Sarah?'

'Yes, it sure was,' she said, smiling. But her eyes looked sad.

'We're home!' I breathed, pushing in the front door, then shutting it after me as the pair of them hurried in, one chasing the other.

Sarah puffed, coming over to fling her bag down by the coat rack, saying, 'Mummy! You sit down! I'll do the cooking. What are we having to eat?'

'No, darling! You keep that mutt out from under me feet. I have everything almost ready. Go on! Sort yourself out. Leave me to get on with it.'

I rushed into the kitchen to boil the water for the spaghetti. I pulled out the big saucepan for cooking it, then opened the packet, breaking it in two, and rushed off, leaving it to boil. Then hurried in to stoke up the fire. It was nicely banked up and had settled down to a lovely red glow, giving out great heat. I gave it a bang with the poker and poked between the bars, letting it collapse a little, then put on more coal. It will roar into life by the time we sit down to eat.

Suddenly there was a ring at the doorbell. I wonder who that is? I thought, putting down the poker and placing the fireguard around the fire for safety. Sarah answered the door, and I heard her laughing, then voices.

Camille! I thought, as I stood looking at Sarah's friend. They had been friends since the first day of junior school. Sarah was barely four that first week. She had trotted out holding Camille's hand, announcing, 'Mamma! This is my best, bestest friend, Camille! She teached me to whistle. Look!' and she put her lips together, spitting and making a blowing sound.

'Oh! You're a marvellous whistler!' I laughed down at her, 'And you're a very pretty little girl!' I said to Camille, bending down to her. 'I bet you are really a fairy princess, but it's a big secret. Nobody is supposed to know that! Isn't that true?'

She giggled, showing her lovely sweet dimples, and Sarah and her have been lifelong friends ever since.

'Ah! Camille! It's lovely to see you! How have you been? Come here! Let me look at you. Gosh, you are all grown up,' I said, taking in her lovely long black hair. It is so glossy. 'God! You're gorgeous!' I screamed.

'Thank you,' she said shyly, looking at me and smiling, showing her dimples. She has the most beautiful blue-grey eyes, and they shine out at you, and you can see an immense gentleness in them.

'You are staying for dinner?'

She hesitated, not wanting to impose. I could see that.

'Don't you dare refuse, Camille! I've cooked enough for an army! There's even too much for Bonzo. Oh, where is he?'

'Out in the garden, cooling his paws,' Sarah said, laughing.

'Ah, yeah! The poor thing is probably going mad to see you all! I'll let him in,' I said, rushing to open the front door.

'No, Mummy, leave him out there.'

I stopped, with my hand on the door, looking at Sarah. 'Why, darling? He's dying to get in and see you.'

'Well, I don't want him in here. That brute will drive us all mad, jumping around the place!'

'Sorry, Martha,' Camille said gently, 'but I'm . . .'

'What's wrong, Camille?' I said, looking at her worried face.

'She's terrified of that savage, Mummy,' Sarah shouted, laughing with a half-cry on her face.

'Oh, but, girls, Bonzo wouldn't hurt a fly!' I said, looking at them, astonished. Then saw Camille looking from me to Sarah with a very nervous look on her face. 'Ah, yeah! I understand. Sorry, darling. I forgot you are like me, terrified of dogs. It doesn't matter what people tell you. You never trust them. No, no, leave him out there. Right, girls! Dinner won't be long. Take your coat off, Camille. Make yourself at home.'

'Come on!' Sarah laughed, grabbing Camille by the hand and rushing her into the dining room. 'I have so much to tell you.'

'Oh! I'm dying to tell you everything as well,' Camille breathed, laughing.

They rushed in, slamming the door behind them. I hesitated, then rushed into the kitchen, grabbing the pot of spaghetti and emptying it into the colander. The sauce was heated, and I pushed the thick slices of Vienna rolls spread with the garlic butter under the grill. I poured oil into the deep-fat fryer to make the banana fritters. The batter was cooling in the fridge, sitting in a bowl. I already made that yesterday. It's better that way, helps it to ferment, and I think it tastes better anyway!

I ladled the spaghetti into the bowls and poured on the sauce, then added Parmesan cheese. 'Ready!' I shouted, carrying it into the dining room. 'Dinner's ready, girls!' I said, kicking the door with me foot as I hung on to the tray.

The door whipped open. 'Sarah! It's your favourite,' I laughed, letting her grab the tray and following her in.

'Oh, delicious, Mummy!' Sarah screamed, already eating the grub with her eyes. She landed the tray down and whipped up the bowls, putting one in each place, then let herself drop into the chair, picking up her fork.

'Eat up!' she said, nudging Camille with her elbow, then lathered into the grub like she hadn't eaten for a week.

'Thanks for inviting me,' Camille said, looking up at me all smiles.

'Ah! Camille, darling! Stop acting like a guest. Sure, you are one of the family!' I said, heading for the kitchen again. I rushed back in with my own plate, carrying the garlic bread in a basket after putting a serviette on the bottom.

'Right! Who is going to open the wine?'

'I'll do it!' Camille said, jumping up and rushing after me into the kitchen.

'Yeah! She's now working in a bar,' Sarah roared after us.

'Are you, Camille?'

'Yes! I've got a weekend job working in the village.'

'Ah! You're a wonderful girl, Camille. Your mum must be very proud of you. You've grown into a beautiful young lady.'

'Thank you! I always thought you were great!' Camille laughed. 'I actually wanted to swap Mum for you,' she giggled. 'You were great fun!'

'Ah, will ye stop, Camille! Sarah used to go mad,' I laughed, getting the picture of a little red-faced Sarah screaming at me with tears and snots pouring down her face as I cheated on her while playing cards! Or God knows what else I tortured the poor kid with. 'NO! Our Sarah thought me the demon mammy from hell!' I laughed, handing her the wine and reaching up for the corkscrew.

'Well, we all thought you were great,' she said, looking at me.

'Thank you, Camille. That's a lovely thing to say. Do you know? I still have that present you bought me when you were . . . God! You were only about twelve or thirteen. It was a beautiful bottle of bath salts with a ribbon around the neck. I was really touched by your kindness. Yeah! I keep it on my dressing table. It always reminds me of you, and when you were all uncomplicated little girls,' I laughed.

She stared at me, smiling, remembering those times too.

'You are lovely,' I said, giving her a hug.

'Wine!' Camille shouted, rushing back in and pouring out the wine.

I trailed in behind her, thinking, it's just like old times, with me having that easy relationship with Sarah. Before she went mad to get to her father and flap her wings. Camille is a lovely girl, too, so open and warm.

'I'll just have half a glass, darling,' I said, putting out my hand to stop her filling my glass. 'At last!' I said, sitting down and forking up the spaghetti, wrapping it around, then aiming it for my mouth. I took a sip of wine and broke a piece of bread. 'Delicious! What more could we want?' I said, smiling and feeling contented with having the girls here. It's just like old times.

I leaned over to take the bowl with the Parmesan cheese. 'Anyone want more?' I said, spooning the cheese onto the sauce.

'Yes, please!' Camille said, reaching for the cheese at the same time Sarah reached for the wine bottle, knocking the bloody thing over.

'Oops! Less for us,' she laughed, rescuing the bottle. But it was too late for my linen tablecloth.

She saw me staring at it and laughed. 'Mummy is going to start flapping now over her tablecloth. You always were terrible for fussing.'

'True,' I said, trying to ignore the red bloodstain oozing its way around me linen tablecloth. I grabbed that from Sister Eleanor's, just before they knocked down the old convent. I stared up mournfully at the two of them, seeing them staring back in shock at me. Camille had a forkful of grub stuck halfway to her mouth, with it still wide open, waiting to catch it. Sarah was staring at me with a grin on her face but a worried look in her eyes.

'Nooo!' I said. 'Forget it! Look at it! It's only a bloody tablecloth!

A lovely snow-white, the very best old linen the nuns could get their hands on,' I breathed out mournfully, still staring at it. They stared at me as we all sat listening to my sorrow hanging heavy in the silence. Then they roared out laughing.

Sarah came flying around to the back of me chair, wrapping her arms around me, suffocating me in a hug. 'Aww! Poor Mummy! Listen! It will be perfect again. As soon as we are finished eating, we can soak it in cold water and salt. Don't worry! Anyway! Dad has some lovely stuff belonging to Mona's grandmother. We can liberate that. Or I will!' she laughed, cackling like a witch.

'Don't you dare, Sarah! I don't want that woman putting out a contract on me with the Mafia!' I said, thinking of her father's wife. We spoke on the phone one day and she complained about my daughter, saying Sarah was having some sort of brainstorming, with her partying every night of the week. I clucked, agreeing with every word, then put down the phone, thinking, Oh! There is a God in his heaven after all. Sarah is giving them hell! Ha!

'Ah! Enough! Never mind any more talk of tablecloths,' I said, cheering up. 'Here's to the future, girls. Health and happiness.' I clinked their glasses.

'And wealth!' Sarah shouted.

'So, what are you doing with yourself, Camille?'

'Oh, I'm at college.'

'Really! What are you doing?'

'Well, I've just started this year. Classes haven't really got going yet. But I'm doing economics and politics.'

'Oh, that's wonderful, isn't it, Sarah?'

Sarah nodded, then dropped her eyes, studying her plate. Me heart dropped seeing her looking miserable at the thought again of having to spend another year at school preparing for A levels.

I asked Camille what she might do after college.

'I don't know really, probably something in the bank,' then she tucked in to her plate again.

'Sarah will be going to college next year. Won't you, darling?'

'Of course,' Sarah said, flicking her hair back, giving me a watery smile.

I could see how it pained her, not being able to start college with all her old childhood friends. Now she was starting a completely new life. Oh, well! It's what she wants. Something new, a bit of adventure. A challenge. And, more importantly, escaping my clutches! I had always put the brakes on, letting her go only so far.

22

'Right, girls!' I said, pushing back the chair to stand up and grab the empty dishes. 'Anyone for dessert? Listen! That's not a question! Don't anyone even dare refuse my incredible offerings of banana fritter with chocolate, golden syrup and stone-cold ice cream!' I said, throwing me eye at the pair of them, then watching as they bounced up to take the dishes off me.

'Are you mad?' Sarah screamed, rushing out the door ahead of me, hanging on to the empty plates. 'That's all I've been thinking about since I sat on that plane,' she laughed, slamming down the plates in the sink, nearly breaking the lot of them.

'I'll help!' she said, flying to turn on the cooker. 'Oh, I'm starved,' she moaned, opening the fridge to take out the batter.

'Starved! But you've just shovelled down half a big pot of sauce and most of the garlic bread!'

'Yeah, Mummy! Daddy complains he will need to get a mortgage just to feed me!' she laughed.

'Ohh! You don't need to remind me!' I said. 'Jesus, Sarah! You used to go round telling people I starved you!' I said, thinking of her excuse when she was only a skinny little scrap of a thing. Four years old you were, Sarah, when you told the Simmons, that Christmas we spent with them. You ate all around you at the Christmas dinner. Everyone sat gaping at you. Then you had the cheek to say – when they muttered, "Goodness! You have such an appetite for such a little girl!" – "Yeah," you lisped, "and Mummy doesn't feed me!" you snorted, turning in my direction to give me a dirty look! Remember?' I shouted, still not able to get over the stuff she used to come out with.

'Oh, yeah!' she screamed, laughing like a hyena.

'Go on! Get out! Talk to Camille!'

'Is someone taking my name in vain?' Camille giggled, coming in the door with the tray stacked with more dirty dishes.

'We'll wash up,' Sarah muttered to Camille, getting in me way as she scraped the plates, trying to get a bit of order.

'No! We can't swing a cat in here! Leave it, girls. You two go on inside. Catch up on your news. I want to cook the dessert. Then we can wash up,' I said to their backs as they grabbed each other, trying to drag themselves out the door, slamming it shut behind them.

'Hurry, Mummy! I can't wait to get my teeth into that!' Sarah shouted before banging the dining-room door. The house rattled, and the door nearly came off its hinges.

'Jesus Christ! The noise,' I said, feeling the vibrations. They are worse than kids!

'Anyone want more dessert?' I said, barely able to move with the amount of grub we polished off. 'There's two more fritters left in the kitchen,' I said, looking hopefully at the two red faces staring woefully back at me.

'Oh, God, no!' Sarah moaned, turning her head away from the table.

'No! No, thanks,' Camille said, rubbing her belly and laughing, then standing herself up slowly. 'That was the best meal I've had in ages,' she smiled, coming over to give me a hug. 'I have to go, sorry! It's getting late,' she said, looking over at the mantle clock bonging away on the mantelpiece.

'Oh! All right then, Camille. It's a pity you can't stay longer. Sarah would love to curl up and talk with you, wouldn't you, Sarah?' I said, seeing a look pass between them.

'I'd better go!' Camille suddenly said. 'Bye, Sarah!' and they kissed quickly and muttered something to each other. Then Camille was gone.

'Oh! That was a bit of a let-down. I thought she would stay a bit longer, and you could have a great natter,' I said, heading in to the kitchen.

'No, she has things to do,' Sarah said, sipping her wine and looking miles away.

'Right! Do you want any more dessert, Sarah?'

'No, thanks, Mummy,' she groaned, collapsing her head on the tablecloth.

'OK,' I said, wearily clearing away the dishes from the table and taking them into the kitchen. I stacked them on the draining board ready to start washing up. 'Sarah! Bring in the rest of the stuff off the table.'

She sauntered in with a basket of bread in one hand and a glass of wine in the other. 'Where would you like this?' she asked, holding the basket in mid air.

I looked at her, seeing a change in her mood now that Camille had left. It's getting her down. The thought of all she has left behind. She looks tired.

Ah, to hell with them, I suddenly thought. 'Leave the dishes for a minute, Sarah. Let's go and have a cup of tea.' Then I laughed. 'You can finish off the wine. There's still some left in the bottle. I'm gasping for a cigarette. Where did I leave my bag?'

'Dunno. Probably in the hall,' Sarah muttered, pouring out what was left in the bottle.

I was suddenly lifted, feeling we can relax now. There's no pressure. It's probably just as well Camille has gone. We can sit down quietly by the fire and talk.

I brought in a mug of tea and sat down on the couch, lighting up the cigarette. Sarah was sitting at the table drinking her wine, but she was still lost in her own thoughts. She didn't seem to notice I was there.

'Sarah!'

'Yeah,' she said, barely moving, and listlessly staring out the window.

It was dark now, and I thought maybe I should draw the curtains, keep out the damp. 'Sarah! Come and sit down beside me,' I said, patting the couch beside me. 'There's something I want to tell you.'

'What? What do you want to tell me?' she said, turning around to look at me.

'Do you know Harry? He's your uncle, my brother.'

'Yeah. Which one is he? The tall one, always grinning?'

'Yes!' I said, happy she remembers him, and seeing the picture of him laughing, happy, always in good humour, when he had better days, with his wife and family around him. A terrible sense of loss and sadness washed over me, and I suddenly felt like crying. Tears swam into my eyes, and I lowered my head, staring at my lap. I held back the tears. I don't think this is the right time for me to let go.

'Well, he died, Sarah,' I said, lifting my head and looking over at her. 'We buried him on Friday. That's actually why I'm wearing black,' I said, looking down at my clothes. 'It's as a mark of respect for him,' I finished, wanting her to know he was special.

She didn't respond.

'He committed suicide,' I said, feeling his loss all come rushing back at me. I stared at the carpet, wondering what the ma was doing and how she was feeling. 'So!' I said, continuing. 'Isn't it terrible? He's gone now. Buried two days and he was so young.'

'Oh, Mummy!' she said, landing down her glass and rushing over to sit down beside me. 'What happened? But surely he was so young!' she said, letting her huge big blue eyes hop out of her head. 'Suicide, you said?'

'Yes, he killed himself, Sarah,' I said, seeing her face crease into a collapse, not able to take it in. 'So, that's the whole story,' I said, lighting up another cigarette and moving a bit away to look at her face.

She sat staring at the floor, lost in what I had just told her, shaking her head and blinking slowly, thinking of the horror and the picture of everyone at near collapse. 'I'm so sorry, Mummy. That is unbelievably tragic! But,' she said, slowly shaking her head and thinking, making a decision, 'I am . . . I'm not one bit surprised with that family. How could they be anything else with the parents they have?' she snorted, looking away and staring at the wall.

'Yeah, I know, Sarah,' I said, shaking me head, thinking it was always bound to be coming. There was no stopping it. 'But you didn't really get to know them very well,' I said, thinking how I always tried to protect her from my roots. 'I didn't take you there very often,' I said, looking at her, 'because I didn't want to expose you to that kind of life. Anyway, you certainly didn't like the ma,' I laughed. 'You even hated going near that area. But he was your uncle, and Sally is your grandmother.'

'No, Mummy! She is not! I understand what you mean by blood, but Nanny is my grandmother,' she said quietly, looking at me.

'Yeah, but still and all, blood is thicker then water, and without Sally we wouldn't be here.'

She went quiet, staring at me. A look of contempt passed through her eyes, then disappeared as she stared at the floor.

I stared at her, reading that look. I could feel myself getting smaller, shrinking inside myself. I'm not able to change anything. It doesn't matter how far I've come or what I have achieved. She is always going to have that shame about who I am and where I come from. If only she knew the real truth!

I sat staring out into the darkness, wondering if Sarah and I will ever be truly happy again. I'm feeling completely drained. Parent-and-young-adult relationships are so complicated, I thought. It's hard not to see her as your little girl. Yeah, well, she's not! I thought sadly. They grow up!

'Maybe we should go to bed,' I said, getting up and moving towards the kitchen. I stood looking at the dishes sitting on the draining board, waiting to be washed. Oh, I'm not in the mood to start washing up, I thought, feeling tired and depressed. 'No!' I said suddenly, shouting in to her. 'Let's do something together! We could watch . . .'

Sarah suddenly stood up, walking in behind me. 'You sit down, Mummy. You have done enough. I will do the dishes now. Then I have to go later, Mummy. I'm going to the theatre with Camille and her mother.'

My head saw sparks with the annoyance. 'Ah, Sarah! I was hoping we could sit down together and maybe watch an old film. Remember you used to love that? We would sit together and watch chillers. You loved that, darling. Please! You've just arrived.'

'No! I promised, Mummy! I'm going,' she said firmly. 'It's all arranged.'

'But when? Camille and HER MOTHER!'

'Yes, Mummy! Please don't start a row. I want us to have a good time together. Come on! I'll get the washing up done. I'm worried about you, Mummy. You look tired. Anyway, I think you should go to bed, get an early night. Then tomorrow we can do something together. OK?' she said, putting her arms around me, trying to make the peace.

'Yeah! You are right, love,' I said, squeezing her back in a tight hug.

'Oh! By the way, Mummy,' she said, going a bit quiet as she landed her face on me with a guilty look in her eyes, trying to think of the best way of telling me something.

Me heart stopped, giving me a jolt. I could sense something I wouldn't like was going to come out.

'Eh, I told Nanny and Grandad I was going to stay with them for a couple of nights.'

'When?' I said, feeling everything was going down the swanny!

'Tomorrow evening. Grandad is coming to collect me.'

'Oh, no, he is not! You can spend your last night with them, Sarah!' I snorted, feeling a rage coming over me at the thought I was not going to get much time with her.

'Mummy! I promised them. Anyway, they are my grandparents. I need to see them. I haven't seen them for ages! We will still have time together,' she said, trying to put her arm around me.

'When?' I suddenly shouted. 'How long will we have? Let me see,' I snorted, feeling me heart flying with the rage. 'Not tonight! You're going out! Not the next two nights! OK! So we will have a few days together, I suppose.'

'Eh, actually, I promised to stay a night or two over with my cousins. See Daddy's side of the family,' she said, letting it all out in a rush.

'Right, Sarah! Fuck off! Just fuck off! Don't bother about me! I've managed very well, thank you, without you for the last two years!' I snorted, going mad with the rage, then feeling cold. Thinking, the bloody selfishness of her!

'Look, stop,' she said, making to pull my hands down by my sides to look at me, trying to placate me.

Without warning, and not even realising what had happened, I suddenly pushed her, sending her flying into the kitchen press, saying, 'Take your hands off me!' Then the shock hit me. 'Oh! I am so sorry!'

She was gone, dropping the tea towel, making for the hall.

'Sarah!' I said, feeling as if the world had come crashing down on me. 'Please! I didn't realise! I wouldn't hurt you for the world!' I said, hearing me voice fade away as I watched her put on her coat and reach down to pick up her bag.

'I'm sorry, Mummy. This is no good. Not for either of us! I have my life now. You won't accept that. You still think of me as a child. That's why Daddy and I get on so well. He trusts me and lets me have my freedom. It's better I leave. We can't get along with each other. Not since I've grown up, anyway! You have your ideas; I have mine.' Then she suddenly bent down and kissed my cheek, then whipped open the front door and flew out.

I stood staring, seeing her rush down the garden path, out the gate and vanish behind the big tree overhanging the front wall. Then she was gone.

I stared. Seeing what was happening in slow motion. But I couldn't take it in. I couldn't move. Me body wouldn't get going. I couldn't believe this was really happening. Yet a little voice inside me was saying, *Yeah! You did know. You sensed she was not really with you. One false move and it would blow up!* Yeah! I know now I did. I certainly had felt a sense of knowing, somehow, this was coming. There was that barrier up between us.

Then it hit me. I went tearing out through the gate, screaming, 'Sarah! Sarah! Come back! For God's sake! We can't do this! Where the hell is she?' Me eyes tore up and down the road, then back down the hill again, staring into the dark night. Gone! Vanished! She's gone! Me heart slammed in me chest, then sank like a bomb down into me belly with the fright and shock. No! For the luv a Jesus! This can't be happening!

I flew down the hill, stopping at the corner, flying me eyes down the road. No! No sign of her! She didn't go that way!

I stared for a long time, standing in the cold and the dark, not caring I was turning icy cold. I didn't want to go back to the house, knowing it would be the end. I would have to face the emptiness, knowing I had brought it all on myself! Oh, no! I couldn't let go! I had to keep going until I destroyed everything. So! That's that. It was so lovely having her here with me, close to me.

I could see again the light she brought with her, feel the warmth of her body as she wrapped her arms around me. I could see the cheerful warm dining room with the roaring-red fire, and the white tablecloth with the red candles, flickering their flame against the window, keeping out the dark night. I could hear her laughter and even smell the lovely food.

Then I saw a picture of her face, smiling, happy. Suddenly it twisted, and then in a flash I was left seeing the horror on her face again as I let fly, losing the rag. In an instant, everything was wiped out. All gone! No, Sarah! It hit me like a punch in the stomach. 'She's gone! She won't be coming back,' I moaned, sounding like an animal in pain. 'Gone,' I muttered as I turned me head back towards the house, dragging with me a terrible sense of grief at having lost her again.

23

I woke up wishing I could carry my head under my arm; it's too heavy for my shoulders. My heart feels like a dead weight. I wandered into Sarah's room, hoping for a miracle. Maybe last night was just a bad dream. No! Me eyes take in the room exactly as I prepared it for her homecoming. Her bed is made up, the little cream chest of drawers sitting next to it with the pink lampshade standing on top. The two matching cream wardrobes, but one is made up of complete shelves only.

I bought the self-assembly pack one Christmas week and stayed up until one o'clock in the morning trying to put it together. I painted the walls a light creamy-pink colour and bought a cream carpet. God! I was so proud of my handiwork when I stood back to admire it. Then I locked the door, putting a huge red ribbon across it and presented it to her on Christmas Eve. I had an awful job trying to keep her out of the way. She had to sleep in the guest room. She kept trying to sneak in, but I had the door locked, and all she could hear was me cursing, banging and hammering. 'I love you, Mummy,' she had said, when she finally got her room back. We were happy then.

I opened the wardrobe door, seeing all her clothes neatly folded. She had taken only what she could squeeze into two suitcases when I let her go off on holiday two years ago. She never came home! Only called to tell me she wanted to live with her father.

My eye wandered down the shelves. The shelves I had put in. I opened a big antique jewellery case with all the jewellery I gave her every year on her birthday. It's still there. She didn't take any of it, not even the jewellery I got from her father a lifetime ago. I looked at it, remembering happier days when I wore it. It's mostly silver, and it wasn't expensive; we didn't have much money. But it meant the world to me at the time.

I gently closed the wardrobe, catching the whiff of a perfume I gave her, the scent plummeting me back down the years. 'Mummy, I love you!' Her innocent face smiling up at me when I gave her something special. I lifted my head, trying to blink back tears that streamed down my face anyway.

I stared at the bookshelves on the far wall, with the extended shelf underneath. Her desk. That was a hell of a job to fix. The plaster was rotten. Charlie and me, we had a hell of a job fixing the rawl plugs to take the screws. She used to sit there every evening, doing her homework at that desk. Yeah! I made that for her.

Ghosts! This house is full of ghosts! I wandered out and sat down on the stairs. I couldn't take another step. The life is gone outa me. Suddenly me heart exploded in a sense of terror. There's nothing left! It's all gone! I'm back to being completely on me own.

Without thinking, I opened me mouth and starting roaring me eyes out, crying like a baby. Then I paused to wipe me snots.

What's that? I could hear something. I held me breath, waiting to hear the sound again. Nothing. I wonder if the neighbours can hear me bleating? Fuck them. I can sit here and cry if I bloody well want to, and as loudly as I want! It's my house, and there's no one listening anyway! There's no one to hear me. So I can do what I want!

I was about to open my mouth and have another bawl when I stopped. There it is! An unmerciful howl went up! It sounds like the banshee.

It's Bonzo! He's crying his heart out! Every time I cried, he joined in. I stopped and listened for a minute. He's howling in sympathy with me. 'Ahh, me poor Bonzo!' I shouted. 'Wait! I'm coming!'

I ran down the stairs and tore open the front door, letting him in. Then I locked the door again, hearing the clicking of the key locking out the world.

'Come on! I'm over here,' I said, turning around to sit back down on the stairs. Bonzo came creeping over on his belly, whining and staring up at me with his big, mournful, chocolate-brown eyes. 'Why are you crying, Bonzo?' I mumbled to him. 'No need for the pair of us to be bleedin miserable.'

He gave a whine, then nudged me lap, hoping I would let him rest his head.

'Come on,' I said, patting me lap. I stroked his head, feeling his skin cold. 'You're freezing, Bonzo! Even with the big black fur coat on you! Poor you, left out in the freezing cold. But it's not much warmer in here,' I said, looking at him and shaking my head.

'No! There's no bright light, no TV blaring out their adverts telling me what to buy myself for Christmas or how to make myself happy. Or make myself better looking, or have a happy family, get myself a man, or be the envy of all the other women. No! There's no cheerful, warm, welcoming fire lighting in the grate. That would mean I'm living, and I'm not really alive any more, Bonzo. No titbits for you. I don't want to eat, so I'm not cooking.

'This was all a mistake, Bonzo. I wasted my life. I got what I wanted. To be away from Jackser and Sally, from the poverty, violence and robbing. But it's all the same in the end. I'm more unhappy now than I was then. Ah! I'm not bothered,' I sighed. 'Life isn't really worth the effort. There's nothing left I want from it.'

I stared at Bonzo, and he gave up listening to my monologue, bored out of his skull. He gave one last look up at me, then snorted and gave himself a big heave, then dropped down on the floor, curling himself into a ball, and fell fast asleep. I stared at him, wishing I could bloody sleep.

24

I opened my eyes and stared around the room. Jesus! I never thought I would end up in this place again. The children's home! I stared out the window, seeing the trees still fighting back the storm. Rain lashed against the windowpane, then there came an almighty bang. I felt as if the bed shook. It was the crash of thunder. I waited, counting the seconds. One, two, three. Then a huge flash, a streak of lightning, raced across the sky. The storm is quite close. I wonder what time it is? I need to get out of this place. I feel shut up in here.

I lit up a cigarette, thinking Sister Eleanor will go mad. Well, too bad! I can always go home if she starts, even if I have to walk. I'm not in the mood to be trifled with! Trifled! I wonder where I got that from? I think I'll creep down to the kitchen and make myself a cup of tea. Creep! Jaysus, I'm now creeping around at my age! Stop it, Martha. You don't have to be intimidated by this place. Or that nun! You are a grown woman, not a child!

Hmph! Right! Where's the kitchen anyway? I want to find out what time it is, I thought, as I crept past her room.

'Are you all right, Martha?'

I stopped dead, with my heart lepping. Jesus Christ! That woman hasn't changed one bit! Does she ever sleep? 'Eh, grand, Sister Eleanor! I'm just going back to bed,' I croaked, heading back to the bedroom with a suffocating feeling in my chest.

I'm feeling trapped! I have to get out of this place. It's giving me the creeps. I paced up and down the room, then gave up and climbed back onto the bed, easing my back against the headboard, and started to doze.

'Good morning, Martha! Did you manage to get some sleep?'

My eyes shot from her to the window. It's morning! The trees were still having a mad dance with the wind. But the storm had lost its fury. I swung my feet off the bed and sat on the side wearily. 'Ah, I'm not too bad, Sister,' I said, eyeing her short grey skirt. Very daring! It's now about two inches above her ankles. And the white blouse with a small gold cross that now replaces the huge gold crucifix she used to wear around her neck. It's finished off nicely with a navy-blue cardigan, the kind your granny would wear to bed. Wow! Yippee! The '80s are here! Freedom!

She now clutches a handbag under her arm with real money in it, and she can even go where she likes now, without having to ask permission. They don't even have to go out in pairs any more. In the past, one went to watch the other and report back to the Reverend Mother! *'Psst! She didn't keep custody of the eyes! Nooh! I caught her looking in shop windows.' Horror, gasp, sharp intake of breath. 'But me, I kept me eyes peeled, cast down, even when a dog stopped to piss, eh, urinate, Mother, on the hem of me habit! Tsk tsk. That's not all, Mother! Nope! Not finished yet, Reverend Mother! You may need to sit down! She was looking at men's jocks – knickers! – in the men's section of Cleary's store, while I was busy heading over to the nun's section for our smalls.' Gasp! Hand on mouth. Swoon. 'Sister dear, get me the smelling salts.'*

Oh, no! Not on yer nelly! Our Sister Eleanor has now tripped gaily into the dull '80s. She's now a swinger! Now she goes off on her own and DRIVES A CAR! What next? My God! The Church has gone to pot!

I was sitting on the bed with a smile on my face, getting the picture of Sister Eleanor in the old days and comparing them with how she is now, when I suddenly heard her roaring my name, waking me out of my trance. Gawd! She's still at it. Nothing ever really changes with her.

'Come on, darling!' she says, rushing across the room and sending the window flying open, her eyes whipping around to see what else needs her ordering. Then she grabs me. 'Come along now, pet. We have to get moving. Oh, let me see! What have I got to do this morning?' All the time pushing me ahead of her, keeping up a running commentary with herself, while stopping to pick up a child's coat thrown on the corridor. 'Really!' she mutters. 'These children are so untidy.'

I ignore her and head off down the stairs, looking for the kitchen.

'Now, darling!' she roars, coming up behind me, finally remembering I'm here. 'Have some breakfast. I'll just put on some scrambled egg and a bit of toast,' she says, flying past me into the kitchen.

'Ah, no, Sister. I won't bother. A cup of tea will do me.' I sit myself down at the long wooden table and pull out my roll-ups.

'No, Martha! Now, come on! You need to eat. Sure, you're starving yourself to death! Have just a boiled egg, then, and one slice of toast.' She stands there staring at me with the saucepan in her hand, looking like she's frozen solid, waiting to whip herself into a frenzy of action.

'No, honestly, I don't want anything,' I said, sucking on the cigarette, dying for a cup of tea.

'But, Martha, you are never going to get your health back if you don't eat! You can't go on like this!' Then she reached for the kettle, pouring the boiled water into the teapot, and I was relieved at getting a cup of tea at last.

'I don't know what's wrong with me, Sister,' I said, staring at the floor. 'I can't seem to pick myself up.'

'Right! Have your drop of tea, and I'll be back in a minute,' she said, rushing out the door.

This is really depressing, sitting in this place. I sure have come the full circle! I never thought I would fall this low again. I'm ended up right back where I fuckin started! Except, when I first started out, I had fire in my belly. Life was exciting, even if it was difficult and sometimes I found myself on the streets. But I always had hope! I knew life was waiting for me, and I could always keep going, no matter what happened.

But now it's like all the stuffing has been knocked out of me. Too many things have happened, too many knocks to the ground, especially the last five years. But I managed to keep going, get to my feet and keep moving. But now I can't do that any more. Christmas was OK, but I'm happy it's over. I cooked a small turkey breast and had a couple of friends over for dinner in the evening. But it was hollow. They laughed, and I pretended everything was grand, but the hole in my heart, where Sarah should have been, was paining me. I wonder why things have changed so much between us? She grew up! Maybe we're just too alike, so now we clash? Jesus! It should have been easy. We have always been so very close. No! I don't understand it. I can't figure that out. I wonder does she miss me?

The wind gave an almighty roar, and the windows rattled, frightening the life out of me. I gave a shiver, looking out at the terrible weather. I felt myself getting heavier. The thought of facing back into that house, and the long, dark winter staring ahead of me, was paralysing me with depression. I can't stand the bloody damp, and the cold doesn't help. Especially since I don't even light the bloody fire or even eat. No! I don't think about Sarah much any more. There's just a constant ache inside me, like I've made a fool of myself and everything I've achieved means nothing. It was a complete waste of time. Maybe I should have taken a different road when I found myself pregnant and had to go off to that home for unmarried mothers in the country.

I should have stayed there, had the baby and given it up for adoption, then got on with my own life. I was still only eighteen! I wish I'd had someone just for myself! But I never stood still long enough for a man to get close. I was either afraid, didn't trust them, or I was putting Sarah first. Anyway, there is no divorce in 'Holy' Ireland! Most men of my age are married, homosexual, or ex-priests going around agonising about their 'lost fucking souls'.

'I'm going through the long dark night of the soul,' one of them gasped, giving me 'mother of sorrowful' looks over a lemonade and a pint of whiskey for him. 'Twenty years I gave the Church! I was a priest, you know!' he sniffed, looking mournfully into the bottom of his glass, hoping to find the answer to his soul-searching there.

Not on yer bloody nelly! I'm outa here! 'Eh, I'm just off to the loo,' I breathed, smiling sweetly at his miserable, sorry-looking face, then making a grab for me coat and bag. Bloody hell! Are there any normal men out there? I thought, flying down O'Connell Street and lepping into me car. Glad to get home and shut me own front door, thinking, Ah, no! Who needs a man? Not me! I'm better off on me own. The world has too many problems. Hmph!

Aaah! Shut up, Martha. You'll drive yourself mad thinking like this. Isn't poor aul Sister Eleanor being very good to you? Ah, indeed she is. Gawd! Yeah! When I was really in need of someone, with all that being in and outa the hospital, well, it was her that came flying to the rescue. She was blind bothered and bewildered trying to placate me. I couldn't do any of the things I was used to – flying around like a blue-arse fly, always on the move. No! I had ended up like an aul one of ninety on me last gasp! I nearly went mental. But there she was, flying in with packets of tobacco, clean nightdresses, new! Me favourite biscuits, Kimberleys, to go with me night-time cup a tea. And now! Here I am, over all that.

So why am I still not moving? Oh, I'm going to go mental! Wish I knew what the hell is keeping me down. Oh, shut up, Martha. You could be left, upended, to work this out on your own. Hah! That might have put a fire under your arse! No. Might not. Thanks be to God I do have Sister Eleanor. So, be grateful. Snort! I dropped me chin in me hands, not able to figure out life any more. It's all beyond me, I sighed. How do you get the will to live?

Sister Eleanor came rushing into the kitchen and grabbed my cup. I was left wondering if there was any tea left in the bottom when she dashed it under the tap, rinsed it and turned to me, saying, 'I have made an appointment with a doctor for twenty past nine this morning. Will you come with me and I'll drive you there?'

'What doctor?' I asked her.

She glanced down at the buttons of her coat and coughed, looking very shifty. 'Well! Ahem, cough. They have a psychologist. I looked it up in the book. It's in his consulting rooms. It's private, of course! No need to worry, Martha. The convent will pay. He's very good, Martha,' she whispered, bending down to me. 'So they say.'

'Who?' I roared.

'Well!' she paused, trying to think.

'Absolutely not!' I screeched, jumping to my feet. 'So now you think I'm mad!' I rasped out in a hoarse voice.

'No! No! No! Of course I think no such thing! But, Martha darling, you have to get some help. What else can I do? You won't eat, you can't sleep, you are depressed! And if you go on like this, God knows what might happen to you! Come on, at least listen to what he has to say. Or . . .' Then she stopped to think, holding her forehead. 'OK! I will give them a call to cancel the appointment. Then I will have to see if I can get you an emergency visit with another doctor. See if they can fit you in somewhere with a general practitioner. Wait here!

I won't be a minute,' she muttered, rushing out the door.

'You are in luck, darling. Come on, quickly. We have an appointment with another doctor.'

I trailed out behind her, saying, 'Maybe you are right, Sister. I need to get living again. It would be great if I could lift this heavy weight dragging me down.'

25

We drove in to the surgery, and Sister Eleanor parked the car. As she was rushing me in the door, she said, 'Now! You wait here for me after you've seen the doctor. I have to go on a message, and I'll come back here as soon as I can and collect you. Then I can drop you home. Is that OK with you, Martha?'

'Yeah, fine. Thanks, Sister,' I said, looking down at my red monkey suit. It was styled on the romper suits toddlers wear going to bed, without the feet! Now they were back in fashion for adults. Jaysus! He's going to take one look at me and get me locked up immediately!

I walked up the stairs and onto a landing, heading straight through a door standing wide open. 'I have an appointment to see the doctor,' I said to a bored-looking woman painting her fingernails.

She barely looked at me and muttered from her fingernails, 'What's your name?'

I told her and she said, 'Take a seat over there and wait.'

I looked behind me, seeing a row of grey-plastic chairs lining the grey-white walls, and sat down to wait, feeling very nervous. What am I going to say? What can he do? There's no cure for the way I'm feeling. It's something I have to work out myself. Jesus! What am I doing here? This is only looking for trouble. Once you get involved with the likes of these people, they don't let you out of their clutches. Doctors record everything. So, letting them think there is something mental wrong with you . . . Well! It's like having a criminal record! It follows you through life:

'*Have you ever attended a psychiatrist? Suffered from mental illness?*'
'*Eh, no! Only depression.*'
'*Same thing! Sorry, you have been rejected. No pilot's licence for you. No green card to work in America. No life insurance for a million quid*

for you. You might top yourself, or top someone else!'

Jaysus! The stigma of having been under the care of a psychiatrist . . . well, psychologist – they are all the same to me! – has far-reaching consequences. What the hell did I let Sister Eleanor talk me into this for? I must be really desperate. Forget it! This is no place for me. I'm not getting involved with bloody head shrinks! Fuck! She will go mad. I agreed to see this fella at the last minute. She had to go back again and start cancelling and getting this appointment back.

I stood up, heading for the door. Then the phone rang, and Nail-polish picked it up. 'OK,' she said, eyeing me. She slammed the phone down, saying, 'Doctor's ready to see you. Up the stairs and first door on the left.'

I hesitated, then thought, I might as well see him as I've come this far.

I walked up the stairs feeling very nervous. My hands were icy cold and sweating. I didn't feel very well. I turned onto a landing and headed down a corridor; it was semi-dark. There are no windows along here to throw in the light. I stopped at a row of doors and knocked on the first one gently and waited.

Pause, then a high-pitched voice said, 'Come in!'

I opened the door and found myself looking around a long narrow room, then turned and closed the door very quietly.

The ceiling was very high, and it was a dull, grey room – like my life, I thought, as I headed down towards a big desk piled high with papers and patients' charts. There was a big old window, showing the grey light of the morning trying to creep into the room. It wasn't very successful, and a lamp was glowing on the desk, with a skinny little aul fella squinting beside it, furiously writing away. He didn't look up when I got to his desk. So I stood, looking around, and took in the big mirror that stretched from the ceiling to the floor and ran the complete width of the wall. My breath caught. That's there for a reason! It's obviously for doctors and students to observe patients while not being seen themselves. It's a two-way mirror! They could be in the other room right now, watching and waiting to observe my behaviour, listen to what I say and make their judgement! Bloody swines! They could even be having a giggle at the poor unfortunates having to sit here and pour out their guts.

I turned to the little man sitting in an old high-backed mahogany chair. I could barely see him smothering under all the files. 'My appointment is for twenty past nine,' I said, not impressed he doesn't even have the courtesy to ask me to sit down.

'Sit down!' he said in a high-pitched nasally voice, talking through his nose.

I sat and crossed my legs, leaving my shaking hands sitting limply in my lap, trying to look relaxed and say what was the matter with me. Just keep calm, I thought, looking at him. He was wearing a brown wool jacket over tanned trousers, and his mop of woolly hair stood standing to attention, with a streak of silver running right through the middle, making him look like he got an electric shock. He had a roaring red face, to match the roaring red hair, and the skin was covered in a mass of boils, pimples, blackheads and even warts. Jaysus! I thought, staring at him. This poor little aul fella is even more afflicted than meself. But he was a squirt of a little aul fella, who thought it made him important to leave a patient sitting here while he went on to ignore them, forgetting they kept him in his job!

Suddenly, he stopped writing, looked up at me over the papers and said through his nose, 'So! What is the problem?'

I was taken by surprise, and my heart started banging in my chest, and I thought about the mirror behind me and gave a quick look back. No! I'm not dreaming! It really is a two-way mirror! I froze. My mouth opened to say something, but nothing came out, so I snapped it shut, feeling very foolish, and just stared at him, wondering what I should say. What's the matter with me?

He stared back, taking his time, studying me, looking at my hands sitting in my lap, then watching them wave in the air, trying to articulate.

'I, em, I'm, eh, not well. I . . . I'm definitely not well,' I heard myself saying.

'Indeed!' he said crisply, reading me from head to toe. Going from my greasy, long, uncombed plaited hair, to my buttoned-from-the-neck-down romper suit. Thank God I'm not wearing slippers! I gave a sigh of relief. At least he can't see I'm wearing a long thermal granny nightdress underneath.

I took a deep breath and let my bony shoulders relax. Keep calm.

Keep a clear head. He may be able to help if you start to make sense. 'I, er . . .' I began again, but just dried up.

'Are you depressed?' he asked me, sweeping his eyes again from my bony face down the length of my bony body, looking away with contempt, finding me wanting.

I thought about this for two seconds. 'Yes! Yes, I am, that's the prob . . .' and he got bored with me and started writing again.

'Continue!' he muttered, never taking his eyes off the paper he was scribbling on.

I felt he was treating me with contempt. And I could feel the heat rising from my belly up to my chest. I stared at him, waiting for him to finish whatever was more important than talking to me. He really looks like a little ginger Quasimodo; in fact, he is the spitting image of him, except Quasimodo is better looking, I thought, staring at him.

He snapped his head up, staring at me, his left eyebrow raised. 'Well?' he said. 'What do you want me to do?'

The little runt! I thought, glaring at him. He's no older than myself. 'Well, I'm depressed,' I said, wondering if I really was. Then he raised his arm, like he was going to conduct a symphony, and snapped the sleeve of his jacket up with his hand, doing it with great flourish. My head followed this movement, my eyes glued on him. Then he wrote something down, snapped it off a pad and handed it to me.

'What's this?' I asked.

'A prescription for tranquillisers,' he said through his nose. 'Take one three times a day.'

I stared at him, my mouth wide open, my eyes bulging. 'But they're no good! They won't solve the problem! They will only turn me into a zombie!' I said, my heart sinking down into my belly.

'That is all I can do for you. Do you want them?'

'No,' I said, feeling terribly let down.

'Then I can't help you,' he smirked, with a sneer on his face, watching me get distressed. Like I was something interesting under a microscope.

I felt very humiliated and scared. If he can't help me, and I can't seem to help myself, and drugs are certainly not the answer for me . . . I tried again. 'Can you not listen to me? Maybe make some suggestions?'

'There's nothing more I can do for you!' he said with great authority and finality. 'Now get out! I have patients waiting to see me, and you are simply wasting my time!' and he stood up, pointing his arm at the door.

What a black-hearted bastard. He's so mean, he wouldn't even spare a drop a piss for his aul ma if she was on fire! We stared at each other, eyeball to eyeball, leaving a heavily pregnant silence hanging between us. He is trying to exert great authority over me with the weight of his profession. He thinks himself a great and important man. His steely-grey eyes had no recognition of me being a human being, and there was no humanity in those eyes. I am at my lowest, I reach out for help, and this little bastard thinks I'm not worth the time of day.

'How dare you?' I suddenly burst out, feeling all the rage, sorrow, rejection, and, most of all, knowing there was no help, no hope, nobody cared. If you are down and out, the world will kick you into the gutter! I had fought long and hard all my life to be equal with these people. But show them your weakness and they treat you with contempt. No better than dirt! This man was playing God with my life. He knows I'm down and out, but I'm not worth his time!

He stood up, with his hands down by his sides, clenched in fists, and shouted, 'Get out! Get out!' He screamed, sounding like an aul one in his 'wet-nelly' voice.

'Fuck you!' I screamed, staring and snorting, my bony chest heaving up and down.

He was outraged, livid. 'For the last time, get out before I have you thrown out!'

That did it! I erupted! I stood stock still, then lifted my arm, my eyes darting on his files, and with one clean sweep of my arm cleared his desk. Files went flying in all directions. The lamp popped its bulb, hissed and went out before crashing to the floor.

'My files! My files!' he screamed like a banshee, tearing around to the front of his desk, trying to gather them all together.

I stood and watched him on his knees.

'My files,' he moaned, looking up at me. 'They are all mixed up! How am I going to sort them all out?'

I felt a sense of control. He was on his knees! See how that feels!

I thought, breathing heavily and looking down at him, feeling very satisfied with myself.

I suddenly dropped to my knees, grabbing the files again. I lifted them into the air, mixing them up even more.

'Stop! Stop! My God! She's dangerous! HELP! A VIOLENT PATIENT!' he screamed, and went tearing off out through the door with his arms in the air like he was giving himself up.

I stood still, shocked for a minute by his reaction, then tore after him. 'Come back here, you coward! I'm not finished telling you what I think about you!'

He tore down the stairs, taking them four at a time, screaming, 'SAVE ME! SAVE ME! There's a mad woman after me!'

I tore after him, not knowing why. It was almost primitive, instinctive, like Bonzo chasing after a cat! But he wouldn't stand his ground and face me!

I was on his tail, but could only take the stairs two at a time. So he managed to get into Nail-polish's office and slam the door right in my face!

I could hear him panting and moaning inside, and I shouted, thinking he had locked the door, 'Open this door at once, you bleedin coward!'

I gave it an almighty kick, and the door flew open. It wasn't locked after all, just shut over. I roared into the room, screaming, 'Where is he? Where is that little runt?'

An enormous woman with red baldy eyebrows and blue hair scraped up in a bun, wearing a long hippy frock, was standing in the middle of the room, and I could see hands wrapped around her shoulders. When I looked down, I saw his brown shoes between her two massive feet. He was hiding behind her!

'There you are!' I screamed, racing around the big woman.

She turned, and his feet moved rapidly with her.

'Come out, you fool! I want to have my say to your face. Why are you hiding?'

'Calm down!' the big woman shouted, trying to look authoritative. 'I am the secretary here, and you have no right to abuse and frighten him.'

He literally peeked out from the side of her, then put his head back, terrified, like a very young child.

I screamed at her, 'Why are you protecting that moron? Why is he, an adult, hiding behind you?'

'You have terrified him!' she shouted back, making the little glasses on her nose wobble.

'Don't let her near me!' he kept screaming.

'I don't believe this. You bastards are acting like God! I came here hoping you would help me, but you are the ones who need help! You are all mad! Mad!' I roared.

'Get out!' she screamed.

'Call the police!' the little runt wailed from behind her.

'FUCK YOU ALL!' I screamed, charging out the door.

I tore down the stairs, not waiting to open the front door, just lifted my foot still running and gave it an almighty kick. It swung open, and I charged out, haring across the road and flagging down a little Morris Minor with a confused old man behind the wheel.

'Please!' I panted. 'It's an emergency! I must get home quickly!'

I opened the car door and dived in, sitting myself down, and he stared at me, trying to figure out what was happening to him. 'It's an emergency!' I puffed, still breathing hard.

He took off slowly, looking very worried. I sat still, intent on my mission to get home as quickly as possible.

'Thank you!' I said. 'I live close to here.'

He stopped the car, letting me out. I shot him a look saying thank you for your kindness before taking off again. Racing to get home.

26

I put the key in the door, flying in and locking it. I ran for the kitchen, tearing down every bottle of medication I had in the press and lining them up on the kitchen table. Ten bottles! They are all full. I had just been to the chemist yesterday, and they are filled to the brim. These should do the job, I thought, looking at them. I tore open the fridge, taking out a half-carton of orange juice. This will help them to go down.

I sat at the kitchen table staring at the ten bottles of pills all lined up. Pills for pain – they don't work; pills to slow the heart down; pills for just about damned everything. Who needs them? I never took half of them. But now I will, the whole bloody lot of them. What else can I take them with? I jumped up, rushing over to the fridge again, yanking the door open. Tomato juice! Perfect. Then I spotted the bottle of vodka. I reached up and grabbed it. It's still half full! When was the last time I had friends over to share this? Months! Right, this will do. It should see me on my way. I'll die happy!

I propped the bottles down beside the pills. One last cigarette before I go! These things are going to kill me! Ha, ha, very funny, I sniffed. There's an irony there somewhere. It's not the smokes, it's the living that kills ye!

I rolled the tobacco in the paper and lit up, feeling almost relieved. Dying is easy; I just couldn't get the living bit right. Yeah! I'm glad it's finally over. It wasn't worth the struggle. I sat back to eye what I was leaving behind. The black outline on the white pantry door where I had leaned my head, staring out through the kitchen window into the garden for hours on end but seeing nothing.

So! This is how it ends. Out, out, brief candle! Life is but a walking shadow, a poor player that struts and frets his hour upon the stage and then is heard no more. It is a tale told by an idiot, full of sound and fury, signifying nothing. Yep! That is me, all right. All hot air and going nowhere! Yeah! Too bloody true it is.

I opened the bottle with the pink slow-your-heart-down beta blockers and popped two into my mouth with a sip of juice. Ah! Nice, sweet! Then I raised my glass to the empty room. To Sarah! You gave me so much love and happiness, with your trusting innocence and the belief I was the greatest thing since sliced pan. I could do nothing wrong in your eyes. You were my little companion. My little shadow. We did everything together. Oh, the laughs we had. Having you filled me with a power and energy. A deep, raw, hungry need that drove me forever upwards to succeed. A fierce need to protect you, make you feel safe and warm. Nothing but the best was good enough for you! That could only have come from being your mother.

Oh, yes! I was fiercely protective of you. But you deserved it; you were entitled to it. It was your birthright. So, I think I tried, Sarah! I know I caused you a great deal of pain. I used to see the way you would look longingly at other children's fathers.

I had sixteen years with you, being your mother. Sixteen years! You reached that magical age. Now the difficult years should have been behind us. We should have been able to start reaping the rewards of all the hard work. Working sixteen hours a day to give you a nice home with all the frills. A private school! And what did you think of all that?

'Oh,' you said, 'I am going to live in England with Daddy and his family.'

'But what about school? You will be sitting your final exams in two years, darling! Then you can study in England if that's what you really want!'

'Mummy, please! I want to live with Daddy now!'

'But why?'

'Because I want to see what it's like to live in a family!'

I looked at her, seeing the pleading in her great big blue eyes. She was desperate to share in her father's life. She needed her father now. Why not? It is so very understandable. The poor kid always felt the lack of one.

'OK, darling. I won't stand in your way. But you have to promise me. No going mad, gallivanting to parties!'

'No, never!' she smiled, staring at me with the eyes shining in her head.

'You have to study!'

'Don't I always? Oh, Mummy!' she said, coming to wrap her arms around me. 'You don't have to worry about me. I promise I won't let you down!'

'No, darling. I know you won't,' I said, holding her tight and stroking her long soft hair, kissing her head and face. 'You have always been a good girl. My God! You know how proud I have always been of you.'

'Yes, Mummy! Thank you for being the best mother in the whole world. I really love you, and I'm going to miss you,' she said, getting tears in her eyes now the thought of really leaving home was hitting her.

So that was that! It was a slow descent after that. I had nothing to keep me going. Only me little . . . well! . . . big hairy mutt. That eegit nearly broke me heart! Getting me into trouble with the neighbours! Bursting the poor kids' footballs after they came in to collect him for a game. They would drag him home again, crying it was their special ball. They had it signed an all! Little five and six year olds. Then look down at him and wonder how he could be so mean! The hairy mutt was cute enough to know he had done wrong and sat there looking very mournful.

Then trouble erupted with the nuns across the road. He started sticking his nose under the nuns' skirts in the local convent when they were minding their own business, walking up and down getting their prayers. He would sneak up behind them and shove his nose up their skirts, not meaning any harm, it was only his way of saying, 'Hello, and where's me dinner?' He does that to men, too; they get it in the balls! No matter how many times I gave him a bang on the nose, he would just look hurt and do it again. His way of saying sorry!

Yeah! He got himself banned by the nuns. Up until then, he could go over for his dinner and bark at the back door. The kitchen nun came out with scraps of lovely lamb chops. But it was the Reverend Mother that got it this time, so that was that! He's barred!

Even you began to see him in a different light. Yeah! Your father turned up to collect you for the weekend. I had persuaded you to take the mutt. 'Ah, go on, darling! He's your dog. Just think, he'll be able to play with their dog. The little fat corgi!'

'Mummy! He's not fat!'

'No, but still and all. Think of all the exercise that dog will get trying to keep up with our Bonzo. They can play together. I'm sure your father will be delighted! Dogs need plenty of exercise, you know! If they get fat, they can drop dead of a heart attack!' I said, looking shocked.

'He's not fat, Mummy! I told you!' she snorted, letting her face screw up with disgust at the insult to her father's dog.

'No! No, he's not! But take him anyway, love!' I said, looking at Bonzo, with the big chocolate-drop eyes looking mournful at the thought he might miss out on his outing. He sat on his arse with his ears flapping, swinging his head from her to me, knowing well not to make a move until he saw which way the wind was blowing.

'He'll liven up the place!' I said, stroking his head for being so good. 'Ah, go on, Sarah! Take him. Your father is going to be delighted with all the enjoyment he gets outa him once he gets to know him!'

Her father turned up, getting the land of his life. He stared down at the dog straining at the leash. Then stared in disbelief as Bonzo took off, tearing himself and Sarah down the path, straight out the gate. Bonzo has had enough! All that fuss! he's thinking, and now I might not even make it out the door! Action! Show them who they're dealing with. Here I come!

'Wait! Stop, Bonzo! Down, boy!' Sarah screamed, skidding along the ground as he pulled the arms outa her.

I sucked in me breath, thinking, Jaysus! Whatever I'm feeding that dog, it's doing him a power of good. 'Ah! See how excited he is to be going with her! Sure, they can't be parted,' I droned, looking up at him.

'Hmm!' he said, taking off after the two of them, then turning back to give me a sour look.

I gave him a big wink, snapping me thumb in the air, then flew in, banging the door behind me.

You came back from that weekend dragging him home by the scruff of the neck, saying, 'He's in disgrace, Mummy! They never want to set eyes on him again. He dug up her new exotic plants, the ones she just put into the garden, then started a row with Hafner, the corgi – they fought all the time. Then Hafner started peeing inside the house, to protect his territory, and Bonzo did the same. Then on Sunday, he jumped up on the table in the conservatory, where she'd left her cake to cool. It was supposed to be for our tea that evening, Mummy! Do you know what he did?' she said, looking shocked to the roots of her toenails.

'No, darling. What did he do?' I said, looking sad and shocked too.

'Bonzo jumped up . . .'

'. . . and lurried the lot down his neck?' I said, interrupting her.

'Yes!' she whispered, puffing out her disgust and horror, then stared at me with an outraged, 'Tsk, tsk!'

'Does that mean he won't be able to go on your next visit?' I said, wanting to make sure.

She stared at me with an outraged look on her face, reminding me of a Reverend Mother who has just been told to fuck off! Sarah drew in her breath, getting her little nose all pinched, then tried patiently to explain how badly Bonzo had behaved.

'They were cheek to jowl the whole weekend, Mummy. That's what Mona called it. Stuck together side by side! Poor Hafner was terribly upset. He was on the move all the time. He couldn't rest even for one minute because Bonzo might do something to mark the house as his territory! That's why they kept wee-weeing, then fighting!' she explained, exploding air out through her nose, making the dust fly.

'Oh, and she was very cross, Mummy! And cross with me for bringing him, and she said you did it on purpose! And Daddy got into trouble for listening to you. And everyone was very cross, Mummy! It was terrible. The weekend was a washout!' she said, copying something I might say. 'Dreadful, Mummy!' she whispered, shaking her head at me, looking the mother of all sorrows. 'All Bonzo's fault,' she sighed, now shaking her head at the memory. Then she ran outa wind and sighed, 'Ohh! But now I'm really happy to be home again.'

Me heart melted hearing her say that. 'Aw! Sugar plum! Mamma's little chicken! I'm sorry. That lump won't be going anywhere for a while. Ah, never mind. Come over to me and I'll give you a big hug!

'Now! I have something lovely to cheer us up. Wait until you see the lovely surprise I have for you. Look! Special Holly Hobby writing paper and envelopes in a lovely Holly Hobby box! And rubbers and pencils to match!'

'Oh, Mummy! I love you!'

Poor Sarah, there were times, too, when I was hard to take. I would cross the line too far into her childhood. Like the time I watched her putting on the new roller skates she got from her father. I grabbed one and whipped it on me. Then took off, flying up the road, telling her, 'You have the other one and we'll race!' She chased me up the road, crying her eyes out, wanting the skate back.

It was times like that she wanted a mother who was more sedate. Acted their age! I was no longer interested in going out with some gobshite for dinner then running home for me life because he was only interested in me body. No! My idea of relaxing was sitting at home watching the telly, laughing me head off at *Fawlty Towers*, with Bonzo snoring beside me on the couch. Then on Saturday, hammering around the grounds of the nuns' convent across the road, playing hide and seek with the mutt. I would wait until he took off ahead of me at sixty miles an hour, then I would drop behind a tree. No problem to him! He came thundering back, heading straight for me. I couldn't put him off me scent. Not until the day I hid behind the nuns' oil tank! He spent about twenty minutes flying in all directions. I laughed like a two year old, watching him.

I had no end of fun with the dog and kids – Sarah's friends. I used to play cards with them, roaring me head off if I lost. In the summer, we played badminton in the back garden. We tied a brick to each end of the clothesline, then strung it across the garden walls. This was a serious business. I played to win, so did Sarah and her friends. They would line up against the garden wall, waiting their turn to play the winner. If I sent a shuttlecock flying into the rockery, then it was in. If Sarah sent it there, it was out! I screamed like a banshee! She screamed louder!

Oh, yes! This was a serious business. I was a shocking cheat! The neighbours! Oh, very respectable. They objected to my language. No! I didn't behave like the other mothers. I didn't have coffee with them. I played with their kids! I was an adult, having the best childhood of my life. Sarah was mortified. She had to live with me. The others thought I was the greatest thing since sliced pan! I was a novelty for them. They didn't have to put up with me carryings on. They even used to bring me little presents and whisper they wished their mummies were just like me!

I glanced down at the pills and emptied out four this time – not wanting to overdo it, I might get sick! – and popped them into my mouth.

The final straw was Harry. I know that now. I was limping along up until then. Well, sort of. I thought I was just down in the dumps, winter blues. But with you, Sarah, now up and gone, leaving me time on my hands but not full health to enjoy it, I started to sink. I no longer had a purpose in life.

When my mind finally got the message, it stopped making huge plans. I would travel! Make a new life. Yeah! Happy days!! But my body wouldn't oblige. I had no energy. My mind finally settled down, watching and waiting for the body to recover. It didn't happen. So the mind gave up and went into a long snooze.

No more reasoning, no rationale to call upon. But the emotions! They blazed into action. It was as if I had been taken over by the dark side of me. The completely negative side. I was raw emotion, and it was a particularly malignant cancer. Hatred for myself oozed through my veins. I was completely in contempt of myself. Indifferent to any pain or suffering I was enduring. Hell-bent on destroying myself for failing, and making sure it was a very slow death.

You're no good! the negative me said. *You can't work. Not much good for anything really, are you?* it sneered. *No! Don't invite friends. It will tire you out and you'll only bore them. Ah! It's too much effort, don't bother about anything. Uh, uh! No need to get dressed! Who is going to see you? It's not worth the effort. Save your strength. Food! Eating? I don't think so. Just let go! There's no need to prolong the agony. That's right, just give up. Anyway, you don't deserve happiness. Who are you? You are fooling yourself! You are nobody! What have you achieved in your life? Let me see! See what? Your best efforts amounted to nothing. Nada. You are a fraud. A little nobody who thought she could fool herself and everybody around her. But deep down you know you are still the street kid! You will never escape that.*

What are you doing now? No! You cannot go into your best room. You will upset all the order you have imposed. The room is immaculate! Everything is perfection. When all else failed, you still had your little nest. This is what you dreamed about. Civilised living. Safe, clean and peaceful. No more chaos and filth and terror! So! Do not disturb, or you will have nothing! Everything will fall to pieces, and you will land back right where you started with not even a pair of shoes for your feet!

My God! Deep sigh! You must take care of the house! That will keep away the terrors waiting to stalk you!

You will lose everything! Plunge back to the never-ending nightmare of the streets! The world will piss on you! You will die in some doorway, bereft and lonely. With no one to care. Anyway! The room is too good for the likes of you! The house is too good for you! You didn't make it!

No! This is not the picture you carried in your head through all those bad days long ago, and even when things were bad later on. No! The picture you had was of a house with lots of happy people in it. A lovely man who was gentle and loved you, and happy children. Everyone contented. Everyone safe. Lots of love going around, and people laughing. You in the middle of them all, taking care of everyone.

It was finally when the deafening silence and the coldness of the house hit you that you realised it wasn't a home. Just a house, and you were never going to get that family you always craved. It just was not going to work out. When that finally came home to you, then you gave up and started to punish yourself, because you are a failure.

Nope! No more pleasure for you. Put that cigarette out! And no more drinking cups of tea. You are no longer entitled to any pleasure, and, I underline this, no more books! You will not be allowing yourself to read!

So what's left? Nothing! I have painted myself into a corner! There's no way out! It looks like ye won, Jackser! But! I'll still get ye, you mad bastard! I'll be back te haunt ye! Night an fucking day! I'll be there to watch you die roarin! And fuck you too, Ma! I wish you had died at birth! Then I would never have been born! And you, too, God! Because you never really existed!

I grabbed the bottles of pills, emptying them onto the table. Fuck this! I shoved handfuls into my mouth, taking a sip of vodka with the tomato juice. 'They call this a Bloody Mary!' I laughed wryly, holding the glass in the air, crying, tears flooding down my cheeks. 'Delicious! Pleasure again!' I sobbed, shoving more pills down my throat. Yuk! My head shivered. Ah! They taste disgusting; there must be a better way to top yerself than this.

I got the picture of Harry flying through the air. Harry! You too! THE BASTARD GOT THE LOT OF US! Even Charlie! He will be next. After you and me, Harry. The others live in a twilight world.

No! Fuck it. Don't let him get you, Charlie! Don't let the ratbag win! I carried you long enough! Yeah! I'm going to make him fucking fight. Where's me notepaper! He'll have to listen to me dying wish.

Dear Charlie,

Stay off the drink. Get back on yer feet! Or I'm comin back te haunt you, Charlie! Do this for me! I never asked you for anything! Remember, I'll be watching you, and I'll still be looking out for you, Charlie. You can always find me. I'll be before you and behind you and beside you. Nothing can really separate us. I just got tired. Sorry about the quick exit! Now! I want you to be positive. That means you are to look on the bright side. Do you understand that? Pay attention to these words. This is important.

You are the last one standing! Think of this, Charlie! You are the only one to survive! You're the winner! That proves, Charlie, just how powerful you are, really strong! OK? You are very intelligent, Charlie. Use it, and remember! No matter what happens. No matter how low you get. I'm walking beside you. So! You are never to do anything that would harm yourself. Wait until you see Jackser planted! THIS IS MY DYING WISH! I expect that from you! You owe me! I carried you long enough! So! Stay fucking sober! Au Revoir! It's French for 'see you again'. Yes, I know you know that, Charlie. I love you! Remember, I'm watching you!

All my dying love, Martha xx

I stared at the paper. My hand just about made it. The letters are dancing around the page. I threw the pencil down; it's too heavy to hold. Everything is getting dark; the bleedin room is spinning. I grabbed out to hold the table and take a swig of the vodka. Got it! I'm spinning through the air, the bottle flying with me. Never was much of a drinker! It's gone to me head! Oh! Smack! I'm after landing on the fuckin floor.

My whole life started flooding past me. Down, down, back all the days of my life, then stopped. Little Martha! *'Youse won't get the better a me!'* she was screaming.

I stared at her. 'Ah, but they did, little one. They did,' I whispered.

My mistake was I gave too much, tried too hard. I should have kept something back for myself. I always was a gobshite. It's too late now. I'm sleepy, lovely!

27

My eyes flickered open.

'Drink this! Ah! You've spilled it down your front!'

Hands are holding my head up for me to take a drink. I see water flowing from my mouth.

'I'll have to change you again!' the voice belonging to the hands moans. Then nothing.

My eyes open. I stare into the face of Charlie, my half-brother, sitting on a chair beside my bed. My bed! So I am still on this fucking planet.

His mouth opens and his eyes widen. Then his brows knit together and he leans into me, saying, 'Wha happened? Ye killed yerself, ye know!'

Hope! Maybe I am dead after all. My eyes sweep around the room. They stop at a machine beside my bed. I am attached to this machine. Waves fly across it in an uneven line. Like they are drunk! My head moves to the left. A big box, the top half glass, is beside me on the left. I see nurses working there. I turn again, trying to figure out where I am. It doesn't look like I'm dead.

I see a window on the far side of the room behind Charlie, with a bed pushed into the corner beside it. Another machine stands next to it. It is blank. A man lies very still, his head turns a little, and he catches me staring at him. Our eyes lock for a moment. His face is dark red, but mostly purple. Then his eyes flicker, and he looks wearily away from me and stares up at the grey sky.

My eyes move down to stop at another bed next to his. A man lies sleeping, strapped to another machine. He's wheezing heavily. My eyes fly back to Charlie. No! I'm definitely not dead.

'Well, ye nearly did!' Charlie is complaining. 'The police called te the door last Thursday night, tha was eight days ago! I gorr an awful fright. Thought they were after me for somethin! Then they asked me was I yer brother. I said, "Yeah!" and they said I have te get te the hospidal straight away. When I got here, you were in a bad way. You were hiked up to a machine, an the doctors told me ye had a fifty–fifty chance of survival. They said ye were brought in aroun half past one in the afternoon. An they spent the day pumpin ye out. But at aroun half past eight tha night ye had a cardiac arrest, they said. An they had te rush ye up here, Intensive Care!

'When I got here, God, ye looked bad! I was sittin on the chair here when suddenly the machine went mad. An the nurses came tearin over an sent me flyin out the door, an they were shoutin, "She's in cardiac arrest! She's now gone inta respiratory failure!" The nurse jumped onta the bed an was kneelin over ye, punchin yer chest. Then a doctor came flyin in the door wit other doctors tearin in behind him, an they slammed the door shut on me, tellin me te wait downstairs. Ye've been gone for over a week, Martha!' he said, digging his knuckles into the bed, trying to make me understand. 'They only took ye off the ventilator this mornin!

'Ye're very lucky te be here! By all rights, ye should be up lyin six feet under, in Glasnevin Cemetery, next te Harry! I didn't think ye were goin te make it!' he snorted.

I stared impassively. He stared back at me, shaking his head in confusion. 'They rang Sister Eleanor tha night, ye know. She said they wanted the next of kin. An she wasn't yer next of kin. An they were wonderin why no one was claimin ye! You were left here on yer own. An be the time ye got bad tha night no one had still come in te enquire about ye! She had a job tryin te find my address. Tha's why she contacted the police. They managed te find me!

'God! I got an awful fright altogether! I don't like the sight of the police. I kept thinkin I was in trouble for somethin! At first I wouldn't tell them who I was. An they kept askin me was I Charlie Long or not! Then I said I was, an they kept lookin at me, wonderin wha I was up te.' Then he gave a half-smile. 'I didn't do nothin at all, Martha! That's the funny thing! But they always make me nervous!' Then he pointed over at a locker sitting on the left side of me. 'There's yer tobacco an papers, an yer lighter.'

My eyes lit up. A smoke!

'I left them there fer ye!'

'Thanks,' I whispered, straightening my mouth in a smile.

I was very tired and closed my eyes. When I opened them again, it was night. I could see the darkness through the window. The man in the corner was being wheeled out under a sheet, and a nurse was stripping the sheet off his bed. It was covered in pink dye. Doctors were shuffling out of the room, their hands hanging limply down by their sides. Their heads dropped. 'We lost him,' they muttered.

I stared at the shape of the body lying under the sheet as they wheeled him out. He was alive this morning. Now he's gone! His machine was switched off. He wasn't strapped to it. They must have thought he was going to be OK. Life is a bitch! That poor man was probably desperate to live, had a lot to live for. Now he's gone. Here I am, desperate to die, still here. What a sick joke!

One of the doctors stopped at the end of my bed. 'You're back with us,' he beamed down at me. 'We had an awful job bringing you back, you know! You went into respiratory failure. We had the medication bottles. Goodness! They were all full! We saw the labels with the date. You took a massive overdose! Enough to stop an army. But we pulled you back! Yes!' and he stopped to pause, thinking about it. 'I remember you from the endocrinology ward. You were in here for months.'

I stared at him, remembering him too. He was a houseman, and he always seemed to be working. He used to walk around haunted and hunted looking. Banjacksed from lack of sleep.

I lay motionless; the only thing in action was my eyes, watching him.

'Welcome back to the land of the living,' he shouted, waving at me, grinning as he loped out the door with his head going ahead of him and the rest of him following.

I lay with absolute stillness, my mind off in limbo. My eyes staring at nothing. I dimly registered poor human wrecks lying around me, their bodies wanting to take their last gasp, their minds holding a tenacious grip on this life. They were helped by machines carrying them through until their ailing bodies could recover and they could get both feet back in this life. It was a minute-by-minute, hour-by-hour, constant battle between staff in this room and Death, which would suddenly appear and try to snatch away a patient.

Staff fought with ferocious and grim determination to hang on to their patients' lives. Machines were whipped into action, a body was grabbed, pyjama top ripped, buttons flew, pillows shot across the floor, the alarm sounded, alerting everyone, especially doctors trained in the mastery of fighting this foe: 'Death is back!'

They came thundering into the room, white coats flapping out behind them. Everyone knowing their place and racing against time. Death's best friend! The guardians of this room won more battles, then lost. And a gloom would hang over the staff, seeing their charge wheeled out, lost to Death.

But I'm still here, and Death got pissed off waiting to see if this time he could get his hands on me. Once again he'd failed and went off sniffing to pick up the scent of some other poor unfortunate who didn't even want to know him. Though I did try to help him!

I lay serenely puffing on my tobacco, watching with interest the machine I was strapped to wave back at me like a drunken sailor. I eyed the cylinders of oxygen next to the beds and wondered mildly if the room would blow up. Nobody said a word. I was gratified by this. A little curious, though, as to why they let me get away with it. Perhaps I sent out a menacing air, lying in my bed with utmost placidity.

It's morning again. Nurses appeared at my bed and clicked off the brake, wheeling me out of the room. 'We're taking you out of Intensive Care, Martha!' the nurse shouted happily down at me, pushing me along the corridor, then waits for the lift. There's two of them. When the lift opens, one steers from behind and the other pushes from the front.

'Did ye hear the latest on Ryner?' the one with the long, curly, dyed-red hair asked the one behind me with the Afro hairstyle. Her cap sat on top of it, looking like the leaning tower of Pisa.

'No! What's the crack?' asked Pisa, smiling and jutting her head towards the redhead in case she missed anything.

'Well! If he didn't go and buy the biggest bunch of roses ye ever saw in your whole life and leave them sitting up in the office for your woman Babs! You know?' Red said, when the other one wrinkled her nose, looking puzzled. 'The one with the long legs that go all the way up to her arse! She's down in Urology!'

'Oh! Do ye mean the one with the lisp?'

'Yeah! Yeah! That's the one.'

'God! I can't stand that one!' Pisa said. 'She fancies herself no end!'

'Anyway! Let me finish!' Red said, getting impatient at her story being interrupted.

'Yeah! Go on! Go on!' Pisa said.

Red took in a breath, then stopped. 'Where was I?' she asked herself. 'Oh! Yeah! So, we used Tipp-Ex and rubbed out Babs' name, and what did we do?' Red paused, making her face look sorrowful. 'We put aul Frosty's name on it, saying, "From an Admirer." She questioned us up and down the place. "Who left them in? When? Are you sure you didn't see who it was?" Nobody knew anything, of course. "No, Sister! It was probably a patient," I said. Then she got red in the face and barked at me, "A patient wouldn't say 'from an admirer'!"

'Poor aul Frosty, she went around for the rest of the day in a daze, and she was killed looking at every man that walked into the place.'

Pisa screamed, laughing and grabbing her knees.

'God love her!' said Red. 'The only pleasure she gets is going to bed with *The Catholic Messenger*.'

Then they nearly knocked me out of the bed. Slamming it out through the door before it was properly opened, banging into it. I shook like a jelly, hanging on to me tobacco, hidden under the bedclothes in case someone decided to take it off me.

They rattled me along a passage and into a big ward. 'Here we are!' the redhead shouted down at me, beaming at a load of people sitting on sofas around a table.

'How're ye, girls!' a tall young fellow – he looked about seventeen years old, with a mop of brown curly hair, wearing a dressing gown and slippers – shouted at the nurses.

'How's it going, Pascal? Are you still here?' roared the redhead again. 'Gawd! You must love this place.'

'Ah, no, Nurse! It's you I'm tormented thinking about that's keeping me awake nights, tossing and turning in me bed of pain! I hope you're saving yourself for me!'

'Ah, Pascal darling. As much as I would love to get me hands on you, sure, your mammy would annihilate me for robbing her little baby! An me a grown woman!'

Then they turned into an empty cubicle, screeching laughing, and heaved the bed, rattling and shaking it against the wall, jamming it into a corner, making my head wobble and my teeth knock together. Fuck this, I thought, why don't they watch what they're doing? They're going to give me brain damage, the bloody eegits! Then they stood on the brake, locking the wheels of the bed, and followed each other out. I was left staring straight ahead at a long desk, but there was nobody there. I heard the gang of people follow the nurses out of the ward, then it was quiet. Looks like I have the whole place to myself.

I turned my head, staring at the wall. Lying with absolute stillness. My eyes glazed over, and I felt an icy calmness. My emotions were frozen. Nothing bothered me. I had said all I wanted to say, and people no longer interested me. I was biding my time, knowing next time I would succeed. My mind, now free of its burden to find reasons why I had stopped caring about life, meandered quietly and gently, looking at the mistakes I had made. It paused, settling on my absurd notion of joining the respectable middle class.

By the time I got up there among them, it was too late to turn back. These people were not real. They politely ask you, 'How are you?' and I'm supposed to say, 'I'm great, thank you. And how are you?' and show my white Gibbs toothpaste smile. When in fact I could be carrying my head under my arm or just about to blow my brains out. But so long as I say everything is OK, then everyone can pretend we're all having a marvellous fucking life!

You look into their eyes and see their pain. They try to guard it with a twist of the lips, looking a bit like a smile. And they see the pain in your eyes, then I see them look away. I see it, because I'm looking for it. I want warmth, to feel valued. But there's only coldness. Only a machine going about its business. I am on a different planet. These people have been trained like monkeys; being 'respectable' is everything. Getting to the top of the tree is the goal, or climbing the social ladder they call it. They never become real people.

The inner city, where I spent my early childhood, they were real people. Yeah! I smiled to myself, thinking of the day I got fed up with the people living around me. I was feeling very low that day. Really lonely. I got into the car and drove into town. I parked it on Parnell Street and found myself wandering down Moore Street, where all the fruit and vegetables are sold.

The women are very tough. Out in all weathers. They would take the head off you if you touched their fruit or said it wasn't up to scratch. I was standing with my back to a shop window, a butcher's, when one aul one stopped to have a chat with another aul one. One of them had two black eyes, and she tried to hide this with a scarf on her head pulled down low over her forehead. I spotted her straight away, and she threw an eye at me to see if I was listening before she opened her mouth and got down to the business of telling her friend what was on her mind. I pretended to busy myself rolling a cigarette and not notice them. But making sure I could hear everything that was being said.

'How're ye, Mary?'

'Ah! Jaysus! Don't ask me, Nelly luv!' they greeted each other.

'Go on! Tell us! Wha ails ye?' Nelly said, folding her arms and hitting Mary with the back of her hand to encourage her.

Mary paused, lifting her big chest and giving it an almighty heave, taking a deep breath in through her nose, looking like she had a bad smell under it, and started. But first throwing her eyes from side to side, in case she saw someone coming along that might know her and hear her business.

'Ah! Holy God! Mornin, noon, te night! I'm tormented wit him comin home drunk an upendin the place. An lookit, Missus! Where do ye think I got these two black eyes from?'

'Well, if it was me!' Nelly said, heaving herself up to her full four feet seven inches and standing five feet wide, straightening herself up and folding her arms under her massive chest and taking a sharp intake of breath. 'Listen!' she said, tapping Mary's shoulder with the stub of her finger, then pausing to take in a gulp of air. She clamps her lips together, dropping her jaw, raising both eyebrows together, and says slowly, making sure not one word is lost, 'I would pick up the frying pan or wha's left of it, or the bleedin milk bottle, an I'd land him such a smack on the head he'd be sent flyin inta tomorra!

Tha'd put a stop te his gallop! Don't ye agree wit me, Missus?' Then she lifted her head back, holding it in the air, staring at Mary to see her reaction, and admire how treacherous she was.

Mary blinked, thinking about it, then got a fright, seeing herself getting splattered if she tried that, and smiled weakly, saying, 'Ye're right there, Nelly. I'm too soft! Tha's my trouble.'

'Well! I'm tellin you now!' Nelly said, leaning into her and gently tapping her on the hand with her finger. 'Take my advice, an better still, wait until he's sleepin an he won't know wha hit him!'

Then they ran off, screaming laughing, telling each other to 'Mind yerself now! An I'll see ye again!' and everyone is happy. Caring and sharing their worries. I watched them go, feeling a terrible longing inside me to be a part of them. I had lost something along the way. I knew I wasn't a part of them any more, and I felt empty, lost.

I don't belong with the people I'm living among now. It is like being stranded in no-man's-land. I don't know where I belong. My values are middle class, but I identify more with the city people. I understand them. But they wouldn't understand me. I would only have to open my mouth and one earful of me speaking with my BBC accent and they're gone! Looking back at me with suspicion.

Yeah! I taught myself to speak by listening to the radio! I decided I might as well go for the 'Oxford' as opposed to the 'Dublin Four' brigade. They're a load of chancers! Culchies trying to pass themselves off as 'West Brits'. The landed gentry! Posers! Bit like meself. Still, I suppose I'm really a loner.

My thoughts were interrupted by the appearance of the young fellow with the curly hair.

'Hello! I'm Pascal!'

I blinked acknowledgement.

'This is the psychiatric ward.'

I blinked, shocked.

'Don't worry,' he said, reading my face. 'You will like it here. Once you get used to it. The nurses are very nice.'

I blinked by way of thanking him. But I didn't want to hear any more and turned my head away from him. So he wandered off, looking for someone else to talk to.

Suddenly there is activity around the desk. A doctor is roaring down the telephone. 'She can't stay here. We are sending her over to you.' Pause. 'What? I don't care! She's not staying here. We don't have the facilities. This is an open ward. She's a very high risk!' Then she screams, 'You have the facilities! I already told you! You are not listening! She's too high risk to be kept here. You will take her, and that's that! We are sending her over to you by ambulance, and that's my final word!' Then she slammed the phone down, balling her hands into fists down by her sides, and roared up at the ceiling, 'Jesus! Bloody cretins!'

Then her bleeper went off, and she unclipped it from her pocket, looked at it, then said, 'Oh, shite!' and marched off, looking like she was going to wring someone's neck.

That's me they are having the row about, and whoever it is that's at the other end of the phone is not too impressed by my imminent arrival. Hmm! Too bloody bad. Then it occurred to me that nobody had consulted me about whether I wanted to move or not. Of course I'm a high risk! Too bloody right I am! But that is for me to decide. I was mildly curious about why I hadn't jumped up and confronted your woman about pushing me around. They should at least come to me and explain, giving me some input into what is going to be happening while I am 'safely in their care'.

'Dear, would you mind awfully going to another psychiatric establishment? You see, we know you intend to top yourself at the first given opportunity, and therefore we believe the most suitable place for you would be the nearest loony bin! Hmm! So, what do you think?'

Then at least I would have the opportunity of telling them to shove that fucking idea up their arse. I'd probably get carted out in a straitjacket. But it would be worth it. Who the fuck gave them licence over me? Hmm! You did, Martha, by getting caught. So now they own you. Yep! This is what happens when you put yourself on the 'Loony Red Alert' list.

I heard the rattle of the tea trolley and looked up. A fat woman with four shades of colour in her hair – black-and-grey roots, probably original blonde going down, and the rest turned a pinky-red. She brought the trolley to a grinding halt at the foot of my bed and shouted down at me. She was wearing a navy-blue wraparound smock with white dots, and she roared, 'Do ye want tea, luv?'

I hesitated, and she whipped the cover off a dinner plate and leaned over to me, showing me cold roast beef, tomatoes, potato salad and lettuce.

I sat up, showing the first bit of interest in anything since I had my swansong back home in the kitchen. It looked delicious! A part of me definitely wanted it, but the perverse side of me insisted I suffer. *No grub*, it muttered. I looked at her.

'Go on, take it!' she said, slamming it down on the tray and pushing it up towards me. 'It'll put hairs on yer chest!' she laughed, grabbing her tea trolley and heading off down the ward again.

Just as I was about to reach for it, two men appeared in navy-blue uniforms, pushing a wheelchair, followed by the doctor who had been roaring on the phone.

'Right you are, my dear. Hop down and jump in here!' they shouted happily to me, pulling out a blanket and waiting for me.

I threw back the blankets and swung my feet out of the bed, standing up. My legs turned to rubber, and I held on to the bed.

'Ah, wait! Let her have her tea first!' one of the men said. A baldy fellow with glasses.

'Oh, no!' said the doctor. 'She's to go over to St Oliver's. She will get her tea there. Now!' said the doctor, leaning her head forward, boring her eyes into the men. 'When you get there, tell them she is expected, and if there are any problems . . .'

'What sort a problems?' asked Baldy, looking very suspicious, then looking at me, wondering if I was dangerous!

'If they don't want to take her, do not, and I emphasise this,' she said, slamming her fist into her left palm, 'under no circumstance do you take her back here! Refuse! Because I suspect they will try to weasel out of their obligations. Tell them she is in their catchment area.'

I was sitting in the wheelchair, staring at me tea, me mouth beginning to remember what it was for, while they discussed me as if I was a parcel. I stared up at yer woman, with her long narrow face and beaked nose, and thick straw hair that refused to sit down and behave itself. It stood out in all directions. I opened my mouth, beginning to break my vow of silence, and even took in a sharp breath, ready to tell her to go and fuck herself, when she turned tail and headed off down the ward. I stared after her, watching her short, fat legs wobbling against each other; they looked like tree trunks! Then I snapped my jaws shut. What's the point? It would only give her the satisfaction of knowing she was right.

We pushed off down the ward and about ten pairs of eyes lifted off their plates and stared after me.

'Byeee!' roared Pascal. 'Pity you can't stay! You would have loved it here!'

I lifted my hand, waving my fingers at him, and we turned out the door and headed out of the hospital and into an ambulance.

The evening light was bright with watery sunshine, and it hit me between the eyes for a second. I blinked, shutting my eyes, then opened them. It was lovely to be in the fresh, crisp air again, and a sudden pang hit me. I wanted to have my old life back, the one before Sarah grew up to gallivant off without me. And she still only a little chicken! And the bloody health. I suppose that would come back if I gave it a chance. But I can't seem to get the strength to lift myself or find a reason to live. Then they rolled me into the ambulance.

'Up you get,' Baldy said, 'and sit down here.'

The other fellow handed me a bunch of daffodils. I looked at them, wondering where they came from. 'They're yours,' he said, nodding at me.

I stared at the flowers, wondering who had brought them. The only person who came in to see me was Charlie, and he wouldn't buy flowers. Anyway, he wouldn't have the money. I shook my head, blinking at him as a way of thanking him. Then he slammed the doors shut and went around to the front, and jumped in to drive the ambulance. We were motoring.

I sat on the side of the stretcher, clutching my bunch of daffodils. I felt very removed from everything and everybody. At home, I had been terribly isolated and had no one to share anything with. I would have loved to belong to someone, have someone who meant the world to me, someone I could trust. Life is not that simple, though. Things have to be done, like earning a living and looking after a child.

We had great times together, Sarah and me, wandering up and down the Alps when she got her summer holidays. Nearly getting nabbed by the police for crossing the border with the edelweiss plant in my rucksack. '*Nein!*' they screeched. '*Das ist verboten!*' I picked it walking along the Tyrolean Alps in Austria.

We were in and out of museums in Florence, with me refusing to pay to get into any of them. Shockin! Culture should be free. So we sneaked in! I had no money! We were doing the Grand Tour on fresh air. That didn't stop us, and it gave us plenty of laughs.

I waltzed around the Continent on the old adage 'necessity is the mother of invention'. Sarah must have her education! So, I staggered up to the guard with the gun in his holster at the entrance to the Papal Apartments, clasping my forehead and gasping for *'Aqua! Aqua!'* while he runs off to get the water for the young woman with the long flowing hair down past her arse, in the tight shorts and Roman sandals, with the little blonde girl and her long, flowing fair locks. Sarah stood watching, roaring her head laughing at my acting.

'Andiamo!' I mutter, as I grab her hand and we dive in, joining the English tour tripping around the Sistine Chapel.

Then it was another year, and we were seen to be taking a bus tour from Ireland to the Dordogne. It was cheap. The bus had been scrapped back in 1940, and they had to push it, belching black smoke, across the Continent, looking for parts. The 'Group' were a shower of religious maniacs who insisted on saying Mass twice a day and praying for a safe journey clutching their rosary beads, looking at the sights out the window of the bus when it was actually moving under its own steam.

When we sailed from Cork harbour to France, Sarah and I travelled in great style. It was the height of summer, and the sun was splitting the rocks. The ship heaved, blew its horn, then staggered out to sea, stuffed to the gills with passengers. The religious maniacs discovered they had to sleep on deck. The French passengers swarmed around the reception desk, buzzing like demented wasps. *'Allez! Allez!'* they screeched to the receptionist. *'Arrêtez-vous, idiots paysans!'* they hissed, snorting insults at each other over all the pushing and shoving. Then it was back to waving wads of money at the receptionist, with the lot of them all desperately looking for a cabin. Nothing could be had. *'Fermé!* Closed! We are full,' roared the receptionist, flapping them all off like a load of chickens.

I wandered off up to First Class and occupied an empty suite with a sitting room, four double bunks and a bathroom. They had very kindly left us a bowl of fruit and the keys of the cabin.

We sat munching on the fruit while I waited to see if the cabin would be claimed by anyone or the staff would check. The door was opened by the private stewardess, and I sat both impervious and imperious, giving her a cold stare, pained with the whole business of being rich and having to slum it in a so-called first-class cabin.

'Oh! You are late arrivals!' she announced.

'Yes,' I murmured in a bored tone.

We wait to see if she will check. Half hour later, nothing happens! I grab the keys. 'Right, darling! Follow Mummy. We are going to find something to eat, and this is our new sleeping quarters!'

We wander down to the religious maniacs, looking for the grub they promised as part of our package.

'Where's the paté and the other "exotic delicacies" you promised us?' I ask the aul fella with the rotten black teeth who is running the trip.

'Over there!' he points to a battered old tea chest.

Sarah and me peer in. Squashed, mouldy, damp tomato sandwiches. Bloody disgusting!

'Come on, darling. Follow Mummy!'

We wander into the cafe and trace the long queue snaking its way painfully slowly around the ship. I stop to look at what they are serving – greasy, half-cooked chips and sausages. Disgusting! And look at the prices! 'Follow me, darling!'

We wander to the dining room, with the black-suited, bow-tied waiter waiting to bow and greet the more discerning clients, with the money.

'Look at the prices, Sarah!'

We glance in and see an enormous round buffet table groaning with every conceivable dish to tempt the tired and jaded palates of the bored rich, and all to be enjoyed sitting at a table draped with a white linen tablecloth with a view of the great ocean.

I took a deep breath, straightened my shoulders and whispered to Sarah, 'Follow me, darling.'

I swept past the waiter, who bowed and glanced, watching me move imperviously and imperiously past the cash desk then sweep over to a man sitting down minding his own business with a white napkin tucked under his two fat wobbling chins. He was happily slobbering over a plateful of foreign-looking grub. I tapped him on the shoulder, screeching, 'DARLING! HERE YOU ARE!'

His mouth dropped open, showing something with legs dangling out. '*Mon dieu!*' he puffed, dropping a bit of what looked like a frog's leg, landing it straight into his lap. He stared at me with the eyes bulging outa his head.

'Sorry! My mistake!' I said, bending down to him. 'I thought you were that handsome brute of a friend of mine! Really sorry,' I said, leaning into him and patting him on the shoulder.

He smiled, and I weaved off, throwing an eye back to the waiter. No problem! He's taking no notice. We dined on frogs' legs, salmon, and had a bit of everything. Then went back for more and more, till we burst! It was a buffet!

'Don't feed me any more!' Sarah complained, looking half dead with the eyes closing.

I casually threw out to the missionary nun travelling with the group – she was back home from China for a well-deserved rest – 'Oh! You are sleeping on deck? Well, we have some spare beds in our suite. You are welcome to stay with us!'

'Oh, really! Would you mind if I invited my friend, the other missionary priest? He has nowhere to sleep.'

'No problem. He is very welcome!'

Sarah and I were in bed early, roaring our heads laughing.

'They think we are rich, Mummy! And if the staff come knocking on the door in the middle of the night, the nun and the priest will get arrested!'

'Yeah! Shockin!' I clucked, laughing me head off, thinking, I can imagine the disgrace! *Priest found sharing luxury cabin with nun. They had an innocent woman and child in tow. The unfortunate mother said, when charged with the other two culprits, 'It was all a misunderstanding. We all thought the other was paying!'*

We sailed into the dining room in glorious sunshine the next morning, after a luxurious bath, me wearing a long, red gypsy skirt and a white-linen peasant blouse, with the hair streaming out behind me. I was showing off my tanned legs at the front, but they looked like milk bottles at the back. I managed that by lying sprawled on my back in the back garden. I never turned over, not wanting to miss even a bit of the sun on me front. I did that every evening. Rushing out to grab the last of the dying sun after I limped home from my 'executive' job. That job didn't even pay enough for me to get the bloody bus home. I had to hitch.

Sarah was wearing her boiler suit. She looked lovely, very cute!

'Look, Mummy! There's our new friends!' she said, pointing over to the window at the two grinning faces waving happily at us, stuffing their big gobs.

'They didn't invite us!' I muttered through gritted teeth, smiling back at them.

'But they think we're rich, Mummy!' Sarah leaned into me, sounding like an old woman full of wisdom.

'Yeah! Suppose so,' I said. 'Maybe we should charge them a few bob! They can afford to eat here,' I said, thinking. We were travelling on a wing and a prayer!

Happy times, I thought, slowly lifting my head.

There were many happy memories. Life was one big adventure. There was nothing we didn't do. Down to RTE, the national television studios, and into the subsidised canteen on a Saturday night for our tea, then sit back and watch all the stars stuffing their gobs before they went on *The Late Late Show*! Sarah loved it.

Yeah! We were always on the move, up to something. Out to the Phoenix Park to ride on the flea-ridden nags. I got a book from the library on horse riding, and the two of us studied it. We got our 'seat' in no time and became quite competent horse riders. Until I took a tumble, got concussed, and that was the end of me dreams of joining the hunting fraternity in the area.

Myself and Kitty, a friend, we would lunch in the local pub afterwards, leaving the bill for a friend of mine. He'd made the mistake of telling me to 'Just call in and tell Joe, the owner, you are a friend of mine. I'll pick up the bill!'

Ah! Great times. Yer man never did succeed in getting me into his bed! It was par for the course then. Men thought because you had a child and were not free to marry then you were fair game. No! I had a higher price on myself than a romp in the sack and a few meals. I never did meet a man I could trust. They all seemed to want something from me.

28

The ambulance man jumped down to open the doors. 'We're here!' he said, jumping back in to collect my yellow plastic bin liner from the hospital with the red romper suit and granny nightdress. 'Hotel Paradiso!' he cackled.

I climbed out, still clutching my bunch of flowers.

'I'll take them,' he said, reaching for my daffodils.

'No! Let go!' I snatched them back and jumped down, landing on the concrete ground in my bare feet. I have no slippers.

I looked down at myself wearing a bright-orange dressing gown, a pair of pyjama bottoms miles too long and ten times the width of me. I had to tie the waist in a knot. A top with half the buttons missing around the chest, exposing everything, with the hospital logo written all over the front. No belt for the robe, and it was too tight anyway. I was so thin from starving myself I could be marked absent if I turned sideways, so it must have belonged to a midget.

'Right! Follow me!' he shouted, thinking I was deaf as well as probably mental.

I padded in behind him and we waited while he rang the bell.

The door was opened by a long skinny monk. Well, he would be, I thought, gazing at him, if old age hadn't bent him in two. His head was trailing the ground.

'This is the patient from the general hospital for admittance here,' said Baldy, pointing to me then standing back.

The monk made no move to open the door wider, and just stared from the ambulance men to me.

Baldy stood with the smile frozen on his face, waiting to do battle. The monk kept looking at us. I got fed up waiting and pushed past Baldy, saying, 'Open the door. Outa the way, please!' and pushed past the monk into the wide, carpeted entrance hall.

The men stepped in behind me, leaving my yellow plastic bag in the hall beside the monk, and handed him a brown envelope. The decision was made for him, and he shook himself, gave a watery smile to the men, closed the door, picked up my bag and said, 'Follow me.'

I trailed behind him down the long wide passage with red carpeting. 'Why must you young people take yourselves in here?' he said, shaking his head that was nearly tipping the carpet. 'You should be out enjoying yourself!'

'Don't you dare speak to me! I did not give you permission to speak to me,' I boomed, astonished at hearing myself. Listening to meself sounding like Queen Victoria.

He went into an office with a high ceiling and a mahogany bookcase. It was stuffed with books: *St Thomas Aquinas and the Lives of the Saints*, *Nursing the Mentally Ill*.

'Take a seat,' he said, pointing to an old, well-padded mahogany chair.

I sat down with the chair pointing to the bookcase. My eyes wandered up and down the titles. He sat behind a lovely big old rosewood desk. It was groaning with papers and books.

'Tut, tut!' he muttered, reading whatever was said in the brown envelope. Then he stared down at me over the small round glasses sitting on his nose.

I stared back, folding my arms and letting my head drop forward, daring him to say another word.

He shook his head from side to side, very slowly, and tutted again, saying, 'Oh, you are a very silly girl!'

'I didn't ask for your opinion!' I snapped, hearing the crisp Oxford English drip from my tongue again. Hmm! I thought. This is obviously the tone I adopt for doing battle with the Establishment, or any idiot who thinks they can push me around.

He pulled down a massive big ledger book and started writing down details from the brown envelope.

That's it! I thought, watching him. I am now a marked woman! I can just see the questions when I have to apply for something that requires a bit of sanity. For example, a job as a nanny in New York. *'Are you of sound mind? Have you ever been in a loony bin? Sorry, I will rephrase that. Have you ever spent time in a mental institution?'*

'Eh! Noo! I was only visiting, well, went for a short holiday. Nice place. You can let your hair down!'

My thoughts were interrupted by the monk pushing back his big old cushy armchair, the castors squealing on the wooden floor.

'Come along now!' he said, waving me out of my chair and herding me out the door. He took off at a fair lick, me trotting behind to keep up. His long brown robes with the white-knotted rope tied around his waist kept flapping against his brown leather sandals. His big head, with a mop of snow-white curly hair, was swinging along the floor as we headed up an incline in the passage. It was glass from ceiling to almost floor on the right side all along the passage. It looked out onto a very lush garden, almost like a jungle, with huge palm trees and all sorts of exotic plants and shrubs. It was so dense you could get lost in it.

We stopped at a lift, and the monk reached over and pressed a button. We stepped in as the doors whished open. More carpet, and the walls were dark smoky glass. This place is really upmarket. I bet it's private. They need not think they are getting any money out of me! I haven't got two halfpennies to rub together! So fuck them! Maybe they'll kick me out faster when they find that out. Yeah! If I know the Church, that's exactly what they will do. On the other hand, they could send me to Grangegorman, where me poor aunt Nelly used to end up when she had one of her fits. Jaysus! I'd never live that down!

The lift stopped and swished open. We stepped out onto a landing with a wrought-iron banister rail curling down a staircase, carpeted, of course, in bright yellow. I looked up to a ceiling-to-floor window going down the length of the building. The monk headed for a glass door, turned the handle, and we were standing in a big reception area with a long desk and nurses looking busy, writing and talking on the phone.

'Ah! Sister Mulberry,' the monk said, heading over to a steel-grey-haired woman with a short-cropped hairstyle and wearing a dark navy pinstripe suit. He handed her a file and pointed to me, whispering into her ear. She listened carefully, leaning into him, watching me, her eyes flicking up and down me, taking my measure.

I pulled myself up to my five feet nothing, crossing my arms, staring at her, taking her measure.

She nodded her head when he was finished giving her a blow-by-blow account of my 'character'. 'Thank you, Brother,' she said, as he moved away, smiling and heading out the door again.

I watched him as he removed a big bunch of keys tied to the rope hanging around his waist and picked out one, opening the door and swinging it shut behind him.

Fuck! That door is locked. I'm locked in!

'Nurse!' barked Sister Mulberry to a little blonde-haired nurse busy writing up charts at the desk.

'Yes, Sister?' breathed the little nurse, dropping her pen and rushing over.

'Take this new patient down to room seven and admit her.'

'Yes, Sister,' said the nurse, dropping her eyes and turning to me and smiling. 'Come on down with me, and I'll get you settled in,' she said, taking my arm and walking me down into a wide-open sitting room with a huge plate-glass window running in a square around the whole floor. I could see it was looking down onto the same courtyard on the bottom floor. You could walk around the full length of the corridors here and see everything that was happening on this floor. This place has eyes everywhere! There's no escape! They can watch you all the time.

We walked past doors on the left, and a big woman with long, curly, black-and-grey hair roared at me as we passed, 'What is your name, my dear?'

I looked over at her sitting on a couch with two massive arms wrapped tightly around a big brown-leather handbag. It looked the size of something I would bring on me holidays to carry all me stuff!

'Are you all right, Petunia?' the nurse shouted, smiling and waving at Petunia.

'Nurse!' screeched Petunia, suddenly hauling herself to her feet and trying to steady her big bulk. 'I am going to walk backwards for Christmas!'

'Ah, you're too late, Petunia. Christmas has come and gone!' smiled the nurse back at her.

Petunia stood rocking on her feet, trying to digest this piece of information. I stared and ran into the nurse, who had now stopped to open the door into a room.

'Sorry!' I mumbled, trying to get my senses back. Holy God! Where the bloody hell have I landed myself?'

'OK, Martha. You take this bed,' she said as she headed down a long narrow room. There were two beds in the room, each with a curtain screen you could pull around for privacy. The other bed was empty. I looked around, seeing a huge picture window at the end of the room. My bed was right beside it. The walls were cream, and the lockers were cream, and the metal bed was low and cream. They looked new to me. The curtain screens were a light pink, and the duvet covers a light rose with white flowers. The floor has a light dusky-pink carpet.

I was surprised, but cautious, not intending to get too comfortable. I'm out of here at the first opportunity.

The nurse sat down on a chair beside my bed and said, 'Now sit down here, Martha. I need to get a few details from you.' Then she slapped the side of the bed, smiling at me.

I sat down on the side of the bed with my hands in my lap waiting for her to begin. She looked at a clipboard with forms attached, then took in a deep breath and said, 'Right, Martha, are you on any medication?'

'Yes, daily for my thyroid. I don't have it with me, so I need to get some.'

'Are you on any other medication?'

'Nope!'

'Have you ever been in a psychiatric hospital before?'

'Nope!'

'Are you attending any doctor regarding a psychiatric illness?'

'Nope!'

'Do you have any other medical condition?'

'Nope!'

'Are you suffering from depression?'

I hesitated. 'Nope! OK, I'll qualify that,' I said, remembering the reason for my failed exit from the land of the living, and my sortie into the Intensive Care Unit. 'Maybe a little under the weather,' I said. 'Depression? Definitely not. I am feeling better already, and very glad to be alive,' I said, creasing my face up and jamming my lips together, making a smile.

'OK,' she said, smiling and putting her clipboard on my locker. 'You can climb into bed now. You must be tired,' she said, pulling down the covers on the bed. I was relieved and gladly swung my legs into the bed, feeling shattered. It felt like the day would go on for ever.

'Would you like something to eat?' she asked, bending down and smiling at me.

I thought about it and decided I was hungry. 'Yes, please,' I said, shaking my head, feeling very comfortable.

'What about scrambled egg and toast?'

'Lovely! Thanks, Nurse,' I said, wrapping the duvet around me and lying back on the pillows.

She skipped out the door, and I looked out the window. The view of the fields was lovely. Huge sweeping lawns as far as the eye can see. With great old oak trees and shrubs dotted around the borders. God! Maybe it's not so bad here after all. I could probably do with the rest. I certainly need to build myself back up again.

I was feeling lovely and relaxed when the door opened and the nurse came rushing in with a tray. 'There you are now!' she breathed, laying the tray down on my lap.

I looked. A big plate of buttery scrambled egg and toast with lots of butter. And a pot of tea.

'Tuck in to that,' she said, pouring out the tea for me, 'and the doctor will be in to see you shortly.'

My lips were beginning to open into a smile when the door suddenly opened and a head vanished back out again as quickly as it had come in. Then I heard a disembodied voice shout. We looked up at each other, the nurse staring at me puzzled. Then the head appeared in the door again, just open enough to allow the head to squeeze through.

'Get her to lock-up, Nurse! Get that patient to lock-up at once!'

I stared, not understanding, and the nurse was looking from the head to me. Then I looked again. A doctor was waving his hand, pointing his finger at me. 'You are not supposed to be here! She's the one a Dr Herman Hero warned us about. It's in his report. She's dangerous. She destroyed his office and caused terror in the surgery.'

My heart started pounding and a rage erupted through me. 'You fucking bastard!' I screamed at him.

'Get her out!' he barked at the nurse, waving his hand at her then to me.

I felt all the rejection come flying back. He's treating me like I am nothing. Not even fit to live. My head flew down to the tray on my lap, ready to heave it at him.

He saw what was coming and slammed the door shut. As he took off down the ward, I could hear the dull thud of his shoes on the carpet and his voice giving instructions was now fading away. I stared at my tea and then up at the nurse. She looked a little confused, and said gently, 'Do you want to eat your tea first?'

I shook my head, mumbling, 'No, thanks, Nurse, I won't bother.'

Then the door flew open, and two nurses came stamping in and made straight for me. 'OK. We're transferring you,' and they whipped me out of the bed and marched me out the door and along past the sitting room. I glanced over, seeing a lovely dining room with round tables and a long picture window looking out onto more greenery. We stopped at another door, a red steel one, and a nurse stood each side of me, pinning me in. I felt myself going very cold inside and hard.

They unlocked the door and marched me in. I stood in a wide-open area, looking to my right at a long desk going the length of the corridor. The desk was completely surrounded by thick glass. Nurses and men in grey suits and white jackets milled around inside. My head shot around to take in the two rooms on the left.

'Come along,' the nurses said, taking my arm and marching me along the corridor.

As we passed the first room, the door was open and a girl, she looked young, but I took her in at a glance, judging she was probably around twenty-six or twenty-seven. She stood in the entrance of a bedroom with two beds. We stared at each other as the nurses stopped to talk to a man in a grey suit who appeared out through a door from the other end of the corridor. Her face was creased up and looked half-frozen, as if she had been crying for ever and she would like to go on crying but had run out of tears and was now exhausted.

Her huge big blue eyes stared out of her head with a glazed expression. They looked almost lifeless as she stood staring at me.

But I could see a flicker of interest as she blinked, trying to take in what was happening. Thick snots had dried around her nose, and her mouth was open, showing thick white mucus around the corners as she started to moan, trying to squeeze out more tears. It was hard going, and she lifted her face to the nurses, showing them her best efforts.

'Nurse! Nurse!' she moaned. 'I want to go home.'

The nurses marched past, ignoring her, and marching me into the second room. 'This is your room, Martha!' they said, waving at a three-legged bed collapsed at one end.

I looked around the room, taking in the lumps gone out of the wall, and black skidmarks, like someone had tried to run up it with cobnailed boots! They probably threw the bed at it too. There was a huge picture window at the end wall, but nothing else. The nurses turned briskly and walked out.

I wandered down to the window, looking out. There was an enclosed field surrounded by high walls and huge old trees. It was probably the orchard and kitchen garden in another life. When the aristocrats owned it. Before the Church got their hands on it, picking it up for a song when the landed gentry legged it, running for their lives during the civil war back in the 1920s. Trust the bleedin Church! Where there's poor, there's brass and slave labour! And they keep their distance. They don't involve outside help. They run a world within a world. Yeah! No wonder they survived for two bleedin thousand years! They surely are making a few bob from this place.

I haven't clapped eyes on that Sister Eleanor one either. Not since she dropped me off with that fucking loony doctor. Hmm! That's their style: dive for cover when there's trouble afoot. Don't get involved. She just comes running to do her little bit of 'social work'. The nuns help the 'poor unfortunate girls' by doing their 'works of charity and mercy'. Then get back to their convents, thinking, we do our best for our flock.

Fuck you, Sister Eleanor! It wouldn't have hurt you to come and see me in that hospital. But you didn't want to get involved. You have nothing to do with me, really. I am only your 'act of charity'. Well, I survived without ever having to ask you for help. So you can stick your 'charity' up your religious hypocritical arse. And stop using me to justify your robbing, power-crazy, money-grabbing fucking religious organisation. You just caught me at a vulnerable time in my life, that's all. But it won't be happening again. I'm no fucking victim!

I walked up to the door and grabbed hold of it, slamming it shut. It gave a satisfying bang! I turned to walk back slowly to the window and the door shot open. A man in a grey suit and glasses stood rigidly holding on to the door, one leg balanced in the air, still hanging outside the door. His eyes whipped on me, then swept around the room. Satisfying himself the walls were still standing, he swung the door wide open and swooped out again.

I stared after him, saying nothing. Jaysus! So this is where they lock the baddies. In the pecking order of madness, I was the craziest one here! Along with that poor girl with the puppy-dog, tragic eyes next door. She doesn't look crazy to me, just tragic. But we seem to be the only two locked up.

I sat down on the bed and it wobbled. Ah, Jaysus! Do they expect me to sleep in this? No way! Not with the money they're going to get for keeping me locked up here against my will! I snorted to meself. Right! I need to think! Make a plan. You silly cow! You've really gone and done it now. Landing yourself in the power of the authorities. When they get you into the system, you are locked in for life. It's very hard to get out of their grasp. I can't believe I was so stupid! I spent years paddling my own canoe, and did quite well. Then just when I should have been sitting back, reaping all the benefits of my hard work, I end up here!

Right! No more fucking around. Fuck! Oh, Sarah! If you could see me now! I don't think you will be making mention to anyone in a hurry. *'Oh! How is Mummy? Well! Actually she is locked up in the loony bin!'* Oh, bloody hell! You will never live this down. Me little girl, the light of me life! What have I gone and done to you now?

The picture of her up on the stage at her school play. She was barely six, and they were putting on a play for the parents in honour of their First Communion they were about to make. I turned up late and planted myself on a seat right in front of the stage. All the other parents gave me filthy looks from the side benches they were stuck on, back against the far wall, well away from the stage. I waved up at Sarah, who was standing with a black shawl wrapped around her shoulders over a lovely long white frock. She was wearing a huge black hat with a veil over it.

I kept waving and smiling. But she didn't smile back, just kept staring at me, looking very worried. Then there was a scurry of activity behind me, and a bishop wearing a black suit with a big cross around his neck and a huge ring on his finger came and sat next to me, taking the empty seat beside me, and beamed at me. He had a mop of brown curly hair, and his blue eyes danced in his head with devilment. 'It's my lucky night!' he whispered, leaning into me. 'I get to sit beside a pretty girl!'

Then the principal of the school, a nun, appeared and glared at me. She wanted her seat next to the bishop. 'Hello, Sister!' I beamed, then looked back to the stage, waving at Sarah again. When I looked back at the nun, she was creeping off to sit at the benches on the side, pushing the parents up to make a bit of room for herself. The bishop and me watched her progress, and when she was sitting down and shifting her arse to make them move up more and get herself comfortable, she clasped her hands inside her robes and glared at me with her eyes spitting venom and her face roaring red from the rage.

I spoilt the highlight of her year. Robbing her place, sitting next to the bishop. He leaned into me again and whispered, 'You'd better watch yourself there. You have blotted your copybook. She's not going to forget or forgive you in a hurry!'

I snorted laughing, and he was tittering, enjoying himself. Then he whispered, 'That little girl with the long fair hair is very lovely, isn't she?' he said, looking at me. 'And she's a great little actress!'

'Yes!' I said, gasping proudly. 'That's my daughter.'

'Oh! Now I see where she gets her looks from,' he said, grinning at me, flashing his snow-white teeth.

'You're a right smoothie!' I whispered, thinking, me an the bishop, flirting! Great gas! Even the other ma's will get something. Think of the gossip over the coffee! Sharp intake of breath! Jaysus! Holy war!

'Ah! But no! That hair of yours is absolutely gorgeous!' he whispered. 'The length of it!'

I was sitting on it, and he looked, asking me how long it was.

'About a foot off the ground,' I said, answering the same old question. It was a great conversation piece. Like having a cute little dog. People always stop for a chat, oohing and ahhhing over the dog. Yeah! People always made comments about my hair. Especially men. It is unusual, I suppose, especially in Western countries.

'It's like pure silk, and it's so well groomed,' he said, staring at it.

'Yeah!' I said, feeling me chest puff and me nostrils flare. Gawd! What a man! No eunuch! He's a bishop! He uses it for stirring his tea.

I leaned into him, saying, 'If you'd seen me last night, trying to get a night's sleep, tossing and turning with a load of spiky hair rollers taking the head off me just so I could sit here looking lovely next to you, the bishop no less!' I beamed at him, flashing my pearly whites, flirting like mad, causing gasps of horror and outrage, with all the earwiggers leaning in for a listen.

He roared laughing. And people around us started tut-tutting. '*The bold hussy! Leadin that poor bishop astray!*'

I looked over to the bench where the nun was sitting, and a row of stony-faced women glared back at me. Hah! I thought, they're all jealous I'm sitting in the place of honour, having a party for meself! Then we all stood up and applauded loudly. I was thrilled with Sarah. She's a natural-born actress, I thought. But Holy Jaysus! She gave me an awful flea in me ear as we drove home.

'Mummy! How could you? You took poor Sister's seat next to the bishop! And she was so looking forward to the bishop coming. And you made a show of me with all the other parents watching you laughing with the bishop like he was a real man! He's very holy and he's not supposed to chase women. Only nuns!'

I will never forget the hysterics! I fell around the place laughing, and she cried her eyes out. That hurt! Wiping the laugh off me face. I could understand: children don't like to stand out! I just happened to be young and cut loose from a man, and thought life is great fun. I was bleedin daft as a brush. There was no putting the skids under me.

29

I came out of my daze, smiling to myself. Yeah! Life is what you make it. So, what now? I have to find a way of getting back on my feet. Discover that drive I used to have for wanting to know what's around the next corner. Hmm! First thing is to get out of this place. That is not going to be easy. I'm in now! They can keep me here as long as they like. I'm now fully in their power! This is bleedin serious. Unless . . . *Think!*

I could play their game. Yeah! I could use reverse psychology and grovel! Become a model patient. Brilliant idea! I could tell them I'm very happy here. It's a lovely place. And I'm glad to be away from the outside world. Now I won't have to bother meself about making decisions. And having everything done for me is just marvellous! The only worry is, I'll say, how long do they think I could stay here? The longer the better, I'll tell them. But I'm a little worried because I don't have the money to pay for this place. And I don't have insurance. I could whine to the nurses that I'm really worried that doctor might send me home. Right! That's Plan A! What's Plan B? Worry about that later!

I heard voices outside the door. 'Not now, Mabel!' someone said, then a nurse rushed in the door and landed a tray down in the middle of my bed. I watched as she tried to stop the tray toppling over. 'Oh, for goodness' sake,' she said, whipping up the tray and looking around the room for somewhere to land it. Her beady little eyes strained themselves as she gaped out of a fat round face, trying to decide where best to put the tray. She muttered to herself as she staggered from one foot to the other, turning herself, not able to decide what to do with it.

'Out of the way, please!' she said impatiently, staggering past me and slamming the tray at the head of the bed close to the wall. 'There's your tea,' she muttered to me as she pushed past without even looking at me.

I watched her go, feeling myself getting very cold. Who the fuck does she think she is? Treating me with contempt! My eyes rolled back to the tray. I leaned over, taking a look. A small teapot – get about one cup of tea from that. Two slices of buttered bread cut in a triangle. A small fat sausage, it burst in the cooking – they must have cooked that last Christmas, it looked like rubber. And its companion, a dried-up piece of leather that had died a hard death as a rasher!

I poured myself a cup of tea and walked up to the window. I stared at the high granite wall covered in ivy and the huge old trees stripped bare, braving the winter elements. Still surviving, still growing, slowly but surely. Stronger and stronger with the passing of time, against many odds. They stood there giving joy, comfort and pleasure during many a long summer evening to generations of people now long dead and gone. In another time, long forgotten now, children chased each other around those trees, tripping in their long dresses, squealing and laughing. Women with long frocks and wide-brimmed hats sat on benches and supped lemonade. They nibbled cucumber sandwiches and laughed, then went quiet as they remembered a long-lost love. Then they pined, feeling the sun go down on their joy as the cold winds of pain crept deep inside them. Or cried when someone was sick and probably dying, with no cure for anything then!

They thought their world would last for ever. Life would go on. But it only takes one incident to change a whole way of life for ever. The death of an only son, say, in France, during the Great War. All the male staff go off to France, encouraged by His Lordship to 'do your duty' for 'king and country'. They, the young staff, go more for adventure. Then it's all over. The guns grow silent, the dust clears. The poison gas is blown in the wind, leaving nothing but an eerie silence. Neither man nor beast stirs. Nor bird in the sky. All lie dead, some mangled together among the tangled debris of shells and machine. All is devastation. A few with greed and avarice rode roughshod over a neighbour. It triggered a world out of control.

The parents live out the twilight of their days without staff or son and heir. They are now lying dead on a patch of green in a foreign land among so many of their own countrymen it could be called 'Little England'. The world had changed for ever. The house lies dying, waiting for the earth to reclaim it. But this place found a use.

Yeah, people have had to put up with some really terrible things happening to them. Shame on you, Martha, for being such a wet nelly.

God! If you're there, then listen to me! For a start, look at the state a me! I'm in bleedin threadbare order. And I'm stuck in this place! I wouldn't mind if I knew why I'm still here. There must be a reason! But I am still here, staring at those self-same trees that go on regardless, and they will, if left alone, go on long after I am pushing up daisies. So why am I huffing and puffing? And why did I let myself get knocked down?

I stared at the trees, their huge trunks going hundreds of feet into the air, giving shelter to this lovely enclosed garden. I leaned out; it must be a least an acre. I wonder what those trees would say to me if they could speak? Giving me the wisdom of their age. They would probably look at me with bored but kindly wise eyes, and slowly wrap their leaves around them and bend their heads and say, '*My dear,*' taking a deep slow gentle breath, '*it is natural to fall. But you don't stay down. You jump up and dust yourself down, and charge into battle again. Your destiny was indeed to do battle, just to survive, my dear. So be it. Each of us is unique. But you railed and pushed and shoved any obstacle that dared get in your path. You moved around it when you could not go through it. You did not stop to take a breath and look around to see if there was something on your path that might have helped you. Friends, or a mate, perhaps. You blindly went, sometimes staggering, but keeping your eye on your goal. When you did reach your goal, it wasn't what you thought you wanted! You never stopped along the way and asked yourself what was really important to you. Not even when you fell so hard this time. You had brought no resources with you to pick yourself up. Now you were alone. Isolated on your little mountain. And the elements destroyed you, without the shelter and protection of people around you, loved ones, my dear. You are not an island. So now, my dear, it almost cost you your life! Take time. Just be still. Life is a great gift!*

'*I have seen you all come and go over the centuries, and when your huffing and your puffing dies away, they put you in the ground, and a new batch emerge, no different from the last lot really. Perhaps you all make more noise, move faster, shout louder, but it is all the same to me. I stand here, soaking up the power and strength of the summers, giving my pleasures to you people, and battle the winters, determined to hold my place here on this earth. Time, my dear. Time is everything. Yours is short. People have a short lifespan. Do try not to hurry it or waste it. Just enjoy it. Now! I am old, my dear, I wish to conserve my strength. I would like to be still.'*

I lifted my eyes slowly away from the trees, taking a slow, deep sigh, feeling a lovely sense of peace, and drifted over to the tray on the bed. I put the cup down and lifted the tray, putting it on the floor against the wall at the end of the bed.

'Bastards! Let me go!'

I stopped, my heart giving a thud. What's that?

I rushed out the door just in time to see Mabel, the girl in the next room, being dragged along the floor by three nurses. A woman wearing a blue smock and leaning on a sweeping brush was standing holding the door open. I looked at the metal bucket with the wheels holding her mops and detergents. She flew out as soon as I opened the door.

'Nurse!' the aul one complained, her beady little eyes taking in the sight of Mabel being dragged through the door, kicking and cursing, great big snots pouring out of her nose.

'No! No, please, Nurse. I want to go home,' she begged, letting her head fall, with her eyes closing in exhaustion, but still refusing to give up the fight to escape out of this place. She screamed and fought until her strength finally left her. I stood and watched as she was dragged into the bedroom, then the door was slammed shut. I could hear them wrestling her onto the bed. Then one of the nurses came flying out and made for the door at the end of the passage and shot into the office.

Your woman with the bucket gave me a suspicious look and turned sideways, keeping her eye on me, and locked the door into the passage by slamming it shut, making sure I couldn't escape out of lock-up!

I watched as she tested it to make sure it was locked. Then she picked up her bucket and blew a curly lock of grey-and-black hair out of her eyes and waddled off on her short fat legs, heading for the end door.

She took out a bunch of keys, keeping herself sideways to watch me, then opened the door, keeping her knee on it to hold it open. I stood staring, envying her that freedom, and felt annoyed she had the power to lock me up. We kept our eyes locked on each other. I could see a malicious glint in her eye, enjoying her little bit of power, knowing I would give my eye teeth to leg it out that door.

I watched as she picked up the bucket and wriggled through. A trickle of energy was beginning to flow through me, preparing for action, and for one split second I was about to leap forward and dash through, but the door slammed shut, and the moment was lost.

I probably wouldn't have got out that way anyway, I mused mournfully. Mabel tried to escape through the other door, so that's probably the way out.

The nurse came flying back, carrying a tray with bottles of stuff. She hurried into Mabel's room, and I could see two nurses sitting on the bed, with Mabel giving them an all-out wrestling match. Her eyes looked terrified when she saw the nurse come dashing in with the tray. Then the door was slammed shut in my face.

I stood staring at the locked door. So that's what happens if you give them any grief! They have the power of life and death in this place. Those bleedin drugs could kill you, or at least turn you into the living dead. You wouldn't know what's up or down any more! Bastards! They have the ultimate control over you here. Well! Nobody's controlling me!

I turned and headed over to the desk, stopping and looking in through the thick glass. There were two nurses and a fellow in a white jacket and white trousers sitting on chairs and standing around holding up the walls, laughing and joking. Enjoying themselves!

I knocked on the window; they ignored me. Then I banged harder, and heads looked over, then looked through me and went on with their carrying-on as if I wasn't here. 'Bastards!' I snorted, looking around for something to bang the window with. Nothing! I looked down at my bare feet – not even a pair of shoes!

Then the door opened again into lock-up and a man in a grey suit came through. I shot off like the wind, heading for the door. 'Not so fast!' said the tall, skinny fellow with the thick glasses, whipping the door shut, giving me a smile and trotting past me.

I follow him, and he stops, looks at me, then points me to my room, saying, 'No, you don't! Into your room, NOW!' Then he turns tail, heading for the end door.

I sidled down after him anyway, and he opened the door, giving me a glimpse of male patients wandering like zombies up and down a passage. Then he squeezed himself through the door, all the time watching me and giving a smile like an eegit that said, *Lookit me! I'm in charge of you! Aren't I great!*

'Fuck face!' I muttered after him. Then I went back to the window and started knocking again. They simply ignored me! Bastards. Then I wandered into the toilet. A little wash basin and a toilet bowl – that's it. No toilet brush to bang the window with. So I flushed the bowl for something to do. Then turned on the tap. Plenty of hot water. More than I have at home. I have to light the fire to get the back boiler heated before I can get hot water. The bloody electric immersion is gone. It costs too much money to replace.

I heard activity outside and rushed out, not wanting to miss any excitement. The three nurses came out, leaving Mabel conked out in the bed.

'Excuse me!' I said, looking from one to the other.

They looked at me, then went on chattering and walking off to the office as if I didn't exist.

I watched their backs, feeling fury at their ignorance. But cooled down rapidly, thinking of poor Mabel. I certainly don't want the same treatment.

'May I take a bath?' I threw at their backs in my politest-of-polite voice.

One of them looked back. An anaemic-looking cow, and she had no eyebrows and very thin, long, stringy, mousey hair tied back with a slide. 'No! Now go to your room, please!'

I watched her as she whirled back to the other two gobshites, who looked at her and laughed.

Just as they were about to go through the end door, I wailed, 'Then at least give me a bed to sleep in. The wheel is missing on that one!' I roared, pointing at my room.

'Later! When we get time,' your woman shouted back before slamming the door shut.

I was left standing with my mouth hanging open, looking at nothing. Four walls, two doors and the big partition bullet-proof glass office window, with bodies moving around behind it. You couldn't even hear what they were saying. And that's it!

I sat down to wait for Godot at a little grey-plastic table shoved into a dark corner of the corridor. Because that's what this is really. The women's part is on the right, and the men's is on the left. And Mabel and I are stuck in no-man's-land. Oh! You really have done it this time, Martha. Getting yourself locked up here! How could you be so bloody stupid?

It didn't take you long to forget just how controlling the authorities can be once they get you into their clutches, you fucking eegit. You better than anyone should remember how fast they were to whip children away from their mothers and even lock up the fucking mothers in homes as well if it didn't look as if they could take care of themselves. Jesus Christ! The rule has always been: no matter how poor you are, no matter how low you fall, you never let yourself get into the hands of the bleedin authorities. Then they just hand you over to the Church, and they fucking lock you up!

I took in a huge breath, running my hands through my matted hair, thinking, when is the last time I combed this? Then I snorted the air out through my nose, making a huge noise. I listened to it, there's nothing else to take my attention. Bloody hell! If I still have a shred of sanity left, I'm going to lose it in this place.

I was feeling banjacksed but too wound up to relax and get some sleep. Then the door opened again. A nurse was coming through. I hopped up without thinking and skated towards the door, sliding along the carpet in my bare feet. She calmly shut the door, locking it, and swept past me, giving me a look with her eyebrows raised like I was a dog who wasn't allowed into the house.

I wandered to the middle of the floor and sat down, watching both doors now, ready to make it before they knew what happened. Better than doing nothing. It will keep me occupied, trying to get the better of them gobshites. I think they only give you that poison, their bleedin drugs, if you start roaring and shouting and look as if you've lost your mind.

The door at the end of the passage opened, and I spotted the long, skinny fellow with the jam-jar glasses coming through. I took no notice, staring across at the desk with my hands in my lap, looking like I was contemplating my belly button. I lowered my head, watching him heading for the female ward, then I lifted myself up slowly, walked over to the desk, watching him put the keys in the door, then he started to turn the handle, and I was off.

I shot like the wind, lightly flicking his arm out of the way, and I was through.

'Stop! Get her!'

I was gone, flying like a blue-arse fly. Heading for the door at the end of the passage! Eyes at the desk close to the door for freedom looked up, moving slowly towards me. Too late! I was at the door, jamming the handle to open. Locked! I turned. Two men with their white coats flapping out behind them, with nurses tearing up the rear, were barrelling down towards me. The group behind the desk, two nurses and one in a navy-blue check uniform – she looked like she was in charge – shouted at the two nurses, 'Grab her, for heaven's sake!'

I went between the two nurses and tore right, lashing down a corridor. I could see the white coats bombing down the other side, and the bloody two nurses racing behind me. I shot into a room and slammed the door shut. No lock! This is fucking ridiculous. If I could get home, let's see what they could do about it then. I haven't committed a fucking crime!

The door opened, and the nurses came in, shouting, 'Do that again and you'll stay in lock-up for a very long time! Wait until Doctor hears about this.'

The others skated to a stop when they saw me being marched out of the storeroom. I grinned and waved at them. Fuck you! You are all going to get a run for your money. I shall keep you lot on your toes, I thought, letting myself be led back to my room.

'I'll do a deal with you!' I said to the white coats, as they led me into the bedroom. 'Fix that bed, and I will lie down like a model mental patient,' and I grinned, showing my white pearlies, 'and go to sleep! How's that?'

They looked at me, then looked at the bed, and the little fellow with the mop of short blond hair said, 'OK, but you must promise, mind!'

'Cross my heart and pray to die!' I drawled out, seeing the irony lost on them. They looked very hard done by, having to run the length of the top floor! Cretins! I thought, watching them amble off to get me a new bed.

So! What was all that about? I mused. Ah! It was fun! There's no way you are going to get out of this place, carrying on like that. But still, at least they noticed you, and now you might get a decent bed.

I slumped back on the pillow, feeling exhausted. That burst of adrenalin cost you your reserves of energy. I closed my eyes and before I knew what was happening I was being shaken awake.

'Time to get up!'

I lifted my head off the pillow, wondering where I was, seeing a fellow in a grey suit pushing in a locker and leaving a carafe of water on top.

'Up for breakfast!' he said, pushing out a trolley with bottles of water crashing around.

I sat up, staring around the room. It's morning! Another bloody day in this place. Another day to get through on this godforsaken earth! I felt the old familiar sensation of my heart sinking into my belly, the flutterings of anxiety in my chest, then a heavy weight settled down inside me, pulling me all the way down into despair.

30

I feel lost and alone, frightened, like a young child who has been left, forgotten, abandoned. I don't belong to anyone; there is no one to claim me. There is an emptiness around me, like silence; no echo of warmth, no other human to connect with. It has been like this for a long time now, and I know no one will come. I am completely alone, just me and my emptiness. I don't matter, and I'm not bothered any more. I don't want myself, I'm not worth the air I breathe, and I don't want to be around people. I want to be left alone to die. A coldness settles inside me now. I don't think or care or worry. Nothing and nobody can touch me.

A nurse put her head in the door and said, 'Breakfast!'

I slowly swung my legs out of the bed and padded out the door, the nurse watching me. She moves out of the way, letting me know she's in charge and I'd better get moving.

The end door opened, and I followed the nurse through onto a corridor. We turned right into a dining room overlooking the courtyard. 'Sit here!' she said, pointing me to a table with two men already sitting waiting for their breakfast.

There is row after row of tables with men of all ages in dressing gowns and slippers being served breakfast by nurses scurrying up and down with bowls of cornflakes and plates of sausages and rashers and snow-white eggs with soft yellow yolks on top. Toast is put into toast racks, and there are little bowls of marmalade. And another nurse pours cups of tea from a huge kettle.

'Do you want a fry?' a big fellow wearing a grey suit and white shirt and black tie asks me.

I give a little shake of my head, declining, and he passes the fry to the fellow sitting beside me.

'Can we have more toast, please, Brother?' the fat fellow beside me asks, stuffing a rasher into his mouth. It has to fight for room with the whole egg and half a piece of toast, along with the sausage he's now forcing in, and now he says with a mouthful of food and an empty plate even before the Brother has moved off, 'And second helpings, Brother!' The food was shooting everywhere on that last demand. Oh! I've had enough of this.

I stood up and walked out into the passage, waiting for someone to open the door so I could get back to my room. I looked down the passage with the glass all round, looking over to the sitting room of the female quarters, then back to the potted plants and huge metal pots with palm trees. Then I wandered down to stand outside the office and stared in through the glass surround at the day staff taking their orders from the grey suits, who I now knew were Brothers.

My eyes fell on a very distinguished-looking man in his mid thirties. I stared at him. He's not Irish. He had long blond hair with streaks of gold running through it, and it was combed straight back off his forehead and curled at the end over the collar of his white-and-royal-blue striped shirt. He was wearing a charcoal-grey pinstripe suit with French pleats gathered at the waist, with a very sharp crease in the leg and the trousers turned up at the bottom. The outfit was finished off with handmade black-leather shoes. He felt my eyes boring into him and looked over at me. I nodded my head to the door, indicating I wanted him to open it and let me out. His incredibly green eyes, they looked like emeralds, fell on me for a minute, then he slowly lowered his sweeping-brush eyelashes, hooding his green eyes, and looked away, dismissing me as if I was a bad smell, and went back to settling his mind on the business of what the group were discussing.

I waited. Nothing happened! He's ignoring me. The bloody bastard stared straight through me. He is simply treating me with contempt. Creep! He has no class!

A white coat came along and opened the door. I followed him through. 'Bath! I would like to take a bath, please,' I murmured to the white coat's back.

'Ask at the desk,' he shouted back to me, pointing to the desk.

'I would if they would take any notice of me,' I muttered to myself, strolling over to Mabel's room.

I looked in the door. She was prostrate in the bed, unconscious. Her head was lolling to one side with her mouth hanging open and white stuff foaming out of the corners. I stared at her. Jesus! Is this their idea of helping people? Or are they helping themselves to have a quiet life?

I wandered over to the desk and knocked at the glass. Heads swung in my direction.

'I would like to take a bath, please!' I shouted. They looked bored and swung away again.

A white coat came flying through the door. 'I would like to take a bath, please.'

'Ask one of the nurses,' he said, flying out the other door.

Another grey suit. 'Could I have a bath please, Brother?'

'Eh, yes! Ask one of the nurses.'

More staff came. 'Bath! Canihaveabath, please!' I breathed out in one sentence. My head was swinging on my shoulders, watching the traffic. It was like Piccadilly Circus at rush hour. No one took any notice of me. So I waited for the next batch. As soon as the door was opened by a white coat, I followed him through the other door, saying, 'Thank you very much!'

I nearly made it. He pulled me back just as I was through into the women's quarters.

'Where are you going?' he asked.

'Just for a bath!' I said.

'No! Back you go!' and he pushed me back in.

'Fucker!' I screamed after him in frustration, justifying their claim for my lock-up.

I was about to head into the men's quarters and cause a stir when the door opened and a little round nurse with black curly hair came straight for me, saying, 'Come on, Martha! Before you drive us all to distraction, I'm taking you for a bath.'

Ah! I exist after all, I thought, following her happily out through the door into the women's quarters.

'Now! Hang on and I'll get you a towel. What else do you need?'

'I have nothing, Nurse.'

'Comb, soap, shampoo? OK! I'll get some from one of the patients,' she said, rambling off.

I rushed into the bathroom and turned on the hot tap. I grabbed a facecloth, giving the bath a wipe, making sure it was clean. Never know what you might catch! I thought, putting in the plug and watching with satisfaction as the boiling hot water poured in.

'Here you are!' she said, dropping a towel, soap, shampoo and even talcum powder, toothpaste and toothbrush and a comb. 'You can change into these,' she said, handing me a pair of yellow-striped pyjamas with St Oliver's screaming across the front, letting everyone know I was a pauper! A loony pauper, at that! I looked at them.

'When someone comes up to see you,' she said kindly, 'you can ask them to bring you your own stuff.'

'Right!' I said, wondering if and when that would happen.

'I will be sitting outside waiting for you,' the nurse said, letting me know I shouldn't lose the run of myself with the excitement of getting out of the lock-up.

'OK! Thank you very much, Nurse. It was very kind of you,' I said, slamming the door and locking it, then diving into the bath and hopping up and down, getting burnt alive! I grabbed the cold tap, trying to balance my toes under it. It was bloody scalding. I never did have any sense and take my bloody time! Then I lowered myself gently into the water, gasping. That's better – the only good bloody thing I can say about this place.

I poured half the shampoo onto the top of my head and ducked it under the water, washing away weeks of grease. Jesus! You could fry rashers on this hair, it's so greasy! I took my time, letting the water out and pouring in more hot water. Ah! This is the life. I can take my time. I'm not rushing anywhere. Then there was a bang on the door.

'Will you be much longer, Martha? I have the meds to give out!'

Me exhilaration dropped down into my belly and out through my toes. I could always leave her sitting out there! There's not a thing they could do about it. I laughed to myself. Drive them all mad if she wasn't so nice!

'Coming, Nurse! I'm just rinsing my hair.' I reluctantly pulled the plug, mixing the hot and cold water, and sticking my head under the tap to rinse off my hair, then climbed out of the bath.

'Thanks, Nurse,' I breathed, wrapping the towel around my head and following her back to lock-up. I sat on the bed for the rest of the morning, patiently trying to get the tangles out of my hair. It is waist-length, and I'm wondering if it's worth all the bloody bother. Years ago, I got fed up with it – it was nearly tipping the ground. So I took myself into the hairdresser's on pure impulse, foolishly asking them to give me a nice new hairstyle. I came out looking like something out of *Charlie's Angels*. Raging I was! They charged me twenty-five quid. They cut it in one piece to sell it on again. That was the first and last time I ever showed my nose inside a hairdresser's.

Grand! It's finished. I let it hang down to dry naturally, and wandered into the toilet to admire myself in the mirror.

'Jesus! The state of you!' I muttered. I look like a bleedin skeleton! 'Serves you right for not eating,' I snorted, turning away from the mirror in disgust, and wandered out to the passage and sat down in my corner, still waiting for Godot.

31

'Lunch!' roared a white coat at me as he passed through, stopping and coming over to herd me into the dining room.

Right! I'm having my dinner! I thought, making for a table with a view of the courtyard. The room filled up quickly, with men shuffling in, some wondering where they were, others not caring, the pain written in their faces, eyes haunted by demons, and some having a private party all to themselves, laughing their heads off at nothing! Hmm! I took a deep sigh, looking around, wondering where the grub was. That bath had galvanised me appetite into action.

A stocky fella in a grey suit looking a bit like Quasimodo, with the long arms and the head to match, slapped down plates with bacon and cabbage and parsley sauce to the two men sitting opposite me. I waited patiently. He went off and came back carrying more plates to the table behind me. Then in front of me and beside me.

'Excuse me!' I said, when he came back to leave a glass of milk to the table beside me. 'May I have some dinner, please?'

He looked at me then through me, and went off about his business. I watched him serving everyone but me. I was beginning to boil. Then I suddenly jumped up, shouting, 'Keep your bloody food! I don't want it.'

He glanced over at me and gave a slight smirk.

I erupted in rage and went tearing out of the dining room and raced for the big metal pot with the palm tree. With the anger surging through my veins, I lifted it, swinging it around like one of those Highland pole-throwers in Scotland. Faster and faster it went. In my ring-a-ring-a-rosy with the palm tree, I could see forks stuck in mid air, halfway to open mouths, eyes on stalks, and Quasimodo in his grey suit making a mad dash to stop me.

When he was two steps away, I let fly. Crash! It smacked into the wall, battering the bucket and scattering the moss peat and palm tree all in different directions. Then I tried to leg it!

Quasimodo grabbed me in a wrestler's clinch, fixing my arms down by my sides and bending me in half.

'Let me go, you big overgrown gorilla!' I puffed.

He squeezed me tighter.

'OK! I give up! Let go! I'm not resisting!' I panted, the life squeezed out of me.

Other nurses came running to dig him outa the fray, but it was me who needed fucking rescuing!

He released me.

'You great big bastard! Call yerself a Brother? The size a you! Using your big ignorant carcass to annihilate me! It's no wonder you couldn't get a woman, so you come hiding in here!' I was heaving up and down, trying to get my breath and tell him what I thought of him. Two of the nurses marched me back to my room, and I sat down rigid, not moving an inch.

The hours passed; I sat without moving. Then the darkness crept in. Heads poked in the door from time to time. I just stared out at the darkness now coming down quickly. I stood up, arching my back, the stiffness in my bones giving me an idea of what it is to be ninety years old, then wandered over to the window and stared out. A mist was beginning to waft over the trees. It looked cold and damp out there, but I would swap it for this place any day.

I can handle that bastard, but it's fucking cruel to behave like that in a place like this, where people are so vulnerable. There's no way I'm setting foot in that dining room again. Let them do what they like! It would have been nice if he had smiled, said something kind, maybe asked me if I was OK. Treated me like a human being. But no! He deliberately ignored me. Probably because I refused breakfast. So he gets his kicks out of making people miserable, then tried to use me for wrestling practice. Twisted bastard.

Still, Martha, the eegit had to stop you, otherwise you would have gone for the dishes next. After you ran outa plants!

Yeah! But your man ignoring me had only reinforced my feeling of being terribly alone, that's why I let fly. I wish I had someone who just cared about me. But life is not like that. People are always wanting something out of you. Well! They can all go and fuck themselves! I'm not giving to anyone any more.

'Tea time!'

I looked around, seeing a nurse putting her head in the door and switching on the light. 'What are you doing standing there in the dark?' she asked, putting out her arm for me to follow her into the dining room.

I said nothing, just stared over at my bed.

'Do you want any tea?' she asked, tapping her fingers on the door impatiently, waiting to rush off.

I shook my head, heading over to the bed. She rushed out, and I switched off the light and climbed into bed, feeling very weary. Another day over. I heaved a sigh of relief, closing my eyes, and pulled the duvet around me, feeling myself falling into sleep.

'Wakey, wakey!'

I sat up scratching my head, watching the lanky grey suit with the long, narrow face and a nose to match, with the jam-jar glasses, pushing his carafes of water. They were rattling all over the place and making enough noise to wake the dead.

'Up you get,' he said, leaning on his trolley, waving his arse in the air, pushing himself and the trolley out the door.

No mention of breakfast! Good! They've giving up trying to get me into the dining room, and I've given up eating. Except for a cup of tea. When I can get them to give me one. Right! What excitement have I lined up for today? Smoke! I grabbed my tobacco and started rolling. Where would I be without these? Thank you, Walter Raleigh! Without you introducing us to the cancer weed we would be all dead and buried for the want of a bit of comfort! Yep! Always me favourite bit of comfort.

I stood up, snatching my wash things, and waited patiently by the other door, hoping for someone to let me out then be prepared to do the guard duty required when I take a bath, in case I managed to find something to break the bullet-proof glass or throw myself down onto the courtyard! Hmm! Not my style!

'Martha!' The little blond-haired white coat came strolling up to me, looking all businesslike. 'You are now to follow me!'

I followed him into Mabel's room.

'In that bed!' he said, pointing to the window.

I looked at Mabel sitting on the side of her bed, following first him, then me, with her huge blue puppy-dog eyes. She was drooling, spits coming out of the side of her mouth, and there was something green around her nose.

'Absolutely not!' I screeched, walking out of the room. 'I like having my own room!'

'Come on! This is your new room. Now be nice to Mabel!' he shouted, waving at Mabel. She looked like she was going to cry again.

'This has nothing to do with Mabel!' I roared, looking at Mabel.

She gave me a smile, showing me more spits, thick ones, coming out in bubbles.

I rushed back into my own room, slamming the door, and tried to grab the locker, pulling it in front of the door.

'Come out of there! This is not your room any more,' he shouted, heaving in the door, me trying to stop him by leaning into the locker. But I was too puny. No feeding in me. 'Do you want to swap beds?' he asked me, bending down ready to move my bed.

I gave up. 'No!' I said, giving out a big sigh. 'I'll move!'

'Good girl,' he said, grabbing my arm and rushing me into Mabel's room.

'Nurse! Don't call me . . .'

'Brother!' he said, interrupting me. 'I'm Brother Marcus!'

I looked at the size of him. He looks about twenty-five!

'Well, Brother! I don't like being called "girl". It's patronising! And just for the record, I'm older than you.'

'Why? How old do you think I am?' he asked, grinning.

'Anything from twenty to twenty-five!' I said. 'So! As I was saying . . .'

'I'm thirty!' he said.

'Well, anyway,' I said, ignoring him, 'You can call me . . .' I was thinking the formal 'Miss' was now gone. I looked at him, feeling very frustrated at losing my self-respect and being treated like an idiot by these morons. 'Just don't call me girl!' I screamed.

'Certainly, madam!' he laughed. Then he was gone out the door.

I wanted to scream. I looked down at Mabel staring up at me with her mouth open, dribbles everywhere. 'Mabel!' I said, marching down to my new bed by the window. 'This is my area, and down there is yours! OK?'

She shook her head, agreeing with me.

'And don't speak to me. I don't want to talk!' Then I climbed into the bed, turning on my side, and stared out the window, fuming! I hate change!

32

I was just dozing off with a thought rolling around in my head: Go for your bath! Go and take your bath! Later! was my last thought, feeling very lazy.

I woke up with the sound of a piercing scream. My head shot up in the bed, my heart pounding. Whatwasthat? Then I looked to where the noise was coming from.

Mabel had her bed turned upside down, and she was wrestling with the duvet. She got herself tangled up trying to shred it and everything else she could get her hands on.

'Mabel!' I shrieked, and the frenzied movement in the duvet suddenly stopped, and she tore herself free, pulling the duvet from around her head, and stared up at me from the floor. 'Stop that fucking messing at once!' I glared at her. 'I am trying to get some sleep here!' I said slowly and with menace.

Her chin started to wobble, then her mouth opened ready to give another blast!

'Don't you dare open your mouth! Now get up from that floor and put that bed back.'

Her eyes flickered, uncertain whether she was on safe ground.

'Now!' I roared.

She leapt to her feet, fastening her eyes on me, and started to lift the bed, bending down quickly to lift the bedclothes from the floor and hump them back on the bed, still all the time never taking her eyes off me.

I sat still, glaring at her. 'And the locker!' I said, pointing.

She turned in a flash, grabbing the locker from the floor and righting it.

'Now! Make up your bed and tidy this place up, and when I get back we can go and have a shower,' I said, marching out to the toilet. 'OK?' I stopped at her bed, waiting for a response, and she shook her head up and down, the steam gone out of her. 'Now give us a smile!'

She stared at me, not ready to give up everything.

'Go on!' I bent my head to her, and she opened her mouth, giving a beautiful smile. I stared at her. 'Mabel! You have a beautiful smile, and you are really very pretty! Smile more, and the world will smile with you. Now! Get yourself ready. I'm going to get the nurse to let us out.'

'OK!' she said timidly.

I came out of the toilet and sauntered over to the desk and banged on the window. A tall hatchet-faced nurse with thin balding hair swung around and snapped, 'What do you want?'

'Bathroom, please! Two of us need to keep the regulation standard of hygiene. We need someone to let us out.'

'I'm busy!' she snapped. 'You will have to wait!'

'No problem, Nurse. When Mabel's relatives come to see her, I'll make sure to tell them she wasn't allowed to take a bath! You were too busy keeping her sedated and not taking care of her basic needs!' I snorted, slapping my hands rapidly on the desk, drumming out a lovely beat.

Hatchet-face gave me a piercing stare. I stared back with a Mona Lisa smile, then turned my head slightly to the left, raising my eyebrows, and continued my stare.

'Oh! For God's sake, come on then,' she said, tearing her keys from around her belt then storming out of the office and coming in through the end door. 'You would persecute Jesus off the Cross!' she snorted at me, rushing past to open the top door.

I charged into the bedroom. 'Quickly, Mabel! Grab your stuff. We're getting out for a bath.'

I bent down to grab my own stuff from my locker. Mabel started getting very excited, her eyes lighting up, and she started to giggle. 'Now, Mabel,' I whispered, grabbing her and holding her arm companionably as we raced for the door, 'No messing! There's more than one way to skin a cat! Don't buck the system! Play it! We'll be fine. We'll get out of here!'

I tore into the first bathroom, slamming the door, and I could hear the nurse fussing with Mabel, telling her not to lock the door.

Two hours later, when we finally had enough of the bathroom, we unlocked the doors and came out looking like two boiled lobsters.

Hatchet-face just pointed us back through the door into lock-up. She had lost her voice. It was from all her squawking and banging and threatening. Eventually, she had just given up and started sighing and tut-tutting, making it sound like she was on her last gasp.

So now, after our wash and polish, we sat on Mabel's bed, looking at all her lovely stuff.

'Help yourself,' Mabel said.

I dipped into her make-up bag, helping myself to her face cream, rubbing it on my face, and splashed Miss Dior perfume behind my ears.

'Put your stuff in your locker and let's go and sit outside,' I said, swooping up her things and standing up. 'Come on! Let's go and torment the nurses!'

We went outside and I said, 'Mabel! You bang on that end of the glass and tell them you want to see the doctor! Ask him how long more they are going to keep you locked up here! I'll bang on this end.'

Mabel looked unsure. 'But I haven't seen the doctor in ages! Not since they locked me up here!'

'How long ago was that?' I asked.

'I don't know! About a week ago,' she said, thinking about it.

'WHAT? That's bloody terrible!' I was shocked. My heart started pounding. So I was right! They can and will do what they like with you! I was not having this. I started pounding on the glass.

'What is it?' roared Hatchet-face.

'I would like to see the doctor, please.'

'Ah! Don't be annoying me,' she barked. 'He's busy!' Then she went back to her conversation.

I stared, my blood beginning to heat up. 'Mabel!' I roared. 'Start banging!'

Mabel watched me and started banging with her knuckles. 'Come on!' I said, waving to Mabel and racing into the bedroom.

I whipped open her washbag, taking out a small tin of Vaseline and a hairbrush with a wooden handle for Mabel. 'Save our knuckles,' I said, handing the brush to Mabel and rushing out again.

We stood at each end, making an unmerciful noise on the glass, beating out a din. Hatchet-face swung around, looking at me, and screamed at Mabel, 'Stop that at once!'

'Keep going, Mabel!' I shouted.

Mabel kept banging, getting into the swing of things, laughing and enjoying herself no end. She was banging and batting her eyelids in time to the noise, and Hatchet-face lost her rag and gritted her teeth and came rushing out of the office.

'Down here, Mabel,' I whispered.

Hatchet-face came flying at us, and another nurse came pounding behind her. She made to grab Mabel by the neck of her dressing gown, and I stood in front, saying calmly, 'Nurse! We really would like to see the doctor, please. I have not seen one since I got here. Mabel has not been looked at by a doctor in a whole week. It is your duty of care to ensure we get the best possible help that this hospital can provide! Now, we would both like to see a doctor to discuss that matter. Hmm? This is a very reasonable request. Now, please attend to this matter. Mabel here is costing her relatives a lot of money! They will be coming up to see her any day now. Isn't that right, Mabel?'

'Yes,' whispered Mabel.

'Well! You won't be seeing the doctor for a long while!' beamed Hatchet-face, her eyes dancing in her head with venom. 'Furthermore, I am the Ward Sister here! Now get back to your room or I am going to report you both to him! Go on, whoosh!' and she grabbed me, trying to steer me in the direction of the bedroom.

'Wait a minute, please!' I snapped. 'Why won't the doctor see me?'

'You may ask him that when you see him!'

'When will that be? And what about her? She's been stuck in here for weeks!' I roared.

'She's not your business!' roared Hatchet-face. 'Now don't bang on that glass again!' Then they stormed off, Hatchet-face looking back with murder on her red face.

I was fuming. 'Come on over here, Mabel!' I wandered over to the corner and sat down on the chair, thinking.

'Why did they lock you up, Mabel?' I asked her.

'Because I kept trying to escape!' she said, looking down at her nails. 'And I keep crying!'

'What's wrong with you?' I asked her gently.

'I got very depressed after I had my baby!' she said, tears coming into her eyes. 'And I tried to kill myself!'

'No! Don't cry, Mabel. In this place it only gets you into trouble. We have to start trying to get ourselves out of this place. We can't afford tears, Mabel! They only weaken you,' I said, looking into her sad blue eyes. She looked like a frightened kitten.

'How old is your baby, Mabel?' I asked her, smiling.

'She's five months old.'

'Ah! You are so lucky! Who is looking after her?'

'My mother,' she said, looking devastated.

I pulled back, not wanting to upset her. 'Look! Let's just enjoy ourselves. We'll . . .' I tried to think what we could do. Then the end door opened and a nurse wearing a grey pinstripe suit and another one in a blue-and-white striped uniform with a frilly cap standing to attention on her head marched past. We both stared at them.

'How are you, ladies?' I mocked.

The one in the pinstripe suit lowered her head, looking down at me over the top of her glasses, then stopped and stared, nodded to me, then looked at Mabel and said, 'How are you today, ladies?'

'Oh, we are fine, thank you. Mabel is in great spirits, aren't you, Mabel?' I nudged Mabel, showing her my teeth.

'Oh! Yeah! Yeah!' Mabel grinned, nodding to me.

'Yes, indeed!' I continued. 'Everything is great! The food is great! The people are great,' I said, nodding to Hatchet-face, who was leaning over the glass, looking very worried, watching us and then looking at the Matron – or whatever she is!

'Yes! Yes!' the Matron said, nodding her head and looking at the blue stripe.

'The place is great!' I intoned, as they drifted out the door. 'But one complaint!' I pointed my finger at the closing door. 'The excitement is a bit too much for us! Our poor fragile minds!'

Mabel started laughing, and Hatchet-face leaned her hands on the desk, peering over at us, saying something to the other nurse, who then shook her head at us, pressing her lips together. I waved, giving them a big slow wink! Mabel started shrieking laughing. It was lovely to hear her laugh. She tinkled, sounding like crystal being clinked. I beamed at her. 'Yeah! We need to get ourselves a good laugh, Mabel!'

The end door opened, and a tall, skinny, gangly fellow wearing a denim jacket and brown corduroy trousers came creeping over towards us. 'Hello!' he said, looking down at us with his hands dug deep down into his pockets.

'Hi!' I said slowly, looking at him.

His eyes were sunk in the back of his head, and his puffy grey face looked like it hadn't ever seen the light of day. He kept twitching his nose and just stood staring at us.

'My name's Rory!' he suddenly burst out. 'What's yours?' Then he shuffled from one foot to the other, looking very uneasy.

'Mine's Martha, and this is Mabel.'

'How're ye, Martha? How's it goin, Mabel?' he waved and nodded to us.

'How is it you are able to wear your clothes, Rory?' I asked, staring at him.

'Ah! I was just down in psychotherapy. But I caused a bit of a fuss, and they brought me back up,' he said, snuffling.

'How do you get down to psychotherapy? I mean, what do you have to do before they let you go there?' I asked.

'Well!' he said, twitching his nose and blinking, shaking his shoulders.

I held my breath, waiting, looking at Mabel, and she looked at me, and we both stared at him.

'It's like this!' he said, shuffling like he was about to do a tap dance. 'When you get your clothes, then they let you go! They take you down.'

'Who?'

'Nurses! They bring you down!' he said, looking at me like I was thick.

'Yeah, Rory,' I said slowly. 'But when do you get to have your clothes?'

'I don't know,' he said, scratching his head, looking very confused and trying to work it out. 'They just give them to ye!'

'Right! I see,' I said, not seeing any bloody thing.

Rory planked himself down beside us, leaning his back against the wall, and stretched his legs out. Mabel and I stared at each other and gave a big sigh.

'Jaysus! Any more excitement today, Mabel, and I'm going to lose my mind!' I said, dropping my face.

Mabel burst out laughing. Then Rory started laughing, thinking he had said something funny. I looked at him, then at Mabel, and she roared her head off. So I started too. Then Hatchet-face came through the door and said, 'Like to share the joke, boys and girls?'

'Yeah! We just heard the doctor has been admitted as a patient! They're bringing him up here to lock-up!'

'Tut! Not funny!' she snorted, giving me a dirty look.

We roared laughing as she flew through the other door, banging it hard behind her and making sure we heard her locking it, to show us our place.

'Frustrated aul bags! Jaysus! That one is haunted and hunted! Creeping around like an aul nun!' I roared at the slamming door. 'She loves her fucking job!' I snorted.

They roared laughing, and I threw myself into the chair, rolling myself a cigarette to cheer myself up.

'Nothing ever happens here,' I breathed out, muttering. Then suddenly I jumped up and started to do the Russian polka, landing on my arse and shooting out my legs. I used to do that in the convent as a kid, when we put on plays at Christmas for the nuns. 'Hup!' I screeched.

The others jumped up, and Rory started to do the clodhoppers' dance, lifting his legs high in the air and stamping his feet, shaking his head and screeching, 'Hi diddle de de!' Then Mabel and I flew up and down the passage doing a tango.

A nurse started banging on the window. 'Stop that noise!'

We stopped to look.

'I can't hear myself think with the lot of you!' she screeched.

I laughed, staring at her. She glared at me with her squashed face; her nose was buried in a mound of flesh. Then I started singing loudly, 'Take her up to Monto, Monto, Monto. Take her up to Monto!' then she shook her huge mop of grey frizzy hair – it looked like Phyllis Diller's, the mad comedienne – and shot out of her office, making straight for us. The end door flew open, and she came barrelling in screeching, 'Rory Ryan! Get back to your own ward!'

We watched as a shower of men came pouring in behind her. She left the door open in all the excitement!

'What's happening? Is there a party?' asked one fellow, his eyes flying around the room, dancing in his head.

'Everybody out!' she roared, waving her arms at the lot of us.

I made for the door with Mabel on my heels.

'Not you!' she screamed after us.

We stopped, looking back at her as more men pushed their way in. The tall skinny fellow in the grey suit with the jam-jar glasses came rushing in behind them, pushing everybody out of the way, trying to make his way to the mad nurse. Then the other door opened and three nurses dragged in a tall girl with hair flying all over the place, screaming and kicking. 'Fuck off! Let me out! Bastards! You arseholes, pricks, motherfuckers! Load a wankers!'

We all stopped to gawk! Then the women came in to see what was happening. I pinched Mabel, laughing. Jaysus! The excitement is mighty.

More nurses came thundering into the room, skating to a stop and looking around at the confusion.

'Quick, Mabel! Let's go for a walk.' I grabbed her and flew out the end door, flying along the passage and into the women's quarters. 'Not a soul in sight! They must be all in lock-up,' I said, swinging my head to Mabel. She had a big smile on her face.

'This is the best thing that's happened since I got here,' I muttered, heading into the sitting room. 'Look, Mabel! They have a colour television!' I stared at the screen, then we looked out the window across to the men's wing, and nurses were flying up and down, trying to push men back to their rooms.

'Let's hide!' I suddenly said. 'After all, we're in the loony bin, and you can get away with anything here. Act the eegit. It's what they expect!'

We ran down to the nurses' desk and hid inside the opening. 'Watch what happens, Mabel!' I giggled. 'They'll never think of looking for us in here! Gawd! This is great gas,' I twittered. Imagine acting like this at my age! Better late than never, I thought. I'm catching up on my lost childhood. I was enjoying myself no end.

'Try everywhere!' We heard running feet, and Jam-jar giving out the orders. 'Did you check the storeroom?'

'Yes, nothing!' Then heavy breathing as feet slapped past us.

'They're looking for us!' I muttered to Mabel.

She put her hand to her nose, trying to stop herself laughing.

I gave her a tap. 'No! Don't give the game away,' I snorted, laughing out through my nose. She was getting very red in the face, trying to keep in the laughing.

'Sound the alarm!' Jam-jar roared. 'They're not up here!'

We could see their trouser legs and a fat pair of hairy legs stuffed into flat black laced-up shoes. They were worn down on the outside, as if the walker walked with a waddle from side to side. I shook Mabel, pointing at the legs. She squealed into her hand. I pushed her head down into her stomach and chewed my fist.

There was a big bang and a sound like a foghorn blasted into the room. I shot my head out, and yer man's head was turned away from me. I grabbed Mabel and ducked around the desk, heading for the men's passage. She dived after me.

'Colditz!' I breathed, snorting laughing. We ducked into the storeroom, closing the door quietly behind us, then I leaned out. Nurses were heading up the men's passage away from us.

'Quick!' I grabbed her, and we flew up behind them, ducking down so we wouldn't be seen from the other side. We raced to the end door as the last pair of heels sailed through, locking it behind them. We dropped down behind the door and sat, waiting for someone to open it.

Rory wandered up the passage, staring at us. Then he stopped and it hit him! 'The nurses are gone bananas looking for you two! Hey! Hey, Nurses!'

'No! No, Rory!' I wailed, hissing after him. I looked back at Mabel and her face was turning purple from laughing.

'Here they are!' puffed bloody Rory. He was running and pointing, with nurses and grey suits and white suits on his tail. They rushed past him, sending him flying out of the way, screaming before they even reached us.

'How dare you? How dare you disappear? You are in a lot of trouble,' screamed Jam-jar, yanking the two of us to our feet.

'Excuse me! How dare you scream at me? Take your hands off me at once.' I pulled my arm away, totally indignant. 'What are you talking about? Disappearing! We have been sitting here bored out of our skulls, waiting for one of you lot to open this door!' I roared, pointing at the door. 'We have been locked out of lock-up! How dare you lock us out?' I screeched.

Jam-jar whipped out his keys as more nurses came flying down to see what we'd been up to. 'Where did you find them?' Hatchet-face puffed as she came steaming down, out of breath.

I looked disdainfully at her and marched in behind Jam-jar. 'Come on, Mabel. These people need sedating! They are absolutely hysterical.' We trotted in behind Jam-jar, who was having a quick conference with the rest of the creeps.

We marched into our room, leaving the door open to hear what they were saying.

'That one is a bad influence!' moaned Hatchet-face.

'I agree with you there!' whispered Jam-jar. 'We should separate them.'

Mabel was laughing, and I said, 'Don't let them hear you. Play them at their own game. There's nothing they can do. We're already locked up! Fucking gobshites! We'll think up another wheeze to keep them on their toes as long as they keep us locked up here!'

'Oh my God!' Mabel laughed, throwing herself onto the bed. 'You know what, Martha?' she said, looking almost normal, life coming back into her eyes. 'That's the first time I've laughed in months. No! I haven't laughed like that for years.'

'Well, Mabel, when in Rome, do as the . . . act like a lunatic!' I roared laughing, walking over to my bed, feeling absolutely exhausted but satisfied. 'That gave them a run for their money, Mabel,' I sighed, feeling a bit weak. 'I'm going to take a break. Call me if there's any more excitement.' The last thing I heard was Mabel giving her tinkly laugh.

33

I lay back against the headboard, oblivious to the sounds going on around me. I glanced down at the book sitting on my lap and picked it up, dumping it on my locker. I can't concentrate. It's a load of rubbish anyway. Cutie! Cutie! Bloody nonsense. About a little boy and his adoptive parents, and their overwhelming joy! Written by a chancer who fancies himself a writer. Just because he has a high profile in one area, he thinks he is a bleedin genius! Mabel can have it back.

I took a deep breath into my croaking lungs, giving out a big snort, and glanced out the window. Patients were slowly walking around the grounds, being trailed by bored nurses looking at their watches and wrapping their coats tightly around their necks, then moving up faster behind the patients, who were in no hurry to get back in.

I was going nowhere, just getting weaker all the time. I'm not able to eat. There is a devilment in me that won't allow me to move on. A feeling I don't deserve to live. Something inside me wants to deprive me of all pleasure. That includes eating. I no longer believed anyone would want me for myself. What I really wanted was to have someone to share my life with. Nobody complicated, just a simple, honest-to-God, caring man. One I could trust and know he would never turn his back on me.

That's not going to happen. All the ones I've met are now married at my age, mid thirties, and they are just on the mooch for a bit of stray. Not my style! I want someone all to myself.

'Look what I've got!' Katie came flying into the room, stopping at the end of my bed. She propped one arm against the wall and tucked her left leg under her, brandishing a bottle held high in the air. 'Vintage wine!' she screeched. 'Take a look, Martha!' she gasped, planking herself down on my bed, showing me the bottle.

'Con brought it in to me today. It's St Valentine's Day. And a huge box of chocs! I left them at the station, for the nurses.'

'Ah! Isn't he so good? Yeah!' I said, looking at the label. 'Baron de Rothschilds. He didn't spare any expense, did he?' I said, looking at her.

'No! We're mad about each other,' she beamed, her freckles crinkling across her button nose, and she swept her long, wavy, sandy hair back from her lovely grey eyes. They always sparkled; she was full of mischief.

We got along like a house on fire. That's unusual for me. I don't normally bother about women. I don't take them seriously. I laughed suddenly! The ma put me off women, and Jackser makes me wary of men! I shook my head. It's never occurred to me before! Hmm! You learn something new every day. But in here, I have time to do nothing else but be around women, and it's a nice feeling. Easier than being with men. Men! They're hard work. You have to be on your guard all the time. Because usually they are only after the one thing. But with women I can now have fun. Act silly, talk, say what I like, and almost be a child again. I'm doing things in reverse order. As a child, I was like an old woman. In here, I act like a child. That's the beauty of this place. You can just be yourself, people don't blink an eyelid no matter what you say or do. So the childish side is coming out in me.

Katie looked at me with her grey eyes beginning to mist over with tears. She was talking, and I shook my head to empty it of thoughts, and leaned into her to listen.

'Poor Con looked lost without me. He said if we couldn't celebrate at home, then we would celebrate here.'

'How long are you married, Katie?'

'Three years! We were really happy, then I had the baby two months ago and went mad!' Then she laughed. 'They had to drag me in here last week!'

'Don't worry, Katie! We saw you.'

'Yeah! Poor Con! He came in from work that evening and I was flinging dishes at the wall. Then I started throwing them at him. I blamed him for getting me into the mess. He was terrified. He couldn't get back into the kitchen until I had run out of things to throw at him. Ah! You should have seen the kitchen, Martha! It was wrecked. God!' she said, scratching her head, 'I can't believe how insane I went.

'My poor mother turned up, creeping into the kitchen, wading over the wreckage, and sat down beside me at the kitchen table, listening to me rant and rave about what a shit Con was! Poor Con. I really miss him and the baby. But Jeremy is being looked after by my mother. She probably won't hand him back. I'll have to prise him free!' Then she laughed. 'So! What about this?' she said, brandishing the wine.

'Drink it!' I said.

'No probs,' she said. 'What about a bottle opener?' She looked at me, squeezing her lips together, her eyes twinkling. 'The nurses let me have it knowing I wouldn't be able to open it.'

'Leave that to me!' I said. 'See if we can bribe one of the kitchen staff to open it for us, or, better still, we'll sneak in and get it ourselves.'

'Yeah! Great idea!' Katie roared. Then her face dropped. 'How do we get to the kitchen? We can't get out of here without an escort.'

'Yeah! I hadn't thought of that,' I said, seeing us locked up here. 'Where's Mabel?'

We looked up as a nurse stood holding Mabel's clothes.

'She's gone to take a bath,' Katie said.

'Right! There's her clothes,' and she dumped them on the bed. 'By the way, Martha. Sister is not going to allow you to go on refusing to eat.' She stopped to look at me, shaking her head and wagging her finger at me. 'She intends taking you on herself!' Then she was gone, skipping out the door.

I took no notice. Then Mabel arrived back, dancing into the room, singing, 'Freedom! Eat your heart out, you two! I'm getting out!' she chirped.

'What?' Katie and I roared, tearing our eyes back from each other to land on Mabel, screaming, 'How? Where?'

'Out for walkies!' smirked Mabel. 'While you two prawns were flaked out last night, I spent half the night nice and cosy talking to the staff nurse on night duty. I kept her company, droned out my life story. I now see the error of my ways and, hey presto!' she waved her arms at the clothes. We were gobsmacked.

Then a vision appeared and filled the doorway with his broad chest. He was built like a tank. The distinguished prat! I thought, looking at his gorgeous sleek blond hair with gold running through it. It was combed straight back, curling up at the collar of his black-leather tight-fitting Italian jacket. His emerald-green eyes, hooded with thick fair eyelashes, penetrated out of a chiselled cream-and-gold face that looked like it was carved out of a lump of granite. My eyes dropped to his 'give-us-a-kiss' lips that Cupid would stab you with his arrow for!

My eyes slowly dropped to his huge barrel chest straining out of his crisp white French-linen shirt, and maroon-silk tie, down to his grey pleated-at-the-waist trousers turned up at the bottom, neatly covering his black handmade laced shoes. I took in a sharp breath, my mouth hanging open, and leaned out of the bed to get a better look at him.

'Katie! Who is your man?' I gasped in a whisper, trying to get a breath.

'He is not for you, dearie!' she grinned at me. 'He's spoken for!'

'Married?' I asked, feeling the burst of central heating fly rapidly out through my toes.

'God has grabbed him for himself!' she continued slowly, grinning at me.

'Whadoyamean?' I gulped, not understanding.

'He's a monk!' she sniffed. 'Yeah! He's a gorgeous bit of stuff! Nearly as tasty as my Con,' she said, eyeing him.

He walked slowly, ever so slowly, taking slow-motion panther-like steps into the room, and lifted his arms wide, holding out the palms of his hands, and said, smiling at Mabel, 'Mabel, Mabel! You are not dressed! Come! We have a date! You must be ready. I am impatient to be with your company! I will wait for you!' Then he joined his hands with such delicacy, putting them together in the air as if he was going to pray. 'The sun shines just for you. Come!' Then he turned and looked at us, giving us a fleeting glance, penetrating us with his incredibly green eyes. Then his eyelashes drooped, hooding his eyes as he flicked them over the garden.

We watched him turn away with the ease and grace of a ballerina. Then he did a slow-motion glide out of the room, waving his shapely arse very slowly from side to side.

I forgot to breathe, finally letting myself let out a big sigh. 'Mamma mia!' I screeched. 'Where's he from?' I asked, swinging my head from one to the other.

'Russia! From Russia with love,' sang Katie.

'Well! You can parcel him up and send him by Mail Express post haste, specially for little ole me. Because, girls,' I said, jumping out of the bed and rushing over to see if I could get another look at him, 'I have just found the cure for myself!'

Katie laughed, saying, 'What about God?'

'He can fight me for him!' I said, grinning, feeling the life coming back into me.

34

I was sitting on my bed, yawning and wondering if I should climb in and have a sleep, when the 'Vision' appeared in the room and stood looking at me.

'I would like to give Katie her medication,' he said in a wonderfully singsong, musical, manly, deep baritone voice. I stared, listening with my mouth open. 'Please! You will help me?'

He held a glass of water gracefully away from him, and his open palm held tablets. Mabel was missing. That just leaves me and him and the bold recalcitrant Katie! I was out of the bed in a flash, trailing behind him, watching his arse slide from side to side and his long golden hair flick from the side down over his right eye. He glided into the room, with me puffing in behind him, all excited.

Katie was lying on the bed, nursing her bottle of vintage wine under her pillow, and grinned up at him, saying, 'Forget the pills! Let's get us a corkscrew and we'll open this!' and she whipped out the bottle.

The monk grinned, lighting up his whole face, and the room, and me! I was alive again! Energy started hurtling through my veins, reminding me what life was really all about.

'Katie! Katie! You must! Take this! For your baby and of courrse your husband!' He held out his hand with the medication and said, 'I beg you! Pleassse!'

I couldn't bear to see him struggling with the bold Katie, and I was mad jealous it wasn't me he was begging!

'Come on, Katie! Sit up!' I said. 'Give them to her! She's going to take them. Sit up, ye messer!' I said, laughing to Katie and dragging her up.

She took it no problem and winked at me, saying, 'Marta, Marta!

Why you no have to take de medication yourself? De lovely monk could then take care of you too! Ha, ha!'

'You are naughty, Katie!' he said, wagging his finger at her. 'Why do you like to tease me?'

I nearly collapsed onto the bed, drinking in his wonderfully Russian handsome manliness. He turned, ignoring me, and wafted out the door, my eyes glued on his back.

'God! You've got it bad!' Katie laughed.

'I can't get over him. He's so aloof, so distant, yet seems very in control, masterful!' I gasped out, trying to steady my breathing.

'Hmm! Nor can half of the women in this place,' Katie snorted. 'Martha! I'd be careful of that fellow!' Katie suddenly said, looking ominously at me.

'Why?' I burst out, feeling a sense of disappointment. 'You don't like him?' I asked.

'No! There's something . . . I don't know!'

I stared at her, trying to see what she sees. 'Ah! You don't like him because you have your own fella. And a lovely little baby and your . . .' I didn't finish telling her she had a doting mother and a father. 'You are very secure, Katie! I suppose I would be too, if I was in your position. I certainly wouldn't be wasting my time running after him!'

'So what are you going to do with him when you catch him?' she asked, staring at me, looking very serious.

'I don't know! It's just the hunt! I want him to notice me. That's all!' I said, thinking about it. 'It's not very serious, just something to grab on to. That's all. Any port in a storm, Katie.' It was giving me something to cling on to, I thought. A reason to live. Then, when I'm on my feet, I'll be flying again! Meanwhile, it's great fun.

Now I know what men get out of chasing women. I thought of all the men who had chased me just so they could get me into bed! They didn't succeed. It wasn't me they wanted, just the challenge. But they love the excitement of it. Turning up for a date, covered in beads of perspiration.

I thought of 'Trilby', an aul fella in his fifties. He was an aul bachelor. But he had plenty of money behind him. He was a district justice on the country circuit. He even proposed marriage, knowing full well, of course, I couldn't take him up on his offer even if I had wanted to. I'm still married to Sarah's dad.

Yeah! It's fun being chased, too. But there's not much chance of that happening now. I looked down at myself. Jaysus! I look like a skeleton. I still can't eat!

We were all sitting out on the passage, at our little table in the corner, when the male patients started wandering in and sitting down on the floor beside us.

'How long have you been here, Jack?' I asked an emaciated-looking fellow. He was the colour of death, and his face was lined with pain. He couldn't have been any more than forty. But he looked like he'd had too many lifetimes.

'About a year now. Yeah! I'll be a year here this coming March,' he said, thinking about it, looking very pained.

I stared at him, feeling his pain, and wondering how he manages to keep going. 'How long have you been suffering from depression, Jack?'

'Oh!' he said, stretching out his legs and thinking about it. 'It started in my thirties. I was a sales rep for a pharmaceutical company. I was travelling all around the country, away from home. My wife wasn't happy, and I didn't get to see the kids much. She was rearing them on her own practically!

'I was under a lot of pressure to perform, get the sales figures up, or I was out of a job. There were plenty of people standing in line behind me, ready to step into my job. So I had no choice really!' he said, taking a deep drag on his cigarette, keeping the smoke in his lungs, before slowly releasing it. I watched it curling up into the air. Then he said, taking a deep breath, his eyes staring into the beyond, looking into another world, 'I came home one day to an empty house. Too empty! I knew something was wrong as soon as I got in the door. I waited, thinking she was out shopping, hoping! But I had a feeling in my gut. Normally she would be at home with a bit of food keeping warm in the oven. It was a Friday evening. She knew I was due home.

'I remember putting the kettle on and looking in the oven; of course, there was nothing there! The oven was cold, and so was the house. It was freezing! I suppose that's what alerted me to something being wrong. Anyway, I started to light the fire when the phone rang. It was her mother. She wanted to know why she hadn't come over to meet her. They were all supposed to go into town, looking at Communion frocks for Hannah. That's my little girl,' he said, looking at us with terrible pain and sadness pouring out of his soul, and staring at us through his kind, soft, blue eyes, now fading from premature old age.

'I couldn't think where she might be. Her mother said she would ring around her sisters and see if she might have dropped in to visit one of them. I jumped into my car to go out and look for them. All the time feeling a terrible fear in my gut. I knew the shops would be closed. It was well past six o'clock now.

'Well, to cut a long story short,' he said, lowering his head and taking another deep drag on his cigarette, 'there was a knock on the door, that evening. Ten minutes to ten exactly. I looked up at the kitchen clock on the mantelpiece as I rushed out to open the door, hoping it might be Evelyn with the kids, hoping she might have lost her keys. When I opened the door . . .' Then he dropped his head again, going silent for a minute.

We waited. Holding our breaths. Then he lifted his head, looking at us each in turn, and said slowly, 'Two policemen were standing there. "Mr O'Connor?" they asked me. "What's wrong? Is it my wife?" I asked them before they had a chance to even get in the door. "Can we come in?" they asked me quietly, leading me into the hall. I knew something was wrong! I just knew something terrible was after happening. They told me she had gone down to the Quayside, down along the Liffey, and thrown herself and the three children in.

'I never went back to that job. I cursed it! I blamed myself for everything that had happened. I kept at the job because the money was good. We were paying for the house. The repayments were heavy, and good jobs were hard to come by. But in the end, it was the finish of all of us, that job! I've been in and out of this place ever since. They've given me electric shock treatment. It's terrible! You lose your memory. Oh! I wouldn't let them do that to me again.' He shook his head. 'Don't ever let them do that to you,' he said, warning us.

'We may think we're badly off,' I said quietly to everyone. 'But there's always someone worse off than yourself. No wonder you're in here, Jack! I don't know how you kept going,' I said, putting my hand on his shoulder.

'Yeah! You've had it very rough,' the others muttered to him in sympathy.

We looked up as a priest came heading in the door and steamed over to us. 'Good morning, ladies! Morning, men!' He nodded to the men, taking a big white hankie out of his long habit pocket and dragging it across his forehead, wiping the perspiration pouring out of him. He beamed at us with his big red face and tried to loosen the three big chins fighting for room inside his thick white-plastic dog collar strangling his neck.

'How are you all this morning?' he roared at us, like we were all deaf.

'Ah! Not good, Father!' I moaned. 'Are you here to give us succour?'

'What?' he said, leaning down to me, wondering if he heard right.

'This terrible madness is getting the better of me. Do you think, Father,' I said, looking up at him, 'they'll ever find a cure for madness?'

I looked up, staring at him, waiting for an answer. He stared back, trying to figure out where I was coming from. 'Would religion help me? Do ye think, Father?' I pushed.

'Oh! Ah! Indeed it would. Pray! Prayer is the best medicine we have,' he rushed on, satisfied now he was on firm ground. 'Would you like me to give you a blessing?' he asked me, and turning to the rest of them, raised his hands in a blessing.

'Ah! I don't think so, Father. I'm going through a very superstitious phase at the moment. I might get ideas inta me head that you've put a curse on me or something!' I said, looking very worried at him as I made a job of thinking about it very seriously, then nodding at the others. 'You never know!' I said, looking very serious. 'These things do happen!'

The others all nodded their heads, agreeing with me.

'Ah! Not at all! Not at all,' he roared, throwing back his huge head and shaking his big belly at us, roaring his head laughing, getting redder in the face and nearly turning purple. He took a fit of coughing, and someone rushed off to get him a drink of water.

'Sit down there, Father,' I said, pointing to Mabel's chair. 'Go on, Mabel, get up and let the poor priest sit down, and you a young one.'

Mabel jumped up, a big grin on her face. 'Let's have a bit of fun,' I whispered to the others.

'Father!' I asked him, when he'd settled down and finished coughing. 'Father! Do you remember when the Pope used to send them Crusaders to the Holy Land? The Knights Templars, I think they called them. Lovely men they were,' I said, shaking my head. 'I knew them well! Of course, the doctor doesn't believe me,' I said, looking sadly at the priest, leaning into him, telling him this in confidence.

He stared back at me, shaking his head in agreement, looking very sad.

'But you haven't seen the doc . . .' shouted Mabel suddenly.

'Shut up, Mabel,' I said, giving her a pinch. God! She's always one step behind! I thought. I stared at her. 'Remember the doctor was roaring at me the other day that it was all part of me delusions!'

Mabel stared, and I dropped my face. 'Yeah! Oh, yeah!' she said, her face cracking in a smile.

'Yeah! So be quiet and listen.'

She shook herself and settled down to listen. I coughed, to get meself ready, then ended up spluttering, wheezing and more coughs. Then, with a final splutter, I sniffed, trying to clear me watering eyes, and waited, getting me breath back. Now I was ready.

I looked up at the priest, seeing him staring with his mouth open, waiting for me to continue.

'Go on!' he barked, beginning to lose the rag.

'Well!' I puffed, thinking as I went along. 'It was back in the tenth or eleventh century, I think!'

'What about them?' he asked, impatient for me to continue.

'What I want to know is, why did he send them there to the Holy Land?'

'Ahem! Eh!' he coughed again, trying to think. 'Because it was the Holy Land!' he said. 'Where Christ was born!'

'Ah! So the Pope wanted it back for the Christians! Is that it?'

'Yes! Yes, of course,' he said, shaking his great mound of white hair.

'But they ransacked the place! Raped, burnt, pillaged and brought back all the great treasures to Rome for the Pope!'

'Ah! It wasn't for the Pope himself!' he interrupted, smiling happily. 'It was for the good of the Holy Roman Catholic Church!'

'But they murdered! How else do you think they got the stuff?

The people weren't waiting to hand over the goodies, you know,' I rasped at him. 'They waged war!'

'Ah! That's a long time ago now,' he said, getting to his feet.

'No! Wait. Sit down, Father! This has me wondering for a long time. What I can't understand is, the Ten Commandments tell us "Thou Shall Not Kill!" Yet the Church was massacring the poor Turks wholesale! Whadeye think about that?' I asked him. 'Is there one law for the Church and one for us?'

'Ah! It's very complicated,' he said, puffing, trying to get himself standing.

'Then, naturally, the bloody Turks start coming after us. The Infidels! Unbelievers! Wanting their stuff back. They got as far as Spain. Luckily they were stopped by the Polish Empire. That destroyed the Poles, of course,' I said mournfully.

'Then the Spanish jumped into the fray. The Spanish Inquisitions started up. They were looking under the beds for Muslims, and everyone ended up on the rack, tortured and murdered by the monks! You lot!'

'Hah! I hope you don't think I'm personally torturing anyone,' he laughed, thinking he was funny.

'Oh! I don't know about that,' I said, looking very suspiciously at him. 'I think I remember you giving the orders when my poor granny – she was only minding her own business,' I snorted, giving him a dirty look. 'Anyway! She was after making butter, and was giving the poor cat – he was black! – the drop of cream left over. Well! They got their hands on her, and you were the one giving the orders to stretch her even more when she wouldn't admit she was a witch! That poor woman didn't know what they were talking about. She didn't know whether she was coming or going!' I said, getting agitated and staring at him. 'And you look the same now as ye did then. Strutting around in your long brown habit with the cowl pulled up around your head! The same one the monks running this place wear!'

He puffed himself into a standing position and said, 'Lovely to talk to you all. God bless now!' and he flew out the door, roaring at the nurses to let him out.

'It was definitely you!' I roared over at him. 'And I bet you are all still at it,' I snorted.

'Thanks very much, Nurse!' he gasped, as he flew past her.

Hatchet-face stood at the door, watching him fly up the passage, then looked at us suspiciously as we fell around the place screaming laughing. 'You sound like a pack of laughing hyenas,' she said sourly, giving me a dirty look.

We screamed even louder, rushing to get into the toilet. Jack threw back his head, giving a huge laugh, and shook his head, saying I was an awful woman, tormenting the poor aul priest like that. You could hear us laughing miles away, and the nurses pressed their noses against the window, trying to look around to see what we were laughing at. Then Rory stopped laughing and asked me, 'Did he really stretch your granny on the rack?'

We started thumping the floor, trying to get a breath. Jaysus! Laughing can kill you, I thought, wiping the tears from my eyes with the sleeve of my orange dressing gown.

35

The lunch was over and I didn't go for any. It's been over a couple of weeks since I ate anything. So I was lying in bed taking it easy when the nurse, the one with the squashed face and beady little eyes, put her head in the door, and said, 'Come on. We're moving you.'

'Where to?' I asked in shock.

'Next door. You're being moved out of lock-up.'

My head spun around the room, looking at my view out the window and my bed, and what about Mabel and Katie?

'No!' I roared. 'I'm not moving. I like it here.'

'Don't be ridiculous!' she said, making for me in the bed and yanking me out by my arm.

'Let go! I'm not moving from here.'

'Yes, you are! Now come along quickly, I have a lot to do.'

She marched me out the door and through into the women's quarters. I followed her into the first room and looked around at a similar room. This one was nicer, though. It wasn't as worn out as the other one. I looked at the first bed – it was empty, probably nobody sleeping there – and headed for the one at the window.

'Now! When you get someone to bring in your clothes,' she said, 'you will be able to move about. You can go down to psychotherapy with the staff.'

Then she was gone. Back to the men's ward. They are in charge of lock-up! I was going to miss them. Even her and Hatchet-face! I climbed into the bed and stared out the window.

The view was different. You could see miles and miles of lawn and huge oak trees stretching as far as the eye could see. I saw houses in the distance, where people were living their lives, going about their ordinary business, free! Free from the pain of living. They must be! Or they'd be in here. They're out there enjoying their children, talking to their husbands, eating when they want to, and being able to eat, and driving their cars! I thought of my own home, lying empty, waiting for me to come back and put life into it. Bonzo! Poor Bonzo. I wonder how he is? I hope the neighbours or somebody is taking care of him. He'll miss me! He will be wondering where I got to when I'm not there to let him in after his travels.

'Martha! Martha, wake up!'

I opened my eyes, looking into the face of a strange nurse. She was smiling at me. I rubbed my eyes, looking around the room. I must have dozed off.

'Hurry!' she said. 'Put your dressing gown on and go out and see the doctor. He's outside waiting to see you.'

The doctor! I thought, sliding my feet out of the bed and opening the locker and taking out my dressing gown. I wonder why he wants to see me after all this time. Maybe I'm getting home.

I rushed out, following the nurse, feeling my heart banging away like mad inside my chest. I looked around, seeing her heading over to talk to a man in a grey suit with grey round glasses and a thin white face. It looked very lived in. I'd say he was in his sixties or late fifties.

I trotted over to him in my bare feet and sat next to him on the long padded seat in an alcove behind the dining room.

'Well!' he said, pushing his glasses down on his nose and turning around to look at me after examining a brown folder under his arm. He stared at me for a minute, his eyes twinkling. 'What have we here? I believe you frightened the hell out of a doctor,' he said, looking at me with a smile playing around his mouth.

I looked at him for a minute, sizing him up. 'Nah!' I said. 'He was "Abbey acting!" Over the top! His reaction was way out of proportion to what actually happened.'

He shifted himself and folded his arms, making himself more comfortable, then said, 'Oh! So what actually did happen?'

'Well!' I said, taking a deep breath. 'He valued his paperwork more than he valued me, so I was jealous and upended the lot!'

He raised his eyebrows slowly, wondering about this, then I continued, 'Also! He's a self-important prat who doesn't know his elbow from his arse. He didn't understand I put a high value on my life, I was desperate to live. He put out the last flicker of hope by treating me as a nonentity. I desperately needed his help to stop the depression I was in from killing me. Instead, he snuffed out the light, leaving me in darkness. I belted home and nearly succeeded in losing my life. So that's my story.'

He stared at me for a long time, searching my face, penetrating my eyes, watching my hand. Then he said, taking in a big breath, 'How are you now?'

'Dying! I'm dying. I can't find the will to live,' I said, looking at him.

'Right!' he said, and marched off.

I watched him go, wondering why I told him all that. I sat on the bench, thinking of going back to bed – I was feeling quite tired – when over strolled the Russian monk in his slow march and sat down beside me. 'What is your problem?' he asked me without any preamble.

I looked at him. His face was clear of all emotion, just his green eyes, being hooded by his lowering eyelashes, gave a quick glimpse of a sharp intelligence as he stared, trying to penetrate into my inner thoughts. I gave him a penetrating stare back, wanting to read him.

'Why are you here? Why are you not living out there?' he said, shaking his head down in the direction of the far-distant houses.

'I don't know! I don't really know!' I mused, thinking about this very direct question. 'I spent my life looking after other people, and when I needed someone, there was no one there. I don't know why I can't go on living. I want to, but I can't,' I said, shrugging my shoulders, wondering what was holding me back from moving forward.

'Then you are altruistic,' he said, looking at me with interest, his face leaning more towards me.

I thought about the meaning of the word and shook my head, reluctantly agreeing with him. 'Yes! I have been altruistic. Giving without looking for a return, until now that is. But I'm lost when I have no one but myself to look after. I'm not used to that. I don't know how to,' I sighed. 'All my life, other people have been dependent on me. That's how I'm programmed! Just to take care of other people. That's what must have kept me going!'

Then he got up and walked off without another word! I was left looking at his back, watching him walk down the ward and head off. Hmm! He didn't even say goodbye, or I'm going! It must be a Russian thing.

'Come on! You have to eat.'

I ignored her.

'Listen! Look at me.'

I looked up at the staff nurse, her face pained trying to think of a reason why I should eat the salad sitting on my plate for tea. I stared at it: white cold chicken sitting next to a tomato cut in half and a piece of lettuce with potato salad. I never did like salad anyway, I thought, looking away from the plate to everyone staring at me, wondering how I could refuse such lovely grub when they were all making short work of theirs. The nurse looked around in frustration, then rushed over, grabbing an empty chair, and pushed the fat one sitting next to me out of the way, banged the chair next to mine and lifted up a fork and said, 'OK. I am going to feed you myself if I have to.'

I started to laugh, and she got red in the face, saying, 'This is no laughing matter, Martha! You are going to end up in hospital with tubes stuck into you, and they'll be force-feeding you. Now! Come on. Just take a little. I don't know how you are still on your feet. You are getting very weak. Just look how thin you are!'

I looked, seeing an emaciated me. I was locked into a death wish, but I couldn't say this to myself – actually admit it. I am really paralysed by whatever is the matter with me.

'I'm trying to get thin enough so that I can escape out through the keyhole,' I said, looking at her with a serious face.

The blonde woman with the coiffured hairdo sitting in front of me burst out laughing. Then the rest of them started. 'What did she say?' patients asked on the table beside me. There was muttering, and they all started laughing. The fat woman with the red freckled face and the mop of curly hair sitting next to the nurse started choking and her face turned purple.

'Oh! Now look what you've done!' roared the nurse at me, slapping your woman's back.

The other patients thought this was very funny and started roaring their heads off laughing. Then the Russian monk came marching up to me with his hands behind his back and said, 'You and I must have a serious talk.'

I looked up at him, trying to read him, and he wagged his finger at me, saying, 'Yes! You have to behave yourself.' Then he marched off, swaggering his arse from side to side.

'I look forward to that,' I muttered to his back. The staff nurse gave up, and I wandered back to my room, climbing into the bed feeling very tired.

I sat up, looking into the distance at the houses, wishing I could be out there, leading a normal life with no worries. But I don't think I'm going to make it. I'm still in my early thirties, but I feel as if I've lived too many lifetimes.

36

'Ah! Hello, Martha!'

I looked up to see where the familiar screech was coming from. Sister Eleanor was rushing over to me in the bed and dumping down a bag with loads of stuff.

'Now,' she breathed, pulling out a new pair of pyjamas; they still had the Dunnes Stores tag on them. 'These should fit you,' she said, lifting them up to show me. Then she stopped, wrapping the stuff to her chest and whispering, 'Oh! Holy God! What has happened to you at all? Sure, you've wasted away to nothing. Are you not eating?'

I started to feel me belly turning hot with annoyance. 'I'm fine! And if you were all that worried, how come you didn't get to see me when I was taken into Intensive Care?'

She stared at me, creasing her mouth, knowing I was speaking the truth. I know she always dives for cover when there's trouble. The nuns always keep away from that. So I expect it. But what I don't understand is why she is taking such an interest in me now. I could have done with this sort of attention when I was a child in the convent. I worshipped the ground she walked on. But she had no time for me. She was the first person in my life I ever tried to get close to. But it just broke my heart. Most of the time she ignored me. Until I started to scrub and polish floors down on my hands and knees.

They took me out of school to work in the convent as soon as I hit my fourteenth birthday. The judge who sent me there specified and underlined it – I was being sent there for an education. But I knew it wasn't a reality. I was only in the fifth class of primary school. I sat there in a fog of confusion, tying myself in knots, trying to work out what Irish and maths and geography was all about.

But then the words 'Take out your English readers!' Ah! This is more like it! I had taught myself to read! I guzzled up the warm feeling when the teacher praised me no end for even being able to read the book, then pointedly ignored the windbag convent children hissing, 'Yah! Notice box! Suck-up! Eegit!' Then sat down for more, with the day scholars telling me, 'Gawd! Ye're great at the reader! Wish I was as good as you! Here! Have one of me gobstoppers!' I sat sucking while the papers and rubbers flew past my ears, the convent children losing the run of themselves with rage because I got sitting next to the coveted day scholar and her sweets. But that one class was to be my lot in the world of education.

Yep! I had skipped all the other years that come before and after that. I had never really been to school. By the time I got to the convent, it was too late. The nuns need their quota of slave labour to work in the kitchens, nursery, cleaning the institution, and someone to look after their part, which was the convent, chapel and convent kitchen. Plus answer the door and phone. That job fell to me. I had been practising my 'speaking voice'. Developing my manners! Ingratiating meself into the nuns' inner sanctum.

Yep! I landed meself the plum job. Oh, no! Nothing I wouldn't do for a bit of warmth from the Sister Eleanor. A bit of praise thrown in my direction every now and then sent me into a frenzy of pot walloping, scrubbing and shining floors. Anything for a bit more of that! I made 'Wee Slavey' in the *Bunty* look like an idler. Most important too, of course, it got me away from the venom of the other kids. I was an outcast, a street kid among the rejected, the unwanted, the abandoned children dumped in an institution. They were all in it together! Me, I was a blow-in!

I was sweeping the children's dining room, or refectory, one day when the secondary schoolgirls were sitting down eating during their lunch break. One thundering bully started to try and get a rise out of me. I had had many a run-in with her and her gang! She now left me in peace after I grabbed hold of her in the dormitory one day as she and five others tried to corner me and beat the hell out of me. I took her down with me as the bodies piled on top of us. I held her by the hair, with my knees throttling her throat, and wouldn't let go until she called off her 'hounds'. They were pummelling me and only stopped when they saw their leader was getting the worst of it!

Now the best she could do was speak out of the side of her mouth about me to her gang.

'When we leave school, girls, we are all going to get great jobs! Unlike some!' she shouted in my direction. 'They will end up in the back of restaurants, pot walloping in the kitchens.'

I paused, feeling a cold determination run through my veins. Never! I will work hard and I will rise to the top! Just wait and see. I will show the lot of you! I vowed. Oh, brave words! We were all brave then.

We left one by one, each following the other out into the big wide world. Alone, young and foolish! But we had hope in our hearts. Intoxicated by our new-found freedom. We were all grown up! Sixteen! The magic word that got us free from state control. We all set off on the same mission: to find love and security. To have a home we could call our very own. But first: find a job and keep it. I didn't. I kept getting fired! I crept back to the convent, looking for food and shelter. Only for a few days until I was off again after finding a new job. 'No! Sorry! Goodbye! Find your own way! We have no further responsibility for you,' Sister Eleanor was able to tell me. Quite stony-faced, too, she was!

I was confused. I had worked on my knees scrubbing floors, and it was all to please her! I thought she cared about me. No! She had only valued the work I had done for her. I meant nothing to her. She was rejecting me. I had left myself open for nothing.

She turned me away from the door. It sliced my heart open. I knew then I had been used; I was worth nothing in myself. It was like it had always been. I'm only as valuable as what I can give. It hurt me very deeply. More so, I think, than Jackser or the ma ever did. I had gone soft in my need for affection.

I went back down the avenue of the convent carrying my heart, the weight of it dragging my head down to the ground. It was even heavier than the suitcase I clutched in my hand. The feeling of rejection and terrible loneliness was making me feel very old and very much alone in the world.

Some of the girls faced into tragic lives. Life continued to be unkind to them. Some died young, well before their time. My idea of bliss was a mother, a family. That wasn't going to happen now. It was too late. I was a grown-up of sixteen years old, with the desperation for love a starved waif has for grub. I didn't know where to look. Men only use you, and women let you down! What to do?

I did find love when I most needed it and least expected to find it. He filled my soul, penetrating my heart very deeply, right to the core. But it was not to be. He went his way, and I went off to face a world with a hole in my heart that could never be filled. The pain it left was like having open-heart surgery without the anaesthetic.

I went on to have a child. I called her Sarah. I had little to offer her father. No matter. We were both young. He went his way, leaving me the gift of Sarah. My spirit gave up looking for love. But the loneliness never really left me. I could never leave myself open to people again. Sarah was relying on me, and I couldn't afford to go through that sort of pain again. I simply looked on everyone with a jaundiced eye. Especially men! I carried a torch for only one man. Who knew what the future might hold? My love lasts a lifetime. So may his yet! I had hoped.

My grief at Sister Eleanor turning her back on me – that rejection slowly turned to mistrust. I never again worked hard for anyone. If I could make money for others, I didn't. I made it for myself and Sarah. For her, really. She was the great driving force spurring me on. Anyway, I had to work on my own, because I kept getting fired.

Now she comes when I'm a grown woman and it's too bloody late. I don't trust her! Particularly after she didn't bother to come and see me in Intensive Care. I could have been bloody dead. And the only one who could claim me is bloody Charlie. He can't even take care of himself! He always relies on me. I'm still his mammy!

That fella couldn't organise a piss-up in a brewery! I would probably have ended up in a pauper's grave! No funeral! I wanted to go out with Louis Armstrong singing 'What a Wonderful World'. That always makes me cry! Then Edith Piaf singing her heart out. Her voice blasting out of a ghetto blaster, singing, '*Non, je ne regrette rien*'. Finally, as they wheel me out of the church, to take me to my final resting place, they can play the song from *Midnight Cowboy*: 'I'm goin where the weather suits my clothes'. Lovely.

Yeah! A funeral like that poor black woman got in the film *Imitation of Life*. Her rotten daughter rejected her because she was black and only a servant! Some daughters should be drowned at birth! The young one wanted to pass herself off as white, so she pretends her mother doesn't exist, leaving her poor mother to die of a broken heart! I cried buckets at that. I insisted on watching it with my friend Lucy when they showed it again over the Christmas. Me and Lucy sat on the sofa with me staring, waiting for the sad bits, my mouth open, ready to cry! I could see the poor mother and me had a lot in common. Both of us losing our daughters in a very cruel way. Well! Mine left home, leaving me with nothing to mother. And she still only half-baked!

I waited for Lucy to remark on that, but it passed completely over her head. Cretin! She has no kids yet! But the poor mother had a huge funeral, with everybody from the neighbourhood coming from far and wide to squeeze into the church. It was crowded because she was respected and loved by everyone, except the daughter!

A huge choir sang, and the area outside, never mind the church, was covered in flowers. With everyone screaming their lungs out in pain at the loss of the lovely mammy! I held me breath waiting for the young one to turn up! She did – at the last minute. She was the last one to find out! She threw herself on the coffin, prostrate, and sobbed until her heart was broken. Serves her right! I hoped Sarah would throw herself on my coffin, weeping and gnashing her teeth! I could leave her a note sayin, 'I'm gone! Ye're too late!' Hmm! Lucky I didn't manage to top meself. At least now I can organise my own funeral.

Hmm! Poor Charlie! He's actually more intelligent than me. He told me that when I was sent away he had to go to the convents to get the bread. But when he got anything extra, he didn't bring it home to the ma. He ate it himself! 'Tha way, Martha, she wouldn't keep after me te get her more. Like she did te you! I saw how she tormented ye when ye brought anythin home. Always wantin more the next time. So I wasn't goin te get caught like tha!'

'Yeah!' I said, shaking my head. 'That was a very good idea! But I always liked to keep the ma happy.'

'Yeah! Well, tha was your mistake! I never made tha mistake! They thought I was too stupid, so they didn't expect anythin from me.'

Yeah! My little Charlie! He ran away from them when he was still only a kid. No more than around ten or eleven years old. He survived the best way he could, sleeping rough. I caught up with him when I was still only a teenager, just after I had Sarah. I've been looking out for him ever since.

Yeah! I taught him the facts of life and warned him about women! Yeah, we stuck together, I still mammy him. But his spirit was broken long before I found him again. Intelligence is not much use to you when the life is gone out of you.

'Where are you? Are you listening to me, pet? Martha!'

I snapped my head up, clearing me eyes, trying to come back to my senses. 'Yeah? Sorry! What were you saying?'

'You were miles away!' she said, staring at me with a puzzled look and a half-smile frozen on her face. 'Are you all right?'

'Yeah, yeah! I'm grand. Sorry, me mind just wandered,' I said, not wanting to give her any information because I'm wondering what her real game is. Nuns do nothing for nothing. They always have a hidden agenda.

'How's the house, Sister Eleanor?'

'Oh! I don't know, pet,' she said, leaning into me, looking like butter wouldn't melt in her mouth.

'So you don't know what happened to the dog, Bonzo?' I felt like crying. It wouldn't have hurt her to check on the bloody dog. My house is on the way here, for God's sake!

'Do you know where my house keys are?' I asked her, beginning to panic at the thought of all I had left behind, and now anything could have happened to the house.

'Yes! Oh, yes! I have them safe, Martha.'

'Oh, great!' I said, feeling me worry ease a bit.

'And look what I have got for you.' She held up two packets of tobacco and papers. That cheered me up.

'Thanks,' I said, taking them out of her hand.

'Would you like me to call to the house and check if everything is all right?'

'Yes! Yes, please! Will you do that? When can you check?'

'I'll do it straight away after I leave here,' she whispered, slapping and squeezing my hand.

I gave her a watery smile. Still not trusting her. She will put herself out for you, providing it does not cost her anything! No, I'm not putting myself in the position again, thinking I can rely on her. She could turn on me any time! But still and all, I'm glad she's here now. I'm just grateful she can keep an eye on things for me. Even come up to see me and bring me the odd bit of tobacco. It's better than a kick up the arse!

'While you are there, Sister Eleanor, will you pick up a few things for me? Some clothes and wash things, and my make-up bag. That's on the dresser in my bedroom. You can put all the stuff in the suitcase; it's on top of the wardrobe.'

'I'd be delighted, Martha darling!'

I cringed, hearing her say that. It sounded so insincere! But she was the only one who seemed to bother; everyone else has their own lives to get on with. I suppose she thinks it's her duty to 'help the girls'. It didn't give me much confidence, seeing myself on her list of charity cases.

'I better get back to the convent, Martha. It's getting late, and I'll come again soon.' Then she leaned over to kiss my forehead and started to move to the door.

'Sister Eleanor!'

She stopped at the door, looking at me.

'Will you check and see how Bonzo is? I'm worried about him.'

'Where would I look, Martha? Sure, I don't know,' she said, hesitating.

'Try the neighbours!'

'Right so,' she said, smiling. 'I'll do that. I'll give a little knock to next door and see if they know anything.'

'Thanks, Sister,' I said, cheering up.

'Goodnight now, and God bless!' she said, waving at me before tearing out the door.

I opened the bag, taking out a small box of chocolates and a packet of biscuits. And there was a long thermal nightdress, probably like the one she wears herself, I thought, wondering what the Russian monk would think of me in this!

37

'G ood morning!'

I opened my eyes, hearing the rattle of the water jars.

'Are you awake?'

I looked up, squinting, seeing the Russian monk staring down at me, looking like he was examining an interesting specimen.

'You must go to breakfast now,' he said, pushing the trolley out of the room.

I turned over on my side, snuggling down into the warmth, my eyes closing, drifting back into oblivion. I gave a big sigh of contentment just before I started to sink deeper.

'OUT OF THAT BED!'

My heart leapt with my head swinging off the pillow, seeing red, and I leapt up, finding meself sitting on the side of the bed before even I knew what was happening.

I was grabbed by the arm and swung onto my feet.

'Dressing gown!' the voice boomed. It was whipped around my shoulders, my arms pushed through. I was swung towards the door, prodded in the back and pushed through it.

'Dining room!' roared the Sister.

I looked back at her in her dark-blue frock with white pinstripes and a white-linen collar, with a starched-linen Anne Boleyn bonnet on her head and a black belt around her waist.

'Yes! I am behind you. There will be no more nonsense out of you today, my lady!'

I swept past the other stragglers. The Dragon lady was causing a wind behind me that sent me moving faster on my feet.

'Come along, ladies!' she said, sweeping up the slow, bothered and bewildered, and piling them all behind me.

Nurses flew around, delivering plates on the tables and giving a quick look to Dragon lady before rushing off to get more plates. A plate was slid under my nose as I sat down. I looked at it. Two rashers, two sausages, a nice-looking fried egg – soft! – and one fried tomato cut in half. Toast was slid into toast racks, everyone keeping an eye on the Dragon lady.

I looked up to see the monk gliding past me, hanging on to one plate, held high in the air, with the other hand in his pocket. He had a 'Mona Lisa' smile on his face as he glided past me. And when I caught his eye, down came the thick-brush eyelashes, and when his eyes appeared again, they were looking away with disdain. All this without moving a muscle in his face!

The plate was swept from under my nose, sailed through the air, and a voice said, 'Come along, madam!'

I looked up to see the Dragon lady marching down the room and landing my plate at an empty table. She sat at one end and pointed to the other end. 'Sit!'

I sat down, looking at the plate, not hungry any more. My stomach closed up.

'We will sit until you eat! Now begin, please,' and she pointed to the plate.

I looked at it, then looked away. Nurses were giving sly glances, and the staff nurse gave me a little wave and a wink, then nodded her head slowly up and down as if to say, 'You won't get the better of Sister!'

This annoyed me. Oh, yeah? We'll see about that! I sat back in my chair and folded my arms slowly, and settled my eyes, quietly examining the Dragon lady, who sat facing me.

She sat with the stillness of a statue and eyeballed me back. Her white face had never seen make-up, and the skin was pulled tight around to her ears. Big faint freckles crept across her nose and dotted her forehead. Her ginger hair, now turning silver, was rigidly disciplined to stay in a straight line, with a parting in the middle, and rolled into a knot on the back of her head. Not a muscle moved in her face, nor was there a flicker in her fading grey eyes that showed tinges of green.

'I can't,' I said, breaking the silence between us. I pushed the plate away with two fingers.

'Why not?' she snapped

'If I knew that,' I said with a sigh, 'I wouldn't be here.'

She stared at me, her eyes flickering with interest. 'You are stubborn,' she said crisply, 'and you allow people to dictate your emotions! But you chose to punish yourself. Please engage your brain. You have a good brain, but you are not putting it to good use at the moment. If you die, you will not have options. Disregard your emotions in this instance and use your brain. Allow that to take control, and if you do rationalise you would like to die, then you will have that option. Now, you are running out of time. It is almost three weeks since you ate, and you are very weak. We may have to send you to hospital, where you will be force-fed.' She allowed air out through her nose and folded her hands on the table, letting her piercing eyes bore into me.

'I have no reason to want to live!' I said, thinking of the futility of bothering to face day after day.

'Nature does not allow time to stand still. Eat, and your time will come. Give yourself one option. Wait for that time. Nothing ever stays the same. Start by eating a piece of toast.'

I picked up the toast without realising what I was doing and started to nibble it. It was dry and cold. I picked up the knife and started buttering it. It tasted a bit like straw. My taste buds were gone. Then I dipped it in the egg, and it felt nice to be eating. I finished the toast, washing it down with tea, and sat back.

'Nurse!' the Dragon lady dropped her head to a little dark-haired nurse who was standing beside a patient at the next table. 'You may take away that plate,' she said, nodding to my plate.

The nurse rushed over, grabbing my plate. 'Let go! I'm not finished,' I said, thinking they were very presumptuous, and glared at the Sister. 'I'm not finished! I said coldly, annoyed with her.

I sat munching on my rashers and dipping more toast into the egg, enjoying the pleasure I had allowed myself. It's not just weeks since I ate. It's been a very long, long time since I allowed myself the pleasure of eating this much food. I finished everything on the plate, mopping up the last of the egg yolk with the last of the toast – four pieces! I enjoyed that, I thought, staring at the empty plate, then lifted my head to look around me. The dining room seemed crowded somehow.

I looked around, my vision clearing, and the Sister was sitting with a cat-that-got-the-cream look playing around her face. Hatchet-face was standing next to her, and Jam-jar from the men's ward.

There were grey suits and white suits and nurses and most of the male ward staff were here! The kitchen women were standing and staring, and all the patients were bloody looking at me. More people came pouring in the door and started whispering to each other and staring over at me. Wonder what's happening? What are they looking at me for? Then an arm wrapped itself around my neck and Katie screamed into my ear, kissing my cheek. 'You ate that! You ate the lot!'

'Oh, yeah!' I said, understanding. 'I'm eating! She annoyed me!' I pointed to the Dragon lady, who said nothing but just shook her head at me, smiling.

God! I'm eating again. Now I won't be so weak. Ah! I thought. The tom-toms were in action. They're just happy I'm eating after all this time. Word spreads fast in this place! Then it hit me. I'm in a place where people care whether I live or die! I'm accepted! They see the madness coming out in me. They see me at my worst! Yet to them I'm still Martha. Suddenly, hot tears started pouring down me cheeks. For the first time in me life, I know what it feels like to belong. Yeah! Even if it is the mad house!

I was lying on the bed reading when I felt the air change around me and a shadow come creeping in. My head shot around to see the Russian monk stalking into the room. I watched him make his way on feet lifting and softly landing on the carpet. I have never seen an Irish person walk like that. It is the way the Italian gigolos walk when they're pushing the old ladies in their wheelchairs along the French and Italian Riviera. I have seen them. The women stare out through Gucci sunglasses, keeping their expensive freshly coiffured wigs in place, with an ugly-looking rat sitting on their laps that's supposed to pass for a dog. They puff and clench their false teeth on long silver cigarette holders and get Gigi the gigolo to run, upsetting his hairdo, because a couple of hairs are blowing on his lovingly nurtured head. Now his swagger is ruined. Because he has to take a few extra steps to get himself moving. 'Sugar Mammy' has demanded he run to the nice little man there and fetch her a cornet. *'Where, my sweet little rose petal?'* he squeaks, turning his head slowly, anxious to do her bidding. *'Don't you see? The little fat man! He is serving ice cream from his little cart.'*

'What are you reading?' the monk asked, bending down to look at the cover.

'*War and Peace,*' I said with due gravity, feeling incredibly intellectual. I could just as easily be caught reading *The Beano*! I kept that thought to myself.

'So!' he said, lifting himself to his full height. He's not that tall, I mused, looking up at him. Then he stuck his barrel chest out. But he is so – I took a sharp intake of breath – incredibly well packaged. The lunch I just had – second meal of the day – was doing its work. Getting my life force moving.

'Sorry! What did you say?' I asked, shaking my head, the mind always wandering.

'You like the Russians?'

'What Russian?' I stared at him, my eyes crossing in confusion.

'This book!' he said, stabbing my book with his big thick index finger, then waving his hands, looking very annoyed.

'Oh! You mean Tolstoy. Oh, yes, eh, I like the Russians very much!' I said, giving him the once-over. His lovely blond hair, it changes colour every time I see him. Today it's definitely all gold! And his 'Oh! I'm so sleepy' eyes are pools of raw sex! I stared at his face – gold! No! It's honey-coloured, and his nose is chiselled to perfection. What a handsome brute!

'Have you read this?' I asked, trying to get a breath.

'But of course!' he said, waving his hands. 'I have studied all the classics,' he said, putting the full force of his eyes on me. Searching through my eyes, trying to get to my soul, looking for my secrets. My eyes glued to his every movement. If his hand moved, my head shot to follow it. If a muscle twitched in his face, I caught it, drinking him in.

God! I've got it bad. Never before have I chased a man. No, definitely not. I'm usually running for my life in the other direction! This is great fun!

He walked over to the window, gazing off into the distance. The distance between us was too great for me; he had walked three feet away from me. Without taking my eyes off him, I climbed out of the bed, leaving one foot between us. I'm not brazen! I don't like to let men know if I'm interested. I prefer they first nail their colours to the mast. I can't cope with rejection, and I don't like humiliation. So I keep my emotional distance. Let them do the running!

'Why are you not out there? Why must you be here?' he suddenly boomed at me, with his plummy, deep velvet voice still singing off the walls and bouncing back to land in my ears again. I followed the sweep of his big strong hand, attached to the powerful masculine arm, and sucked in air, my head giving a sudden rattle with the breath getting caught in my windpipe. I leaned on the window, looking down at the small specks of houses.

'I don't know,' I said, feeling my heart sinking down into my belly. 'But I ate this morning!' I said, smiling up at him, feeling hope creep up my chest.

'Yes, I know,' he said, keeping his face still, speaking quietly. Then he turned and wandered out the door as if we had not spoken to each other! I watched him go, still trying to make him out.

38

I woke up, giving a big stretch, curling my toes to the end of the bed, or at least trying – I'm not that long.

'Come for breakfast!'

I lifted my head, squinting in the direction of the voice. The voice came from the arse waving at me as it pushed the water-bottle trolley out the door.

'You must get up now,' the arse said, in a mournful monotone.

The Russian monk! I felt cheered. The sight of him makes my day.

I leapt out, grabbing my dressing gown, heading off to the dining room. Right! Where will I sit? My eyes peeled around the room and fell on a glamorous-looking blonde in her forties. She was sitting next to an elderly woman in her sixties who was talking away ninety to the dozen. But the blonde wasn't paying a blind bit of notice to what the woman was saying. She was more interested in giving me her attention, or more, the long rubber rollers I had plastered all round my head.

Sister Eleanor had finally managed to stagger in, bringing me up a huge suitcase full of stuff. She must think I'm moving in here permanently. But it's great having my own stuff. I marched over to the table with the blonde, and she stared up at my hair rollers with the ends pointing up to the ceiling, giving the impression I'm giving the V sign to everyone.

'Hi!' she said, giving me a flash of her snow-white capped gnashers.

'Hi!' I said. 'What's for breakfast?' I asked, sitting down next to the old woman.

'I'm having the bran, with a fry-up,' said Blondie, pointing at her plate. 'It's good for the bowels!'

'Yeah!' said the aul one. 'There's an awful lot of cancer of the bowel these days. I think I'll have some. BROTHER!' and she turned around with a mouthful of sausage and gave an unmerciful scream. 'Can I have a bit of bran for me bowels!' Spitting sausage everywhere and spraying me.

I jumped up, saying, 'Aw, fuck! Mind where ye're bloody spitting!' and rushed around the table, planking myself next to the blonde. She was screaming laughing, and I grabbed the serviette and started wiping my face. I was disgusted and glared at the aul one.

'We were all young once,' she snarled at me, jiggling her false teeth up and down. 'Your turn will come soon enough, an be the state of ye, you won't have long to wait!' she sniffed, pointing her fork at my skinny body. Then she dug her fork into a big fry-up, loading her mouth with half an egg, sausage and a bit of rasher. Then dripped it down her chin, landing a bit of egg after it. I watched it flop onto her big chest, and she bent down, ready to lick it up, but then thought better of it and used the fork to scrape it off, losing her false teeth, and the whole lot landed on her plate. The blonde went hysterical, leaning herself into the table, screaming with the laugh. Then she landed her elbows on her plate, bashing her fists on the table, trying to get a breath. I watched the rasher clinging to her black mohair jumper, and the lovely white-pink egg ending up all squashed.

The aul one muttered, 'The curse a Jaysus!' as she rubbed the bits of runny egg off the teeth and shoved them back in her mouth.

'Ah, fuck this! I'm not sitting here!' I looked around for somewhere else to sit. Too late! All the tables are full. The nurse clapped down a plate of rashers and sausages and fried egg for me, and a bowl of bran for the aul one.

'Are you all right, Maggie?' the nurse said, taking the plate from Maggie.

'Will ye leave me to eat me breakfast in peace?' she said, grabbing back the plate with the bit of rasher left.

The nurse grinned, throwing the eye at me to see if I was going to eat. I was starved and started to make short work of it before she even left the table. Even Maggie was not going to put me off eating all around me.

'Where did you get those rollers?' the blonde asked me.

'In the chemist,' I said, looking to see what else I could eat.

'Your hair will hang in long sausages,' the blonde said, laughing and eyeing my curlers.

'Yeah! I'm hoping to play Bette Davies in the remake of *What Ever Happened to Baby Jane?*' I said, keeping my face neutral.

She started laughing like a horse neighing! Then Maggie waved a slice of toast with half a pound of butter lathered on and roared excitedly, 'I saw tha fillum, years ago! Me an me poor husband did. He's dead now, Lord rest him! Tha one tried te kill her poor sister! An she in a wheelchair! Helpless she was! Yeah! I remember it now.

'We sat eatin tubs of ice-cream, an yer woman was after the sister's house! Tha's right! It's all comin back te me now,' she said, staring into the distance, with her eyes fogging over and her mind flying back down through the years. 'It was over . . . Oh my God! It must be twenty years or more since that fillum was made.'

'Plates! Give me your plates, ladies!'

My head shot up and I was staring into the eyes of the Russian monk. He flopped down his big bushy eyelashes, turning away from me with a bored expression. I was disappointed – not even a smile! Blondie swished herself around, sticking out her chest and crossing her legs, showing off her silk Christian Dior chocolate-coloured frock that clung to all her curves, and gave him a big smile, showing off her horse's gnashers.

'Ohh! You're back on duty, Brother Sebastian.'

'Yes!' he said, giving her a come-to-bed smile with his sleepy eyes, and letting them sweep all over her curves!

She ran her greasy hands all over her belly and up under her ample knockers, sighing. 'Oh! You feed us too well here. I'll have to go on a diet when I go home!' she breathed in a whiny, little girl voice.

I looked at her with disgust. You would think an aul one her age would have more sense! Carrying on like that!

I was raging. Then fuck-face, the Russian, gives her a big grin, and says, 'I think you will get all the exercise you need from your husband when you get home!'

I was shocked and stared at his face. He was staring, with a glint in his eye, and forgetting to collect his dirty plates, as he busied himself getting comfortable, crossing his ankles and leaning his arm on Blondie's chair.

'Oh, so you like married women?' I snarled, glaring at him.

'Of course! They are more fun than the young girls!'

Blondie cackled like a witch and had the cheek to put her arm around his shoulder and bring his neck down to whisper in his ear.

I watched him listening, his arm going around her waist. 'Ohh!' he said, lifting his head and widening his huge green eyes. I never really got a good look at them before. 'You are a very naughty girl!' he said, waving his finger at her.

'Ah! There's many a sweet tune played on an old fiddle!' crowed Maggie, sucking on her false teeth and drawing up her arms. Then she wrapped them around her chest, as she lifted her shoulders, giving her head a shake, showing a glint in her eye. 'Oh, indeed, there is!' she muttered, watching the two of them enjoying themselves no end.

I sat glaring at the monk with my arms crossed, my hair rollers standing up on my head, knowing I would have to do something about this before the blonde one grabbed him from under my nose. 'Where are you from, Maggie?' I asked, ignoring the two.

'I live over this side now. But I was born an reared in the Liberties.'

'Ah, no? So was I!' I said, looking at her, delighted to meet someone who wasn't originally a culchie.

'Well, ye certainly wouldn't know it te listen to you! Where'd ye get tha accent from, might I ask?' she said, looking like I had committed a crime.

'I gave meself elocution lessons, Maggie!' I said, looking at her lived-in face, as she chomped on her false teeth, narrowing her eyes with suspicion, trying to make me out. 'It's a long time now, Maggie. I'm living over this side for years.'

'Whereabouts did ye live?' she asked me, narrowing her eyes to slits, not believing me.

'Just off Thomas Street.'

'Oh, yes! I know tha well, very well indeed. Sure, I used te go te school in Francis Street. Oh, yeah! And all them before me. Oh, indeed!' she said, lifting her chest and leaning her head over, nodding it slowly at me, wanting me to know she's an expert, and there'd be no fooling her on the Liberties. Then she went quiet, letting her mind wander and her eyes fix into the distance, getting lost in her memories.

'OK,' the monk said slowly, with a big sigh of contentment as he lifted himself up off the blonde's chair after nearly suffocating himself with his head stuck in her big chest while supposedly only leaning over her shoulder, feeling the mohair, wanting to know what kind of wool it was. 'It is time to move, ladies.'

I gave him a filthy look and took off out of the dining room, saying goodbye to Maggie. The blonde stood up, balancing herself on huge high heels, and pulled down her silk frock that was nearly exposing the top of her knickers. Then she bent down and ran her hands the length of her legs, pulling her nylons up, exposing her meaty thighs, and wriggled her arse to let her frock sink down, trying to look sexy. Then she coaxed her hair to stand up in a wave on the top of her head.

I was looking back with my mouth hanging open in disgust. 'She thinks she's bleedin Marilyn Monroe!' I snorted, heading out the door. And she giggled, clattering out of the room behind me, saying, 'I'd better get ready for occupational therapy. Brother Sebastian has just told me he's taking us down.'

My heart gave a leap! Right! I'm going down there too. I took off for the bedroom, grabbing my washbag and towel, heading into the bathroom for a quick bath. When I get out, I'm going to make myself look gorgeous. My heart started leppin with excitement. It's me or the blonde! No way is she getting her red-nail-polished bony fingers on him!

I galloped from the bathroom out of breath, still trying to steady my pins after starving myself for so long. Now for the make-up bag. I emptied the lot onto the bed, whipping up the make-up and wetting the sponge, trying to smooth it all over my face. I squinted into a little hand mirror and relaxed my face, hoping to see beauty. 'Jesus!' I gasped, staring at myself with disappointment in the mirror. I look like someone resurrected, plastered with make-up, and now there's a grinning skull leering back at me. I might look better with eye shadow. Deep brown for the lids, now lighter gold above that. I stared – not bad! Now white-pink for under the eyebrow. Hmm! Now two layers of mascara! I blinked. Aah! Fuck! I smudged my eyelid!

'You are coming now, please, with me, to therapy?'

My head swung around in shock. Ah, fuck! The monk! I stared with my black eye, watching his eyebrows raise slowly, his eyes dancing in his head, his mouth ready, wondering if it was worth a good laugh. Then he decided it wasn't worth the effort. He lowered his lashes and his nostrils flared as he lifted his face away, heading back out the door.

'Oh, yeah! Don't go without me!' I roared at his back. 'Sister said I'm allowed down today!' I mewled, the steam going out of me, feeling very foolish.

'Yes!' he said, looking back over his shoulder. 'But if you are not ready in . . .' and the creep looked at his watch, as if he could go off quite happily without me, then looked again at my black eye and said, flapping down his brushes, covering his eyes and turning away, leaving me with the heart sinking inta me belly button, feeling disappointed I couldn't make meself good looking, '. . . ten minutes, we shall leave without you.'

Ah, go and fuck yourself! I wanted to scream with annoyance, embarrassment and humiliation

I swung back to my mirror, staring, trying to figure out what I was doing wrong. I can't get that glamour look of the blonde! 'A thousand curses on the lot of them,' I snorted, roaring at the door, then whipping my face back to the mirror and staring. Right! Rub it gently with the finger. This is excruciating, trying to rub off the black without taking off the eye shadow and starting again.

I was anxious to look beautiful and get moving before the blonde had too much time with him. Now, suck in the cheeks. Jaysus! I looked like death warmed up! Now, brush on rouge from the cheeks to the brow, a little on the chin. Lovely! Then I sucked in my lips. Now for the lipstick. Try putting on different colours, see what it turns out like. I peered closely at the result of four different colours. It's sort of green, looks a bit like gangrene of the mouth. But it's different! Yeah! Leave it on. I peered in the mirror, blowing kisses at meself. Hmm! I look interesting. Right! Get moving.

I threw everything back in the bag, then had another look at meself, staring in the mirror, still not sure. Huge haunted and hunted eyes stared out of a skeleton that looked like a tragic figure just arriving out of Auschwitz.

No! Not really the picture I had of myself standing aloof, sucking on a long silver cigarette holder with a black More's cigarette sticking out of the end, examining the monk through grey smouldering eyes and blowing big wafts of smoke into his face, watching him squirm, but unable to turn his head away, mesmerised by my beauty!

Yeah! A woman of mystery. A bit like Marlene Dietrich. I could even get her height if I wore twelve-inch knee-high leather boots. Yeah! I better start eating. I need at least two stone to get me up to eight stone. Eight and a half would give me the sexy curves of the blonde!

Right! Out with the curlers and on with a white high-necked Victorian blouse and a black dress. Eleanor thought it was a jumper. I stared down at my matchstick legs smothered in a pair of winter black tights. Not bad. Could be worse! Then I lifted the front of my hair and gathered up the lot, pinning it back with a ruby-encrusted slide I bought in Harrods. The only thing I bought there! Now for a dab of Christian Dior perfume behind the ears in case I think of something sweet and interesting to whisper in the monk's ear. Hmm, if I can distract him from the blonde!

Then I raced into the bathroom to get a look at myself. Grand! The hair looks classy and Victorian, with the neck encased in the lovely blouse. A black silver-buckled clip-together belt wrapped around my waist and black Italian slip-on shoes finish the look. Not bad! Pity about the legs, though. They need a bit of feeding for the shape. I lifted my shoulders, taking a deep sigh of satisfaction – I hadn't seen myself looking nice for a long time – and wafted out to find the monk.

Everyone was standing and sitting around waiting. A few visitors were talking to the patients. One of them turned to smile at me. I lifted my chin, giving a smile, not really interested. No sign of the monk, or the blonde for that matter! I wonder where they are?

'Hello!' the visitor said, making her way over to me. She had steel-grey hair, cropped short like a man, with a long pointed nose and an anaemic, narrow, sharp-looking face.

A nun! I thought, looking down at her long grey skirt with the white blouse and small cross pinned to her grey cardigan. You can tell them a mile away. Now that they've given up the habit and taken to exposing their heads and showing their tree-trunk legs, they still can't disguise the fact they are all nuns let loose. They have that haunted-and-hunted look on their face, and in their eyes. That tells you they have never lived in the real world. Their eyes lack depth, and their manner is simpering, letting you see they are emotionally girlish and even naive. But then again, I have met some who could rule the world, they are so strong and powerful! And very well up in the ways of the world. But not too many!

'I'm Sister Joan,' she said, handing me her limp white hand to shake.

I grabbed it, giving it a good shake to wake her up. She looked a bit dozy, with her lazy 'I have all the time in the world to listen to your problems' face. She leaned her head towards me, dropping it sideways, smiling, and said, 'What is your name?'

'Nelly Dean!' I said, giving her a poker face.

'Oh! What a lovely name,' she simpered, reminding me of the kind of snotty-nose kid I wanted to kick up the arse because they were so spoilt. 'I haven't heard that name for many a long year.'

I smiled with my chin lifted, saying, 'Yes! It's a family tradition. From the matriarchal line. At least one female is always called Nelly. After a great aunt! Back in . . . Oh, I don't know, some time in the 1700s. She was hanged for cutting her husband up into a lot of little pieces.' I shook my head, staring at her, then shaking my head again in disbelief, thinking about it.

She kept nodding her head up and down, her eyes bulging at me, looking very serious, and couldn't wait to hear was there more.

'Yes!' I said sadly. 'But that wasn't the end of it. Another Nelly brought a meat cleaver to the confessional box and made mincemeat out of the priest for telling her she had to put up with her husband's brutality.' I leaned into her just as she choked on a breath, her mouth open and her eyes bulging.

'He gave her twenty-three children,' I whispered, shaking my head and staring into her eyes. She held her chest. 'And it was after the last one!' I gasped. 'Straight after she was churched, you know!' I said, puffing out a breath in disbelief. 'You know, Sister? When they had had a baby, they weren't allowed to move out of the house, not even cook, until they were blessed by the priest. It was called churching, because women were dirty! They had sex to have the baby. Shocking!' I gasped.

'Yes!' she gasped. 'I have heard of that old tradition.'

I stared at her head going up and down and all round, supported by her left shoulder. She looked mesmerised. 'I'm the last Nelly!' I said.

'The ma thinks the name will die out in the family, especially after me!' I slapped my chest in disgust. 'She thinks it's an unlucky name!'

'Yes!' she said, losing her breath, nodding hypnotically. I was staring so much, fascinated by her reaction, I felt like nodding in unison.

'So have you, eh, had some misfortune?' she asked me, shaking her head the one way now, up and down. Her eyes looking very sympathetic.

'Ah! Indeed I have,' I said, looking very sad. 'I thought all nuns were really the banshee and were out to get me! I had a compulsion to get them first, you know?' I said, watching her eyes blink, then cool down, the heat from the excitement of my family history rapidly vanishing and alarm bells going off in her head, making her eyes guarded. Then she straightened up and looked around the room, making sure she wasn't alone with the patients, and eased herself away from me, trying not to alarm me. She kept sort of smiling, but her mouth didn't open, and it certainly didn't reach her eyes.

'Yes! Well, it was nice talking to you all,' she said, waving at us and heading down to the desk, interrupting the nurses in the middle of an argument. They were arguing about who had to come down with us to supervise. No one wanted to go.

'Ah, Esther! I was down there the last two times. No! It's your turn now. I have to get these reports done! Look!' and she banged her hand on a sheaf of papers, blowing the hair out of her eyes and looking like she would throw the lot of them at Esther, who was taking no notice of your woman. She was busy examining the size of her fat arse. She leaned herself back, craning her neck.

'Do you think my bottom's too big?' she asked, turning the other way for a better look.

'And you'll have help from what's his name,' Orla rambled, staring at her mound of papers, taking no notice of Esther's fat arse. 'Yeah! Your man, the Russian monk!' she said, lifting her head to Fat-arse, then looking down at the papers again, hoping they'd vanished. Then she started to rub her belly, saying, 'Ooh! I think I'll ask Sister for the afternoon off. I don't feel well,' she moaned, getting lost in her own world, staring miserably at her papers and hoping for a way out.

'Oh, all right then! But get them moving,' Fat-arse suddenly said, straightening herself up.

I was listening and started to make for the door. The nun was standing around the desk, waiting for one of the nurses to let her out, and she moved closer to the nurse, not making eye contact with me. She was busy examining the floor, feeling my eyes boring into her. That'll give her something to think about! I was dying to laugh out loud and tell her I was joking, but I think she's beyond that. She looks like she could do with a sweet cup of tea, or maybe something stronger.

Bleedin nuns live in cloud-cuckoo land, with no idea about what goes on in people's lives. I suddenly lifted my arm and shouted, 'Yehoo! Sister! Will ye come and see me again? I don't get many visitors, not since the last time anyway!'

Her eyes searched mine, hers looking really haunted.

'Did I tell you? I got a black belt in karate! That's probably why they had me in lock-up for so long,' I said, looking mournful and thoughtful. 'I was only practising that time! But . . .'

'Goodbye now!' she said, waving at me, her head swinging around to look for the nurse and get the bloody hell out of this place.

I stood looking quite benign, my hands joined together at my waist, a pleasant smile on my face. Then I gave a big sigh, looking around me, knowing she was keeping an eye on me.

The rest of the pack, a priest and another grey-haired nun, came rambling up to the door, shouting, 'Goodbye now!' and waving like we were all lunatics, very pleased with themselves they had done their good works. One of the nurses let them out, and my nun was down the stairs and way ahead of the others as soon as the door was opened.

'I'm ready!'

I got a bang on the arm and looked up to see Blondie grinning down at me. I stared at her from her big black stiletto high heels to her shimmering purple-velvet trousers – they clung to her body, showing her arse and thighs and everything! – up to a low-cut silk blouse, showing a creamy, well-fed pair of knockers being gently caressed by a diamond pendant wrapped around her neck and sitting snugly between the twins. My heart sank. Ah, fuck! I can't compete against that!

'Are we going yet?' she sang in her little girl's voice, giggling like an eegit.

'I think we're probably waiting for the "Queer Fella",' I said, feeling savage with that monk.

'Who's that?' she asked, grinning at me.

'The Russian monk,' I muttered.

'Ohh! He's gorgeous!' she said, looking around for him.

'He's not interested in women,' I said. 'One of the nurses told me he's gay! Just pretends to like the women!'

'No! I don't believe a word of it!' yer woman nearly choked. I watched her face turning sour, letting her eyes wander off to picture the monk locked in a mad clinch with another monk, kicking off their sandals and wrestling out of their brown habits.

'Yep,' I said, looking very disappointed. 'I was after him myself, you know.'

'Really?' she said, hanging on to her pendant and looking very worried altogether. Too much was happening too soon!

'Well, I'm not really all that interested,' she said, looking around to see if she could see him. 'I'm very happily married,' she said, giving a mournful look at the rings on her fingers. The diamonds on that engagement ring would give you epilepsy, it was so glittering. Then she sniffed, looked down at her sexy trousers, and said, lifting her head and throwing it around the room again, looking even more desperate, 'My husband gives me everything! Of course, he's getting on in age. He was sixty when I married him. I was only twenty-eight!'

'God! That must be twenty years ago,' I said, looking her up and down, saying, 'You really are a lovely-looking woman!'

Her eyes lit up. 'Do you think so?' she said, sticking out her chest and feeling her arse.

'Absolutely! You would never think you were just around the corner from being fifty!'

'EXCUSE ME! I will have you know I'm only in my early FORTIES!!'

'What's happenin? Wha are ye's all shoutin about?' Maggie planted herself between the two of us and stood gaping with her jaw hanging down, her eyes bulging from me to Blondie.

'Do I look fifty to you, Maggie?' Blondie roared, her face looking shocked, with her nose letting out air, then sucking in more air through her mouth, leaving her nose wide open and rigid.

'No! Who said tha?' Maggie's head swung slowly around, landing her eyes on me, looking very suspicious and waiting for me to give an answer.

'Ah, no! I didn't mean you look old!'

'Here!' Maggie roared. 'You shouldn't be talkin! Look at the state a you! You're neither fish nor fowl! Sure, wha man would look at the likes a you?'

'Don't you bloody well dare insult me!' I screamed. 'You aul hag!' I snorted, knowing full well I was in the wrong, but feeling demented at the thought it was really showing now just how bad I was looking.

'Who are you callin an aul hag, you dyin-lookin cow? Hold me back before I kill her!' screamed Maggie, waving her massive arms like pendulums.

Blondie started screaming laughing, and all the other patients started shuffling over to get a better look. The nurses dropped their papers and came rushing over, grabbing Maggie, and looking from one to the other of us.

I was examining my nails, and Blondie said, 'Poor Maggie is having one of her turns, Nurse.'

'Who started this row?' Esther asked, looking at me, her eyes glaring. 'Did you upset Maggie, Martha?'

'No! I was just standing here minding my own business.'

'What is the problem here? Ladies! Ladies, please! You have to behave yourselves,' said the monk, swaggering over, taking his time and bringing his hands together like he was going to pray with all the elegance of an aristocrat.

Blondie's head shot around, her eyes sparkling, and she grinned at him as he made his way over, making to put his hand on Maggie and the other one on Blondie.

'Why do you all make this fuss?' he said, looking gently down at Maggie, leaning his face into her. Blondie dropped her hip into him, laughing, and wrapped her arm around his strong, ample, built-like-a-bull waist. The fucking cheek!

My heart was going like the clappers from the excitement of seeing him and the fury at Blondie fuck-face smooching up to him! And they were not taking a blind bit of notice of me! I couldn't allow myself to lose dignity, so I snorted and marched off to wait at the door. Then I turned and screamed, 'Nurse! Would you kindly get on with your job and take us down to this bloody therapy place?'

'Take it easy, madam!' Orla snorted, marching over and taking out her keys. 'Ready, Esther? Take them down before there's a riot!'

The other nurse turned and shouted, 'Stay together, please. I don't want any of you lot straying off!'

We all shuffled up behind her, me breathing heavily down the back of her neck with the excitement, my eyes glued on the key turning in the lock. Then we were out the door. The big exodus was started! I shot past Esther, my legs going like the clappers down the stairs.

'Back here, please!' Esther roared, pointing her finger at me to stay behind.

39

We all shuffled down behind her, watching our step. People still not awake yet walked into others, and some not even moving were getting walked into from behind. It was a nerve-racking business. I was trying not to get landed over the spiral staircase with the heaving bodies behind me. Some people were impatient and heaved the crowd forward, sending me collapsing onto the back of Esther. I was flattened against the staircase, then lifted up into the air like a blown-up doll. She grabbed the banisters, and I hung on to her meaty neck. I was hanging over backwards and tightened my grip on Esther's neck. I could see I was throttling her; her face was turning purple. She dug her elbows into me, fighting for air, a hissing sound coming out of her mouth. I wouldn't let go. Her neck was the only thing between me and a sailing through the air, ending in my sudden death.

'Help!' I squeaked, trying as well to get my legs wrapped around her. My arse was now waving in the air. 'Jaysus! She's going to send me flying!' I croaked, laughing hysterically with the fright, hearing squeaking noises coming out of my mouth. Then she managed to pull forward, and I went with her, then let go as she disappeared under the mass of these bleedin zombies.

I was determined not to go down, and used Esther's arse as a springboard and dived up for air. She came up with me, bracing herself like the Incredible Hulk, sending me flying against the banisters again! I screamed in fright, instinctively grabbing a hold of her collar with one hand and wrapping my other hand around her neck.

'Why do you not fucking watch where ye're going!' I screamed in terror, right into Esther's ear.

'Let go! For God's sake, you're strangling me!'

I was off the ground again, me clinging to her like a monkey. My legs getting swung around as she tried to free herself. She was clinging to the banisters.

The crowd pushed past, pinning us over the staircase. I was looking down, seeing the distance I would fall.

'Ah! Help!' I dug my feet into her, twirled myself around, letting her go, and I was balancing myself on the stairs, grabbing hold of one of the bodies on the way down, and was now on the move again with the heaving mass.

'I'm too bloody light! This skinny body will be the death of me yet!' I gasped, feeling all the blood draining out of me. 'I'm too easily pushed around. I'm light as a feather,' I jabbered to no one. I was shaking like a jelly.

'Get back here! Wait!' spluttered Esther, trying to scream. She croaked, coughed and tried to get her breath, the veins standing out on her neck. Her face was purple. 'You are all going back up to the ward if you do not do as you are told!' Then she stood up, holding her chest, it was heaving up and down, her nostrils flaring five times their normal size. Then she straightened her hat, jamming it on her head, pulled down her frock and pulled the buckle back to the front. We all stared at her.

'Now!' she croaked, pushing her way to the front. I was in the middle of the bunch. 'Walk in single file!'

We all shuffled into line, politely letting other people get there first. No one said a word. Not wanting to be locked back up in the ward. I flew back to the end. The line was now orderly, people now alert, fear in some of their eyes after seeing Esther and me doing the dance of death! Everyone was watching their step and letting the other person in front get down a step before moving.

We made it to the bottom. Then the quick shuffle started again! Cigarettes were pulled out of boxes and handed around. People feeling magnanimous at the thought of our day out. For some of us it was the first time we had been let out. This was an earned privilege!

We walked along passages with glass from ceiling to floor, looking out onto the beautiful courtyard. Then we arrived into a big room. It stretched for about a mile! On the left, we passed little office boxes with glass surrounds. Men wearing white coats and grey suits sat nattering and chatting up the nurses, who sucked in their cheeks, gazing out into the distance, trying to make themselves look interesting and pretend they weren't interested, but taking in every word and smirking at each other, delighted to have all the men to themselves.

We filed past and their heads shot around to take us in. I could see their eyes narrowing, looking out for the troublemakers, and mentally doing a head count. Then their eyes wandered over to the patients sitting along the benches busily painting masterpieces or doing jigsaws. Some were knitting or making baskets.

I wandered over to talk to an intelligent-looking man with grey hair and glasses sitting on his nose. He was reading a book, then suddenly he stopped to have a conversation with the walls. 'It is all the same! All the same,' he said, waving the book around the room. Then he looked up at the ceiling, saying, 'Heavens above! Only I know this; indeed it is I, Lord!' Then he thumped his chest and examined his book again, to read a bit more. I was just about to move off when he lifted his head, staring straight at me. 'Are you the messenger?' he barked at me.

I stared, wondering what he was talking about, then his eyes lit on the woman sitting beside him doing her needlework. He suddenly slammed the book shut with both hands and clapped the woman on the head with it. 'Wake up! Wake up and see the light!' he boomed at her. The woman grabbed the top of her head, rubbing it like mad, twisting her fat, white, freckled face in annoyance.

I stood staring from one to the other. But the woman never once took her eyes off her needlework. She just went back to pulling the needle through the cloth, bending her head deep in concentration, leaving her head exposed ready for another clouting any minute. Because yer man was now talking to the wall again!

I hurried off, feeling very much mistaken about him and certainly not wanting to get brain damaged. I'd had enough excitement for one morning. This place is definitely proving to be a death trap, I thought, as I rushed out of the room.

I headed on to see what else was happening. The crowd behind me started disappearing to the tables. I walked on, looking to see what was around the next partition. All the space on the right was sectioned off, dividing up the rooms. I walked on, seeing faces look up, men and women sitting together. Yeah! This is better, no segregation down here. You need the men for the mix. Otherwise the women start killing each other after a while if there's no men to take the brunt of our frustrations, I thought, getting the picture again of me and Blondie fighting over a fella!

I walked over to see what an interesting-looking fella was doing. He was playing a board game with another fella.

'Hi!' I said, sitting down next to him. 'What are you playing?'

'Backgammon,' he said, looking at me with icy-cool blue eyes. His hair was prematurely silver, with waves going down the back of his neck to sit below the collar of his shirt. I stared at him. Handsome fellow, I was thinking, looking at his tweed jacket and Brown Thomas wine-wool scarf hanging around his neck.

'Do you like what you see?' he asked, his eyes softening with a smile.

'You have lovely eyes,' I said, smiling, 'and great taste in clothes.'

'Thank you! I like the classics,' he said, making a move on the board.

'My name is Martha.'

'Seamus,' he said, taking my hand and giving a firm but gentle shake.

'Push up! I want to see how you play this game,' I said, pushing him with my bony hip.

He moved up, taking the board game with him, grinning at me, showing a lovely pair of natural teeth. 'You are a brazen hussy!' he said with a glint in his eye.

I stared at his eyes again. They had huge depths of sadness. 'How long are you here, Seamus?'

'Thirteen months, one week and four days,' he said crisply.

I was gobsmacked. 'Good God! Do you have a family? Wife and children?'

'No! I never married. Too busy making money,' he said, slapping down the black checkers.

'What business were you in?'

'I made purple money,' he said, grinning.

'Church?'

'Yes! That's what they call purple money,' he said, laughing his head off. 'Now the money keeps me in here!'

'My credits are running out, I think!' said his partner, looking grief-stricken as he scratched his mop of grey hair then fixed his glasses on his ears. 'I think the VHI will not cough up for much longer.' Then he took a deep breath, gathering his shoulders together, and leaned into the board looking very worried, getting lost in his own world.

We sat quietly staring at him. 'I will have to leave soon!' he said with deep gravity, shaking his head sadly to the board like he was announcing the end of the world.

Seamus smiled gently, putting his hand on the other man's, saying, 'You can come back again when you build up your credits.'

Good God! He must be institutionalised! I gave a shiver, wanting to change the subject. 'Who's looking after your house?' I asked Seamus.

'I have a housekeeper; she's running it. It's a big house on a hundred acres. The land is the remains of an old estate,' he said, looking at me to see what I thought of this.

My interest was piqued. He can't be more than forty! But. Ah, no. He's been in this place for over a year! No, I have enough problems of my own! I stared at him and he grinned at me, knowing what I was thinking. Yep! It looks like he might be on the mooch for a woman. No, not me, sonny! Definitely not me.

'There you are!' roared Blondie, staggering around the corner on her stilts. The height of those bloody high heels! I stared down, feeling mad jealous at the style of her.

'Come on!' She grabbed me by the arm, laughing, and said, 'Let's go and play table tennis.'

'That sounds great!' I cheered up immediately at the thought of doing something interesting. I never played that before, but there's always a first time!

I was up and off. 'Bye, Seamus! See you later,' I laughed to him, and took off after Blondie, who was waving her body down to the end of the room.

'We're next, boys!' Blondie shouted at two fellows as I came barrelling around the corner. One of them was Rory.

'Hi, Rory. Look! They let me loose!'

Blondie roared laughing and grabbed the little white ball as it hopped on the table. 'Come on! Time up! Give me the bat,' and she lunged at Rory.

'No! I'm telling the nurse right now!'

'Let go!' roared Blondie, as she wrestled the bat out of his outstretched arm.

I was busy taking in the other fella. I stood gaping, mesmerised. He was wearing a long wine-silk smoking jacket with a lovely white-silk cravat wrapped around his neck, and he had long, curly white-blonde hair. My eyes landed on his face, watching him stare with his head thrown back, an amused look on his red-bow lips. He had a very aristocratic bearing. His face looks the image of Oscar Wilde, dressed like one of the 'dandies' out of the late Georgian period.

'What is your name?' I asked.

'Henry!' he said, looking me up and down, raising his chin in the air like he was daring me to insult his outfit.

'I love your style, Henry! Very romantic!' I purred, moving closer to him. 'How old are you, Henry?' I asked, my eyes glittering at the romance of him.

'Twenty-four!'

'How old?' I roared, all thoughts of romance slipping away as disappointment leapt in to settle on me chest.

'How old are you?' he asked me, striking a pose, flirting with me.

'Too old for you, Henry!' I said, giving him a sour look.

'Good God, woman! I am not the slightest bit interested in you!' he said, sniffing like there was a bad smell under his nose.

Blondie roared laughing, and I stood staring at him snort his way around the room, trying to look imperious. Then I started laughing my head off. 'What sort of women do you like, Henry?'

'Not your sort, my dear!' Then he pompously picked up another ball and batted it at Blondie, who was falling off her high heels, laughing her head off.

'Cheeky little runt!' I snorted. 'What do you mean my sort?'

'If I wish to cuddle up to a skeleton, I can follow my father into the college of surgeons and have my pick! The place is full of skeletons, you would be right at home there!'

Blondie watched my face turning purple with rage and started stamping the floor, trying to get air. She sounded like bagpipes wheezing out the laughs.

'Give me that bloody bat,' I screamed, steaming over to tear the bat from him.

He put his arm in the air out of my reach.

I stood snorting, hands on hips, watching his movements. Then, like lightning, I bounced to the other arm, anticipating he would swap over, and grabbed it. I waved it triumphantly in the air, and Blondie was collapsed on the floor with her legs crossed, tears coming out of her eyes, just as Jam-jar came flying around the corner with Rory on his heels, pointing me out as the robber!

'I might have known it would be you!' he said, making a beeline for my bat. 'Give it here!' he barked, reaching around my back to take it.

I dived out of his way.

'You are not going to bully my patients!' he screeched, the bit of hair flying off his head to swing around his ear, leaving the bald patch on top exposed.

'How dare you, you four-eyed fucker?' I screamed in rage. 'You are the thundering bully! Come and get it, you little pipsqueak.'

The shouts brought other patients in to see what the fuss was about.

'You are going back to lock-up!' he screamed at me, lunging for the bat.

I laughed, ducking out of his way and letting him land on the table.

'No!' shouted Henry. 'Leave her alone. We are finished anyway.'

Jam-jar didn't hear. He was too intent on getting his hands on me.

I shot out of the room, pushing my way through the patients. They all looked like they were having the best day of their life, with the huge grins on their faces. I ran down the room, heading for the door, and straight into the barrel chest of the Russian monk. His eyes bulged in shock, and his hands immediately grabbed my waist, lifting me off the ground like I was a pound of sugar.

'Let me down, you fucking bastards! How dare you treat me with such indignity?'

'Behave!' his voice rumbled like a bear, then he shook me like a rag doll. The man is a bloody tank. I relaxed into the position of being carried under his arm with my arse in the air. It's just as well I'm wearing thick tights! Anyway, there's no point in resisting.

Blondie was nearly asphyxiated. She collapsed herself against the wall, pounding it with her fists, trying to laugh. Big hee-haws sounding like an asthmatic donkey came wheezing out of her neck as she watched the monk carry me with my legs swinging in the air. Then he twirled me around with the greatest of ease and put me standing on the floor.

Jam-jar came pounding down, hauling himself at me and grabbing my arm. He was out of breath and held me with one hand, flicking his hair back with the back of his other hand, and said, looking white as a sheet, with steam coming out of his nose, 'You are going back to lock-up.'

'No! She is OK. I will take care of her,' the monk said, shaking his head and putting his hand on my arm. I don't know if it's to protect me from Jam-jar or to stop me running off. But my chest was melting with pleasure as I stood quietly by, waiting to see who would win the argument.

'No! She's coming with me,' Jam-jar croaked, pulling me away.

'No! It is OK, Bert! I will take this one,' and he waved his arm at Jam-jar, taking me by the arm and marching me down the room.

Bert stood staring after us, and Blondie flew past me, tapping my arm and saying in a whisper, 'I won't be long, I've got to dash to the toilet!'

She puffed her way out the door, crossing her legs like she had deformed hips, flying nowhere in a hurry on her high heels.

'Do you want a cup of coffee?' the monk asked me, suddenly stopping.

'Yeah!' I said, thinking all my birthdays have come at once.

'Let's go,' he said, taking my arm and steering me out the door. Then he slowly put his hands in his pockets and meandered down the passage.

A door swung open and Blondie came flying out, skidding on her high heels straight into us, sending me smack into the monk's belly, big and all as it is. It was like a rock.

'You ladies are in a great hurry today,' he said, reaching out to grab hold of her, pushing me out of the way with his arm.

'Where are you going?' she asked, looking from me to him. I glared at her, taking in the sparkle in her eyes. No wonder she was in a hurry. She was making sure I didn't get to be on my own with the monk! Her glance didn't stay on me long enough to see me wishing she'd broken her bloody neck.

'We are going for coffee. Come!' said the monk, giving her his bleedin arm.

She wrapped herself around him like a fur coat, curling her arm under his. I was forgotten!

My heart sank down into my belly, and I felt the rage coming up to my chest again. That fucking woman is used to getting her own way. Robbing the monk from under my nose. I stood staring after them, and the eegits didn't even know I wasn't moving. They were too busy nattering to each other about sweet nothings! I thought about telling them to shove their coffee up their arse, but thought better of it. I'm not that much of a fool. Hanging on to me dignity is one thing, but letting the way open for fucking Blondie to have him all to herself? NEVER! Hmm! I'll have to think of something.

I took off after them, wondering if I could squeeze in between them, prising them apart. I eyed their hips knocking in unison, keeping step for step. No chance there! So I whipped up alongside them, and my jaw dropped, the heart going crosswise in me chest at seeing the monk listening to Blondie talk a load of rubbish, while he gazed into her face and stroked her hand, telling her she had piano fingers.

'Oh! You are such a charmer!' she cooed and giggled like a sixteen year old, wriggling her whole body in ecstasy. 'No,' she lisped.

'Oh, it is true!' he purred, tapping the top of her nose gently with his finger.

I nearly got sick. I wanted to kick him up the arse, wearing her high heels, and shove her face down the toilet. 'How old did you say your husband was, Sylvia?' I suddenly asked, dripping with venom as I leaned across the monk.

I watched her grab his hand again, like her life depended on it, and look over at me, the light going out of her eyes. For a fraction of a second, I felt sorry for her.

He shook his head slowly from side to side, not impressed with me, then eyed her. This gave her hope, and she lifted her head, spitting over at me, 'Mind your own bloody business.'

The monk lowered his sweeping-brush eyelashes at me, squinting, and said, wagging his finger, 'Martha! You must learn to behave yourself!'

'Excuse me! I only asked a civil question.'

They moved closer together, freezing me out. I crawled behind them, feeling the fire go out of me too. That didn't work! I'm now the one ending up looking foolish. He's speaking to me like I'm a half-witted child. Fuck ye, Martha! Stop acting like one! You are only making a complete eegit of yourself. Anyway! He's definitely only interested in her. Ah! To hell with them!

I turned tail, going back down the passage, and headed out the door into the grounds. Fields! I looked around. Fresh air! I saw a tennis court through the shrubbery and headed for that. Two women were belting a ball back and forth to each other. It looked easy. But I knew it wasn't. I tried that in the convent when I was a kid. The racket sailed out of my hand at the first attempt. Sister Eleanor came barrelling over to me and belted me out of the court, saying I had no respect for property. Nah! I'm no good at that!

I wandered off, spotting an enormous window looking into a restaurant. It was overlooking a huge water fountain spouting jets of water high into the air and sailing back down into the basin. I headed for the restaurant, walking around the window, trying to find the way in.

I ended up at the front entrance to the hospital, with miles of landscaped gardens and a huge plate-glass entrance. This is not the way the ambulance came in with me. I headed into the foyer, where round leather seats sat in a circle looking out onto the gardens. Patients were sitting smoking and gazing out the window. Then I saw the entrance ahead into the restaurant. I sailed past the big reception desk, getting a suspicious look from the baldy-headed woman manning the desk. She stared out at me from a weather-beaten face, looking carefully at me through her milk-bottle glasses.

I lifted my head in the air, looking like I was only visiting, and made straight through the door into the foyer of the restaurant. I stopped to look at a huge fish tank with ugly-looking black fish.

They started blowing kisses at me. I stared, fascinated, and one stopped to stare back.

'Mind they don't bite you!' a voice said, laying a hand on my shoulder. It was a monk in long brown robes. He whipped off again, flicking his thick silvery hair back off his eyes, and looked back at me, giving a huge grin.

I took up my trot again, marching in the door after him, and stood on the top landing looking down into split levels of great comfort.

The view was magnificent, with the spray from the fountain sailing into the air and landing back into an enormous marble basin. Seats and tables were spread out all along the rooms, with very comfortable-looking armchairs mating with tables, and long-cushioned seats against the walls. People were dotted around the place, and one woman was playing the piano. I made straight for that.

She crooned softly to herself, singing moodily, 'He said he loved me. But he lied!' Then she shook her head slowly in despair, sniffing.

I interrupted her melancholic mood. 'Do you play "Chopsticks"?' I asked her, ready to sit down beside her and bang out a duet. I'm not bad on the aul piano, I thought. I play by ear. I had to! Because I got kicked out of the music lessons in the convent even before I had a chance to get started. Hmm. What's changed? I still can't keep out of trouble!

'So!' I prodded the woman; she was ignoring me. 'A duet!' I had my hand poised over the piano.

She glared up at me with a pair of pink eyes. God! She's done some crying, I thought, looking at her. 'No? No "Chopsticks"?' I asked, bending down to her.

'Get stuffed!' she whispered through gritted teeth.

'Right! I'll come back when you're in a better mood,' I said mildly, taking off on my mission to 'find myself' in this place. Therapy! I need something to occupy me. Forget the monk. He's lost his soul to the blonde. She'll eat him alive! I would have been most definitely a much better proposition. But that's his loss.

I looked around, spotting a long passage filled with light and colour and all sorts of exotic plants and tropical trees growing in big pots. I headed straight for that. Out of the restaurant and into another foyer and grabbed hold of the door into what looked like an orangery! Lovely! Wrought-iron tables with iron chairs to match. I sat down, having the whole place to myself, and looked out, enjoying the wonderful trees and shrubs outside and feeling like I'm sitting in the middle of the jungle inside, surrounded by tropical plants and feeling the delicious heat intended for the plants. Ah! This is the life.

I shifted my bony arse, finding a comfortable position, and started to roll myself a smoke. Lovely! I stared contemplatively out at the beautiful gardens and enjoyed the peace.

'Here you are!'

I looked up into the face of Nicola Kelly, a friend I've known for years. 'Do you know how long it took me to hunt you down?' she asked, bearing down on me with her huge bulk.

How the hell did she find out I was here? 'Hi, Nikki,' I said, without any enthusiasm.

'I went up to see you in the general hospital,' she said, lowering her well-fed arse into the steel chair.

I looked at her without answering. She didn't seem to mind.

'They told me you were sent here. What happened? Why are you here? Mind you, it looks like the Ritz,' she said, spinning her head around to admire the place. 'But this is a "MENTAL HOSPITAL",' she said, mouthing the words I was supposed to lip-read, her eyes bulging then fixed on me, waiting for an explanation.

'I knew it!' I said, snorting out through my nose and clamping my lips together. 'They told me it was the best hotel north and south of the border to recuperate after an illness. I was led to believe I was only here on me holidays. Now you are telling me it's a "MENTAL HOSPITAL"!' I leaned in, mouthing the words and looking around to see if anyone was listening. 'No! We're the only ones here. Can you believe it?' I said, shaking my head at her.

She stared, looking the picture of worry, then her face cracked up laughing. 'Bloody hell, Martha. You had me going there for a minute!' she said, giving me a poke in the chest. 'But I still can't understand how you landed yourself up here.'

'Ah, shut up, Nikki! You're supposed to be cheering me up. Not putting years on me with your bloody creepy carrying-on! Now! What did you bring me up? Where's the grapes?'

I looked around at the plastic bag thrown on the ground. 'Oh, yeah! I brought you a bit of stuff,' she said, and she took out a big box of Milk Tray chocolates.

I whipped open the wrapper, dipping my hand in and taking out two – the barrel and the Turkish delight – then pushing the box over to her.

'What happened?' she asked, stuffing two in her mouth, keeping one in her hand, and her eyes flicking over the box, deciding what's next.

'Nothing. I just decided to snuff myself.'

'So I heard!' she roared. 'But why?'

'There is no why, I just did! I got tired of living, Nikki,' I sighed.

'I don't understand! You of all people! No, there has to be a reason,' she said, looking into my face.

'I suppose. I don't really know, and I don't really care.' I felt the life draining out of me, thinking about the state I'm in, and the cold dark life and the emptiness waiting for me out there. I didn't want to face it, and I was barely hanging on here. I could easily get up and walk out that front door any minute and end it all without warning.

'Look! Come on! Let's go into the restaurant,' she said, whipping up the box of chocolates. 'It's more comfortable there.'

I reluctantly followed the box of chocolates.

'Right!' she said, dropping herself down into a cushy seat in the corner where we could have a good view of the restaurant and everything happening around the reception and outside the hospital. 'Gosh! It's really lovely here. What's the food like?'

'Good,' I mumbled, grabbing another chocolate for comfort and before she ate the lot.

'It must cost a fortune to stay in a place like this.'

'I don't know. I'm not paying,' I said through the comfort of a mouthful of chocolate.

'Who's paying for all this, then?' she asked, her eyebrows rising to her hairline.

'How the hell do I know? But I'm bloody well not! I haven't got two halfpennies to rub together. So they can sing for it!'

'You are a scream!' she roared, diving on the box and filling her mouth.

I looked, dipping my hand in. 'There's only one left!' I roared, forgetting she can go through grub like a pile of piranhas.

'Stop fretting. There's loads underneath,' she said, whipping the top paper off. 'Oh! Who's that gorgeous-looking thing making his way towards us?' she said.

I followed her eyes, landing on the monk wearing his leather jacket and throwing his long, silky, gold hair back. My heart went like the clappers. 'That's one of the monks. He's Russian,' I said, not moving my lips.

'Russian!' she said, her lips opening in a sexy smile, her eyes running the length of him. 'Ohhh! What a waste!'

'Yeah! He's supposed to be saving it for God, but he's giving it to a blonde bombshell with huge creamy knockers behind God's back! What a hypocrite!' I said sourly. 'Ah! Don't be looking at him, Nikki! He might think we're desperate for him!' I hissed.

She didn't bloody hear me. Her face was frozen in a ridiculous grin, her eyes glued rigid drinking him in. Bloody dazzled by the Russian fool! As he got closer, she lifted her arse an inch off the seat and stuck out her huge knockers, rubbing her hands under them. I watched as she then stuck them out in a fake stretch, pretending to yawn!

'Ye came to see me, not run off with one of the fucking monks!' I roared, red in the face, my temper rising to the ceiling.

She ignored me, keeping her eyes feasted on him.

'Fucking women!' I said, shaking my head to the wall. Imagine making a fool of yourself over an idiot monk! It could only happen in the loony bin! I was very discouraged by all this competition. Ah! I can't be bothered. The man has no morals! He thinks he's God's gift to women!

'I have been searching for you!' he said.

I ignored him, staring with a puss on my face at Nikki, with the huge stupid grin on her face, flashing from me to him.

'Why do you not stay with me?' He moved himself right in front of me, staring down intently.

I stared indifferently into space. Nikki gasped, saying under her breath, 'His voice is soooo sexy! Lucky thing! I'd love a bed here for the night!'

She kept talking under her breath and staring at him with a thick smile on her thick lips. Her eyes were shining.

'Come! You must tell your friend to wait. Lunch is being served. Come!' Then he took my arm and pointed me in the direction of the lift and said, 'Please go now! You must be trusted if you wish to spend more time out of the ward.'

I walked to the lift like I was in a trance, delighted he was with me. Then, when I looked back because of the silence, I discovered I was standing by the lift on my own. The fucking eegit was heading off down the passage over to the monastery where the monks live. He did it again! He never even said goodbye!

Nikki was standing at the entrance of the restaurant. 'I'll wait here for you. How long will you be?' she shouted.

'About half an hour,' I said.

'OK, I'll get some lunch here!' Then she gave a dazzling smile, puckering her lips and throwing her thumb down the passage after the Russian, and raised her eyes to heaven.

I laughed and got in the lift, leaving her there to wait.

40

I walked into the dining room and stopped, looking around for a free chair. Blondie waved me over, 'Come on! I've kept a seat for you!'

I breezed over, sitting myself down. Suddenly there was an almighty blast from behind me, straight into my ear.

'Where were you, madam?'

I looked up into the red face of Esther. 'You are grounded on the ward! Wait until Doctor hears about you vanishing!' Then she slammed down a plate of bacon and cabbage with parsley sauce in front of me.

My mind went blank with shock. 'Oh! Did you not hear I was out in the restaurant with a visitor?'

'What visitor?'

'The one sitting down there now, waiting for me. Did the Russian monk not tell you?'

'No! No one tells me anything! I was tearing up and down all the morning looking for you! You have no right to leave the therapy room, especially without permission!'

'I went with her and the Russian for coffee. He brought me!' I said, pointing at Blondie.

'Well! He didn't mention it to me!' she sniffed, wandering off and muttering to herself.

'Where did you get to?' panted Blondie. 'I had coffee with Sebastian!'

'Sebastian!' I roared. 'So now you're on first-name terms?'

'God! He's a hulk!' she said, ignoring me. 'We wondered where you went to. You should have stayed, then we could have had a great laugh.'

'NO! You mean you actually managed to squeeze me into the conversation?' I looked shocked, shaking my head with sarcasm, but she wasn't listening.

'Yeah! As it was, he went off to look for you, and I was left on me tod!' Her face fell on the dinner, then she lifted her head and glared at me.

'It was only supposed to be me and him anyway,' I said sourly.

'Stop kidding yourself,' she said, her eyes spitting venom. 'You're not his type. He likes blondes!' she said, patting her hair.

I'll fucking land that dinner on her head in a minute if she doesn't start acting her age. My heart was leppin, flying with the rage. On the other hand, I don't want to go back to lock-up. Enough nonsense, Martha!

'Ah! You're right. He certainly fancies you!' I said, smiling.

'Do you think so?' she gasped.

'Jaysus! Will ye listen to yerselves!' snorted Maggie. 'Neither of ye is exactly spring chickens, but ye're talkin there as if ye're schoolgirls!'

'EXCUSE ME! You old cow . . .'

'Martha! One more sign of trouble out of you, and you'll be marched straight back to lock-up!'

I whirled around, seeing Esther appear out of nowhere. She stood over me, waving her finger in my face. I could see this would give her and Maggie great satisfaction. I'm really fed up with this place; it's like being a child again back in the convent. This is ridiculous! I'm used to being my own person. I'm really fed up with myself. How did I ever get to be so stupid?

I clamped my mouth shut and stabbed at the bacon, glaring at Maggie. She smirked and shovelled a lump of bacon into her gob, rattling her false teeth up and down, showing everything in her mouth.

'They have a geriatric unit here, I believe,' I said, turning haughtily to Blondie.

'Yeah, I think so,' mumbled Blondie, shovelling up a mouthful of cabbage.

'It must be full,' I mused. 'Some are being sent up here!' Then I started eating with relish and throwing a sly eye to Maggie. She stopped shovelling her dinner and eyed me. Her fork stopped in the air, her mouth wide open waiting for it. Then the fork moved closer to her mouth, then paused suddenly, her eyes squinting slowly over to me. I examined my meat. 'Lovely bit of bacon, this!' I said to the air.

'Ye'd better not be passin them remarks at me!' Maggie warned, her eyes looking very vicious.

'God, no, Maggie! Sure, you're in your second dotage.'

'Whadeyeahmean be tha?' she roared, slamming down her fork.

'Nurse! Maggie is having one of her fits!' screamed Blondie.

Esther came rushing over. 'What is it now, Maggie?' she said, sounding worn out.

'This brazen hussy is tormentin me!' she said, waving her fork at me.

'Ah, no, Maggie! No one is upsetting you. We are your friends, aren't we?' I said, looking at Blondie, desperation now hitting me. Lock-up, here I come. Oh, God! Why can't I keep my bleedin mouth shut!

'Yeah, Nurse. She's just upset today.'

'Come on, Maggie. Eat up your dinner and get ready for medication or you'll spend the rest of the day in bed.' Then Esther rolled herself off, muttering, 'I'll kill someone before the day is out.'

I looked at Blondie and we both screeched laughing. 'There's saner people locked up,' I said.

'Ye can fuckin say tha again!' muttered Maggie, pushing and smacking a bit of fatty bacon, then seeing it slide off the plate to land on the table. She lifted her head, snorting, giving us murderous looks. She was raging now because she got herself chastised.

'Ah, we were only having a laugh, Maggie!' I said, smiling at her.

'Ah, I know tha, daughter! I get me moods. But none of us mean any harm. It's just good te be lettin off a bit of steam,' she sighed, her shoulders drooping, the weight of the world on them. I suddenly saw a poor old woman, tired and worn out. She's taken her fair share of knocks and suffering, I thought, looking at her. I felt very ashamed of myself for being so mean.

'Yeah! We're in the right place for that, Maggie,' I sighed, feeling old and tired myself. I wondered was it worth it. I was beginning to think I had failed my whole life. I never thought for one minute I would end up in the mad house.

I stood up, feeling very weary, and went over to Maggie. 'I'm sorry, Maggie,' I whispered, leaning down and wrapping my arms around her. 'You don't need the like of me making your life more difficult than it is.' I kissed the top of her head, and she reached for my hand.

'Ah, no, daughter. Sure, I know ye don't mean any harm by what ye say. Don't you go worryin yerself about me. Sure, it's a long aul road we're travellin, an I'm nearly at the end of mine now. Just you make sure te get yerself better, an get out there an enjoy yerself. Ye're a good girl. Sure, ye haven't one bad bone in yer body,' she said, looking at me earnestly.

'Thanks, Maggie,' I sniffed, wanting to cry. 'Thanks for that kindness, Maggie. You're a lovely woman,' I said, stroking her soft wrinkled cheek in my hand and seeing the kindness in her faded blue eyes and the loneliness looking out at me.

I eased myself up gently, saying, 'I'm off now. I better get going.'

'Where're ye goin?' Maggie asked me.

'I have a visitor! I don't want to keep her waiting.'

'See ye later, then! I'll be stuck down in therapy doin the bloody knittin! It's not knittin I need!'

'No!' Blondie laughed. 'It's a roll in the hay you want!'

'Yeah!' I laughed. 'With a blind man!'

'Get out, ye cheeky cow!' Maggie roared, throwing a bread roll after me.

I ducked and it hit the nurse just as she appeared up off the floor after trying to pick up the scrapings of someone's dinner. It bounced off her hat.

'Stop that! Pick that bread up at once, Maggie Ellis!' roared Esther.

I laughed, making for the door, and dived into my room, slamming the door shut behind me. It's all so bloody childish! I'm going backwards! I never had time for this kind of carry-on in my life. Now, when I'm supposed to have more sense, I'm getting childish. Ah, well. It's better late than never. You can do what you like in this place. Everyone expects it, and no one judges you. Yeah! You can be yourself.

I brushed my teeth, staring at them in the mirror. They're a lovely set of gnashers, not even one filling. Then again, you've never been near a dentist, except to get that wisdom tooth out! I combed my hair and put more lipstick on. Fat lot of good that will do you with the monk. He's only interested in that Blondie with the big knockers! Still! I'm not giving up. The fun is in the chase, and it's getting me back on my feet by putting fire in my belly. That's definitely something to hold on to.

Right! You'll do! I skipped out to the sitting room, ready to go downstairs and meet Nikki.

'May I go down now, please, and meet my visitor?' I asked the nurses. They were standing over the medicine trolley, giving out medication to the patients lining up.

'Not now,' they sighed. 'Medication first. You have to wait. We can't leave the trolley unattended,' they sang, handing out tablets and water to a patient hopping from one foot to the other. Everything stops for medication. Everyone must be medicated. Except me! I put enough inside me to stop an elephant! All eyes were now glued on the trolley. Happy hour!

They watched carefully as the patient took the two big pink pills, and Esther said, 'Let me see under your tongue.'

I stood staring, looking into the patient's mouth.

'Now the back of your throat,' and the woman opened her mouth wide, waiting, until eventually Esther said, 'You can shut your mouth now.'

The woman's jaw dropped open, and she roared, 'What about me sleeping pill?'

'I'll give them out to you later, after tea, Madge!' Esther roared into the woman's face. I jumped back, getting the blast in my eardrums.

I was looking at the woman's face. I don't think she's retarded, and I doubt if she's deaf! Maybe just a little confused. Patronising fucker. She's half the woman's age and has half the experience, that's why she's treating the poor woman in an undignified way. Just because they are on opposite sides of the medicine trolley. Then I thought, on the other hand the nurses have more experience than I do around patients. I'm still ending up getting mighty shocked when someone starts acting differently to what I expect. So, yeah! They know what they are doing. And I would be lost without them at the minute. They really do care. Still! I don't see why I should have to hang around. I have a bleedin visitor!

'I'm going downstairs, Nurse,' I said, heading for the door.

'You'll wait until everyone else is going!' snorted Orla, looking up from her charts.

Esther glared at me, daring me to object.

'Fine! I'll just sit here, watching you ladies work, while I take a nap!'

'Do you not get medication?' a new patient asked me, with her hands wrapped around each other, scraping her feet along the carpet and swinging her head from the trolley back to me, anxious not to lose her place in the queue.

'Nope!' I said, flopping down on the couch.

'Why is that, I wonder?' the new patient asked the ceiling, taxing her head over the idea I was being deprived of happy pills.

'They want to observe me in my natural state,' I said, throwing my voice to the nurses.

Esther gaped at the ceiling, sucking in her cheeks and blowing out her nostrils. 'Here! If you manage to stay quiet for a few more minutes, I'll open the door and let you all out myself.'

'Ah, Esther! Now I know what it is I like about you so much.'

'Don't tell me!' roared Esther. 'I'm trying to concentrate here!'

I said nothing, feeling she was ready to upend the whole trolley. That woman could do with a holiday in here.

The door opened and it was a quick shuffle out the door. 'Single file!' screamed Esther from the back, as we pushed and shoved our way down the stairs, trying to get past the ones stopping to have a think.

We made it down the stairs and onto the passage with smoke coming out of the back of my hair. I whirled around, staring into the face of the new patient. She stared back, her eyes crossing, with the cigarette burning red stopped halfway to her open mouth.

'Watch what you're doing!' I screamed, madly putting out the fire in my singed hair. I whipped it around, staring at it, flaking off the singed bits, and roared in an almighty rage, 'You bloody fucking eegit! Look what you've done to my hair!'

The woman started crying, and Esther grabbed me. 'That's it! I've had enough of you. Come on! Back to the ward.'

My chest went cold, and anger and panic went shooting around my belly. I could feel my head turning cold from the shock. Lock-up! Suddenly I was back to me senses. 'Ah, no, Nurse! I'm sorry!'

I turned to the patient and said, 'I'm sorry, please don't upset yourself. I didn't mean it.' I put my hand on her arm, really meaning it. 'I was just upset about my hair! Nurse! Let me go. I'm making progress. It would only set me back if I'm sent back to the ward.'

We stared at each other. 'OK,' she said, relenting. 'But I'm warning you! Any more trouble, and the doctor will be hearing about it. You can't go upsetting the other patients.'

'No! No!' I said, shaking my head up and down, agreeing with everything.

'Go on, then! And don't set foot outside in those grounds,' she warned.

'Absolutely not!' I said, taking off for the restaurant. As I moseyed down the passage, I could see a crowd down outside the chapel. Monks were pouring out, with smoke billowing all around them, and the smell of incense hit my nose.

I put my head in the restaurant; no sign of Nikki. I looked back down the passage to where the monks were, and she was in the thick of them.

'Nikki! What are you doing? Come on! Let's go into the restaurant.'

'Take a look at this!' she whispered, her eyes on stalks, waving at me to come down. She was all excited.

I saw the parade carrying out a coffin and waved at her to follow me, then headed for the front door. 'Come on out this way,' I said, when she came puffing up behind me.

'It's a funeral! One of the monks must be dead!' she said.

'Yeah! Come on this way, we'll be able to see it better.' I galloped out the front door, heading left, then left again, with her on my tail. We stopped to see the procession heading past us along the path, making for the monks' quarters, on their way to the graveyard. A coffin was slowly being carried by six monks, their heads lowered, covered with the cowls of their brown habit. A long procession of monks, their faces hidden, with their hands wrapped inside the sleeve of their wide habits, were singing the Latin laments for the dead. Leading the whole funeral procession was the Russian monk. He was energetically swinging the thurible, sending incense smoke billowing from left to right. I knew it was him, as I could see the golden hair blowing out from underneath the cowl.

I stopped dead in my tracks, gaping with my mouth open. 'Would you look at that?' I said in a whisper, the sight taking away my breath. 'It looks like something out of a Fellini film.'

The Russian lifted his head sideways on seeing us watching him. It probably occurred to him I was not supposed to be out here! The cowl dropped back off his head, letting the wind blow through his hair. It danced around his head, framing his chiselled face, and the pale watery sunshine picked out the threads of gold running through it. For a split second, his incredibly green eyes lit on us. Then he slowly lifted his arm, covering his head with the cowl, his eyes moving away from us and staring into the distance as we watched his face disappear.

'My God! That monk is like a Greek god!' breathed Nikki. 'I have never seen anyone so handsome,' she said, turning her head slowly to me, her eyes wide in her head and her mouth catching flies.

'Yeah!' I agreed in a whisper. 'Fellini would give his eye teeth to witness this scene. It is so medieval,' I said in wonder.

The procession vanished down a path and around a bend, heading for the graveyard. We couldn't follow, it being out of bounds to us – you have to be a monk. I stared down the path, watching as the monks now disappeared. I continued to stare as their ghosts lingered. Then the mist slowly lifted and the air cleared. A faint, distant, ancient memory stirred deep inside me. A feeling of a more brutal and yet sacred past. I stood rooted, time stood still, a feeling of déjà vu sweeping through me.

I shook my head, closing my mouth, and felt the cold breeze lifting me off the ground. I was light as a feather. Just a bag of bones, really. The place seemed lonely now the monk was busy elsewhere, and I looked at Nikki. She looked so substantial, full of life. Living as she wished, working, happy and getting on with life. I could feel the pull of the grave again. A terrible feeling of sadness and loneliness washed over me. I'm tired of living. There's nothing left I want from life. I don't need it.

I turned, heading in the door, Nikki trailing behind me. I stood looking around me, wondering what to do.

'What's wrong?' Nikki asked, following my eyes around the room. 'Are you feeling down?'

'A bit,' I said. 'Sorry, I'm not much company.'

Nikki looked out at the fountain, a silence between us. 'Look,' she said. 'Why don't you sit down over there? I just want to run to the shop. I suppose I better take my car. Look, sit down somewhere, and I'll be back.'

'OK,' I said, making for a seat in the corner and staring out at the fountain.

The emptiness inside me would probably lift if the monk was here. I wonder why I feel so strongly about him. The one and only time I got involved with a man, he too was like a Greek god to me. He still is. Nothing and nobody can or ever will open my heart like that again. When that flame died, I walked a long and lonely road, sometimes with the terror of getting lost in the dark. There was only one other soul with me, and she needed me to lead the way.

41

I had had my whole life ahead of me. I had just started my first job as a junior typist in an office. No more searching through the 'Domestics Wanted' in the *Evening Herald*. Now I was on my way, going up in the world. I had managed to get myself off the streets when Sister Eleanor refused to take me back.

Life was great! I got myself a little bedsit down on the quays, not too far from where I was born. Everything was going fine. But, of course, I got fired! Lost the job. No problem! I landed another job with an engineering place. The two bosses, they were partners. One of them had a terrible temper, but he was old and his bark was worse than his bite. So I took no notice.

He had eight sons, all grown up. They worked in the firm. One of them was brain damaged from a motorcycle accident. He used to arrive in with his wife shuffling in behind him wearing a huge hat, like she was on her way to Ascot. The make-up on her face was so thick, she obviously shovelled it on with a trowel.

'Martha! Make me a cup of tea!' he would bark.

'No! Make it yourself!'

'Mo! You stay here. I'm going down to tell my daddy on her.' Then he would rush next door and bring in a chair for her to sit down. Then rush off down the passage to tell his daddy on me.

Mo sat across the room, staring balefully at me for being mean to her husband. I sat staring at Mo, enjoying the diversion, admiring Mo's lovely clothes and wondering where she bought her hats and why she has to wear so much make-up. The silence thickened. Then she started.

'Will ye go an get Felix for me? I don't like him leaving me on me own,' she moans and whines.

'He'll be back in two shakes of a lamb's tail, Mo. Don't worry,' I reassured her.

Sure enough, old Neddy would give an almighty roar at Felix. 'Will ye get the hell outa here and stop going on about yer bloody tea! OUT!' Then he would put his head out the door, and roar, 'Martha! Martha! Where the bloody hell is that young one? I'm going to fire her!'

I leapt up. 'Yes, Mr Hammond!'

'Why don't ye answer me when I call you?'

'I didn't hear ye, Mr Hammond.'

'Get on the bloody phone and tell my wife to come here this minute and take him home!'

'Who, Mr Hammond?'

'Bloody Felix! Who do you think?'

'Felix! Where's Felix?' Mo moaned from the corner.

'What about Mo, Mr Hammond?'

'ARE YOU TRYING TO TRY MY PATIENCE?'

'Right! And Mo too, Mr Hammond.'

'I'm persecuted with the lot of them. How the hell am I supposed to earn a living with all these good-for-nothing wasters around me? Huh?'

'Tsk, tsk! You have an awful lot to put up with all right, Mr Hammond,' I muttered at him, shaking my head, looking very sorrowful.

He would then turn his huge bulk and stamp back down to his office, muttering under his breath. Then give his office door an almighty bang. Felix came flying back into the office.

'Martha! My daddy said you are to make me a cup of tea or he's going to fire you.'

'Nope! He did not. And if you don't stop tormenting me, I'm going straight up to tell your daddy on YOU!'

'Right! I'll give you two cigarettes.' He took out his packet of ten Majors.

'No, make it four!'

'Felix, gimme a cigarette,' Mo moaned from the corner. She was now slumped, buried under her hat, exhausted from all the waiting.

'Mo, I gave you a packet yesterday!'

'Look! These are all I have left!'

'Martha!' He twirled around to me, always acting and trying to sound like his father. 'I will give you three, and when I come again you can make my tea for nothing.'

'OK!' I grabbed the ciggies, making them their tea. Poor Felix was forty years old, and his wife was in her thirties, but they were so innocent. I had great gas haggling with him every time he came steaming into the office. Nothing ever changed. His father would run him out the door, I would haggle for the cigarettes, and his mammy would come and collect them, promising to take Mo shopping. That pleased him. He adored his wife, and Mammy would buy him something nice, too. It was the only way she could tear him away from the tormented daddy.

I sat in the office, waiting for the switchboard to ring. There was nothing to look at except the four grey walls. I had a desk and a chair – that was it. The little window was high up in the wall, to let in air. So, for enjoyment, I would phone up the secretary – she did the typing for the bosses, and her office was down the end of the corridor next to Neddy. There was only one other female, an elderly lady who did the accounts. She was nice, but very prim and proper. So Becky the secretary would look in the paper for 'Domestics Wanted', and I would phone up looking for the job, while Becky listened in on the extension.

'Hello! Hello!' I would gasp. 'I'm lookin te know if ye want me te come an work fer ye! I'm a fierce hard worker. I love the scrubbin a blankets! And dhere's nothin I like better then dhe gettin down on me hands an knees an scrubbin the aul floors! I do enjoy the aul hard work! I would be cleanin them windas fer ye about every other week! I'm from the heart of the counthry! An I'm a firm believer dha hard work never kilt anybody! Now! Can I have the job?'

Becky and myself howled our heads off, laughing at the gobshites thinking they had got a right eegit coming to work for them. It was a bit quiet after that. But the job was not demanding, and I was happy there.

One day I walked back to the office after lunch with a book in my hand and reached down to switch the kettle on to make myself a cup of tea. I was blown across the room and landed about twenty feet away, slammed into the wall. I had put my hand into an exposed electrical socket. The cover was broken. I lay like a rag doll, sliding down the wall, when the men from the trade counter came rushing up. They picked me up and went to take a look at the wall.

'Lucky you weren't standin in tha puddle a water when ye touched tha socket! Or ye wouldn't be standin here now!'

'Yeah!' I gasped, wondering what happened.

That experience, well, it made me very alert! I'm always wide awake now, always checking everything. Is the gas off? Are the plugs pulled out of the sockets? Jaysus! I drive meself mad.

I would wander home in the evenings, thinking what I would have for my tea. I earned four pounds a week. Two pounds ten shillings went for the rent. That left one pound ten shillings for food, heating and everything else.

I wore my overcoat in the bedsit to keep warm in the winter. Forget the heat. So it was mostly the one-ring cooker that used the money. It was a shilling for the electric meter, so to boil an egg and keep the light bulb going for about three hours, it cost me seven shillings a week. Yeah, and I smoked. That's another reason why me eyes lit up at the sight of Felix.

I passed my old house in the Liberties every evening on the way home. The house had been knocked down, and the land was now used as a car park. There was a fence around it now, and it was all locked up. I stopped every evening to gaze at the hole in the wall where the fireplace had been. That was all that was left standing! The old yellow Georgian bricks were black from age, but somehow they were a tie to my past. I knew I had belonged somewhere once. I felt a bit alone now, out in the world on my own. Having put the ma and everything else behind me, I still had this place. Where I had some happy memories before we met Jackser.

I would wander on, eventually arriving home to my little room with the bed in the corner and the wardrobe and two chairs and the table under the window, and the sink and little one-ring cooker beside it in the corner. It was home.

Then I got a boyfriend. I felt like every other young girl, doing all the normal things they do. Having a boyfriend was one of them. It meant someone wanted me.

The year brought very bad news for me. I stood in the old doctor's room, listening to him as he explained I could have the baby adopted. We stared at each other as he shook his head sadly and told me I should contact the organisation to help unmarried mothers. I could go away and nobody need ever find out about it. When I had my baby, I could give it up and start my life over again.

From then on it was a nightmare, keeping it secret from everyone. If the nuns from the convent found out, they might do to me what had happened to other girls. I could be locked up in a Magdalen convent!

I kept very quiet. Every morning I woke up, for one split second I would forget. Then I would turn over to get out of bed and it would hit me. I am pregnant! Dear Jesus! What am I going to do? I started to vomit straight away, and it never stopped. I lost a lot of weight. I was now locked in a world of my own. The same problem going around and around in my head, day after day, minute after minute.

I went into the Catholic organisation in the city centre to talk to the priest who ran it.

'So! You can go down to our unmarried mothers' home in the country. When would you like to go? The sooner the better. You will be looked after and won't have to worry about people finding out. When the child is born, and the papers are signed, you will be free again.'

'No, thanks, Father. I have a job, and when I start to show the pregnancy, then I will come.'

He sized me up, looking me up and down, seeing I was already showing. 'Come back to us when you are six months pregnant. OK?' he said, standing up and putting his hand on my shoulder and showing me the door. 'Come here, and we will make all the arrangements. You can be gone by the next day.'

'Thanks, Father.' I looked up at his soft white face, his eyes closing down, all business. He held the door, ready to close it as soon as I walked away. I hesitated, wanting something more. But not knowing what it was. Then turned, heading back down the stairs, hearing the priest slam the door shut behind me.

42

I turned my face away from the wind as I stepped out into the dark and bitterly cold morning. I felt dazed. I stood for a minute to get my senses back and let people walk around me and into me. They clicked their tongues in annoyance and stepped around me. I stood, staring at the faces, wishing I was related to one of them. I wanted to cry for me mammy, but there was no mammy. Sally's face wafted into my vision, and I saw her helplessness, and I turned the vision away. Now I know how she felt. But I'm not her, and I never will be.

A girl pushed past me, keeping her head down, and rang the doorbell behind me. She kept her eyes peeled on the ground and pulled the scarf around her head to make sure her face was hidden. She's just like me. I gave a sidelong glance to see what she was like, but all I could see was her bent back. I moved off, wondering what people would say if they knew. But I know the answer to that. They would look at me with curiosity – an Unmarried Mother! Then drop their eyes, closing me out, and be glad it's not them. People don't change. I'd seen it often enough with the ma growing up. And the nuns would be dying to get their hands on me. They certainly didn't like me. I was sent to them because I'd gotten myself into trouble with the robbing. They never forgave me for bringing their convent into disrepute. Yeah! They didn't take my sort, they told me.

They would bung me off to their Magdalen home like they did to some of the others. No way. I'd heard the stories from some of the other girls.

One of them was married now. She'd managed to escape out in one of the laundry baskets and slept rough on the streets of Dublin until she got the money to go to England. I shivered with the fear running through me at the thought of being locked up. I hurried on, wrapping the long, black maxi coat around me I bought myself for Christmas. I paid a shilling a week out of my wages, and by Christmas I was in great style. I had a long yellow scarf to go with the coat, and wrapped it several times around my neck, glad of it now.

I hurried on, down through alleyways that hadn't changed for hundreds of years, the smell of piss and decay turning my stomach, and came out onto Grafton Street. People were very well dressed here. The ones with all the money came here to spend it in Brown Thomas and Switzer's. I looked at their well-fed hatchet faces. It's funny how the rich are always very plain, while the poor always seem to be better looking!

I turned right, passing Bewley's, and the smell of the coffee was nice. I'd love to go in there and buy myself one. I haven't had time to get meself a bit of breakfast yet. But I have to start watching the pennies now. I hurried on, joining the people rushing to get somewhere. Everyone seemed to have things to do, places to go.

I stopped at the entrance to Stephen's Green, looking up at the arch to the unknown soldier. There's no point in wandering in there. It's too cold. I turned away, heading in the direction of home, picturing the empty cold room – it was more like a prison at the moment. I sat on the bed for hours, staring into nothing, worrying. I won't be able to put on the little hot-air heater. It eats the shillings.

I kept wandering in that direction, thinking if I need to buy a half-pint of milk. Do I have bread? I'm not sure if I want to eat anything, it's a terrible waste of money if I just leave it lying. I could feel the fear creep into my belly again. Jesus! What will I do now? What will happen to me? There was no one I could tell. I felt very alone in the world.

I wandered down through Thomas Street, feeling lost. Thinking, there's people here I should know. I looked at the weather-beaten faces of the dealers as they stamped their feet in their fur-lined boots, walking up and down to keep out the cold. Their eyes swung up and down the street looking for customers for their vegetables and fruit. I kept my head down, not wanting to make conversation.

I crossed the road, heading into St John's church to say a prayer, hoping to lift this terrible feeling of having the world on my shoulders, and that everything would turn out right. This was a disgrace. I had gotten myself into trouble, and I would have to pay the penalty.

They fired me from my job when I was six months pregnant. The priest had been right. I was now showing. I hurried down the hill, my stomach heaving. I stopped to bring up the tea and bread I'd just eaten, then pushed on. My heart was hammering away in my chest. Jesus! I'm going to be late for work.

I hurried down the quays, passing the homeless shelter for men. I suddenly stopped as the door opened and a down-and-out grey-faced man walked into me. We muttered to each other, neither of us bothering to make eye contact. He kept his eyes down, locked in his own world, wondering where he was going to go to get in out of the cold and get a bit of heat, and maybe something to drink to get him through another day until the night came and he could go back to the hostel and sleep another night to face another day until he finished his hell on earth.

I was locked in my own world of worry and loneliness and waiting – for what? The baby to be born, this to be over! I couldn't see that far ahead. This hell will go on for ever. It has been a long time since I laughed and felt young and carefree. The worry of meeting someone and the nuns finding out, and the thought I had done the exact thing as my mother, made me feel I have ruined my chances of ever having a better life.

I arrived into the office and Alec was waiting for me. 'You're late.'

I took off my coat, and he stared at my stomach.

'Get me a number,' he barked as he stormed out the door. 'Knutsberg in Holland!'

'Right away! OK, Alec.' I reached for the phonebook and the switchboard rang. 'Good morning, Hammond and Mooney!'

'Yeah, I'm ringing about the job for a receptionist. Is it gone?'

I was stunned. 'What job? There's no job for a rece . . . Where did you see the job advertised?'

'It's in this morning's paper!'

'No, sorry! The job is gone.'

I hung up and rushed down to Mr Hammond. Alec the son was sitting at his desk.

'Yes?' He lifted his round fat face and shrugged his shoulders, trying to make himself look bigger. He was a fat, little aul fella, who was now taking over from the daddy. Even though he wasn't the eldest, he made himself look very busy, and the sons were always throwing shapes around each other. But he made sure to come in every day, and more and more the others were missing.

I looked around. No sign of Neddy. 'Alec! There's a girl on the phone asking about the job for receptionist!'

'Right! Put her through,' he snapped, reaching for the phone.

'But, Alec! There's no job for a receptionist. I'm . . . that's my job!'

'Not any more! You're fired!'

'How? What do you mean? Why?'

'You were late! And this!' He pointed to my stomach.

'I can still work, Alec,' I said half-heartedly.

'You're fired. Now, put any calls through to me that come in about the job. Go and see Mrs Kelly. Tell her to fix up your wages and collect your cards. You can stay on until Friday. That's your last day.'

I stared at him, not able to take it in. He dropped his head and went back to his work, and I was forgotten.

There's no point in arguing with him. I turned away, heading back down the passage in terrible shock. Then I stopped outside Mrs Kelly's door. She was the bookkeeper. I wandered in and stood in front of her desk. She was an elderly woman, and I never spoke to her much. She was too serious to make jokes with Becky and me, back in the old days before I got myself into trouble.

'Mrs Kelly,' I whispered, staring at her. 'Alec says I'm to collect my cards. I'm fired.'

She shook her head and looked down at my stomach, pointing and saying in a whisper, 'When are you expecting?'

'In three months, Mrs Kelly.'

'I'm so sorry! What will you do?'

'I don't know. I'm supposed to be going down to a home for unmarried mothers, but I don't want to go.' I knew it was foolish to think I could avoid it, but I kept hoping something might change.

'Listen, Martha! I will make up your wages now. It will take a little time, but if you come back to me after dinnertime, I will have your cards ready, and you can go home today. Does your family know?'

I shook my head. 'I don't have a family.'

'Who brought you up?'

'I lived in a convent. But I can't let them know. They will put me away.'

She shook her head, agreeing with me. 'What about the home?'

'Yeah, I can go there and leave when the baby is adopted.'

'That's your best bet. I suggest you take the time off now and go and see them. Make arrangements to leave as soon as possible,' she whispered, looking into my eyes.

We stared at each other. I could see the gentleness and the kindness she had for me.

'What about Alec?'

'Never mind that eegit! I will sort him out. You get your coat on and get yourself sorted out as soon as you can. Go on! I will be thinking about you, and I'll light a candle for you. You'll be all right!'

I gave her a little smile, feeling a sense of purpose.

43

The old single-decker bus rumbled to a stop outside the convent. I stepped down, dragging the big suitcase and landing it on the ground. The bus heaved off, leaving me standing in the middle of the country. It's miles from anywhere, I thought, looking around me at the country road. Nothing but fields and trees and hedges. I could get the country smells. I looked up at the entrance gates and the sign over the gate saying 'St Mary's Home'. I picked up the case and headed in the gate.

The suitcase was heavy enough, even though I hadn't too much in it. Just the few things I'd bought myself since I left the convent, and they weren't much good to me now. Nothing would fit me properly. I had to squeeze into them. It must be around the four o'clock mark. It had been a long aul haul down from Dublin. I got the half past nine train down, then had to wait for a bus in the city.

I walked up the dark avenue. It was shaded by trees. The path narrowed as I turned a bend, with the trees leaning over, trying to take up as much room as they could from the path. Jesus! What am I doing? I can always turn back or leave whenever I want. They can't keep me here. I came in voluntarily. I turned another bend, and the entrance stared straight down at me.

I crunched my way across the pebbles laid out in front of the entrance to make a wide path outside the door and stopped to ring the doorbell in the wall. My heart fluttered looking at the big, wide, brown entrance doors leading into a porch. I took in a deep breath and waited.

'Good evening!' A tall, red-faced nun in a long black habit down to her toes smiled at me. Her eyes flicked down to my suitcase and then at my belly. 'Come in! Are you Martha?'

'Yes, Sister,' I said, lifting up my suitcase and feeling my heart sink at the mention of my name and being expected. It feels like I may be handing over control of myself to these nuns again. I stopped, hesitating about stepping through the doors she held open.

'Come along! You are welcome,' she said, reading my mind. Nuns are very cute! They know how to wrap you around their little finger. Then they can be the devil from hell and exercise iron control over you if it suits them and if they can get the power.

Jesus! Jesus! Will I get out of this place again? I wanted to turn and run. But all the time she was pushing me through doors, then whipped up my suitcase as soon as we reached a long dark passage and she stopped outside a door. 'I'll take this.'

Then we were in an office with a big old desk and bookshelves around and a filing cabinet.

'Take a seat, you must be tired!'

I nodded, saying nothing.

'Now,' she said, whipping out a file. 'I just need some details from you.'

She walked over to a big leather desk chair and sat herself down, taking up a pen, and said, 'Now! I need your parents' names and address.'

I stared at her, and she leaned forward, waiting for the information.

'Why?'

'Oh, we need to know about your family history for lots of reasons,' she smiled.

'Yes, but what exactly do you want to know for?'

'Well, for a start, when you have the baby adopted, we try to place the child with a family from a similar background. Even the colour of your eyes and hair – all these things matter to help the adoptive parents. If the child looks like them, it helps them to pass it off as their own. Also, as you come from Dublin, the child would be adopted by people from the country. We can't take any chances of the mother ever seeing her child. Do you understand now?'

'Yes.' But it all went over my head. I couldn't really get my mind to work. I can't tell her about Sally. She doesn't exist any more, and I can't tell her about the convent!

'What is your family address?'

'Look! I am not going to give you that. Nobody knows anything about me. That's the whole point of me being here. If you insist, I'm walking out that door,' I said, white-faced, stonily determined she was not getting anything out of me.

'Well! If you insist,' she said, lowering her pen and looking at her empty folder.

'I do!'

'Yes! Very well then. Now! You are free to leave any time you wish,' she said slowly, her eyes narrowing, taking me in. But looking like I would have a fight on my hands if I tried that.

I stared back just as hard. 'I will leave, Sister! If this place does not suit me,' I said quietly but firmly.

She nodded. 'Now! You may walk out the gates any time you wish, but we advise you do not for good reason. The girls know only too well what happens with the townspeople. They will make it very uncomfortable for you. They know, obviously, you are staying here, and they gossip, pointing and laughing at the girls, and some may even make hurtful remarks.'

'What town?'

'Well, you must have come through it on your way here by bus?'

'But that's a long way off, Sister.'

'No! Not in the country,' she said. 'So it would be ill advised to venture up there.'

I listened, having no intention of visiting the culchies.

'Come along now and I will show you to your sleeping quarters.'

She stood up and picked up my case. 'I will put this away in the storeroom. You won't be needing it.'

I stared at my suitcase walking out the door with the nun and felt I was losing my chance of escape. My whole life was in that case, and I had no intention of losing it.

'Couldn't I keep it with me, Sister?'

'No! Why would you do that? Sure, you wouldn't have anything in it that would be useful to you in your present condition.'

I hesitated.

'Anyway, it would only be in the way. We can't have luggage strewn around the place. When you are leaving, you can ask for it back. Incidentally! Do you have money with you? I must put it away for you to keep it safe.' She stared at me, waiting. 'It could be stolen, you know!'

'OK,' I said reluctantly, taking the purse out of my coat pocket. I had kept my hand on it all the way down from Dublin in case anything happened to it. I counted it out. Seven pounds and four shillings and ninepence. That's what I had left from my two weeks' wages, and the two pounds Mrs Kelly slipped into my wage packet out of her own money. She was a very good woman. It didn't seem like only yesterday I was standing in her office talking to her. Now look where I am.

I handed over the money, feeling I was giving up my last chance of freedom. She counted it, putting it into an envelope with my name on it, and put it in a safe. Then she locked it and said, 'Follow me and we'll get you something to wear.'

I looked around the dormitory. It was tiny. Six beds were nearly head to head in an attic room. I was behind the door. The annexe window was up in the roof, and it only let in a bit of light. I put on the long grey shift she gave me; it looked like a tent with brown stripes. I looked down at my narrow bed with the hairy black blankets and white sheets, and lay down, stretching myself the length of the bed. I was suddenly exhausted and was glad to be off my feet. At least I have plenty of room in the frock. Now I don't have to squeeze myself into my clothes any more – that sure is one good thing.

I lay stretched out and suddenly I felt the baby move. I put my hand on my stomach and felt a big lump squeeze out through my skin. I looked down, feeling it. It was the baby's foot or something. It's having a stretch for itself too.

I held on to the foot, and suddenly I wasn't alone any more! It's a baby! My baby! I laughed. 'Are you enjoying yourself?' I asked quietly. It started dancing up a tango and going mad, delighted with not being squashed any more. 'My baby,' I crooned to it, rubbing where I could feel it bouncing around.

'Tea time!' A head poked its way around the door, waking me up.

I sat up, wondering where I was for a minute. The home! I looked around as the door slammed shut, getting a quick look at a very pregnant girl. Then I made my way down to the dining room by following the herd of girls all making their way to the sound of cutlery and cups being put out. When I arrived in the door, there must have been over sixty girls here sitting at tables for six. I made my way over to a free chair and sat down. I immediately spotted the girl I saw outside the door going in to see the priest a while ago, back in Dublin. She was reading a letter and looked about twenty-five. I wonder how she got herself into trouble? It must be worse for her, being older. I wonder why she didn't get married.

I sat in the smoking room, puffing away on my cigarette. I was in a corner on my own, well away from the rest of the girls. I didn't want to mix with them because we had nothing to say to each other. They were girls from all around the country; there was no one from Dublin. I didn't like the look of some of them; they were a bit rough.

I was shocked to hear them telling each other this was their second and third time! How in the name of Jesus could you make a mistake a second time? Not unless you were like bloody Sally, my mother. No! I don't want anything to do with them.

'I'm due now in two weeks!' one said to the other, sucking on her cigarette, flopping out her legs on the worn-out lino on the floor, then examining her man's pair of slippers that had seen better days. She had walked the backs off them, and her red swollen legs looked disgusting, spread out with her belly hanging down sitting on her lap. She looked about forty but was really in her twenties.

I got up and wandered out of the smelly, smoky room. There were no windows to air the place, and the four dirty-green walls would put years on you. I wandered out to the yard and stopped at a long line of outhouses. It must have been a coach house at one time.

'Hello!'

I looked around to see a girl with brown curly hair smiling at me. 'Are ye looking for the laundry?' she asked, ready to direct me.

'No, I'm just taking a ramble.'

'Sure, ye might as well. It's a lovely day, isn't it?'

'Yeah!' I said, eyeing her belly, wishing I was as big, then I could get out faster.

'When are you due?' I asked.

She slapped her belly, looking at it, and said, 'Five days! Then another six weeks, God willing. Then it's back to the land of the living for me,' she laughed. 'Where are you from? Dublin, is it?'

'Yes. Down here I'm surrounded by you culchies. I'm feeling a bit out of my depth!'

'When are ye due?' she asked.

'Three months,' I sighed.

'Ah! Ye won't feel that going.'

'I don't think I'll last that long in this place. Going into that smoking room is driving me mad. Listening to the others going on about how many they've had and when they're due is putting years on me.'

'Ah, don't be minding them. Some of them are right sluts, but they stick to their own.'

'Where do you work?' I asked.

'I'm a civil servant, so I'm lucky. They give me the time off, and my job is still waiting for me.'

I took in a sharp breath at the thought of her luck. 'That's great for you,' I said happily.

'So long as I don't keep the child, mind,' she said quickly. 'No. I mean, if I marry, I would have to give up the job, because they make us women leave then.'

'Oh,' I said, trying to figure that out. 'Does your mother know you are here?'

'Indeed she does not! I have a friend I post my letters to in Dublin, and she forwards them on. I keep sending home messages to the mammy, down every week from Dublin, of course – that's where I'm stationed. Telling her all sorts of excuses. But I have to be careful I don't let her think I'm on death's door, or, God almighty, she would be up on the next train to take me home. A fine pickle I would be in then!' Her eyes bulged at me, the two of us getting the picture of her getting found out.

'No! You have to be very careful,' I said, feeling for her.

A little girl with long, brown, curly hair down to her waist passed over the cobblestones, carrying a bucket. I stared at her, and she gave me a shy smile.

My friend watched me staring after the little girl. 'She's only fourteen. Barely. Can you believe it? The poor child!'

'What's your name? Mine is Martha.'

'Geraldine! My friends call me Gerry.'

I put out my hand and we shook.

'Yeah!' Gerry continued. 'An aul fella on a neighbouring farm is the culprit. So they say. But she's had her baby!'

'Oh my God! The poor little mite,' I said, feeling shocked and heartbroken for the little thing. 'But, Gerry, why is she not gone home to her mother?'

'I don't know,' Gerry said, thinking about it. 'She's a bit retarded. And the baby won't be put up for adoption because of that. If there is the slightest thing wrong with the baby, it won't be put up for adoption, you know, and they won't let you leave. No, babies who are not perfect are sent into a convent. They don't get adopted.'

We wandered over to the outhouses, and Gerry put her head in the door, saying hello to a very tall old woman. 'How are you today, Molly?'

The old woman was bending over a big old sink, scrubbing nappies. She lifted her head and smiled, 'I'm right as rain, Gerry! How is yerself?' Then she lifted herself to a standing position. I could see she was really stooped from the waist down. 'Isn't the weather great altogether, girls?' she said, beaming out from her dark little room into the sunshine.

'Ah, it is at that, Molly. Take it easy now. Don't go killing yourself!'

'No fear of that,' laughed Molly as we moved on.

'She has been here most of her life,' whispered Gerry. 'Would you believe she's in her nineties?'

I was astonished. 'She's old, right enough,' I said, thinking about it. 'But in her nineties?'

'Yeah! She has a son a priest! But he's dead now. He came to see her once. The poor aul thing still talks about it as if it was only yesterday. But that was over fifty years ago. She spent most of her life here!' Gerry said, shaking her head thinking about it.

I looked back, and she was still bent over the sink, washing away.

'Yeah! They used to lock them up in them days,' said Gerry.

'I don't know about that,' I said. 'I think they still lock them up.'

'Ah, but not here,' Gerry said. 'But you are right. Little Mary may be kept here or sent on to another convent where she'll spend the rest of her days.'

'But it wasn't her fault she got into trouble,' I said, feeling very angry.

'What's that got to do with anything? Her mother won't take her home, so now she's left to them,' and she pointed her finger at the convent. 'She's not wanted, Martha!

'Do you want to come into the nursery with me and see the babies? I'm due back at work. I'm in charge of the nursery.'

'What do you do?' I asked.

'Everything. There's two of us. We feed the babies and clean up. It's a full-time job. But we get to change around. I'll probably get to do kitchen work next.'

I'm not doing any bleedin work, I thought to myself. This sounds exactly what went on in my old convent. In fact, I looked around the yard and then out to the fields, it even looks the bloody same!

We arrived at the nursery, and Gerry went over to a cot and cooed at a little baby. 'This is baby Rose, Mary's little one. She called her after her mother.'

I looked in the cot and the loveliest little baby girl lifted her little body, wanting to be picked up. She bucked and wriggled, and her little legs and arms were like pendulums. I gazed down slowly at her, a huge smile on my face. I couldn't take in how lovely she was.

'How old is she?' I asked Gerry, not able to take my eyes off the baby.

'She's five months old.'

'Ah! Why will they not put her up for adoption? She's beautiful.'

I reached in, taking her up, and her whole body went rigid with excitement. 'Ah, look! She's smiling at me with her gummy little mouth.'

Gerry laughed and went off to pick up another baby to feed, taking the bottles already made up by the other girl working there. 'She's used to different faces. They come and go here,' Gerry said, looking down at the baby she was starting to feed.

'Where's her bottle? I'll feed her!'

'No! You won't be let. They don't like the girls coming in. It makes it harder for them to let their babies go for adoption. That's why they won't let them feed their own babies.'

I stared down at the little scrap in my arms, and it hit me there was nothing wrong with this little baby. Nor, for that matter, was there much wrong with her mother – if anything. She's only a frightened little girl who's pulled in on herself with what happened.

No! I don't buy that story about the old farmer. It's more than likely the problem is closer to home. Must be the bastard of a father, and the mother is protecting him. That's why she won't take her home. And the bloody nuns know this. It's a well-known fact that children born like that are expected to be handicapped. That's the real reason the nuns won't put the baby up for adoption. Bastards! Now two innocent children are suffering while the poxy mother stays quiet, and the nuns will use poor Mary like they did Molly! So, who says they won't lock you up? Tell that to poor Mary! Bastards!

I put the baby down in the cot and tickled her chin, not wanting to leave her. She was desperate for attention. Just then the door opened, and the Reverend Mother – I found out that's the one who 'welcomed' me that first day I came here – came in.

'Oh, hello!' she said, wandering over and staring down at the baby, a false smile on her face, looking at me as if I shouldn't be here.

'Would you like to do a little work, Martha?' she asked me, all smiles.

I twitched my lips in a smile, not saying anything.

'Come out here with me and I'll show you what I would like you to do for me.'

I followed her out into the yard outside the nursery.

'Do you see these weeds growing here?' She bent down and started to pull them up from the cracks in the tiles. 'Why don't you do a little weeding for me?' she smiled.

I stared at the weeds.

'Go on,' she said, poking me with her arm and laughing. 'It will keep you occupied. It's not good to have too much time on your hands. Good girl.' Then she was off.

I stooped down to pull at a weed and then fucked it back on the ground. Get stuffed, you fucking chancer. I'm not falling for that a second time. You can only make a fool out of me once. My days of slaving for the fucking nuns are dead and gone. I stormed off to have a smoke for myself and sit down and think.

Right! I'm three weeks here today, Saturday. That's it! I'm getting out of here today before my baby is born. Otherwise it may be too late. Anything could happen if I stay here. The nuns in my old convent could somehow get to hear and may step in and feel they can do what they like with me. Gerry is wrong. Is she forgetting about poor little Mary and her innocent little baby? Right! My mind is made up. I'm leaving right this minute.

I stamped on the cigarette butt and headed back into the nursery looking for that Reverend Mother.

'She's not here,' Gerry said, looking at me with questions in her eyes. She knew I meant business about something, but I said nothing and just looked in the cot at little baby Rose. She was sleeping on her back and looked so tiny and innocent. I wish I could take her with me. She's going to end up in some fucking convent until she's sixteen, then go off looking for her mother. By then it will be too late. Her mother will be institutionalised! Bastards! Life is really the luck of the draw. Poor Mary. She can't fight for herself, but I'm certainly very lucky. I can run rings around any of them when I don't let my guard down. One thing is for sure! I will never let anything like this happen to me again.

44

The train rattled and shook its way into Kingsbridge Station. I looked out the window, seeing how dark out it was. Jesus! It must be around ten o'clock at night. I'd better get a move on.

I pulled out the suitcase from under the table and made my way off the train and headed out of the station. I was glad I made up my mind to leave today. That place was doing me no good, and no good could come by staying there.

I managed to get the train ticket for half price. A child's fare! The poor aul fella in the station didn't give me a second glance. Maybe it's because he couldn't see me belly. On the other hand, you wouldn't notice, especially when I leave my scarf hanging down the front. I've really lost a lot of weight. I could easily pass for a child's fare. That comes in handy. But, some child! Eighteen years old. Huh! I had more sense when I was eight!

Right! First things first. I headed over to the phone box on the other side of the street and took out my little notebook to look up the landlord's phone number. He gave it to me once in case I ever had a problem. I dialled the number.

'Hello! May I speak to Mr Roberts, please?'

'No, he's not here,' a man's voice said.

My heart did a dive into my stomach. 'Who is this?'

'I'm John, his son.'

'Oh! My name is Martha. I was staying in his house until recently. I had the room at the front of the house. Upstairs. I was hoping he might let me rent it again. Look, I'm badly stuck. I have nowhere to go. I really need the room. Please?'

There was a silence from the other end. I waited with my heart in my mouth.

'OK, this is what I can do, Martha. I will drive over there to the house now. It will take me about an hour to get there. So, you can sleep the night in your old bedsit – it's still vacant – and come into the office in the morning and speak to my father, OK?'

'Thank you! Oh, yes, thank you so much, John. I'm in town now. I'll try to get there before you, but I might have to wait for a bus. So, you will wait for me, won't you?' I asked him, feeling desperate he might just go off if I wasn't there.

'Yes. Where are you now?'

'I'm on Talbot Street.'

'Wait there. It's on my way. Give me about forty-five minutes. Say around eleven, and I'll pick you up from the street. OK?'

'OK, John! Thanks a lot.'

I put the phone down very, very happy to have somewhere to stay, even if it is only for one night. Pity the shops are closed. I could have got a few things in. Milk and bread and a bit of cheese would be nice. I know! To hell with it. I'll scrounge milk and tea from somewhere. Maybe the country girl in the next room. Oh, thank you, God, for looking after me. That man is a wonderful human being.

I left the phone box and started to cross the road. Then I spotted a fella making straight towards me carrying a little brown suitcase. His eyes locked on mine, a mad glint in them, and he quickened his step, heading right for me. I could see the madness in his eyes, and I felt myself going cold all over.

'Don't start with me, you fucking bitch!' he roared straight into my face. There was nowhere to run. The phone box behind me was no good.

Before I could get the next breath, he lifted his suitcase, hammering it down on my collarbone. I screamed as I fell to the ground, and he was just about to start kicking me, raising his foot, and I grabbed my case to break his kick.

'Geraway from tha girl, ye bastard!' A man coming out of the pub just behind me came tearing over and distracted the crazy bastard. I tried to get up before he did me any more damage. Lightning bolts of pain shot through me, and I groaned.

'Go on, fuck off! Or I'll break yer culchie red neck, ye cowardly bastard!'

The little swine slunk off like a dog, and the man bent down as I hauled myself to my feet.

'Are ye all righ, chicken?'

'Yeah, yeah. The pain will ease in a minute.' I wondered if my shoulder was broken.

'Come on!' He took up my suitcase. 'Where were ye goin?'

'I'm waiting for someone. They shouldn't be too long,' I grunted, hoping the pain would ease.

'Where do ye live?'

'I'll be OK. Thanks very much for all your help. I'm getting a lift just across the road.'

'Come on. I'll give ye a hand with the suitcase.' He put his hand out to me, looking up and down the road to see when the traffic eased, then helped me across the road.

I sat down on the steps of an old house, feeling the cold go up me. My head was starting to pain me.

'Ye don't look too good to me,' he said quietly, looking at me very intently.

'No! I'll be all right now, thanks. Don't worry about me.'

'Listen! Are ye sure ye're OK? I'm talking about yer condition,' and he looked down at my belly, seeing I didn't have a ring on my finger.

I nodded to him. 'I'm grateful for all your help. You go on. I'll be OK.'

He hesitated, looking up and down the street, then said, 'If ye're sure?'

'Yeah! Thanks.'

Then he went on about his business, looking back once to see if I was OK.

I felt very old suddenly and very tired, the pain in my head and shoulder not helping matters. Then the car drew up and a man in his twenties jumped out and said, 'Hello, Martha?'

'Yeah.' I tried to stand up quickly and look normal. I didn't want him to think I was going to be more trouble than it was worth.

'Hop in! I'll take the case,' and he lunged for it, throwing it in the back.

We didn't say much driving down the quays, and I could see he was going out somewhere. He smelled of Old Spice men's aftershave.

His hair looked like he had just been to the barber's that day, and it was slicked back with Brylcreem.

The car pulled up outside the house and I got out.

'Come on,' he said, grabbing my case and putting the key in the hall door.

We went up the stairs and stopped on the landing, and I waited until he opened the door and let me into my old room. I waited while he tested the light to see if there was money in the meter. The light came on, and he put the case inside the door.

'Right, Martha. There you go. Don't forget to call in and see my father in the morning. He should be in the office around ten.'

I woke up with my head feeling like cotton wool. My shoulder felt stiff and numb. I eased it around to try to get some heat in it, then put on my frock and shoes. I washed my face in cold water and brushed my teeth and combed my hair, then put on my coat and scarf. I haven't got a key! But I'll call in and see the landlord when I get back from signing on at the labour exchange. That's what Gerry told me to do yesterday when I told her I was leaving. She knew all about these things, working in the civil service. I'm going to need something to live on.

I walked down the quays and finally found the place and the right queue to join. That's what the man in the other hatch told me to do. This is the same labour exchange Jackser used to come to. Jesus! How could you get yourself into this mess? Never mind. Things will be OK. I have my plan.

I was waiting in the queue, and it was moving very slowly, when I started to feel weak. I have had a problem lately with that. It only happens when I stand. I have no problem walking for miles, just the standing. But it is worse now. It's probably with all the worry lately and the travelling yesterday without anything to eat or drink. I still haven't had anything. I was just about to collapse when the girl behind me asked me was I all right. I turned to her, explaining it was the waiting, when she said, 'Jesus! Ye're snow white. Here! Get this girl a glass of water and something to sit down on.'

I was delighted to walk over and slump against the counter. It really was bad this time. All the worry did it.

'Here! Take this. Sit down here,' another woman said, taking the chair the woman behind the counter handed her.

'Did you want to sign on?' she asked me.

'Yes! I lost my job three weeks ago.'

'Right! Have you got your cards there?'

I took them out of my pocket and handed them to her.

'OK, you sign on every Monday. You come in here and go over to that queue.'

'How much will I get?' I asked.

'Two pounds ten shillings.'

Jesus! It will have to do. Two pounds ten shillings!

'Thank you,' I said, standing up and taking my labour card from her.

'Are you all right now?' the women asked me.

'I'm grand, thanks.'

'Well, if you're sure,' they said, not looking very sure themselves.

I walked off, dying to get out into the fresh air and get back to the room and make myself a cup of tea. I'll go and see the landlord first, though. Just in case he doesn't let me stay.

I walked back slowly, thinking, if I pay the two pounds ten shillings I get from the labour, then that will give me a roof over my head. All I'll have to worry about is getting the money for the food and the electrical meter. I walk everywhere, and I don't need anything else, except my cigarettes. I will manage somehow. I can always go into the Rotunda Hospital to have the baby and wear a wedding ring. They won't be any the wiser. Then we'll see what happens when the baby is born. That is enough for the moment. I'll take it one step at a time.

I rounded the corner and turned into the works yard where my landlord has his office. And I went up the stairs and knocked on the door. I was now in a cold sweat and feeling faint again. Just get this over with and if everything works out – please God, grant that he will let me stay – that will solve all my problems for the time being.

'Come in!'

I opened the door and he was sitting at a desk piled high with papers and a black telephone sitting beside his hand.

'Sit down,' he said, eyeing me, taking in my bit of bulge at the front.

I wrapped the scarf around my stomach, knowing it was too late.

'So! What happened?' he asked me, almost roaring.

I sat staring, not knowing what to answer.

'This!' He pointed to my stomach.

Oh, Jesus! The game is up. I'm out on my ear.

'You're a Dublin girl, am I right?' he barked.

'Yes,' I whispered, feeling myself completely drained.

'Now, you've been living in a bedsit. What does that tell me?' he asked the door, looking straight past me. 'You've come out of a convent! Am I right?'

I was shocked. Jesus! He's very quick. I said nothing. Just waited quietly to let him say what he had to say.

'So, who's the father?' he suddenly roared.

I twisted my mouth, thinking.

'It's that gobshite that's always sniffing around you, isn't it?'

'Yes,' I muttered.

'Right! That little bastard is going to marry you. Give me his work number! I'll break his fucking neck when I get my hands on him. Don't worry!' he roared, lifting up the telephone. 'I'm the man for him, the little shite! He won't get out of this!'

I was laughing inside, thinking he was right, and it suddenly dawned on me that was exactly the thing to do. If I get married, then I'll be a respectable married woman Then no matter what happens, the authorities can't touch me.

'I'll talk to him myself, Mr Roberts.'

'Tell him I said he's going to marry you, OK? Or I'll come after him! I mean that! All my kids are grown up now. My daughter is now a married woman. But if anyone treated her badly like you've been messed around, they would be planted!

'So you can stay in the bedsit with pleasure, and if there's anything I can do to help, just let me know, OK?'

'Yes, Mr Roberts,' I said, standing up and giving him a huge smile.

'Here's the keys. Go in and get yourself a bit of kip. You look all done in! And remember what I said. Any trouble from that little fucker, and I'll sort him out.'

I went down the stairs and headed up to the shops. I wanted to buy a few messages. I needed to get meself that sup of tea and bread and cheese I promised myself last night. Then I went into the phone box and called the baby's father. I was going to ask him to come and see me. But as soon as I heard his voice on the phone, I said straight out, 'Listen! It's me! I'm back.'

'Where?' he said suddenly, shocked.

'Dublin. I'm back in my old bedsit.'

There was silence. Then I said, 'Hello! Are you still there?'

'That's great,' he said.

'Yeah! Listen! We're getting married. Straight away. So tell your mammy you are taking the time off work on Monday! We're going to see the priest about arranging the wedding. I'm thinking a week from this Monday!'

There was a stunned silence. 'Hello! Did you hear what I just said?'

'Yeah! Yeah! That's a great idea! I was just thinking the same!'

'Right so. Now, listen to me carefully. When your mammy blows a fit, tell her you're old enough to be a father, so we are getting married no matter what she says! Did you get that?'

'Yeah, yeah! Don't worry about Mammy. I will sort that out with her!'

So we did marry. We separated just as quick. But, no matter. I was still a married woman. Not a respectable one. No! I was now a single mother. But thankfully not an unmarried one. That would have made me and the baby social pariahs! No, I was technically a deserted wife! Just one step up. That got you a raised eyebrow, an inquisitive look. We were a shadowy lot. A hidden people. I didn't meet many others. We didn't openly admit it. We didn't exist really. Because this was 'Holy Ireland'. Marriage was sacred. 'Let No Man Put Asunder.'

So then I started the next phase of my life as a deserted wife. The other women shunned me. Mothers at school. I might rob their husbands! The husbands chased me anyway. I was not under the protection of a man, so they thought I was fair game. They were the hunter, and I was the hunted!

Until now! The monk is the first man I have trusted enough to actually allow myself to become emotionally involved with. I wonder what makes him different? Does he remind me of someone? I suppose it's because he's a monk. Spiritual! That means he's decent. He would be responsible. I would be safe with him. He wouldn't try to use me, or hurt me then throw me away. Also, he's working with the mentally ill. That makes him attractive to me. He would understand me. Not judge me for cracking up. I think he's very mature as well. He always seems so calm and steady.

But nothing can come of it. He has his commitment. He's not interested in marriage. But he's actually helped me without knowing it. For the first time in years, I have been able to allow myself to want to get close to a man instead of always being wary of them. Yeah! Things are not as bad as we think. Looking back on the early days of trying to struggle with a baby – they were hard times.

But now I have my own home. Sarah is grown up, and I'm still in my early thirties. Yeah! Life can be a bowl of cherries if ye don't weaken! Roll on the happy days! Thank God for all my blessings. I'm really very lucky. I just went through a very bad time. But that's all in the past now! Ah, I can't wait to get home and start again.

45

I was still staring out the window when Nikki came flying back in and sat down beside me.

'Here! Hold that,' she said, and rushed up to the counter, bringing back a tray with a pot of tea. 'Now, let's cheer ourselves up with a drop of this.' She pulled out a half bottle of whiskey and poured a big splash into the tea, then more again, laughing.

'Anyone watching?' she asked, hiding the cups under the table.

'No!' I said, whipping my eyes around the room.

'Now drink that,' she said.

The heat hit me straight away as it slid down my neck. I felt a buzz in my head and suddenly the room started to seem brighter.

'Doctor's orders!' she said, holding the cup to mine and laughing.

Trust Nikki to think of a way of cheering me up.

'God, Nikki. We're mad! We still have no sense,' I said, thinking of all the trouble we got into over the years. 'Remember the time we got stuck on the autobahn in Switzerland? The cops picked us up, telling us it was *verboten*! And you started yelling, "We bloody know that. It's the gobshite's fault that dumped us here because we wouldn't travel to Istanbul with him in his bloody truck."'

'Yeah!' she roared. 'That was all your fault. I wanted to go but you said no!'

'Yeah! He lost the rag and threw us out. That was because you'd eaten all his grub the night before, and he got nothing in return!'

'God! Don't remind me. You got the night's sleep on the top bunk while I had to wrestle him the whole night, trying to save my virtue!'

'Serves you right, Nikki! I took nothing from him, so he didn't think I owed him something.'

'What do you mean? You ate the whole bunch of bananas he put out for me!' Nikki roared, still feeling sorry for herself after all this time.

'Yeah! The cops dumped us in the village, telling us not to go back near the autobahn. Then we discovered everything was really expensive. We thought when they said, "*Eine schilling*," that was cheap! Until they took a pound off us. Then it was back onto the autobahn again. It looked like bloody spaghetti junction. But we hit lucky. We got a lift from that man in his big Mercedes, and we took the ferry from the lake in Switzerland across to the lake of Bodensee, in Germany.'

'Ah, yeah!' Nikki said. 'Then we met the mad German, Helmut. He brought us to the Austrian Alps.'

'Yeah! He took me skiing, Nikki, until he discovered I couldn't ski. Then I spent the afternoon on the nursery slopes while you were still sunning yourself back at the Gasthaus, sitting in hair rollers and trying to make yourself gorgeous, hoping to get him off me.'

'Bloody bitch!' Nikki moaned. 'I had to entertain meself with little Adolf, the owner of the inn! His wife kept screaming at him and waving huge knives at me while she was cutting up the vegetables for the evening dinner!'

We snorted laughing into our cups, then my eye slid to the piano. No sight of the melancholic.

'Come on! Let's have a go,' I said, dashing over to the piano. I lifted the lid and started to bang out 'Soft as the Voice of an Angel'. The only thing I could play properly. Nikki banged on the other end, and we played a duet.

A thin, white-faced, elderly man in his sixties came creeping over and sat down at a table beside us. I started to sing softly. I had been in the church choir when I was in the convent. We sang Latin hymns for the Mass. Yeah! Until I got booted out for telling the choir nun, when she asked me: *'Martha Long! Why are you scratching your head?'*

'I have ringworm, Sister Benedict.'

'Out! Get out of my choir, you filthy creature!' she screamed, banging on the gong, looking for Sister Eleanor with one hand, holding me in an iron vice grip with the other.

'Why did you tell her that?' Sister Eleanor roared at me, red-faced. 'You have no such thing!' she said, tearing her eyes and fingers through me head, then looking at my neck.

'Oh! I thought I had. I heard one of the other kids saying they had it, and it sounded interesting to me, like something I might have!'

'Come on! Play "When the Saints".'

'Right!' I said, banging away with two fingers while she banged the other end.

'Oh! Oh! Oh, when the Saints! Oh, when the Saints! Oh, when the Saints come marching in! Tra la la la,' I wailed, not knowing the rest of the words. But it sounded great!

When we finished, the little man came shuffling over with his hands in fists held out in front of him, and leaned into us, asking with rheumy eyes filled with sadness, 'Will ye ever play "If You Were the Only Girl in the World". Do ye know it at all?' he asked us hopefully.

'Yeah! Yeah! I know it!' I said, delighted.

I banged away at the keys, looking for the right note to start. 'OK! You sing,' I said, starting off slowly, playing by ear.

Nikki tinkered away at the other end, getting the key, then we were away.

'What's your name?'

'Tom!' he said.

'OK, Tom.'

I sang low to get him started. Then his voice lifted, 'If you were the only girl in the world, and I was the only boy,' he sang in a very sad, hauntingly lonely old man's voice. It was beautiful, and I felt tears at the back of my eyes, and my chest started filling up. I was back in the little bedsitting room all those years ago. When I was seventeen, living on my own, lying in bed at night, listening to the old man in the room next door sing himself, and me, to sleep every night. He had come back to Ireland after working for years on building sites in England during the war. Now he was living out the last days of his life where he wanted to be buried, he said. He'd left enough money to be taken back to his beloved Sligo. And even had his grave ready. There were no living relatives left there, so he stayed in Dublin.

His voice haunted me, and his loneliness swept through the wall between us and wrapped itself around me, and I felt it mix with mine. We shared that loneliness. For that short while, in the late hour of the night, we were deeply connected, and he probably never knew. But I was young then and had it all ahead of me. I had the

chance of shaking it off me, hoping for a bright future. Whereas he
. . . his was all gone.

I looked at Tom, and tears were spilling down his face, and I
reached out and gave him a hug and kissed his soft cheek.

'Thank you,' he muttered. 'I enjoyed tha,' taking out his hankie
and wiping his eyes.

I laughed through my tears at Nikki, saying, 'It's good to cry
sometimes.'

Tom lifted his head, smiling, and started singing, 'It's a long way
to Tipperary! It's a long way to go! . . . Pack up your troubles in your
old kit bag and smile, smile, smile.'

We were cheering ourselves up, and the room was brightening.
People started sitting around the piano and joining in. Others started
peeling in the door, until we had a concert going. Someone started
singing, '*Non, je ne regrette rien!*'

Ah! One of my favourites! The Great Edith Piaf! We all joined in,
and the old man sang 'I'll Take You Home Again, Kathleen'.

People had tears in their eyes. So had I. But it was a nice sadness –
we were not alone. Everyone was silently, within themselves, sharing
their moments of joy and great sadness.

Then we got raucous and started roaring our heads off, singing,
'AS I CAME HOME ONE SATURDAY NIGHT, AS DRUNK
AS DRUNK COULD BE! I SAW A HEAD UPON THE BED
WHERE MY AUL HEAD SHOULD BE! WELL, I TURNED
TO ME WIFE AND I SAID TE HER, "WOULD YE KINDLY
TELL TE ME WHO OWNS THAT HEAD UPON THE BED,
WHERE MY AUL HEAD SHOULD BE!"

'"AH! YE'RE DRUNK! YE'RE DRUNK! YE SILLY AUL
FOOL!"'

We banged away, singing and laughing and crying, and then the
nurses came in – some of them were here already.

'Tea time!' they roared, clapping their hands.

'Everybody down to the dining room for tea, please!' shouted Jam-
jar, putting his hand around his mouth, trying to make a megaphone
and herding everybody out.

I closed the lid on the piano, and Nikki said, 'That was the best
impromptu party I've had for a long while.'

She stretched, red-faced from all the whiskey she drank. I had about three; she drank the rest. She leaned over, giving me a hug and a kiss. 'You take care of yourself and get back to life. The world is not the same without you.'

I felt a warmth sweep through me and was grateful to Nikki for her goodness at taking the time to come and spend the entire day with me. We have been friends for a long time – fought over men, then when we won, the man was forgotten and we were friends again.

'Bye, darling!' I said, hugging her. 'Now, keep your beady eyes off that monk. Don't you go robbing that fella from under my nose. It's hands off! I saw him first.'

'Ah, now!' she said, with a mad glint in her eye. 'I might just crack up and get meself a bed in here. Jaysus! Can you imagine! The pair of us stuck in here together! Everyone would crack up, and the place would shut down.'

'Yeah! I would go home feeling much better and taking the monk with me!'

We roared laughing, then she dumped the empty bottle in the bin and waved back, walking up the stairs and out the door. I watched her go, still wondering how I ended up here.

You never know what is in the future. People used to think I had it made. Even Nikki. My own home, a beautiful child, car, holidays on the Continent, and no man to answer to. That was in a time when women had to have a man if you had a child. Now look at me! I think now, what I had really wanted was a happy family. A decent man I would feel safe with, one who would love me for myself, accept me and never let me down.

I sighed, wondering if I'll ever be happy. I can't seem to get it right! I looked around at the people all heading up for their tea. Some of them are very gifted people. People who'd had very full lives. Some had professions, others had reared families, and I wondered what went wrong. They looked like the living dead, shuffling along, doped up to the eyeballs, pain written all over their faces.

Some had suffered breakdowns. I still don't know what that really means. Couldn't cope any longer, I suppose. Just riddled with terrible depression, and some are cursed with manic depression.

One woman walked out of here and managed to get on a plane

and arrive in Paris! She didn't even have a plane ticket, never mind a passport. The worst thing was they didn't even know she was missing until they got a phone call from the police. She was discovered when she arrived back at the airport and tried to get on the plane without a ticket after having a lovely day out for herself walking the streets of Paris! She's a manic-depressive, and she was flying high as a kite that day. Jaysus! She sure was. In more ways than one!

I joined in with the moving masses heading back up to the ward, wishing I was going home to a husband and children, planning what I would cook. It's the simple things, the routine of having continuity. The knowing you are wanted and needed. Yeah! That is what I crave.

I crept into the dining room like a snail, my head feeling none the better from the booze. My eyes fell on Blondie having an argument with Maggie. They were pulling the jug of milk between them, slopping it on the table. Blondie was laughing, tormenting Maggie. She wouldn't let her have the milk.

'Nurse! Nurse!' screeched Maggie. 'Sort out tha bloody cow! She's keepin all the milk on her side.'

I crept off, looking for another table. I'm not in the mood for those two. I sat down at the back of the room with the big woman. The one who told me on the day I arrived that she was going to 'walk backwards for Christmas'.

'Good evening, my dear!' she said. 'Do feel free to join me.'

I sat down, glad to be in the company of civilised people.

'Do try the salad. It is salmon this evening.'

I looked at her plate. It looks nice! Salmon and potato salad with a bit of lettuce and tomato.

'Yes! Good idea. I think I'll try that,' I said, looking around for a nurse.

The monk was standing in the centre of the room, balancing a plate of grub in the palm of his hand, and the other one tucked into his pocket. He spotted me and grinned, making his way over to me. For once, my heart didn't go bing-bong-a-bong! I looked at him in a different light. Somehow, he reminded me of a Rolls-Royce without the engine! I needed a real man.

He plonked down a plate in front of me, lifting the cover. I stared.

'Eat! It is good for you,' he bullied.

'I intend to! Thank you!' I said, dismissing him and milling into the salmon.

'I am hearing you were making a lot of noise with the other patients.'

'What did you say?' I asked him coldly.

He smiled, showing his snow-white teeth. I stared. This man likes to get by on his looks. He plays games with people, I thought, my eyes taking in the length of him. Yes, he's gifted with almighty good looks, but I wonder if there is any real substance to him.

I went back to eating my supper, and he wandered off to stop at Blondie's table. I watched him stoop down and say something to her. She gave an almighty cackle and slapped him on the shoulder, screaming, 'Where did you hear that? Oh, you are very naughty!'

I took no notice, turning away, and looked at my companion. She was nibbling on her salmon, taking dainty little bites, and breaking her roll into tiny pieces.

'Where do you live?' I asked.

'Mulberry House, my dear. Do you know, at one time we had an enormous staff to run that house. Of course, we only stayed there for the season.'

'Oh, where did you live?'

'Belgravia, London, my dear! But then we had the old pile in the country. But, of course, that is all gone now. Yes, indeed,' she sighed, heaving in her big chest through the embroidered linen blouse. It buttoned up to her neck.

'You look quite Edwardian, you know,' I heard myself saying, delighted to give her the benefit of my good manners, good breeding, good education! Who're ye fooling, Martha? Anyway, I picked it all up from a real lady, just like this one, when I stayed with her for a few months. She made a huge impression on me. I went on to polish myself, using her as me role model. I reserve that side of me for only the most discerning and civilised, of course. It's not for ordinary living. I would sound like a real eegit! A pretentious prat!

Hmm! Who says I'm not? Anyway, it was something I grew into, after years of developing a bit of culture for myself. Fuck! I'm all confused again! One minute I would be happier with Maggie, the next I'm sitting, wanting to give the impression I'm just like your woman here! Hmm! I'm in the right place! Good, so do what you want.

I leaned into the table, listening intently.

'Oh, yes, indeed! It is just my sister and I, poor Marina, left now to take care of everything.'

I listened to her voice and watched as she waved her arms around in the air.

'Including the cats!' she gasped, looking horrified. 'They really are our children, you know. I do hope she is managing to feed them.' Then she leaned across the table and whispered, looking around to make sure no one was listening, 'She tends to get forgetful, my dear. Oh, it is so beastly my being stuck in here!'

'Indeed! It is a dreadfully beastly place to be stuck,' I said, getting into the swing of being in civilised company.

'I am Lady Petunia Fitzponze!' she announced, extending her hand in friendship.

'Oh! How do you do?' I said, in my finest polished accent. 'My name is Martha.'

'I am absolutely delighted to meet you, Martha,' Lady P. said, picking up her fork and continuing to examine her plate for the tastiest morsels.

My good breeding did not go that far. I took one look at the salmon and forked a huge chunk into my open mouth.

'You must call and pay us a visit,' she said, wiping the corners of her mouth with a napkin. She had barely touched anything, so there was nothing to wipe. 'My sister and I would be delighted to have you visit. You are a wonderfully charming young lady, and sooo pretty! Such lovely hair!'

I was all ears! This lady has definite good taste. She sees something the other ratbags don't see!

'I would be delighted to come and visit you both,' I said, getting quite carried away with my good manners. I had the feeling I was at last meeting someone on my own wavelength. I'm definitely a born aristocrat! There must have been a mix-up in the maternity ward. I got stuck with a pauper. No, worse! Bloody Sally! No wonder things could only get better after that!

'Do you find,' I said, leaning towards her, 'good manners are disappointingly disappearing with the rise of the hoi polloi? I blame the free education, of course,' I sniffed, waving my serviette. 'Now any old Joe Soap can set foot inside Trinity College. And absolutely no breeding whatsoever, my dear!' I said, shocked, forgetting I had never set foot inside a schoolroom and only took a short cut through the yard at Trinity College.

'Absolutely!' she gasped, covering my hand with hers, delighted to meet one of her own. 'I blame the war, of course.'

'Eh! Which war was that?' I asked.

'The Great War, of course! That gave the common man a foot in the door. Nothing has ever been quite the same since!' Then she banged down her serviette and started to get red in the face. Oh, oh! Trouble, I'm thinking.

'Nurse!' she barked. 'Take this plate away at once! Tell Cook the fish is off! It is most definitely not fresh! Servants are so lazy!' she snapped, looking around the room and snorting. 'I shall have them all fired at once!'

I had had enough to eat and took off, saying, 'Thank you so much for the supper. Delighted to meet you!' and legged it out of the dining room. No! That's enough excitement for one day. Jaysus! Nothing is what it seems in this place! You can be having a normal conversation one minute, then the next . . .

I rushed into my room, throwing off my clothes, and dived into my pyjamas. Then I grabbed my wash things and headed off to the bathroom, feeling exhausted. Dying to soak in a nice hot bath.

Oh, that was lovely! I headed out of the bathroom looking red as a lobster and making straight for my bed.

'Yoo hoo!'

I looked over to see Blondie waving over at me from the alcove.

'Are you coming over?' she roared, and slapped the space beside her. 'Come on out! We'll have a laugh.'

I hesitated, then saw she was all dressed up.

'Be out in a minute!' I said, rushing into my room and plaiting my hair for the night. I looked in the mirror to admire myself. A skeleton version of Pippi Longstocking looked back at me. Ah, who cares? I'll get more human looking when the weight comes back. Now! Out to see what your woman is all dressed up for.

I padded over to Blondie and sat down beside her, drawing up my bare feet. I eyed her long black-silk skirt with the slit up to her belly button, showing the tops of her stockings and even the garter belt! I took in her white silk blouse with the low cut showing a gorgeous diamond pendant. Her blonde hair was gathered up in a chignon, with wisps hanging around her ears and little curls framing her forehead. A surge of heat ran through my belly. I was raging! Mad jealous!

'What are you all dressed up for?'

'Oh! Didn't you notice who's on duty?'

'No, who?'

She looked around, smiling, and inclined her head down the room. I followed her eyeline, spotting the Russian snaking his way along the wall with his hands in his pockets. His eye caught us looking, and he flicked away immediately.

'Oh, him! No! I've lost interest. He's only dessert. I prefer dinner!'

'Like hell!' she roared.

'It's true!' I said, wondering who I was kidding. But still and all. My antenna is up. That means danger! 'Somehow or other I get the feeling he's floating around Europe, looking for an opportunity.'

She turned her head, watching him, her eyes narrowing.

'Did you get done up in this rig-out for him?' I asked, throwing my head in his direction.

'No! My husband came to see me.'

'Oh, I missed that. When?'

'He's just gone. Back home to a lonely house. I told him to take it easy on those hills. The roads are very narrow, and with these dark nights . . .'

'Where do you live?'

'Killiney Hill.'

'Overlooking the bay?'

'Yes.'

'My goodness! That's very grand! He must be loaded!'

'Yes, he is,' she said crisply. 'And old.'

'Oh,' I said, picking up her mood dropping. 'Do you have children?' I asked her softly.

'No, only two dogs, Twiggy and Jeff, they're poodles.'

'Did you want children, or did you marry for money?'

'Both!' she said. 'But Dick can't have children. He didn't tell me until after we were married.'

'So, this was a first marriage for both of you?'

'No, he's my first, but I'm his third wife. He's in his seventies, and he had mumps when he was a young man, it made him sterile. So we'll never have children,' she said with a faraway look in her eyes.

'But we do have a large Georgian mansion with big entrance gates on two acres of land. He owns property in half of Dublin. I have a woman to take care of the house. I drive a two-seater Mercedes, and I am stuck in this place!' she said, looking around bitterly.

'So you really wanted children?' I said quietly.

'Yes! I would give it all up tomorrow for a child.'

I looked over to the monk, laughed and said, 'There's your donor!'

She looked up, thinking, and spun her head around to look at me. 'I would in a flash, but what would I tell my husband?' she asked, staring at me, eyes wide.

I laughed. 'Tell him you are the Virgin Mary, and the Angel Sebastian gave you a message, you are going to have a "miracle baby".'

She screamed laughing.

'Look, Blondie! Your husband is not going to live for ever. Meanwhile, you are not getting any younger. So you have to make a decision.'

'He would kill me, or if I did something to hurt him, it would kill him! I don't know what I'm going to do with myself.'

'So, meanwhile, you are hoping to have some fun with the monk, is that it?'

'Yes!' she said. 'What about you?'

'Ah, it was fun. He's very attractive all right, and he has kept me going. But it's wearing a bit thin now. I have to start thinking of reality. It's time to start looking at what I am going to do with my life. My daughter is now grown up. So I think it's time to move on. Start again. Look after myself for a change. But I don't really know how to do that. I think if I'm left to my own resources, I'm not really interested in just doing things for myself. I missed that opportunity when I was a young one. The last time I was free I was just seventeen. Starting off in life! I made a mistake, and this is where I ended up! I suppose I get my sense of self-worth from taking care of other people. That's all I know.'

I looked at Blondie, and she was listening with her eyes. I could see she felt for me.

'Yeah! We are a right pair of eegits, ending up here when we have everything going for us,' she said wryly.

The monk was chatting to two women in their thirties. The dark-haired one with the freckles and the fat face, she was a doctor and never married. Now she's had a breakdown. She comes from a very wealthy background. Her father was a heart specialist and a good businessman. She told me he made some very wise investments. She still lives at home with the ma, and her sister and her husband. They live in a huge house in its own grounds, overlooking Howth.

'Where's Maggie?' I asked, looking around. I knew there was something missing.

'She's gone to bed, having an early night. Tomorrow they are taking her down for ECT.'

'No!' I said. 'Putting electrodes on her head and sending bolts of electricity through her brain?'

'Yes! That's exactly what they do!'

'But that destroys the brain cells and the memory banks.'

'I know! But they still use it on patients,' Blondie said, snorting in air and looking around disgusted. 'Mental hospitals can give you the creeps if you think about it.'

'Yeah! The bastards hold the power of life and death. They even control when you are released. You can be bunged back in any time. Once you're in the system, it's easy to control you. They watch everything. I just want to get out. It's time I moved on,' I said, feeling a shiver of fear run through me.

The monk stood up, his eyes turning in our direction. I could see he was heading over to us. He took that slow walk of his. First, the right leg, lifted into the air, held for a brief second, then he swung it down, bringing up the left leg – it was like a slow march.

'Good evening, ladies,' he said, his eyes melting at the sight of Blondie giving him a glimpse of milky-white thigh. He was staring at the top of her leg encased in a black stocking with a blue frilly garter.

I suddenly jumped up. 'I'm off to bed. You take care and behave yourself!' I whispered, laughing.

'See you in the morning,' she drawled, basking at the sight of the monk eating her alive with his hot eyes.

The monk looked after me, then sat down happily beside Blondie. I could hear them laughing. I had purpose in my step when I headed into my bedroom. It's definitely time to move on. I'm getting out of this place and heading off to the States as soon as I build myself up.

Nikki did just that and had a great time. At least she did until she got herself deported! Silly fool. She was warned not to leave the States until her green card came through. The wealthy people she was working for were going to sponsor her. But, oh no! Our Nikki wasn't satisfied until she took herself down to Mexico for a visit, then got nabbed off the bus by Immigration when she tried to get back in. She was working illegally! Now the bloody fool won't ever be allowed to return to the States. The people she had worked for had to send all her stuff home, and the money she had stuffed under her mattress. Thousands of pounds were delivered by armoured truck. That was hilarious! Pity, though, I could have gone over and joined her. We would have worked together.

So! First thing is to see the doctor and get myself out of here and off home. Then start trying to let out the house. Then apply for a visa – holiday one, of course – and find a job! Fine! OK. I'm happy with that plan. It's a good one and should work out. Next thing is, health! I have to build myself up. Eat plenty, take lots of fresh air and make sure to get a good night's sleep. That means going to bed early. Sleep and I'm away in a hack! Yippee! Watch out, world! I'm coming back!

The door opened and the monk breezed in.

'Why are you in bed so early? Your friend would like your company.'

'I want to get some sleep,' I said, whipping the duvet over me and turning on my side.

He went up to the window and stared out, looking at the dark night and the leaves blowing around in the wind. I ignored him; he's not important to me any more.

'When do you go home?' he suddenly said, looking around to stare at me.

'Soon! I will be going as soon as they let me out. I am going to work on that doctor, convince him I'm no longer a danger to myself.'

'Good! Do you live in Dublin?'

'Yes! I have my own home and share it with my dog Bonzo.'

'Hmm,' he said, thinking. Then he wandered out without saying another word. I stared after him.

46

I was down in the passage, waiting for the doctor. The nurse had said he wanted to see me, and I was to wait here for him. Things are getting better! The doctor wants to see me in his office! He actually asked to see me! Maybe I can go home today, or if not it will surely be soon.

Rory came over and asked me did I want a game of table tennis with him.

'No, thanks, Rory,' I said, moving away and strolling down the hall, not wanting to get bogged down with him. I needed to concentrate and think about what I was going to say. It's better to keep my mind clear for that doctor.

People wandered up and down the passage, wanting to stop and talk. I look like a spare part standing in the one spot for so long. I'm usually on the move, so everyone wants to know what I'm up to. I saw the monk come down the stairs, glance up to where I was standing and move on. I suppose he thought I was going to run up and start chatting him up. But he has been ignoring me since I starting losing interest in him. I'm not bothered with the carry-on of chasing him any more. It has served its purpose. Now it's time to get serious. I want to get home.

I was still standing here when the monk suddenly appeared out of nowhere. He's like a bloody snake, the way he creeps up on you!

'Would you like to play a game of table tennis with me?' he asked, looking a little confused. Probably because I gave up chasing him.

'Perhaps later. Right now I am waiting to see the doctor.'

'OK. I will see you around,' he said, wandering off.

A tall, well-built doctor came marching up and stood right in front of me, with his feet planted flat on the floor, and stared at me without saying anything. Then he looked at a file under his arm, and said, 'Hmm,' with a smile playing around his mouth, thinking. Then he gave me an even more penetrating stare, saying, 'Come along to my office,' making it look like he had made a decision.

He marched off, with me following at a trot. Jaysus! I can't read him. This could go either way. For sure, he must be thinking of letting me home, I hoped, following him for miles.

He stopped at a door, opened it and stood back to let me in. My mind was made up. OK, Martha! You're in charge! I walked in slowly, feeling much more confident.

'Do take a seat,' he said, waving his arm to a comfortable armchair. Then he sat back in his own chair and studied me. 'Yes, yes. You are certainly looking much better. Your hair is beautifully groomed!' he beamed.

It should be, I thought. I had to sleep in head-stabbing rollers to get this look. I was wearing a long green-velvet skirt, which flared out behind me when I walked, with a long embroidered linen petticoat just showing underneath – very elegant, Victorian – with a white-linen blouse and a black belt around my waist. Yep! I'm looking very nice, if I say so myself, I thought happily, watching him taking me in from head to toe.

'Why did you allow yourself to fall so far?' he asked me.

'I don't know. It was gradual. I withdrew more into myself. I was still recovering from a major operation. I nearly lost my life a few times. It came as a shock when my daughter left so suddenly. Everything in my life seemed like it was falling apart. But I didn't see it. I had no insight. I didn't really listen to myself. I was always used to difficulties in my life. I just saw this as one more. So I thought I was coping, taking the dog for his walks, but I was really becoming more and more deeply depressed.

'I saw my daughter's decision to live with her father as a rejection of me. I could have read it differently. Just a simple case of a girl wanting to spend time with her father while she was still young. It was a new experience for her. Perfectly understandable. I could have gone on and relished my new-found freedom. I had earned it. But in my state of mind . . . Well, not only did I make it into a hell for myself but I caused her a lot of pain. We have a very deep bond. It really must have pained her to see I took it badly.

'Our last visit ended badly. Naturally, there was a lot of tension. We were both walking on eggshells. It blew up! So this was all down to me. I was now carrying my head under my arm. Feeling rejected. I turned the rejection into believing I was no good. Nobody would really want me. I was nobody, just useful for looking after other people who needed me for that. But I had no inner resources for looking after myself. I had no conception that I could or should do that. That I was important for just being me. I am not programmed in that way. To myself, I am worth nothing.

'I have existed and felt my worth according to how much I have to offer other people. The harder I work for them, the better it pleases them – that is my reward. Looking at it, I suppose I am a modern-day slave! I can't exist just for myself. There is no worth in that for me. I think if I had a close relationship, I would see my self-worth mirrored in that person's affection for me. But I made a mistake when I was young. I never wanted to repeat that. So I poured all my love into Sarah! I could never trust another man. So really, my problems are deep, but I don't want to start opening a can of worms, bringing up stuff that would destroy me. So I will just have to muddle through.'

'Yes,' he said after a while. 'But what I don't understand is why you just sat and let the train run over you. Most people would move.'

I thought about this. 'I have always been alone! It is not in my make-up to ask for help. I don't understand that concept. I have always had to be self-sufficient. Very few people reached out a helping hand in my formative years. So I don't expect or even think I can get help. For that you have to have a close relationship, a friend, or someone who cares. I didn't have that. So I am limited by lack of knowledge in a lot of ways. I don't trust the authorities. I have no trust in doctors, especially when it comes to emotional pain. Drugs don't help. Talking doesn't help. They can't take away the pain! So when the pain of loneliness, rejection and too many knocks became too much for me, I ended up paralysed. I was not able to get to my feet. So this is where I ended up.'

'Yes,' he said. 'I think you must have someone to talk to. You need to be able to share difficulties. You can't bottle them up. So I would suggest to you that you find some way of developing at least one person you can talk to. We all need this. OK?'

'Yes, I agree. Thank you, Doctor.'

'Now! I am going to allow you to go home for a weekend. Would you like that?'

I was hesitant. Going home? Back to the house? On me own again? Yeah! Home! The reality was just dawning on me. A sudden fear ran through me, getting the last picture of myself there. No! No, I'm not facing that! Go back to that house again? Not in a million years! But how come only a few minutes ago that is exactly what I just wanted?

I looked down at meself, trying to think. I look lovely! I'm really changed. Nearly back to me old self! I'm much more confident again. Life can be great! I can have a great time. Sarah is now gone. Grown up. Off your hands. She's happy! You've done a good job. Now it's your turn. Start again!

Me heart started to lift. Yeah, think of it! I can do anything now. Anything in the whole wide world! What's to stop me? Nothing! Absolutely sweet nothing. Oh, yes! Time to say goodbye to the old; on with the new.

I lifted my head with a big smile on my face, saying, 'Yes! Thank you, Doctor! I would like that very much.'

'OK! Shall we say this weekend?'

'Yes, that would be grand, thanks, Doctor.'

'Today is Tuesday,' he said, thinking. 'You can leave on Friday afternoon, OK?'

'That's fine, lovely, great! Thanks, Doctor,' I beamed, getting all excited.

He stood up and came around, looking at me. 'I think you are looking very well!' he said, looking all pleased they had managed to put me back together again. 'You have made great progress. Now, you should keep yourself well groomed. It does wonders for your morale. You are an attractive young woman. Make the most of yourself.'

'Thank you, Doctor,' I said, grinning at him, feeling delighted me looks were starting to come back. I had gone around long enough looking like a bag lady.

He opened the door wide, saying, 'Have a lovely weekend and enjoy yourself.'

'I will!' I said, tripping off, delighted with myself. Yeah! I'm on the road to recovery.

I swept into the therapy room, looking around for Blondie. The monk came quietly up behind me. That's a first! He's on his own! No Blondie.

Without thinking, I gushed out, 'Guess what?' I stared at him with a grin on my face.

He stared back, shaking his head slowly. 'No, tell me,' he said, giving me a half-smile without opening his mouth.

'I've just seen the doctor!'

'You are going home!' he said, singing the words with his head shaking, then leaning into me with his eyes lighting up, letting a gorgeous smile break out on his face.

'Nope! Wrong!'

'So! What is the good news?' he said, rattling his head, still smiling at me.

'I'm going home this weekend! Brilliant, isn't it?'

'Excellent! So now we will expect to see you behaving yourself!' he grinned, walking off.

I gave myself an extra polish, getting visions of myself looking dazzlingly beautiful when I get to escape out on Friday. Where will I go? Home first anyway. Then, who knows? I have the whole weekend to go where I like. I stared in the mirror and an emaciated corpse stared back at me, looking shockingly white. Lovely! Put more cream on the face – lather it on. Now for the hair. I plastered the head stabbers, or hair rollers as some people call them, all over my head and put a net over them to stop them falling out. Then I stared back in the mirror. Jaysus! Hilda Ogden from *Coronation Street* was staring back at me. But I shall look beautiful in the morning. Wait until Blondie and the monk see me.

I even went around all evening with hot olive oil plastered in my hair. I got a little pot of it from the nurse. Everyone was complaining about the smell. I think that bloody Esther one gave me cooking oil! Anyway, the shine is dazzling! I still can't believe my good fortune. I'm getting back to my old self.

I wafted out of the ward wearing a long gypsy skirt, with my petticoat showing underneath of course. Very fashionable! And a lovely white-linen grandad shirt buttoned up to the neck, no collar. My hair was streaming around my back in curls and waves, and the highlights were dancing around my head – it looks coppery. Yeah! I'm looking lovely.

'Esther! Could you let me out, please? I'm off down to therapy.'

'Come on then,' Esther said, pulling the keys from around her waistband and giving me a sour look. Like she was jealous because I'm all done up and wafting myself around the place, with the meals handed up to me, and she has to work. There's no justice in that!

I sailed out the door, waving and laughing. 'Bye, Nurse!'

She slammed the door shut with an unmerciful bang, raising her eyes to heaven, looking like she had the weight of the world on her shoulders.

I bombed down the stairs, taking them two at a time, definitely feeling my old self again. I could now get down on my own. A trustee! Yep! Things are looking up.

I bounded into therapy, waving at the nurses in their little boxes. They squinted out at me, and Jam-jar gave me a second look. I winked at him, giving him the thumbs up. He wasn't impressed and leapt out of his box, roaring, 'I'm watching you! We want no trouble down here!'

'Yes, dahlink! And I . . . ham watching you!' I breathed, blowing him a slow sexy kiss!

He put his head back in, muttering, 'The cheeky so and so! She better watch herself, that one!'

The other nurses laughed, getting great enjoyment outa him. Jam-jar takes himself and life too seriously! I thought, laughing.

I sailed down the room, spotting Blondie.

'I'm over here!' she laughed, trying to learn to play chess with Seamus.

'Hi, Seamus!'

'Oh, hello!' he said, looking at me with a glint in his eye.

'I'm off to play ping-pong.'

'Yeah,' Blondie laughed. 'Give me a minute, until I grab Seamus's king. Then I'll be up with you.'

Seamus snorted. 'Spoken like a true amateur! A little knowledge is a . . .' Then he stabbed her with his queen and cornered her with his rook. 'CHECKMATE, dear girl!'

'Ahh, no!' Blondie stared. 'How did you do that?' she asked, looking stricken at the board, her eyes swimming around, looking for a way out.

He laughed, giving her a quiet, superior look, then started setting up the board again. 'Do you play?' he asked crisply, rounding on me, hoping to demolish me as well.

'As a matter of fact I do. I used to play with my daughter through many a long winter night.' My horizon suddenly darkened, sadness sweeping through my chest as the memory of those long, lonely nights suddenly hit me.

Then I shook my head, thinking, no! Dead and gone! Then grinned, saying, 'Nope! Sorry! I'm off to play table tennis. Coming, Blondie?'

'Right! I'm off, Seamus!' she laughed. 'Thanks for the game.'

She hurried out behind me, staggering on her high heels. I stopped, pointing down at the heels. 'You can't play in those!'

'Course not,' she said, wobbling on the heels. 'I'll take them off!'

We hurried into the room, and Henry and Rory had beaten us to it.

'OK, boys! Time's up! It's our turn now.'

'Absolutely not! We were here first!'

'Yeah,' sniffled Rory, getting himself a bang on the head with the ball.

I bent down and grabbed it. 'Grab the bat from Henry, Blondie!' I grabbed Rory, swiping the bat before he even knew it was gone.

'You can't do that!' screeched Rory, chasing me around the room. Henry was wrestling Blondie. I dived on him, with Rory still on my heels, jumping into the air behind his back and grabbing his bat with both hands.

'That is not playing fair!' Henry screamed.

'Nope! Life is not fair, Henry. Now out of the way!' I pushed him to one side, and they both stood sulking against the wall.

'Ready, Blondie?' I said, straddling the table. I swung the bat gently, getting the feel. I like this game – it's fun. The bat is light, and it's all in the hand and eye. Years of playing pitch penny – taking the well-polished and much loved 'lucky pennies' off the young fellas as a kid – has trained my eye.

I stand back, watching the ball fly through the air, then relax, get into position, and my eye darts to the spot where I want it to land, which is the corner of the table, and HEY PRESTO! Blondie is tearing around the room like a blue-arse fly, skidding in her tights after the ball.

'Ah! Come on, Blondie! So far, I've beaten you three games to nil! You taught me to play this. Now the student is overtaking the master!'

'I'll play you!' shouted Henry.

'Give him the bat, Blondie, and watch me demolish him.' I was having the time of my life. This game is great. I never played games in my life, really. I had more important things to be doing with my time. Mother of God! I feel like a child, a very happy one. Yeah, I'm having my second childhood!

I hugged the table, whipping the ball back at lightning speed, slicing it against the corner of the table. A queue was now forming. Kids from the junior section were waiting to take on the aul one. Me! I was now staring down at a pale-faced young fella of seventeen. His eyes were like glass, and he was watching me very intently.

'I haven't got much chance against you kids,' I said, laughing. 'You play games in your private school all the time.'

He didn't respond but just limbered up along his side of the table, watching me intently, ready to smack the ball back. He was intent on beating me, like his life depended on it.

'Right!' I said, smacking the ball into the middle of the table. He sent it hurtling back. I dived left, swinging myself around, and swiped it back, slowing down my breathing.

It came singing back, humming past my ear. I leaned back, throwing the bat to my left hand, and jumped, sending it scorching back, aimed for the corner of the table. My eyes were glued, watching as it sliced off and smacked against the far wall. I was delighted. Game, set and match to me.

The poor young fella shook his shoulders, trying to understand how he'd lost. I felt sorry for him, watching him shuffle off with his hands deep down in his pockets. It would have done his confidence a lot of good. But this is survival. I need to boost my own hopes, confidence, belief and energy. I need a reason to live, and I'm getting there!

'I have a present for you,' Henry said, haring back into the room and handing me a little gift-wrapped package. 'I had my sister buy it for you!'

I examined the package, while Henry waited, like this was the most important thing I was missing in my whole life. 'What is it, Henry?'

'A diamante hair slide,' he said, pointing to my curls, then grabbing hold of them, manhandling and juggling them up and down. 'I love your hair!' he sniffed, wrapping my curls through his hands and rubbing handfuls across his nostrils.

'Oh, Henry! You are really good,' I said, feeling very warm towards him. I leaned into him. 'Give us a kiss, you gorgeous thing.'

He went straight for my lips.

'No, no! Naughty boy! On the cheek. We're not engaged yet!' Then I gave him a hug.

'Hmm, you smell nice,' he said, grabbing me in a bear's hug.

'That's yer ration of passion for the day, Henry,' I said, pushing him away and laughing.

Blondie was roaring her head off laughing. 'Tsk, tsk! You should be ashamed of yourself, Martha. Cradle snatching!'

'And you should keep away from that Russian!' roared Henry, red-faced and disgusted because Blondie called him a baby. 'That fellow is up to no good. I have seen the pair of you go twittering around him, and he is dangerous. I'm telling you! I have been watching him. That fellow has managed to get himself out from behind the Iron Curtain, and he does not want to return. He's floating around Europe looking for an opportunity, and he will use you!'

I stared at him as Blondie laughed her head off, saying, 'He's doing no such thing. Ah, go on, Henry! You are just jealous. But never mind. You are a grand little fella, and don't worry, I'll wait for you until you grow up into a lovely handsome man!' she laughed, tormenting him.

Henry grabbed the bat and started bouncing balls off Blondie. She ducked and ran out of the room on her high heels, laughing.

'I'll be seeing you, Henry,' I said, walking out of the room, a cold chill running through me, thinking, the voice of reason? Out of the mouths of babes and sucklings. I wonder! Those very words he's just spoken are exactly what I had been thinking. Yeah! Enough messing,

Martha. It might start off as fun, but these things can develop a momentum of their own. It's all too easy when you are vulnerable. Watch your step, lady!

I saw Jam-jar making a beeline straight for me and I stopped.

'You are wanted back in the ward,' he shouted down to me, waving me towards the door. 'Go up now.'

'OK! I'll see you later, Blondie.'

'I hope you didn't get up to anything!' she said, laughing and wondering what it was about.

'I'll soon find out,' I said, heading for the stairs.

'Get your things together, Martha. We're moving you downstairs.'

'Who, me?'

'Yes, you! But don't look so worried. You will be able to move about down there more freely. St Elisabeth's means you are on your way home!'

I trailed my way like a snail into my room and looked around, then stood staring at my wardrobe. I had this all to myself for nearly the last four months. Everything was in its place. Everything in order. I always have to have that. It makes me feel secure. I can't stand chaos! It means being marooned, drifting around in a canoe without a paddle, and I can't swim.

I don't like moving – change. It means being uprooted. Lost again, left wandering and having nothing I can call my own, nobody belonging to me. It plunges me right back with the aul fella Jackser, trapped in his iron grip. I shook my head, not allowing the picture of my old life to take root. No, never mind him. There's no point in going back to the past. That doesn't exist any more. I felt depressed at the thought of having to change. I like things as they are, I sniffed, my eyes darting around the room, trying to think of a way out. Bloody change always will frighten me. I wanted to sit down and cry and wail like a baby. Angry with the fucking staff for pushing me on.

I know deep down in my heart they are only doing it for my own good. But fuck that! It's too soon. I want to make the change myself, when I'm ready. Oh, dear God! I can feel me heart sinking down into me belly, bringing a heavy weight that is starting to paralyse me all over again. When will this ever end?

Ahh! Jesus Christ! These were supposed to be the best years of me life. Sarah is now on her feet. I'm free again. I kept going all these years looking forward to now. Ohh! I don't understand! Why does my past keep coming back to haunt me now? I sank down on the bed, burying my head in my hands. I'm tormented with these thoughts! I closed my eyes, letting the pictures fly through my head.

47

I remember when I moved into my home. My very first home in my whole life. I couldn't believe it was happening to me. Years of hard work, striving relentlessly, and finally I had arrived. Sarah and I moved in. But I couldn't settle. I kept wandering back to my old flat, where I had lived for years with Sarah. She was only a little thing when we moved in. But I felt my whole adult life was there. All my memories – the good and the bad. The old flat was unlucky, no doubt about that. It had been built for an aristocrat's mistress. Sarah discovered the old tunnel he used to come and visit his little bit of fluff. It led straight through to the great big manor house now lying in ruins on the grounds of the old estate.

Our flat was one half of the whole ground floor of an old Georgian house. It had been beautiful in its day, but we had water running down the walls like the Catacombs of Paris, the black mould turning everything into muck that was left lying under the beds, and the clothes turned green in the wardrobe. The sheets on our beds would have steam rising out of them when our cold damp bodies heated them up. The mice would play ring-a-ring-a-rosy in the frying pan. They had squatters' rights, because no matter how many traps I laid, they bred faster than I could shift them.

No woman could keep a man in that house. The couple who had lived in the flat before us moved out, going their separate ways and swearing undying hatred for each other. Young newlyweds moved in to the flat upstairs – the old widow who had lived there for over forty years died. They put a face on me that would turn milk sour. All that kissing and holding hands! Then it was the removal van and promises to put Mafia contracts out on each other, swearing the other would die first.

In five flats, one marriage lasted thirty years, then they moved into the flat upstairs and he was gone! He legged it with the only single woman in the house, who had moved in next door to them. She had just left home after recovering from a nervous breakdown. The only thing I learned about her was that she was a civil servant, her name was Madge and she didn't like fleas! In fact, she was terrified of them. Only last night she had spent the entire night shivering in the chair when she discovered one in her bed, she confided, gasping and holding her hand to her mouth, her eyes bulging. I gasped, thinking of the mattress walking off with me still clinging to it as a child. We were riddled with fleas, and other things!

I stared as she told me her business, my mouth open and my head shaking up and down, watching her eyes darting around as she talked to me, probably keeping an eye out for the fleas. Then she was gone, taking the dapper little dandy with the silver-head-of-a-lion walking stick with her, leaving his broken-hearted wife to console herself with the woman's husband from two doors down. He was a retired sea captain. The other husbands all died.

I was shocked by the carryings-on of these middle-class, elderly people. They were shocked when I sunbathed in my knickers and nothing else, out in the garden hidden by the hedge. I thought, Verily, it is true what they say. 'The aristocrat's wife put a curse on the house,' I used to go around muttering. But I felt my soul belonged there. I made all my decisions about our lives there, for Sarah and me. I often sat in the kitchen at night. It was warmer than the huge drawing room. I would read and think and even cry with awful loneliness that always came creeping back when I felt overwhelmed with worry. Especially around Christmas. We didn't have anyone we could go to – that was bloody lonely. I felt it for Sarah. I found it difficult enough to get the money for the rent, never mind getting the presents for little Sarah, and the food, and the coal for the fire. Yeah, it was certainly tough going then. But we survived.

One Christmas was really bad. Sarah was very sick. She got infective hepatitis. It was going around the school. I watched the doctor take off out the door after letting me know what I already knew – what was wrong with her. I looked at her lying in the bed, with the tired, pinched, yellow-white face looking up at me like an old woman at eight years of age. She was so tired and couldn't keep anything in her stomach.

I grabbed the phone and rang the children's hospital. 'I want to speak to the ward sister, please,' I said to the voice at the other end, then asked, 'How do I nurse her, Sister?'

'Well, diet is very important. Her liver is not working. So don't give her anything with fat. No milk, cheese, eggs or fatty meat. Absolutely nothing with fat. She needs plenty of rest. It will take at least six weeks for her liver to recover.'

'But she will recover,' I said, 'if I do exactly what you just instructed? If I give her plenty of rest and nothing with fat, and keep her in bed rest for at least six weeks?'

'Yes! Goodbye now,' she said.

'Thank you, Sister,' I said, putting down the phone, feeling more in control now I knew what needed to be done.

I got a piece of paper and wrote down what I could feed her. OK. Meat, fillet – that would be good for her. Brown bread with tomatoes on top. Plenty of good fresh vegetables. Right! Next question is how do I get the money? I can't leave the house. So I won't be able to work. Fuck!

I sat down at the little red-topped round table, looking around the narrow, old-fashioned kitchen. I stared up at the shelf holding the battered old Bush radio that crackled and hissed before springing into life. Then my eyes wandered over to the gas cooker standing in the middle between the two old presses, with a worktop one end and a Belfast sink at the other, listening to the never-ending dripping tap that was nearly company. It broke the deadly silence.

It was beginning to get dark. I looked up at the big, old, high window overlooking the backyard. The grey, damp night mist was pressing its nose against the window, bringing in the dark, showing it was nearly Christmas week. Jaysus! Money! How much have I got? I knew exactly what I had as I reached up to the shelf, taking down my handbag. I opened the little brown purse, counting out the change. One pound and thirty-seven pence. I checked the back of the purse, counting out six ten-pound notes. Sixty pounds. I can't touch that. That's put by for the rent. The rent man will be around in the morning looking for his money. At least that will get us a roof over our head for another month. We can't afford to get ourselves put out on the street.

Right! I'm going to need money for the bottle of gas. I will need that for the Superser heater. Jaysus! That thing eats the gas. It's grand when it's heating, if you sit right up to it. But the place freezes when I have to switch it off. It causes an awful lot of condensation, leaving the air cold and damp. The only good thing about it is you can push it around the place. That bottle is nearly empty. Fuck! That costs five quid.

OK, think! I'm grand for the rent. So we have the roof over our heads. The electric – I keep that to a minimum. Only the lights – and I spare that – and the little fridge. Sarah's school fees are now paid up for the next year. Fine! So all we need, really, is food and a bit of heat! I could feel me heart beginning to hum with fear as an idea was coming to me.

I stood up, thinking as I took out the hot-water bottle from under the sink and filled the kettle, putting it on the gas cooker. Thank God I don't have to pay a gas bill! No, we have all the cooking for free. I won't let the gas company in to cut it off! I think they got fed up coming around and banging on the front-room window, roaring to be let in.

I filled the bottle with the scalding water and crept into the bedroom, walking around me own bed. I held me breath, seeing she was turned on her side, fast asleep. I made me way over, sliding the hot water bottle in under the blankets, tucking them up around her head, leaving only her nose out for air. Jaysus! It's fucking freezing in here. But at least she's snug up here in the corner, out of the draughts. They're blowing in from all directions what with the big old window on one side letting in the cold – it doesn't close properly – then the draught from the hall. Not to mention the kitchen window letting the icy winds blow in from the backyard. Jaysus! One day I'm going to get me own house. Then no one can put us out on the street. That's always me biggest fear.

Right! I better get moving. I picked up the phone and dialled my friend Gean.

'Hello!'

I listened, hearing the excited voice at the other end getting outa breath at the thought it might be someone interesting.

'Is that you, Magdaline?'

'Yeah! Oh, hi, Martha,' she said, letting the excitement out of her voice.

'Ha! Sorry, love, I'm not Terry Ryan! Has he asked you out yet?'

'Tsk! I'm not after him! He's too boring. Besides, he keeps coming out in a nervous rash every time we try to talk to him. Or at least when I do!' she sniffed.

'Well, now! From what I heard, the pair of you are mad about each other. So stand still and let him make the first move. Don't be crowding him with all your friends. Give the poor young fella a chance,' I said, laughing.

'Yeah, but I don't think he's ever going to ask me out, Martha. He's too shy!' she said, sounding very down in the mouth.

'Right! Listen, love! I'm in a bit of a hurry. Is Gean there?'

'No. She's not in from work yet.'

'Oh.' I could feel me heart sinking.

'Will I get her to phone you when she comes in, Martha?'

'No, that will be too late. The shops will be closed. Listen, darling. Would you be able to come around and keep an eye on Sarah for me? Just for a while. She's sick, and I can't leave her on her own.'

'Yeah, sure. Do you want me to come around now?'

'Yes, oh, would you do that for me, love? That would be a great help!'

'Yeah! I'll just tell Mum, then I'm on my way.'

'Oh, thanks, darling. You're a real lifesaver!'

'See you in a few minutes.'

'Yeah! Bye!'

I hung up the phone and rushed to get my coat on. OK! I need the shopping bags and the money. I better not spend the whole pound. OK! What else do I need? I opened the press on the wall, seeing a half packet of Odlums Porridge. Hmm! I can make that with water. There's no fat in that. Need bread. Only a half packet left. I'll get brown bread, but it's a bit dear and will go fast! Jaysus! I need everything. The press is empty! Pity I couldn't get out to make a few bob this week. No, not with the child being sick. Fuck! There must be a better way of earning a living than going from hand to mouth.

I stepped off the bus and made my way across the path lined with bushes and trees. When I came out into the open area, I could see the car park was full of cars. The area was lit up with the bright lights coming from the big building ahead. It must be the biggest supermarket in the country, with food on one side, then you can wander into the other, where they sell rows and rows of clothes and toys.

I could feel my nerves going. I have an awful fear of big shops. It reminds me too much of when I used to have to go robbing for Jackser. But I have to come here. I need to save me pennies. It's cheaper than the local corner shops.

I pushed my way in through the glass doors, getting blinded by the bright lights, and stooped down to pick up a basket. Then I pushed my way forward, having to fight in through the crowds. It's black with people, all intent on getting their Christmas shopping.

My eyes lit on all the boxes of stuff selling for the Christmas. Tins of biscuits, boxes of chocolates, boxes wrapped with red ribbons holding expensive stuff. The place was heaving with people. I slowly pushed past well-dressed women pushing trolleys of food, muttering to their husbands about what to get next. The husbands followed, trailing behind, pushing cartloads of wine and whiskey, and boxes of crackers and all sorts of luxury stuff.

I made my way to the vegetables. I picked up a net of onions. Jaysus! The price of them. Thirty-two pence for these. There's only six! I stopped for a minute, thinking, letting me eyes wander around the huge shop, watching the wives with their husbands, staggering along with every luxury of food and drink a body could want.

Suddenly, without thinking, I dropped the onions down and made my way back to the front entrance. I let down the basket and took hold of a big trolley. I could feel meself going icy cold, and I started to shiver inside myself. I fixed me face, letting it go still, and stared ahead, making myself go still inside and everything inside me on alert. I was totally concentrated on what I was doing. I wandered along the shelves, picking up the best packets of tea, orange juice for Sarah, mandarin oranges, Bovril, brown sliced bread – Hovis! – six packets of the best fillet of steak. I kept filling the trolley with anything that took my fancy. It's Christmas!

'OK, enough,' I breathed to meself, seeing the trolley was threatening to drop with the amount of stuff stacked high as I could get it. I made my way down the shop and parked the trolley along the side, then went next door to the clothes and toy store. It's all under the one roof. I grabbed another trolley and made me way along the counters and clothes racks.

I picked out a lovely jumper and trousers for Sarah. This will keep her lovely and warm. I picked up nighties and pyjamas, and started filling the trolley. I wandered on, coming to the toy section. That's nice – a lovely white doll's wardrobe for Sindy, the doll who has everything! I picked her up, landing her in the trolley beside the wardrobe. Oh, these are lovely. Packets of clothes for Sindy. A riding outfit with even the whip and boots. A packet with nothing but high-heel shoes, bags and bangles – lovely. I loaded all the different styles of clothes and jewellery for the doll they had to offer. Now the trolley is full.

Right! OK, Martha. Now it's time! I looked around, seeing the crowded shop with everyone intent on spending money faster than running water. I walked off slowly, heading over to the back of the shop, getting lost inside the alcove with the coat racks. I looked around, seeing there was no one heading in my direction. Suddenly I opened the bag, fitting all the stuff in, then stopped, lifting me head to see if anyone was coming. No! Keep going. Me heart was shivering with fear, but I held meself tight, keeping still inside meself, and packed everything into the bag.

Right! That's the lot. I could feel me face heating up with the nerves. I took in slow deep breaths and grabbed stuff off the racks, loading the trolley. Throwing them over the bags. An empty trolley with a full shopping bag would look suspicious! I headed off looking sharp, but not too quick, making my way towards the entrance.

When I got to the end of the row, I looked towards the entrance doors. Fuck! The aul fella in the uniform is standing guard at the middle door. I moved back up, keeping on the inside, where there's not many people, then stopped to examine the price of coats I wasn't interested in. I have to look like a normal shopper. Then I turned, making me way back down again. The aul fella was now wandering slowly down towards the supermarket with his hands behind his back.

OK! Now! I whipped the coats off and grabbed up the bags, making me way quickly, not too fast, towards the entrance doors. I stopped at the big plate-glass windows to look around, letting me eyes take in the length and breadth of the place, wanting to see if anyone was giving me the eye, watching me! I stayed perfectly still, keeping me face stiff, showing no nerves. But me heart is hopping like mad. Everyone seems busy about their own business. No one seems to be minding me. I looked around puzzled, making it look like I was searching for someone I had lost, then sighed and made my way quickly to the front entrance, looking like I had given up waiting.

I took in a breath, holding it, my back and neck tingling, waiting for the hand on my shoulder as I whipped open the door, feeling the cold, damp night air on my face, telling me it was freedom – if I can get moving through it without getting caught! I headed off towards the path leading to the bus stop, with the high wall around the area, keeping the shopping area enclosed.

I stopped just as I got close to the area with the trees and bushes on my left. I bent down, pretending to fix me bag, and lifted me head, taking in everything around me. I peeled me eyes back to the shopping area. No! It's dark around here, no one is coming down this way. Most people shopping here have their own cars; they don't need to take the bus.

Right! I stood up quickly and tore over to the bushes. I looked around. Where's the best spot? I hid the big bags under a clump of bushes, then took notice of the tree. It's the third one in. Right! Move! My nerves started rattling as I made me way back to the shop. There's no turning back, Martha. You have to finish the job! I thought, as me mind flitted on the idea of quitting while I'm ahead. No! Keep moving.

I pushed in the entrance door, seeing the place was really getting crowded. People were at a standstill, waiting for the crowd to shift so they could get moving. I picked me way carefully through them, putting my hand on shoulders, then fitting me way through. People squeezed up to let me past.

OK! Here we are! Me shopping trolley is still where I left it. I heaved it around, feeling the weight of it, and pushed it towards the way in. It was a bit clearer now, with only a couple of people coming in. I stood still, taking stock. No sign of the uniform! No one's taking any notice of me. People are busy milling around, going backwards and forwards, coming in and going out, heading for the doors.

OK! Now is the time to make a move. I headed off, pushing me way through the crowds walking in front of me, then turned right, making my way towards the gap for the way in. I kept me eyes peeled ahead, taking no notice of the checkouts with people lined up to pay for their shopping. The checkouts were lined the length of the shop, leaving only room enough for people to walk past to get in for the shopping.

This is it! Me heart dived up into me mouth, and I held me breath, heaving the trolley into the gap. Suddenly, a crowd of people surged in, blocking me path. I was stuck. Eyes landed on me, and heads dipped, taking in the full trolley load of stuff not wrapped in plastic bags. Before they had a chance to make this out, I was pushing. 'Sorry, excuse me, please.' Then without warning, a tall man in a pinstripe suit pushed his way through, and our eyes locked on each other. 'Excuse me, please!' I said, carrying on about me business. He stopped in front of me, staring from me to the trolley, wondering and waiting as he figured out what was his next move. What's going on here? I could see his head thinking.

'Sorry! I need to get out!' I puffed, pushing past him as he leaned himself away to let me get past. I wobbled to the front entrance and out the door into the cold, dark night of the wintry car park. I could hear footsteps behind me, taking long steps. His hand landed on my shoulder. 'Wait a minute, please. Can you come back to the shop with me?'

Suddenly I was looking up into the face of the man in the pinstripe suit. 'Sorry?' I said, looking puzzled at him.

'The shopping!' he pointed, still not on sure ground. 'You haven't paid for these!' he said, looking shocked, wondering if he was right or wrong.

'I most certainly have paid for these,' I said quietly, keeping my voice steady. 'No! You are assuming that because they are not wrapped in bags, I didn't pay for them. I actually went back from the checkout after paying. I asked the girl for a box – it's much handier than a shopping bag. She couldn't hold up the queue, so I said I would go back in and look for one myself. I couldn't find any empty boxes. So what you saw is not what you are thinking. You're not the manager here!' I said, making a guess. 'I know him. He's very helpful. I shop here every week. He helps me to load up the car when my mother drives me!'

We stared at each other. His bright grey eyes stared at my face, with our eyes boring into each other. It was like a game of poker. I was playing for everything I had. Sarah was lying sick at home in a cold miserable flat, waiting for me to come home and take care of her. Nothing on earth was more important than getting out of this in one piece. He was still not sure. One false move, one flicker of nerves on my part and that's it! I'm dragged back inside!

'Ask the checkout girl!' I said. 'The third one from the end. But first check with the manager. He knows me! If you put me through any difficulty, having to answer for my honesty, it will humiliate me! Certainly it will make . . .' I hesitated, giving a little shake of my head. 'The shop needs its reputation,' I said quietly, lifting my chin a fraction and pinning him with a steely look in my eyes.

With that, his eyes widened then narrowed at the veiled threat. We bored into each other, with him measuring, gauging, trying to get the feel of me.

Don't let go, Martha! Just hold your ground, say nothing, do nothing. Keep still; very, very still. Stand him down. Let him weaken.

We were two people locked in a deadly stillness. Nothing could be heard but the terrible silence as his mind assessed, calculated, worked out the risk. He too had a lot to lose. My only hope is in his hesitation. Right now, I've grabbed the high ground.

I stared him out, daring him. Not letting go of an inch. Or any minute now I may be marched from the sweet freedom of this cold, dark car park, straight back into the blinding light of that shop, with people milling all around, all happily helping themselves to any amount of Christmas cheer a body could want. Then they'll pay up and drive back to their lovely warm homes, feeling very satisfied. Now they are ready for their big Christmas celebrations.

He will have to fight his way through that heavy crowd, dragging me with him. Because I won't go quietly! People will stop to stare. They will tut-tut at the shoplifter, righteous in their disgust at the thief, while they feel for their heavy wallets, bursting with wads of money. Some will probably know me to see.

The police will arrive. I will be taken away in a police car, a statement made out, with a demand that I sign it. Then I will be locked in a police cell, waiting for someone who will never come to bail me out. These days they send shoplifters to prison! Jesus! Jesus! Help me now in my hour of need.

I slowed my breath, tuning into every instinct in me, calling on everything I had ever learned about human nature, wanting to find a way to make him back down.

I slowly closed my eyes, then opened them, pinning them hard on him. He stared back, rock solid. I could see his body was rigid as he sized me up. I slowly took in a long, silent breath, trying to stop the throbbing pain of fear that was threatening to drain the life out of me.

Suddenly, there was a shift in his eyes. I could see him stiffen, his eyes harden into a decision. He's resolving to do his job.

My heart lunged, then roared up into my head, making me see sparks, and the noise deafened me. I'm sure he can see it thundering through my chest and hear the banging. Jesus! The pain is like being hit with a sledgehammer.

Oh, sweet Jesus! He's going to get me arrested! All is lost! The child is on her own! A terrible dread hit me as terror drove out the bravado, the daring, leaving me wide open to collapse. I gripped the handle of the trolley, trying to squeeze the life back into me. I had nothing left but to show him a glimpse of the real me. Please! My eyes pleaded, looking to the man behind the suit, behind the job. See all that can be lost to me. I need the food. I want my little girl to know that Santa has not fogotten her. It is Christmas; we have nothing. I have done what I had to do. Now, a terrible power is in your hands. Just let me be, go my way.

'Please!' I whispered, letting my eyes show all this. 'Please believe me. I have paid!'

Suddenly, he softened, relaxed his shoulders, saying, 'Go on then! It's OK!'

I moved off slowly, feeling meself going weak, and wobbled away with the full trolley. I am not out of harm's way yet! I need to make distance between him and me and this place. He knew! He knew

I robbed the shopping! I'm sure of it! He's not stupid! Maybe a bit of him didn't want to take the risk I was friends with the manager. Whoever he is! But in his heart he knew I didn't pay. He really let me go out of the goodness of his heart!

Oh, sweet Jesus! In my very hour of need, you let a miracle happen! I could have lost everything. Sarah would have been destroyed. That young one sitting there in the miserable, cold, silent flat. Waiting, not knowing what's happening. Desperate to get home to her own house. Then the panic after she sees nothing happening. I didn't come back. Jesus! Never! Never again. Nothing on earth is worth what I just did! But yet, I had to! There's no one else to put the food on the table. That costs money. It's Christmas. A time for children. I don't know anyone I could ask. I never get that close to people. I keep my business to meself. Everyone I know is just someone I know! That's all. Yeah! I had to take the risk!

A thought came into my head. God helps those who help themselves. Thank you, God, for looking after us, I whispered quietly as I made my way to get the bags outa the bushes and land them on top of the trolley. I will have to push this all the way home. Who cares? We have enough now to keep us going. My only worry now, dear God, is that Sarah will be well and on her feet again. Come the New Year, that's it! I will go all out with a vengeance. We have to get a home of our own, come hell or high water! I won't rest until I get that!

Sarah was to sleep soundly through the depths of those dark, lonely winter nights, while I was plunged into an abyss of swirling fear, pain and worry. Always constant, day by day it went on – fighting to keep the wolf from the door. She lay tucked up for the night in her little bed next to mine, sleeping the sleep of the innocent. I was so very protective of her. She made everything worthwhile.

I had been very lucky! She slowly recovered, managing to eat and keep the food down. But by the time that virus had worked its evil, it took away the life of a little girl from the infant class in Sarah's school. They had diagnosed her too late. Just like Sarah.

For some reason that morning, I had woken up and went over to her in the bed. Something told me to feel her liver. It was hard. Then I took her over to the window. Yes! I could see the yellow in her eyes where it should have been white. That is when I rang that doctor. 'Get yer arse down here now!' I hissed. 'She has hepatitis!'

'Nonsense!' the aul git said.

'You better get down here or I'm having you up before the medical council!' I snarled at the bastard. Three times I had taken the poor child up to him! Three times he told me there was nothing wrong! I kept sending her back to fucking school. She ended up looking haggard and worn down, dragging herself around like a very old woman in a child's body. That's when I put her to bed. That's when I rang that doctor.

'Yes, hepatitis,' he said, shaking his head as he wandered back out the door. The old fucker was going senile! Oh, we were lucky! Sarah was just getting back on her feet when I heard the news about the other little girl's death. They had flown her to London by helicopter. But it was too late! My child had been spared, but another poor mother was plunged into a nightmare agony of loss and pain. It would probably have hurt less if someone had cut her heart out without an anaesthetic.

We went to the church that cold, dark January night. Her little white coffin was sitting at the top of the chapel. Everyone had gone home. All the prayers for the dead had been said for her. It was quiet now. Hardly a soul in the chapel. Her little coffin looked so lonely, sitting there on the bier, with her now resting in God's house before they buried her the next day. I closed my eyes, whispering a little prayer to give her Godspeed on her journey to heaven.

'Mummy!'

I opened my eyes, seeing Sarah looking up at me with a haunted look on her pale face. She was shaking my arm.

'What, darling?' I whispered, bending me head to her.

'Why did they leave Emily here? Look! They've gone off leaving her in her coffin all alone! Why do they do that?' she whispered, pointing up at the coffin. 'Do you think she can still hear even though she's dead?' she said, thinking, trying to figure out death.

'Well, she needs the rest here, darling. One last time waiting with God in his house, so her mummy and daddy, and all her family and everyone can say goodbye to her. Then when they've buried her body – because she won't need that any more – then the angels will come and carry her up to heaven.'

'But, Mummy,' she said, not satisfied. 'Why did she die? I got better!'

I sighed, thinking. 'Darling, everyone is not the same. She was only staying here for a little while. She was a present for her mummy! You know how cute and funny she was. She made her mummy and everyone very happy. Now God wants her back, because she has another job to do in heaven.'

'What job?' she said, letting her mouth hang open, with a faraway look in her eyes, taking in everything I was saying.

'Well, God has lots of angels running around him. Maybe Emily has to sort them all out. They can lose the run of themselves, you know! Tormenting each other, laughing and pushing and shoving, getting very noisy and driving God mad because they won't listen to him. So now it's time for Emily to get up there and sort the lot of them out. She can line them all up and get them to do what they're told! That's what children are for in heaven, you know, Sarah!'

'Really?' she said, letting her eyes gape out of her head at the wonder of it.

'Oh, yes,' I said, shaking my head. 'Taking charge of all the angels! That's what heaven children do. They have to make sure they are doing their job of looking after the child they were given down here on earth. That's why a lot of kids get into trouble. Their angels have taken their eye off them, then the bold angel has rushed off somewhere, gone to have their own fun when God is not looking. Then they start playing with each other, letting the poor child they were supposed to be minding get themselves into trouble!' I said, letting air out through me nose, sounding very definite. 'So that's where Emily is off to,' I said, watching her turn her head as the two of us stared up at the little lonely coffin.

But I did get us a house. Yes! All my dreams came true on the one day we moved in there. But somehow my own home was not what I expected. I couldn't settle. I missed me old roots. I used to keep wandering back and staring at the old place – our big, old, damp Georgian flat – feeling very lonely. Me, with my very own house left waiting for me to come home. It seemed very empty, even leaving aside the fact I had no furniture. That didn't bother me. We sat on the floor on cushions and dreamed about what it would be like when I get the money eventually. We would decorate it and get lovely furniture.

I got a do-it-yourself book and made repairs, plastering under the window where the damp patch was, and ended up doing everything meself. Well, me and Charlie did, God love him! I bought a lovely big ceiling rose, after getting it cheap, for the sitting room. Charlie mixed the brown, butter-looking paste to stick it to the ceiling. Then he slapped the rose to it, getting a sudden thought.

'Martha, I can't let go! This stuff takes ages te dry. If I take me hand away now it will smash te the floor!' he puffed, staring at me in shock, with the eyes hanging outa his head.

I stared, dropping the cigarette butt outa me mouth with that sudden, worrying thought. 'What can we do, Charlie?' I said, staring up at him, trying to think.

'I don't know, Martha,' he whispered. 'Ye're always gettin me te do stuff, then when it turns out wrong ye blame me!' he snorted, beginning to get very annoyed.

'Well, now, Charlie,' I said, shaking my head. 'There has to be a way around this. We just need to think. But the most important thing is, Charlie, not to let it drop and smash. So, tell you what! You stay up there holding that tight until it dries, then I'll make us all a lovely dinner when the job's done! How about that, Charlie?' I said, raising me eyebrows, staring up at him with a smile on my face, thinking that was the best thing I could come up with.

'Wha? But tha'll take hours, Martha! Me bleedin arm's droppin offa me already!'

'Well! Have you any better ideas?' I roared, losing me own rag.

'Wait! Where ye goin? Come back, Martha!'

'Listen, Charlie,' I said, rushing back in after getting a great idea to cheer him up. 'Tell you what. I'll get you a nice cup of tea now, Charlie. You can drink it with one hand, and I'll even hold the cigarette for you so you can have a smoke at the same time! How's that?' I said, flying off to the kitchen.

'No, wait! Come back! Bring the sweepin brush. I have a better idea!' he roared.

I left him holding the brush to the ceiling with one hand and sucking on his cigarette butt with the other.

Yeah! Charlie and me. We did everything ourselves that needed doing in the house. Even making bookshelves for Sarah. She ended up with a lovely room. But the empty feeling of loneliness never left me. I missed my old flat. I began to mistrust the idea of happiness. I should have been happy with my own home. But the problems were still the same. I began to feel there was no such thing as being free from worry. It was all in the mind. Nothing makes us happy until we can find the happiness inside ourselves. I couldn't do that.

I began having health problems. When I moaned to the doctor, he glanced up at me and swiped a page out of his notebook and told me to run to the chemist and take these pills.

'What are they for?' I asked lethargically.

'Help you sleep!'

I was back. 'I want to wake up some time! They don't work, I'm still sick. I'm not well.'

Another swipe off the pad. 'Take this and run to the chemist.'

'What will they do?'

'Help you relax!'

'I'm back! They don't work. I've now turned into a zombie!'

Pause, while he thinks, scratches his head. 'Would you like to see a psychiatrist?' His hand is held over his pad.

'It's not in my head. Look at the colour of me! I'm the colour of cigarette ash!' I scream.

'Then if you don't want to take the pills, what do you want me to do?'

He was wrong, of course. I was very sick, and not in the bloody head. I was yet to find out what the diagnosis really was.

So life dragged on. I accepted it when old-age pensioners shot past me when I walked down to the shops. Premature old age, I told myself in the mirror, as a grey-faced old woman stared back at me, showing a severe loss of weight. Along with all the other things happening to my body. That was it! I carried on dragging myself through life like a snail. So getting to find that inner peace, or whatever would give it to me, was looking like a distant dream. I was pissing in the wind! Yeah! So much for happiness just being around the corner when you get what you think you need! No, happiness is a very complicated business! And I find it very difficult to take change that's not of my own making.

I suppose the howls of suffering of that little girl I once was, with her nightmare childhood, still scream in the bowels of my soul at any threat to my fragile hold on security. That little girl deep within me is never at rest. Not any more! She had lain quiet for years, lying in her dark little corner, buried deep in the dark recesses of my mind, keeping all her dark secrets to herself. She could do nothing. I had forgotten her while I was busy barrelling my way through life. I had a dream. Nothing and nobody was going to stand in the way. When I took a knock and was sent flying, I sprang up like a jack-in-the-box, tearing back into the mad arena of life, fighting for my share. Outa me way! I don't listen to people telling me what I can and can't have. I don't hear when they say it won't work. What you want is impossible, they bleat! Rubbish! I mutter. If men can do these things, well, I'm getting my share too!

Women stay at home! Mind the kids! Man the house! Look after the husband! They're the earners. They've got the power. The world doesn't listen to women. Fuck that! We women have a lot of power! We've been wiping men's eyes with our wiles since we all lived in caves. We knew how to stop you dragging us off by the hair of our heads when we hadn't cooked the meat you just clubbed to death. We knew it was bad to feed you too much of that stuff. It only helped you to think. No! Thinking was bad for you! It put ideas in your head. So, less meat for you, more for us women! We had to always stay one step ahead of you brutes! You were physically stronger than us, so, naturally, we had to use our noodle – head!

Yes! Men think us stupid. Emotional. The softer sex. Good! Long may it last. We can continue to run rings around you. That is, until we women can stand equal with you. Some men, they are so arrogant, drunk with their certain power. They don't realise they have been had. When they do, then they shrug, shake their shoulders and smile wryly. Oh, well, I like to indulge a pretty lady, they say. Who gives a fuck? We women always get there one way or another!

So, let your guard down. My power is to lull you into a false sense of security. No, I'm no threat. Only a silly woman who will know you are after my body. That's why I got the job. Never mind. I can handle you. You will get a run for your money! You will enjoy hunting me, the beads of perspiration dripping from your brow as you chase me around the place. That's when I make my exit. I am fast on my pins. So the game is always played according to the men's rules. Fine! I understand the rules. Outa me way! I want a house. A home!

I pushed and shoved, getting shoved back, laughed at. But I got my house! Sometimes I was drunk with exhaustion, but then I was alive!

Now I don't know where that Martha is gone to. She left, leaving behind a frightened old wet nelly. Someone who was afraid to live but not afraid to die. Jaysus! When did I start to disappear? It must have been so very gradual I never noticed. Maybe when I got what I wanted? A home! Became middle class. Then I discovered I am not what I wanted to be. I will never be middle class, which is what I pretend to be. I don't really even like them. Too much hypocrisy!

Yeah! My identity is really lost to me. I can't find an affinity within any of the social groups. But the pull of who I once was is growing stronger as I move away from the pretensions of the middle class. I have been living a lie to myself, and that is what is robbing me of who I really am. This is an empty persona I have wrapped around myself. I am a fraud! On the outside of life, living on the fringes, not wanting to fit in. I felt like an outcast, not belonging to anyone or anything. I had no identity. Yes, I am ashamed of Martha Long, the street kid, robber! The little nobody! Yet I think this child in me is trying to tell me something. Yes, the truth of me could lie somewhere there in her. She knows this – that is why she is coming back to haunt me. She knows I need her help.

Yes, it seems as I was growing weaker, becoming more disillusioned with life, losing heart, the child in me was coming back to haunt me. Now she is growing stronger by the day. One day I will have to face up to it! Yeah, I think that is at the root of my problem.

I came back to my senses, blinking to clear my vision. I felt a little lighter in myself. Like I had discovered I am not so bad after all. The street kid I once was – she wants to help me. I felt a stirring in my heart for her. Like I wanted to protect the little nobody. She is you, Martha! Or once was. Not now. No. But you are a part of her, and she is a part of you. Yeah! I thought, getting a picture of meself down through the years. We are really a lot alike. I don't think I have changed so very much. Just developed a lot more. But she was a lot more honest. She knew who she was. Martha, the little street kid! I shook my head, smiling, thinking of her, then let the thoughts go back to where they belong. Somewhere waiting to come back and haunt me.

I looked around the room, then stood up. Right! I better get moving. It's going to take me hours to get this stuff sorted out. Bloody hell! Where did all this stuff come from? I stared at the wardrobe, bulging with everything I owned. Better get packing. The sooner you start, the quicker you'll be finished.

Right! Ready at last. I lifted the heavy suitcase and wrestled with a big plastic bag stuffed with clothes, trying to wrap me arm around the width of it. Forget it! I thought, dropping it on the floor, then started again. I picked up the plastic bag, deciding to drag it, lifting the heavy suitcase with me other hand, then made me way out the door.

'Jaysus! This is like moving house!' I puffed, as I staggered down the stairs, trying not to trip and break me neck. I'll be bleedin banjacksed by the time I get this lot down. I still have even more left, waiting for me back inside the room.

'Nurse! Wait for me!' I shouted, roaring me head after the skinny nurse's arse, seeing her vanish outa sight, then hearing her make her way along a passage without me. I'm really going to lose the rag if that one thinks I'm going to trail around the hospital looking for her! The fucking skinny cow wouldn't give you the steam off her piss if you were on fire, never mind offer to give us a hand! Fuck her! 'Where is she?' I moaned, feeling tortured with all this upheaval. The creep! She ran off and left me. Right! Let her come and find me.

I sat down on the stairs and rolled meself a cigarette. Now she will have to climb all the way back up these stairs, because I'm not going to answer her when she discovers I'm not trailing her shadow. Fuck her! I'm in no mood to be trifled with, I thought, sitting contentedly sucking on me cigarette, feeling better now, knowing I won't be the only one getting discommoded!

48

'There was no need to take that attitude with me! I can't be in two places at once! I'm really upset you called me those terrible names. I have feelings too, you know!' the skinny staff nurse moaned, nearly crying with all the insults she got after leaving me sitting on them stairs with nothing to look at but a bleedin blank wall!

By the time she bothered to come back, I had changed me mind. I wanted to stay up here. 'I'm not moving! Do your worst! Send me back to lock-up!'

I thought that was a good plan. I hatched it up after smoking me way through three bleedin cigarettes, poisoning meself. I think they use lock-up to 'punish' the troublemakers, or the ones having a major wobbly. I suppose mine was just a little wobbly, because it didn't work. I'm raging! She's raging!

I tuned in again, hearing her still crying. 'I'm surprised at you! I thought you were more ladylike,' she sniffed, still not able to get over her sorrow at the insults outa me while she heaved, pulling the guts outa me, trying to get me and the bags moving.

I tuned out again, leaving her to talk to herself. My concentration was all going into getting me and the heavy bags to the new room.

I trailed behind her, wondering was this an exercise in her getting her own back. She must be taking the long way. Surely we have walked ten miles already! She pushed open a door, walking us down a dark, old-fashioned passage, then stopped, pushing in the end door. I hurried in, dying to get a look. Me mouth dropped open, and I stopped stone-dead. Where's the luxury?

'St Elisabeth's!' she hissed, clenching her teeth, letting her eyebrows stand up. 'You're going to love it down here,' she flew, running the words into each other.

I slowly shifted me head, letting it swing around the room, then back on her, seeing the malicious grin on her face. My mouth opened, but nothing came out. I'm gone into complete shock.

'Bye now,' she breathed, curling her fingers. Then she was gone! Flying out the door, banging it shut behind her.

I stared at the two battered old beds with the matching battered chest of drawers and skinny wardrobe. Then my eyes peeled on the old sash window getting the light blocked out because a red brick wall was nearly pressing up against it.

'Fuck this!' I snorted, losing the rag. I'm not staying here. I know me rights. They're not getting rid of me that fast. I'm still in need of intensive care! How long was I up in that other place? Four months? That's not long enough. Some of them are up there for the last year. Right! I'm going to see about this! Who do they think they are? Pushing me out the door and I'm not even halfway ready!

I whipped open the door and marched down the passage. 'Excuse me!' I said, looking at the bent head busy writing up charts, sitting in her little office.

'Yes,' the voice murmured, without lifting her head.

'Listen, would you ever get on the phone and tell that lot up in there,' I said, pointing to the ceiling, 'they may come down to collect me. I'm not staying here! I'm in no fit condition to be . . .' I tried to think. 'It might put me over the edge, all this discommoding! I need to be comfortable! Feel happy in me surroundings! Already I can feel meself . . .'

'What?' she said, lifting her head.

I stared into the steely-grey, odd-looking eyes, with the red face and the cheeks hanging down to her chest. Jaysus! It's Sister Hornblower! Everyone runs for their life!

'Are you telling me you have not settled yourself in yet?' she snorted, heaving up her huge chest.

I stared at the silver watch dangling on the chain pinned to her chest. 'Eh, that's what I just said,' I croaked, losing me nerve.

'I mean, have you unpacked yet?' she barked, standing up and moving to wave her finger at me, landing it down to point back down the passage.

'No! I'm not staying,' I said, sounding reasonable.

'Well!' she said, lifting her watch to look at it. 'You have ten minutes! Then I will come down and get you myself. You are not allowed up here during the day. You have to stay down in occupational therapy. Now! The clock is ticking!' she snorted, staring at me over the little granny glasses sitting on her nose. I stared back, with the two of us having a Mexican stand-off. Then she broke the silence.

'Don't be ridiculous!' she breathed. 'Have you listened to yourself? You don't want to become institutionalised!'

'No!' I snapped.

'Exactly!' she snapped back. 'Use that backbone. You have more than enough. Now, straighten yourself up! No more nonsense. Go on! Off with you!'

'Right!' I sniffed, heading meself off back down the passage.

I suppose she's right, I thought, pushing in the door, landing me eyes on the room again. Jaysus! I've nothing to look at, no view. Bleedin hell! Look at the beds. I sat down, giving it a little bounce, and me arse went straight down through a hole in the middle. At least the room is empty. Good! That means I have it all to meself. But one thing's for sure – they are serious about getting rid of me. There's no mistaking that!

I started to unpack, hearing someone knock on the door. 'Come in!' I shouted, wondering who this was. The nurses never knock.

My eyes landed on the monk, seeing him push open the door, putting his head in. 'I have been looking for you!' he said, sounding a bit fed up.

I watched as he ambled in then stood throwing his head around the room, digging his hands into his pockets. 'So!' he muttered, shaking his head, looking like he was thinking.

My heart leapt with excitement, then dropped, seeing his green eyes sweep past me with a bored look. Oh, enough of this, Martha! It's time to get serious. You had your fun chasing him, now it's time to get back to real life.

I sighed, feeling me heart jerk at that thought. 'I have to get this stuff put away and get out of here,' I said, letting him know I wanted to get on with me business.

He said nothing, so I lifted a bundle of shirts and bent down, putting them in the chest of drawers.

'You should be going home soon,' he suddenly said.

I nodded my head to him and carried on putting things away. He still stood there, making the silence in the room feel very heavy. It felt like a pregnant silence. With things waiting to be said or left unsaid.

Then I heard him drawing in his breath, pausing before he said something. 'Would you like to take a walk in the garden?'

I hesitated, stopping halfway to pick up stuff off the bed. I wasn't expecting that! My head whirled around, looking at him. He shook his head, drawing down his mouth, making it look like it was a good idea he just thought of.

'When?' I said.

'Whenever you like. After lunch?' he said, looking at his watch.

'OK! Might as well get myself a bit of an airing. I feel like Dracula!' I said, laughing. 'But I will probably go up in smoke. It's been months since I saw the daylight.'

'OK! I will see you downstairs around two-thirty,' he said, making a move for the door.

'Yeah, that will be nice. Thanks for asking me,' I said, smiling happily.

'Yes, fine,' he murmured, shaking his head, giving me a little wave. Then he was gone, out the door.

I stood staring after it, trying to make out why his sudden interest. Then it hit me. What does it matter? I will be going home soon, so that will be the end of that. No need to go getting all excited, Martha. He's not someone who has something to offer, or me to offer him. Exactly! Get back to your senses. The game is over. This place is nearing the end for you! So start thinking like your old self! What was that? Jaysus! It doesn't matter. Right! Galvanise yourself into action, finish this job and get moving. It must be nearly din-din time. I'm starving! Wonder what the eating place is like down here? Hurry! You'll soon find out.

I stood back, admiring me new little nest. My books sat on my locker, next to the lamp with the pink shade burnt in the middle. Everything was in its place. All my stuff was hanging nicely in the wardrobe just waiting for me to run my eye over it and decide what I will wear for the day! My perfume, Chanel No. 5, along with all me make-up, sat lined on top of the dressing table. Lovely! It looks more homely now! I sighed, taking in a big breath, letting it out contentedly. Jaysus! I hope no one moves in here with me. I'll cause holy murder! They might even start robbing me stuff! Then there will be a murder committed! I snorted to meself, feeling me belly go on fire with the thought of the imagined thief! Bloody hell! Stop, Martha. You're going nuts! Getting all . . . Jaysus! The ma used to say that when I was little and we lived in the homeless hostel . . . Stop! You're driving yourself nuts!

I blinked, trying to settle me senses again. Clear me head. Right! Get moving. You're grand! I gave a big sigh and shut the door behind me, then walked down the dim passage. I hurried on, getting a lift at the idea of seeing my new surroundings. I'm even getting taken for a walk with the monk. Or maybe he might be taking more than just me. Wonder if Blondie will be tagging along? Maybe he likes the idea of two hungry women hanging off his arms! Bet he does. That fella is a chancer! I think he loves himself. He's not blind to all the women in this place panting whenever he walks into the room. Jaysus! I've even seen some of the nurses licking their lips, letting their tongues hang down to their belly buttons when he smiles at them! Still! It should be good for a laugh. Especially fighting Blondie for him. Yeah! That's the best bit!

I grabbed the end door, pulling it open, and stopped to look in at the nurses' office, then jumped back. Hornblower was still sitting there, looking like she was plastered into the place.

'Off down stairs with you, please! You took your own sweet time before you came mincing down here, looking like a tourist!' she snorted. 'I expect you to obey my rules,' she said, staring at me with one steely marble eye. The other one was blue!

I leaned in me head, getting a better look. Now I could see them in the light. Yeah! They're two different colours. Like them Dulux dogs! I wonder if she was born like that?

'Providing you do not break my rules, we will get along fine!' she fired at me, knowing I wasn't really listening.

'Oh, oh, yes, Sister,' I simpered. 'You won't have any problems with me.'

'That's NOT what I've heard!' she barked. 'Now run along!' she said, waving her hand at me like I was a child or a dog.

I shot down the stairs, making for the dinner. I could really have given that one a piece of my mind. Treating me like a child or a halfwit. That's what I don't like about this hospital. They treat you like you're mental or a halfwit! But the grub is gorgeous. The smell of it was wafting up the stairs. My belly rumbled. It was only one floor down, and I was walking along the ground-floor passage in no time. Gawd! I'm feeling grand now. This new sense of freedom is lifting my spirits no end!

That was a lovely, gorgeous dinner. They get even better grub here than they do upstairs. Lovely! I'm really feeling satisfied after that. Right! I better get a move on. I took me time in there, eating me way through two whole dinners and double portions of all the different desserts. I hope your man hasn't taken off without me!

I turned into the restaurant, spotting the monk surrounded by a gaggle of women, with Blondie in the middle of them. She waved me over, laughing. For a split second my heart took a dip, and I stopped dead. Ah, ah! Stop the nonsense, don't be childish, Martha. Everyone is entitled to their ration of him.

Right! I danced down the steps, heading over to them. The monk stood up, saying, 'Goodbye, ladies! I will see you later.' Then he started walking in my direction.

He's leaving them sitting there! Maybe it's just him and me. Great! The less the better. More ration of him for me!

I turned, heading back to the door, waiting on the corridor outside.

49

'Come!' he said, when we got outside. 'We will take the path along the trees.'

'Lovely!' I giggled, sounding like a schoolgirl. Then in the next breath I was feeling disappointed. No Blondie! Looks like you've caught his interest, Martha. After all your running. So, what next? I went blank.

We walked along the paths around the orchard, dipping under the hanging branches of the trees. I used to look longingly out at this place from my room in lock-up. That seems like a century ago, another lifetime. Suddenly I felt a great sense of ease sweep through my body as I looked around at the peaceful garden. The lovely, old, red-brick high walls, with the trees, bushes and shrubs. The whole place pulsed with life. Ghosts from a long-ago era hung in the shadows, giving me a sense of timelessness. A time to be born, a time to live, laugh and cry. Then, when your time is up, a time to die.

I had a feeling of déjà vu. As if I had done this before. I felt very much alive, walking slowly side by side with the monk.

'My name in religion is Sebastian, but my birth name is Sergei.'

'Oh!' I said, looking into his handsome face, staring at his green eyes softening with a smile playing around his red, beautifully shaped full lips.

'Yes!' he said, inclining his head towards me, his strong handsome face creasing into a smile. 'Call me Sergei!'

'Sergei.' I rolled it around on my tongue, my heart fluttering with the romance of it all. It is like something out of *Anna Karenina*, I said to myself, feeling breathless. Then it hit me like a bolt of lightning. His green eyes, his chosen path – a monk! Religion! So very like someone in another time, another place. So all along, this was the draw for me. He reminds me of someone I would have given up my last breath for. But the similarities stop there. He would be a very poor substitute for Ralph Fitzgerald! The only man on earth I have ever truly loved.

'We Russians make the best writers,' he said, gently waving his arms. 'Our history is one of long suffering. We have something to write about. The West! Bah! The people are sated! Too soft. Their underbellies are made of mush! Life is too easy for these people.'

'So why are you here?' I asked.

'My boss, the general of the order, sent me here from Rome.'

'Why?'

'He wishes me to observe. Then a new hospital will be started in a more remote part of the world. We are well established around the world. So now we will go to those parts which are still quite primitive. Yes, it will be good to go there,' he said, a faraway look in his eyes.

'So what were you doing in Rome?'

'I was living there, in the Vatican. That is where we have our headquarters.'

'How did you get to Rome?'

'In my country, I was assistant to the provincial. That is the boss of our order in that particular province. When the general of the order was on a world tour, I met him. He thought I would be useful to him. So he took me to Rome with him.'

'Did you meet the pope?'

'But of course! Every morning I would see him walking in the gardens.'

'He's Polish,' I said. 'Do you speak Polish?'

'Yes, but of course!'

'How many languages do you speak?'

'Five – Italian, German, English, Polish and, of course, my native tongue, Russian.'

I was beaming at him, feeling terribly impressed.

'So now! What do you do when you leave here?' he asked, giving my heart a nosedive.

'I don't know,' I said half-heartedly. 'I will probably rent out my house and head off to America. New York. I have nothing to keep me here,' I said, my voice trailing off.

We walked on, both of us lost in our own thoughts.

'Why don't you get married? Have children?' he suddenly burst out, stopping to look at me.

I stared at him, the thought never really surfacing to my head. 'I never thought it an option.'

'You are young, you can still have more children. What age are you? In your thirties? Take a husband! Bah, there is time for you still!'

'But husbands are not easy to find,' I laughed. 'Most Irish men my age are married, separated, gay or ex-priests! I don't want a man with a wife and children in the background. That's too much baggage! I have enough problems of my own,' I said, trying to convince him, but wondering was I really trying to convince myself.

I never really thought about marriage. My heart was never in it. How could it be? I loved only one man, I thought, seeing his face, hearing his voice, then sensing him, even back through all that long ago time. When I closed my eyes, I could feel his arms wrapping around me, drawing me into him as he whispered, 'I love you, darling!'

Even now, I could feel my heart break at the loss of him. Yes, even after all this time. No, that pain never really eased. I just accepted it.

'I am still married in Ireland,' I said quietly, wanting to end the conversation. 'My ex got a foreign divorce. That's how he married abroad. But it's not valid here, because we don't have divorce.'

'So it may be wise for you to go abroad,' he said, looking at me. 'You must look to the future. If you stay here,' he said, dropping his mouth and lifting his shoulders, 'you will have a very limited opportunity.'

'Yeah, that's true,' I said, feeling a bit empty inside. Knowing that made sense. But if I had sense, I wouldn't have ended up here, I thought.

I looked over, seeing we were nearing the front entrance. People were on the march, all heading down the corridor in the same direction. He stopped, then looked at his watch. 'It is time for supper. OK?' he said, giving me a cheery little wave, then wafted off.

Oh, he must be off duty, I thought, seeing him head away from the hospital. Wonder if he will be back this evening? I would enjoy sitting with him and Blondie – it would be good to have a laugh, sit in company. Huh! I sure need it after that conversation. It was a bit too heavy-going for my liking.

'Too bad! Too bad!' I muttered, making me way in the door.

I moved in with the crowd, all slowly moseying their way down to the dining room.

I looked at all the new faces, seeing people staring ahead, lost in their own world. The pain deadened on their face after years of finding no way out or no one to share it with. Some people had friends – they managed to poke their heads above the suffocating pain and laugh and smile, and meet each other's eyes, knowing they wouldn't be judged because their minds let them down.

I suddenly felt a bit lost. I had moved on, leaving my friends behind. Now I was back to feeling empty. I wanted to be up sitting with Blondie, looking into her face as she waited to hear what the monk and me had got up to. I would tell her about the miserable conversation we had, then roar laughing when her eyes lit up, knowing that's not what we had in mind at all when we got him to ourselves. Even if I didn't really know myself what I wanted to do with him.

Yeah! We could share each other's hopes and expectations. I still desperately need that. I'm not on me feet yet. This pain, this torment, this terrible dark pit I keep falling into over the last few years. Well, it's not over quite yet. My heart is heavy with the loneliness at the minute. I can't bear the pain of wandering on my own, having to look for a way to fit in, to be with people who care and matter to you. Or worse, giving up caring. Living in a no-man's-land between this life and death. I had reached that. Now I am here.

This is what this place is all about. They throw us a lifeline, allowing each of us here to sit out our pain, then wobble up to grope and stagger around, desperately trying to find our way out of the darkness. We can touch each other, bonded by the same pain. We can look into a face and see our own pain mirrored in the haunted eyes of a thousand-year-old young man of twenty. It does that to you. That look, that touch we give each other tells us we are not an outcast. We know, we understand, we accept each other.

I walked over to join the queue waiting to be served the evening supper at the counter. It is like an upmarket restaurant. There is even a menu.

'What would you like?' the woman behind the counter asked me.

'I'll have the steak-and-kidney pie, please.'

'Vegetables?' she asked, holding up the ladle.

'Yes, please.'

I carried my tray down and sat beside a man talking to his friend.

'It's hard going!' the bald-headed friend said, dipping into his mixed grill, dropping a bit of bread into the soft egg yolk.

'Yeah!' the man said, looking very pale and worn. He had premature lines carved into his forehead, and his thin sandy hair, coming down in wisps around his ears, needs cutting, I thought, looking at him. He can't be any more than forty. But his slight frame makes him look very neglected. He could easily be mistaken for sixty. The poor fella hasn't worn too well.

'How will I ever get through this?' the thin man asked, dropping his fork and looking around him, seeing nothing but his inner pain.

His hands were balled into fists, and then he closed his eyes and held his head over the table.

'One day at a time, Frank! One day at a time. Just take it easy,' his baldy friend said, putting his arm on the man's shoulder and leaving it there. 'But right now, minute by minute, my friend. You will get through this! I promise you. We are all going through this together.' Then he looked at the man's plate. 'Have your bit of grub. It will give you strength.'

The man opened his eyes, staring at his food, then looked at the door, thinking, and his friend watched him carefully.

'Come on. Let's go. We'll go upstairs. This is a bad moment for you.'

They both stared, locking eyes on each other. Then the friend stood up, pushing back his chair, and led the thin man away, taking him firmly by the arm.

'Alcohol!' an elderly man with a chubby white face and silver hair said, nodding to me from the next table. 'They're up on the top floor,' he said, pointing to the ceiling. 'They're kept separate from the rest. They have their own unit.' Then he shook his head sadly and concentrated himself on eating his grub.

I took in a deep breath and looked down at my own grub. Poor man. There's nothing worse than alcohol. It really is hard to beat, and they destroy everyone around them, including themselves.

I wandered out of the dining room, seeing very few people around. I could see in the distance, down towards the end of the long passage, a man here and there, slowly walking backwards and forwards, trying to ease themselves. I spotted a man rushing in and out of an alcove, having a whole conversation with himself. He was completely content, getting lost in his own world. Nothing would bother him now unless someone came along and disturbed him by trying to start a conversation. He can only cope with one person at a time and that's himself.

I walked past empty rooms, seeing billiard tables looking abandoned and dusty from old age and lack of interest. 'It's like a morgue down here,' I sighed. Everyone must be upstairs on the wards, getting their medication. Then the ones with visitors will be getting ready. Might as well go up and take a lie down on my bed. Nothing else for it. Maybe a bit of rest might give me a lift.

My eyes opened slowly. I looked around the dark room, feeling the cold. I must have fallen asleep. I jumped out of the bed, taking off my clothes, and headed for the bathroom. Right, Martha! A hot bath and a good night's sleep, that's what you need.

I walked along the seedy corridor, looking up at the bare light bulb hanging from the ceiling as faces stared up at me from chairs propped against the wall. Jaysus! This place hasn't seen the light of day for many a year. The carpet is worn into the floorboards, and the walls are grey. I think they were probably yellow at some time.

I turned a corner and headed in through a door, making for the bathroom. I stopped dead. Ah! Jaysus Christ almighty! The bathroom! What bathroom? I looked around. A great big rust-bucket bath with a dripping cold tap! I looked at the corner and saw a grey-plastic chair to put your things on, but it was swimming with water. Will I go up to the top floor? Nah! It's too far this hour of the night. Besides, I'm too banjacksed, and anyway, they would only chase me out. Maybe another day.

I bent down, putting in the plug, and switched on the hot tap. Better clean it out first. 'Jaysus! I'm too tired for this,' I muttered as I swung into the room next door that passes for the laundry room. One whole washing machine for all the patients. But you have to find it first, with the mound of clothes buried on top. I grabbed a rag, looking for some cleaning stuff. A bottle of Jif! That will do.

I rushed back in, cleaning the bath, and then let the hot tap go full blast. The taps are huge, probably the first ones brought out in Queen Victoria's time. The water thundered in, steam rising, and the room started to heat up a bit. It was very chilly in here. I dived out of my pyjamas. Ah, fuck! The chair is wet. I stood holding my night things in my hand, wondering what to do with them. I'll hang them on the back of the chair. I picked up my washbag from the dirty wet floor and put it sitting on the chair, taking out my washcloth and soap, then dived into the bath.

Ah! Oh! It's fucking hot! I leapt up and down, holding on to the sides, cooking myself alive, then leapt out. My feet are roaring red. I stood looking at them, then switched on the cold tap. That will teach me to wake up! I climbed back in more carefully, then lowered myself down. Ah! That's better. I better get organised next time I come in here.

'That was nice,' I breathed, as I walked along the dim passage. The same faces stared at the same spot on the opposite wall. Jesus! This place would definitely put years on you. We are supposed to be nearly cured down here. But they look like they've given up altogether! It's the shock of losing all that luxury we left behind upstairs.

I opened the door onto my corridor, looking forward to climbing into my bed. I turned into my room, falling over a body stretched from the hall into the room.

Jesus! I screamed with the fright, not seeing where I was walking. I tripped, my head making straight for the wall, and lashed out my arms to save myself. I tumbled over the legs, twisting, and fell backwards, landing on the left side of my bony arse.

'What the fuck are you doing here?' I screamed at the big mass of dough, with the two small eyes buried in the middle of what must pass for a face. They stared back at me, alive and shining with malevolence and menace.

I jumped up, putting on my bed light and throwing my things onto the bed, and marched over to sort out whatever was lying on its side. The head propped up on its outstretched arm stared down the hall, watching the door at the end.

'Who are you?' I screamed at a woman of about twenty-five, and about twenty-five stone in weight!

She stared at me with her lips puckered up, like a nine-month-old baby does when you take its lollipop. I could hear a heavy breathing noise coming from the little button nose buried in a mound of flesh. Two little holes flared up and down, and the beady little eyes glinted with menace.

I stepped over her, stood and gave a piercing scream down the hall. 'NURSE! NURSE!!'

The door opened and a harassed-looking nurse stood with her hands on her hips and her foot propping open the door, and shouted down at me, 'What is it, Martha?'

'Please remove this person!' I was bulling with rage at having my privacy invaded.

Now this, coming after losing my lovely room upstairs! My bathroom, my friends, and whatever else I lost. All in the one day! And now fucking this! No way! 'Get her out of here!' I screamed.

The nurse came flying down, kicking the door shut first with her right foot, muttering, and let out a roar before she even hit the body. 'Molly Murphy! If you don't get up off that floor this minute, I am ringing your mother to come and collect you tonight. You are not going back up to the intensive care ward, and that is that!'

Ah! She doesn't like the new suite they offered her. I don't blame her! I moaned, muttering to meself and sniffing with disgust at me new living quarters.

The nurse stood over the body of Molly and lowered her head. Then, with the hands on her hips and the legs stretched out to balance herself, she threw her head back to the ceiling and gave an unmerciful scream. 'GET UP! NOWWW!'

I rushed over to my bed, with the noise enough to waken the dead, and dived in, pulling the covers over my head, deciding to ignore the whole thing. I could hear the muffled arguments going on outside the door. I lifted my head. Good! The nurse had closed it. Then I saw a bag on the other bed. They are going to move Molly in with me! No chance! They have their work cut out for them if they think I'm going to let that happen.

The shouting got worse, and I jumped up, throwing the duvet back, and padded over to the door, opening it, and looked down at the mound on the floor. The two little blue eyes flicked over to me. I could see them spitting with venom. They stared at me with a glint of daring.

'Leave her, Nurse! Let her sleep there for the night. She's comfortable down there, aren't you, Molly?' I said, looking down with a smirk on my face.

The little round hole closed, tightening into a mouth, then it opened, saying, 'Fuck off, you!'

'She's well cushioned, Nurse. Ignore her. She's just looking for attention, stubborn little bitch! Probably gives her mother hell.'

The mouth opened and a blast of 'Ahaaaa!' came screaming out like the banshee. I went in and closed the door. The nurse took off without another word, slamming the end door after her. I dived into bed, taking a big sigh at the sudden quiet. I started to relax, feeling the lovely warmth, and I was now sliding down into a lovely, deep, welcoming sleep. 'Ahhh! Yes!' I sighed happily. This will cure all me ills and rejuvenate me when I wake in the morning.

Me heart leapt! Wha'ass that! The door started to vibrate, with Molly drumming her feet against it. I took a leap out of bed, whipping the door open, looking down on Molly.

'Kick that door once more,' I said, quietly enunciating each word through gritted teeth, 'and I will give you such a kick up your fat arse, you won't know what hit you! Then I will drown you in icy-cold water with a pot from the tearoom, and you will regret you ever messed with me! Do we understand each other, Molly?'

She stared at me, her eyes beginning to pucker through the flesh, widening.

'DO YOU UNDERSTAND THAT?'

Her head bobbed up and down, with the eyes blinking. I marched in, slamming the door shut, muttering, 'Spoilt bitch!'

It's morning. The nurse put her head in the door, smiling, and said, 'Breakfast, Martha.'

'Thanks, Nurse.' I lifted my head, yawning, and stretched. The sun was trying to creep around the window, but it looks like a lovely day. I jumped up, ready to face it. Yeah! It's going to be a nice day. I'll go and have my breakfast, then take a bath and see how the day goes – just take it step by step. There's no point in worrying about nothing. Oh! Where's Molly? I looked over to the other bed. Her stuff is gone! Then I whipped open the door. She's gone! There's no sign of her. Yeah! Happy days. I've got the room to myself again.

I polished off the grub quickly, because I was anxious to be on the move. Finished! I was out the door taking the stairs two at a time and into my room to give my teeth a quick clean, then brushed my hair. That will do. I'm ready. All I need now is a coat. I opened the wardrobe, taking out the long red coat with the wraparound belt and deep pockets, and changed into a pair of black boots. I better tell the nurse I am going out.

As I opened the passage door, just about to walk past the nurses' office, hoping Hornblower wouldn't be on the prowl – she might try to stop me – I heard a familiar roar.

50

'**M**artha!'

I looked around, wondering who was calling me.

'Where have you been all morning?' Blondie shouted, laughing and looking wide-eyed as she ran down the stairs. She jumped the last two, trying to balance on her six-inch high heels, grabbing a hold of me to steady herself.

'What did they want you up in the ward for yesterday? You never came back! Are you down here now? And listen! Where did you go with himself?' she laughed, her eyes shining, dying to know what's going on.

'Well, I have been booted out of upstairs! I'm now down here. I can go where I please, wear what I want. Look! All dressed up in me outdoor clothes. I'm going out for a while.'

Her eyes narrowed for a minute, letting a feeling of envy cross her face. Then she laughed. 'Oh, I'm delighted for you! That means you will be going home soon!' she roared, giving me a tight hug.

Yeah, home, I thought, laughing with the nerves. 'Yeah! You're next, Blondie! Out the door. Then they'll beetle around, tearing out barbed wire, and wrap it around the place to keep us out! So, better get yer skates on. Grab the monk while you can!'

'Why? What were you up to yesterday? You never told me,' she roared, giving me a suspicious look. 'He didn't invite me to join you, wherever the pair of you went,' she sniffed, feeling sorry for herself.

'Ahh! Don't get excited, Blondie. Jaysus! He's a long string of misery! I came staggering back here last night looking for something to hang meself with! I'm keeping away from that Russian. That fella would put you in an early grave,' I snorted.

She roared laughing, delighted to hear I hadn't got me hands on him.

'No! He's still on the loose,' I said, sniffing with disgust at all that huffing and puffing I did, hunting him down day and night. Jaysus! The idea of it. I shook my head, not believing the carry-on of me.

'Listen, Blondie! Here's what you'll do!' I said, bending over to whisper. 'Just grab him! Grab your Gucci handbag and floor the Mercedes outa here. Take him home with you to Dick. Tell him the monk has to stay with you. For, eh, medicinal reasons. Or, he's the new pet. A companion for the parrot, or whatever you have.

'Now! While Dick is trying to digest this, give him the works. Tell him the hospital says you need private care. A monk! They're harmless. Are you getting this?' I said, nudging her, with the big smile plastered on her face.

'Right! Now! They're willing to loan him out. They have plenty to spare. He's your new private nurse. And, eh, Dick will have to move outa the bed, into the spare room. You need to fit another bed in. Two singles. Then the monk can wear the carpet out in the middle. Rushing to nurse you,' I said, flicking an eye on her big chest.

'I don't think Dick would be too happy with that arrangement,' she said, getting a faraway look with her eyes all shiny. Really thinking about it!

'Ah, ah! Put them dirty thoughts outa yer head,' I said, giving her a push.

She staggered back, and I tried to catch her. We ended up plastered on the floor, with her hanging onta me.

'Let go a me fuckin good coat!' I roared, laughing and crying as she tried to pull me down and get herself up.

'Stop that horseplay! Get up off that floor, you two!' a voice barked.

I whipped around, seeing Hornblower tearing down the passage.

'Come on, quick! She'll stop me going out!' I puffed, grabbing Blondie by the arm, trying to heave her up.

'Mary Ann! Put your knickers on the inside of your trousers! You can't wear them like that!' Hornblower roared.

A heat hit me belly and came roaring out in a big laugh. I pushed Blondie away as a high-pitched laugh came squealing out of her. 'Fuck!' I said, crawling away on me hands and knees. 'Me good coat is ruined. I'm getting outa here. Come on if you're coming!' I croaked, tearing meself up off the floor.

Then I saw her lift her head and glance down the passage, smiling as she made to turn away from me. I looked, following the direction of her eyes, seeing the monk coming towards us.

'Ladies! Ladies! Why are you not down in therapy?' he sang, giving the pair of us a big sexy smile, showing his dimples.

I whirled around, looking at Blondie. 'Oh, Brother!' she gasped, sucking in her stomach and heaving out her chest. I eyed her staggering over on the big high heels, sliding the arse from left to right. 'We're just going down for coffee. Are you coming down too?' she breathed, grabbing his arm and sliding her chest to lean up against him.

'Yes! Come,' he said, waving his head at me, then taking off down the stairs with her.

'No! Can't,' I said. 'I have to go and collect my car.'

'Oh!' he said, turning around to look at me. 'You are going home. Now?'

'Yeah!' I said, looking at him, seeing him thinking.

'Hmm! You would like company?'

'What? I can't go out!' Blondie puffed, letting her eyes hang out on stalks, worried she might miss out on something.

'Well, I'm going now,' I said, not really interested in him tagging along. I wanted to go on me own.

'Of course! Please yourself,' he said, shrugging his shoulders with the eyes closing as he dismissed me with a wave of his open palms. Then he said slowly, resting his eyes on me, 'I am off duty this afternoon.'

'But I'm not allowed out!' Blondie roared.

'Look, I'm coming straight back, Blondie! Jaysus! I'm only going to collect me car!' Then I pushed past them, saying, 'See you later. If I go now, I'll be home . . . Back here before lunch. Bye!' I waved, seeing Blondie's face light up and break out into a huge grin, delighted she was getting him all to herself.

'No, wait! One minute, please!' I heard the monk shout after me.

I looked back to see him coming down the stairs. 'Come,' he said, putting his hand lightly on my elbow, guiding me down the stairs.

'What is it?' I said, looking at him, seeing him smiling at me.

'We will talk downstairs.'

Blondie came rushing down after us and stood beside him.

'I will meet you for coffee. Wait for me, please,' he said, smiling to

Blondie, then guided me towards the entrance door.

I looked back, seeing her hesitate, then take off, wondering what this is all about.

'Friday evening, I am going to visit my friend. Would you like to come with me?' he said. 'Or maybe you have made other arrangements? You have a car, I need.' He waved his hand, shrugging his shoulders, giving me a huge grin. 'You will eat! My friend will cook!' He shrugged, pulling down his face, still smiling.

I looked at him, wondering why he was asking me. 'Why?' I suddenly said.

'What is why? You amuse me!' he said. 'You have a car! Maybe this is not good? OK! There is not a problem.' Then he waved at me, taking off.

'Hang on! Yeah, OK, that will be nice,' I said, shouting to his back.

'Good! We will leave some time after six,' he said, turning back to give me a big grin and a wave.

I took off out the door, feeling very happy with myself. Oh, brilliant! Date with the monk! Right! I better hurry to catch a bus, I thought, steaming out the gates, not wanting to miss me dinner.

'Right! Here you are,' I muttered to meself, humming it out in a tune. I could feel me heart keeping time as I pushed open the gate of my house, then stopped, sweeping me eyes around, taking everything in. I eyed the grass; it was in need of a bit of work! The weeds were everywhere, with long scutch grass. It was the month for growth – early April. My eyes scanned the house, looking up at the windows, then down to the porch doors. It looked neglected, lifeless and lonely. Like it was waiting for me to come back. I'll have my work cut out for me, getting this place back into shape.

The windows need cleaning. I'll have to wash the curtains and throw open the windows. Polish and dust the rooms and leave open all the doors, letting in the light and air.

I stayed where I was, staring at the house. I was seeing a ghost of myself. The one who was dragged out of here half-dead. She soared across my vision, deep within my inner eye as I stared. She was very grey, she didn't belong to the living at all. Fear swept through me, and I hurried up to the porch, opening the door, and grabbed the post.

Then I locked the door quickly, desperate to get away.

I'm not ready to face it back here yet, I thought, still feeling I was on shaky ground. Yeah! It's natural, Martha, I puffed, wanting to shake off that old feeling of how I used to be. Still am sometimes, I thought. Oh, don't start! Relax. This is your home, Sugar plum. 'Home sweet home!' I hummed, heading into the garage.

I opened the doors, letting in the light from the early spring. April. The start of new life. Suddenly! With the familiar scent flowing in from the trees and shrubs outside, I walked out, listening to the birds screaming to each other, busy building their nests. I took in a deep breath, smelling the warm, fresh spring air, and felt the vibrations of new life swarming into being.

Memories of happier days, being young and full of life. Tearing into the garage and out of the car, slamming the doors shut behind us. Me and Sarah. The last journey before getting ready to go off to the Continent. Or a night out with friends, or just rushing in to cook a meal and sit down to watch TV with Sarah. That smell, and the sound of the birds, brought the memories rushing back.

I felt my heart lifting and my mind clear. I'll be OK! I'm in the driving seat now. I'm not dependent on anyone. I'm getting out of that place soon. I'm just about ready. Yes, yes, I bloody am! Suddenly I could feel me old self coming back to life. Oh, yes. Oh, indeed, very yes!

I jumped into the car, switching on the engine. Come on, you beauty! Start up! I don't want to miss me dinner. I sped off to the hospital, feeling carefree. All me worries seemed to fly out the window, leaving me light and airy. Oh, have wheels will fly! Definitely. Now I can be in and out of the hospital like a blue-arse fly. Just rushing back to get my meals handed to me. It will be like living in a hotel! Yeah! Until they put their boot under me arse, sending me flying out the door.

51

I stood admiring myself in the mirror, wearing a lovely red-wool skirt with a French grey-silk striped blouse, with an emerald brooch pinned into the top buttons. A black, silver-buckled belt snuggled around my waist, and my feet were beautifully shod with a pair of black-patent four-inch high heels and black stockings. Ohh! Don't I look lovely? I put on the fox-fur jacket I'd rescued from the St Vincent de Paul when a friend was going to get rid of it. I flicked my shiny long hair off my face, grabbing hold of it and lifting, letting it drop down around my shoulders. I had to spend the night in spiky hair rollers, crucifying myself to get these curls! God! I hope I look a million dollars, because I'm thinking I do! So, with the extra four-inch heels, and the head grown another four inches, I'm ready for anything.

I staggered off on my high heels, trying to get into a rhythm and not break my neck. I made it down the corridor and turned back, heading back up the stairs again after forgetting to tell the nurses I'm off for the weekend.

I put my head into the office. 'I'm off now, Nurse,' I said to the blondie nurse with the hair curling around her shoulders. A young doctor sat keeping her company, and I was delighted to see his eyes light up at the sight of the lovely me.

'Hi, Doctor!' I mewled, waving a limp hand at him, flirting.

'Where are you off to?' he said, with a bit of longing in his lovely grey eyes, looking like he wished he was off somewhere too. He had dark-brown curly hair and lovely white skin.

'I'm off out to meet a couple of nuns and say a few decades of the rosary!' I said, lowering my eyelashes thick with mascara at him, hoping I looked demure.

'Like hell you are! Not dressed like that! Are you not taking me with you?' he asked, looking very woebegone.

I looked at the nurse, and the grin disappeared clean off her face, and she snapped, 'I expect you back tonight on time!'

'Ah, ah! The doctor says I can go wild for the weekend. Obviously no one told you that.'

'Well, be back when you're supposed to be back and not after!' she snorted.

I roared laughing, looking at the doctor rolling his eyes and turning to the nurse saying, 'Right, Mammy! We'll call you every hour! Just to let you know we're OK.' Then he jumped out of the box and came rushing around to give me his arm, heading me towards the stairs.

'Don't be such an eegit!' the nurse roared, losing her rag altogether at the thought of losing the doctor. She's been chasing him night and day for months. All I ever heard her say was, 'When's Dr O'Reilly on duty? Did you see Dr O'Reilly? I think he's gorgeous!' she'd gush, sitting and moping, pining for him to turn up.

'I'd better get a move on,' I said, taking my arm back and heading carefully down the stairs, not wanting to make that nurse's day by tumbling the length of them, then ending up splattered, with me head twisted in the wrong direction, showing a terrible look of surprise and shock written on me poor frozen face. Yeah! And the smile still plastered to it. And why? All because I lost the run a meself! That's why. What with the monk on one side asking me out, and the doctor throwing me the eye on the other! Well, Jaysus! I must be really gorgeous and sexy altogether! No, Martha. You're not Marilyn Monroe! Forget about wagging the arse down these stairs. 'Take it easy,' I puffed, watching me hand turning white with the death-lock grip these banisters are getting.

'Have a lovely weekend!' he roared after me.

'Thanks, Doctor, I will. Bye, Nurse.'

'See you,' she muttered.

I headed off out the entrance door, seeing Baldy the receptionist giving me sour looks. She didn't approve of patients going off gallivanting for the weekend, enjoying themselves, while she's still stuck behind the desk, married to her job. 'Do you have a pass?' she roared after me.

'Yes! Check with the ward nurse on duty,' I said imperiously, then galloped off on my high heels, getting used to them now.

I sat into my car and turned on the engine, then rolled a cigarette, feeling a great surge of contentment flooding through me. Yeah! I'm on the move again. The future is looking very rosy, I thought, as I drove down the avenue, turning out the gate. There's Sergei. He was walking up and down, his hands in his pockets.

I pulled up beside him. 'Hi, Sergei!'

'You kept me waiting!' he growled. 'You are twenty minutes late.'

He got into the car, huffing and puffing, then started again. 'I am always on time. I do not keep people waiting. Time is very important. This is not good.'

'Sorry, Sergei. But I didn't wake up looking like this! Twenty minutes late is not bad considering all the beautification I gave meself! You look nice too,' I said, seeing his lovely black Italian-leather jacket and the white-silk open-neck shirt.

He sighed, shaking his head, giving me a smile without opening his mouth. Then he tossed the back of my hair and aimed his hand, saying, 'Drive! The evening will be over!'

'OK! Where to?'

'First, I wish to visit the docks. A ship is there, and the captain is my friend. I know him from home. We are neighbours.'

'OK,' I said, heading off to the docks.

'We're here!' I switched off the engine, looking up at the huge ship.

Sergei jumped out, saying, 'You will come with me to meet my friend?'

'No! I am not going onto that ship,' I said, looking at it, remembering the talk about women who went on ships looking for sailors to sell themselves to. Half-remembered memories of my mother doing one such thing. I shook my head firmly. 'No, you go on. I'll wait here.'

'But why? This is nonsense! You must come and meet my friend.'

'No, thank you, Sergei! I don't like ships.'

He went off, and I sat, lighting up a cigarette, watching him go up the gangplank.

Time passed, and still no sign of him. I was about to start the engine, taking off and leaving him there, when he came strolling across cool as a breeze, no hurry on him. He was carrying two bottles of vodka, one under each arm like a pair of babies. He grinned at me and threw himself into the car.

I was huffy. 'You took your time! It's freezing cold sitting here, you know!'

'Oh, please. I am sorry, my friend, the captain, we got talking. Ohhh, do not spoil your face! Show me a happy one!' he laughed, holding up the bottles to admire them. 'Look! This will warm you. Eighty per cent proof! Almost pure vodka! Better than the rubbish they sell you here!' he said happily, looking down to admire them.

'Right! Where to now?'

'OK. Now we go to see my friend. Wait! Here, I have the address.' He reached into a black-leather wallet, pulling out his notebook and handing it to me.

I glanced at the address. Mount Street. We set off, heading up the quays, and I said, 'What is your Russian friend doing in Ireland?'

'He is stranded here. My friend is an engineer and was commissioned by an Irish businessman to complete a job for him. He took people from other countries, but now he refuses to pay. The others have managed to get their money, but Boris has yet to receive his. It is a lot of money. But they do not pay him one penny. I have been helping him, bringing him food and giving him money. What he needs, I will get it for him,' he said, lifting his shoulders, holding his hands out.

I looked at him, seeing the concern on his face, and I felt myself warm to him. This started to cheer me up. By the time we got there, I was almost back to my earlier great humour.

'That is the house there,' he said, pointing to a black door.

I parked on the other side of the road. Sergei immediately jumped out, heading around to open my door. 'Oh, thanks,' I said, beaming at him giving him a little bow.

'No need!' he said. 'We Russians treat all women with respect.'

He waited while I stopped to light up a cigarette then followed him across the road. He rang the doorbell and the door was whipped open in a flash.

'Boris!' Sergei boomed at a tall Russian with a black beard and incredible sky-blue eyes. He grabbed Sergei in a bear's hug. The two of them slapped each other, looking like they wanted to beat each other to death, babbling in their own tongue. Then the bear stood back, speaking in Russian and looking down at me with his eyes twinkling. 'Who is your friend?' – I assume that is what he is asking.

'This is . . .' Sergei said, thinking, '. . . my driver,' he grinned at me. 'Martha! Please, I would like you to meet my good friend Boris!' Then he bowed at me, waving his hand. 'Boris!' he rumbled. 'My friend, Martha!' Sergei said, then walked past the Russian.

Boris stopped in front of me, stood up straight with his knees together and bowed to me from the waist. He took my hand in his huge paw and said, 'Martha! I am honoured to meet you.' Then he kissed my hand, holding it like it was delicate china and I was royalty, and swept his arm behind him, standing aside to let me walk in.

I minced in on my high heels, taking care not to slip on the hall rug, and tried to look regal, getting carried away with the notion I must look royal or something, to get that kind of treatment from Boris. I walked into a sitting room with a dining table in the centre. It was covered with a green heavy tablecloth and set for dinner. I looked around at the fire roaring in the fireplace, and a long round couch in the alcove under the bay window. A lovely warm pink glow came from a ship's lantern sitting on a side table by an alcove, with two deep-cushioned armchairs each side of the fire. Sergei brandished the vodka, laughing and speaking in Russian as Boris came thundering into the room, saying something in booming Russian.

They both examined the bottles, eyeing the proof content. 'Would you like some vodka, Martha?' Boris said in his deep rumbling voice.

'No, thank you,' I was about to rumble back, getting carried away with the whole thing. 'Ahem!' I coughed. 'No, thank you!' and a bloody squeak came out. I was nervous. I glanced over at Sergei, who was shouting at Boris to open the bottle and laughing and pointing at the kitchen. Boris flew out, saying we would eat soon. Then suddenly Sergei turned in my direction, saying, 'Come! Make yourself comfortable. Please. Let me take your coat.'

'It's a jacket, Sergei, fur!' I said as he took it off me, then held it up, giving it a puzzled then disgusted look.

'Hmm! Fur, no! This is something a rodent would grow on its back,' he said, hanging the jacket on the back of the chair, wiping his hands to get the hair off, then dismissing me fur with a wave of his hand.

I exploded with the insult. 'Excuse me! I'll have you know that is pure fox fur!' I shouted, going over to lift my jacket and give it a rub, then shaking it to get the fur standing again.

'Bah! Come to Russia. You will buy real fur! And a hat, and, what do you say in English, for your hands?'

'Gloves?' I said.

He waved his fingers, dropping his mouth. 'No matter. You will see, then, real fur!' He wagged his finger, dismissing me with a wave of his hands by slapping them together.

'What part of Russia are you from, Sergei?'

'Moscow. Now! We must attend to more serious matters.'

'Like what?' I said, wondering what he was talking about.

'Eat! Drink! Sing! Dance!' he laughed, grabbing my hand and spinning me around, then flying me back to him in a bear's hug!

'Oh!' I said, getting wrapped in his chest then lifted off me feet to be carried over the room and landed sitting on the sofa.

Then he bent down, kissed his finger and landed it on me lips, saying, 'Behave! No fighting! I will go to see what we eat,' then he vanished out the door, leaving me in a fog, wondering what just happened.

Jaysus, yeah! Romance! *Anna Karenina*! Gawd! That was lovely, I thought, trying to get my breath, then reached down to me bag for another smoke.

Boris came barrelling in, brandishing three glasses. Sergei ambled in behind carrying a bottle. Then they were on the bottle like greased lightning. '*Na zdorovje!*' or something like that they said, as they toasted each other. They smacked their lips, Boris still holding the bottle at arm's length, admiring it as Sergei watched him from his chair at the dining table. He enjoyed seeing Boris feasting his eyes on the bottle of strong vodka. Then they threw back their heads, emptied their glasses, then it was another round and more toasting each other's health. I took a tiny sip outa mine, feeling it burning its way down me neck, setting fire to me belly. Jaysus! That's dynamite! I thought, putting the glass down beside me on the little wine table.

Then Boris rushed out and came flying back in again carrying two big soup plates held with dish towels, and landed them down on the table. 'Eat, Martha!' he said, pointing to the soup and rushing over to guide me to the table. 'I have a special drink for you. Maybe when you have finished your dinner, hmm?' he said, raising his huge bushy eyebrows.

'What is it, Boris?'

'Ah, it is excellent!' He gave me the thumb and forefinger, kissing them together! '*Da*! You will like it!'

'I don't drink much, Boris, and certainly not strong vodka. I'm not used to this stuff,' I said, holding up me glass.

'Not to worry! This is baby's milk,' he boomed, flying out again.

My head shot to Sergei, saying, 'We shouldn't really be eating the poor man's grub.' I whispered, looking at him with his head dipping in and out of the chicken stew, then wiping his hands on the teacloth.

'Eat up! It is delicious. It is impossible to refuse Russian hospitality,' he spluttered, brandishing half a chicken in his hand.

Boris was back, carrying his own dinner in one hand and a basket of bread in the other. Drinks were splashed into glasses, held and clinked together. '*Na zdorovje!*' they boomed.

I examined my dinner. Potatoes, chicken, carrots and onions, and other stuff, with peas and all sorts of herbs. I sipped, breaking a bit of bread, and munched on a piece of chicken. 'Delicious, Boris!' I said. 'You are a wonderful cook.'

'It gives me immense pleasure, Martha, to see you eat and enjoy!'

God! He really is a gentleman, I thought, seeing the pair of them lapping up the stew, pausing only to take a drink and wipe their hands on the tablecloth. Then they started to roar at each other in Russian. Arguing and waving their hands. If I didn't know better, I would think they were going to kill each other. Then they stopped talking, letting the conversation die away, and just sat quietly, staring at the table, with the two of them lost in their own thoughts. Suddenly, Sergei whipped his head around and stared, giving a big sigh, and smiled at me, saying, 'Now we will have some dancing! Boris and I will show you some Russian dancing. Boris!' he commanded, flinging out his hand, saying something in Russian.

Boris leapt up, and the two of them started to pull away the dining table. 'Excuse me, please, Martha!' Boris asked me with the civility of a gentleman, while Sergei carried on attempting to lift the heavy table himself. He whipped it around, hitting me in the hip without noticing.

'Fuck!' I muttered, rubbing my side, then glared at Sergei, waiting to see if he would notice and apologise.

'What?' he said, whipping his head to stare, seeing me rub my side.

Suddenly I was whipped through the air and settled on me sofa again. 'Please! Do not stand in the way,' he said, sounding annoyed.

'Fuck off!' I muttered.

He stopped and stared at me under his eyebrows. 'No! Do not speak to me like that, please,' he said, shaking his finger at me. Then he went back to hauling the heavy table, with the two of them pushing it against the wall.

'Hup!' The two of them bounced their arses on the floor, Boris slapping his arse and kicking out his legs. Sergei bounced around, his long golden hair shimmering with the light caught from the rays of the fire. God, he is a handsome brute, I thought, staring at his fine physique and incredibly handsome face, crowned with a head of massive golden hair. Looks don't usually attract me. I prefer the more caring type, calm and steady, with great depth – that's what attracts me. Someone, now, with the nature of Boris. He is mature and civilised, very genteel. Sergei is a bit of a dark horse. He's hard to read.

They stood up, more vodka was poured, then the bottle was nearly empty. I was thinking of moving myself off back to the hospital. No point in going to the house now. I would need to light the fire, and it's far too late for that. I get tired easily because I'm still underweight. I'm only six stone. Yeah! I have got to get the health back. I'll eat as much as I can, and get lots of fresh air and do plenty of walking. Jaysus! When is he ever thinking of moving? I'm bored outa me skull. They keep talking in their own tongue. Fuck! I'm feeling banjacksed.

Then they started to hum a tune; I recognised it. I started to hum, then sing, joining in very quietly, staring into the fire. 'Those were the days, my friend, we thought they'd never end. We'd sing and dance, for ever and a day . . .' My voice started to trail off on hearing the Russians joining in in their own language. Then my voice picked up again, singing along as they sang in Russian. We smiled at each other as the song came to an end. Then they said it was a Polish song, and very old.

'Would you like a drink, Martha?' Boris asked, leaning towards me with the most almighty gentle blue eyes. I looked at him, seeing a nobility in his bearing. Gawd! He truly is a gentle giant, I thought, never having met the like or size of him in me whole life before.

'No, I won't, thanks, Boris.'

'Come! Take a drink, you need to relax!' Sergei said.

'But I have one,' I said, holding up my nearly full glass. 'No, thanks, Boris. It's too late. Besides, I have to drive back.'

'Nonsense!' bellowed Boris. 'That settles it! You will sleep in my guest room, and Sergei can camp in with me.'

'No! Honestly.'

Boris shot out of the room, coming back in just as fast with a glass filled with creamy white stuff that looked like Bailey's Cream.

'What is in it?' I asked, taking it from him and examining it.

'Drink it,' Boris said, quietly. 'It is good, they give it to babies.'

I tasted it, taking a little sip. It tasted good!

'No, no! You must drink it down. No sip!' complained Boris. 'Drink!'

I drank it down. 'Finished!' I slurped, leaning over to put the glass down on the table beside me, then suddenly the top of my head blew off!

I slumped over the side of the armchair. I was paralysed! I have never been drunk in all my years. But now I was incapable of moving. My arms and legs felt like jelly; I didn't have a skeleton. The room flew around, and I was aware of them watching me with interest, looking astonished. Jesus! What happened? My head is swinging around by itself.

Sergei said, '*Jesu!*', or something in Russian, then he came towards me. I could see him moving to bend down and pick me up.

'Tut, tut! You should not drink. It is not good for you,' he moaned, carrying me off in his arms.

'Put her in the bedroom,' Boris said. 'She can sleep it off.'

I woke up, lifting my head from the pillow, wondering where I was. Then it came back to me, as I looked, seeing the strange room through the early-morning grey light trying to creep in through the window. I stretched, feeling hot and damp. Fuck! I ended up sleeping in all me good clothes. Ohh, me head. I lifted it gently, hanging over the edge of the bed. Where's me shoes and coat? Fuck! I'm never again having anything to do with them fucking Russians. Mad bastards! Them and their drink.

Oh, I'm so thirsty! I need a drink. I threw back the bedclothes and staggered out the door, wondering which way was the kitchen. In here! I groped in, hearing the snoring. The pair of them were hanging out each side of the bed. I squinted, trying to see properly. I feel like throwing a bucket of cold water over them. Swines! Them and their 'baby's milk'!

I tried a door further down the hall, finding the kitchen. Me head swam, trying to settle me eyes on a glass. That will do. I rinsed the vodka glass, guzzling down nearly six glasses of water. Ahh! That's better. Now to find me stuff, and get the hell outa here!

52

I brushed my teeth and headed down to take the lift up to the top floor.

'Hi! How are you?' beamed Esther, a big smile plastered on her face at the sight of me.

'Hi, Nurse! Did ye miss me?'

'Oh, the place hasn't been the same since you left. It's like a morgue!' she said, twisting her face, looking grief-stricken.

I bounced over, giving her a slap on the arm. 'Bloody liar! You couldn't wait to get rid of me!'

'True! Oh, very true!' she laughed. 'But you're looking well,' Esther said, smiling. 'You are certainly not the same girl we had to keep under lock and key.'

'Ahh, I wasn't that bad!'

'Not half! You drove us all mad!' she screeched. 'Now look at you! But you still need to put on a lot more weight.'

'Yeah,' I said, looking down at my matchstick legs.

Right! I'm off. I wandered down the ward looking for Blondie.

'Where's Blondie?' I asked two women sitting on the sofa, staring at the wall. They shifted their eyes to show they heard me, then their faces dropped even longer, and they went back to now staring at a spot on the carpet. Hmm. I walked on, looking in the dining room. Nope. Not a sign of her. Two girls were finishing the cleaning up, chatting away companionably. Then I heard one say, 'Do ye know tha Russian monk?'

'Yeah. Oh, yeah! I think he's just gorgeous!'

'Yeah, well, I thought so too. But do ye know wha? He really annoyed me, he did! The other day he was passin me when I was workin outside. I was fixin the plates on the trolley, an he asked me how I was. Right?' She stopped to make sure the other one was giving her all her full attention.

The other one folded her arms, shook herself, stared, fixing her eyes, and said, impatient to hear the rest of the story, 'Yeah, right! Go on! I'm listenin. I'm all ears. Now go on an tell me!'

'Well!' your woman continued, taking in a big mouthful of spit and swallowing it. 'I started to tell him all about meself. Ye know, how long I'm workin here, an all tha. Thinkin it was great he stopped te talk te me. An do ye know wha?' she asked, her mouth hanging open and her eyes bulging. 'In the middle of wha I was tellin him, ye know, he just walked off! Walked off! I couldn't believe it! I stood waitin for him te come back, watchin him, but he just kept goin. Right in the middle of me conversation! No!' she slapped the table with her cloth, rubbing the hell out of it and shaking her head, 'I never liked him after tha!'

'Really?' said the other one, her eyes staring into the distance, trying to picture this. Then she said, 'Yeah, it's a pity. I thought he was lovely.'

Hmm! Good old Sergei! He can be very cold, all right. Maybe he thinks he can dine out on his looks. Or maybe it's a cultural thing. Russians have different ways from us, I thought. Who cares? He's part of this place. I'll be leaving it all behind very soon. Maybe I'll tell that doctor I'm ready to go home. Yeah! Time to get back to normal living. Right! Now to find Blondie. I haven't seen her for a while. Wonder what she's up to?

I wandered over to Blondie's room, putting my head in the door, seeing her lying very still with her head facing out the window. Something's not right, I thought, as I walked over quietly. She stared out the window, with her face looking like marble.

'Hi, Blondie! What's up with you?'

Her head turned slowly, looking at me with dead, lifeless eyes.

'What's wrong with you? Why are you lying there?' I breathed, looking in shock at her matted hair. She wore no make-up and her skin had turned the colour of ash.

'I'm not bothered,' she whispered hoarsely, sounding like all the life had gone out of her. Then she turned her head back to stare at the window.

'Blondie!' I gasped, not able to take in how this could have happened to her. 'Are you not well?'

She nodded her head slightly, giving a blink, showing she couldn't care less.

I pulled over a chair, sitting down next to her, blocking her vision of the window. 'What's wrong?' I asked slowly and quietly.

Tears came rolling into the corner of her eyes, and I watched it drop onto her cheek.

'Come on!' I said, stroking her head.

'Sebastian has dumped me. He's not interested any more,' she said quietly, lifting her hand to rub her cheek, then started sniffing, sounding like she had a cold. 'We used to talk all the time. Go for walks, play table tennis. Now he just walks away, takes no notice of me when I see him.'

My heart was sinking lower as I watched Blondie. She really is collapsing. I hardly recognised the woman lying in the bed. She looked like an old woman. Someone who had seen better days. Fucking Sergei has done this to her. He's an insensitive bastard!

'I don't think he's worth it, Blondie,' I said, feeling the weight of the world on my shoulders at not being able to dig her out of this. I sat thinking. Staring at her. Trying to work out if there was something, anything, that would get her going again.

I shook my head. No! I recognise this. Nothing on earth will shift her in that state. What she wants, I can't give her. Neither can a filthy-rich old man. He can throw the world at her feet. Wrap her in furs, diamonds. Jaysus! She wants for nothing. But it's all fool's gold because she has nothing. No! He can't compete with a fella like the monk. Throbbing with life, virile, he can give her a child. Challenge her! Ooze her insides with his energy. Share his passion. She wants to feel alive. But the monk? How deep is he really? I shook my head, not able to work it out. For sure, he has his life in the Church. For me, it was just a game. I needed the challenge to bring me back to life. But it looks like Blondie depended her life on him!

I felt heavy. I couldn't work out what to say any more. So I stood up, pushing the chair against the wall.

'Listen, Blondie,' I said, bending down to kiss her on the wet cheek. 'Don't give up hope. There's better days around the corner. We have survived this far. I'll come back and see you. Then when we get out, we can start going out together. You can come down to my house for dinner. We can go out. Do anything we want! Have plenty of laughs. Maybe we can put a Mafia contract out on poor aul Dick! No, forget that. Listen! Leave it to me! I'll work something out. But, one thing's for sure, we don't need the bleedin monk anyway! He probably thinks it's for stirring his tea! Huh! Would you agree with me?'

She grabbed me hand, shaking it on the bed, letting a heavy sigh come out. It was supposed to be a laugh. I looked into her eyes, seeing the tortured pain. 'I know what you want, Blondie! You can get that. But not the monk. So say a decade of the rosary, giving thanks to God you escaped him! Anyway, he told me he was, eh, gay,' I said, thinking that was a good idea.

'He did?' she said, suddenly finding a bit of life inside herself.

'Yeah!'

She stared at me, watching my face, not believing me but wanting to.

'Course he bleedin did! Sure, wasn't I only out with him just a few weeks ago. He brought me out to meet his boyfriend.'

She stared at me, letting her nostrils squeeze, beginning to doubt me.

'Listen! Would I tell you a word of a lie, Blondie?'

'Yeah, you would,' she said, giving a half-laugh.

'Well! Here's what happened . . . Yeah! Stone drunk they got me! Then when I woke up – you won't believe this!' I snorted, letting heavy air out through me nose. 'They were in bed together! Wrapped around each other!'

'No!' she said, letting her eyes hang out on stalks. 'Were they doing anything?'

'Eh! You don't want to know, Blondie. Believe me! I was after him meself. You should know that!'

'God! Who would have believed it?' she said.

'Tea time!' Esther said, coming into the room, smiling at us. 'So! You two are still thick as thieves!' she said, looking pleased to see Blondie taking more interest.

'Right! I'm off down to get me tea. Don't want to miss anything. The good stuff is gone if you don't get there early!' I said, standing up, seeing her lifting herself, looking like she was just waking up from a sleep. 'Give us a kiss,' I said, bending down to give her cheeks a smacking kiss.

She grabbed me neck, saying, 'You're a treasure! Thanks! But I don't know whether to believe you or not,' she smiled, giving a little snort.

'Right! I'll prove it to you when we see him again.'

'How?'

'Just wait and see,' I said, thinking, I wonder what I'll come up with? Ahh! I'll think of something 'Right! Bye, Blondie! Don't go getting into any trouble without me!'

'Go on, out!' Esther said, pointing me at the door.

Right. I was out the door, galloping down for me tea. OK! I should be home by this time next week. I'm nearly sure of it, I thought, flying into the dining room, getting the smell of lovely grub.

53

I was walking along the orangery on my way up to the top ward to see the girls. Blondie is still not out of her depression. She has good days, then she collapses again, poor thing. But she will get there; it's just going to take time. Mabel is still in lock-up. She is getting worse. Now she has given up completely. She won't eat or drink and keeps screaming and trying to get out. She's determined to kill herself, so now they have her under constant sedation. Jesus! She's so young and pretty, with everything to live for, including a family and a husband. I wonder why the thought of her little baby waiting for her doesn't give her the strength to live? But at least Katie is on the mend. She's down here with me. Two out of four – it's something, I suppose.

I was just turning the corner when the consultant with his helper, the registrar, stopped and grinned at me. 'How are you now?' asked the consultant, beaming at me.

'Oh, very well, Doctor, thank you. I'm anxious to get home and get on with my life. I think I've been here long enough, don't you?' I asked, smiling at him.

'Yes, yes, I do,' he said, smiling, his eyes narrowing, watching me closely.

I waited, letting him see what he wanted to see and come to his decision. There was a long silence, then he looked at the other doctor, murmuring with his head turned away from me.

I stepped back, giving them some privacy. The other doctor grinned at me, then straightened his back, giving his shoulders a jerk, then blinked, waiting for the consultant to speak.

'Yes! We are going to let you go home next week. This is Wednesday! Say Sunday or Monday. How does that suit you?'

'I'm delighted!' I said, beaming at them. My heart started racing. Oh! I am so glad to be going home at last.

'Are you over that nasty bug you caught?' the other doctor asked me.

'Yes, I'm much better now, thanks,' I said. 'It knocked me flat, but I'm up and running now.'

'I know! You had a fever of one hundred and two.'

I shook my head, remembering.

'Nasty business,' the consultant said as he moved off, anxious to get going and get out of the place as soon as possible. 'Well, good luck now! Take it slowly. Do not go trying to take on too much at once,' the consultant said.

'No! Absolutely not!' I said, waving them goodbye.

I beetled back to my room, getting money for the phone to ring Sister Eleanor, dying to let her know the good news.

'Oh, that's wonderful news, Martha. I'll pop in this afternoon, or maybe tomorrow, and take the house keys from you. I can run up and air the house before you get home. Oh, it's marvellous to see you back to your old self!'

'Yeah, Sister! It's wonderful to be able to enjoy life again,' I said happily.

I rushed back to my room and started to pack away my things. Jesus! The amount of stuff. It's going to take a freight train to get me out of here!

Then the door of my room opened. Sergei came in slowly, closing it behind him. I stared at him. He was looking a little pale. I hadn't seen much of him for a while. Not since that last time, when I ended up legless. He's been missing lately. No one has seen him around the place. People said he was out sick.

'So, you will be going home,' he said, seeing me taking the stuff out of the wardrobe and land it on the bed.

'Yes! That's it. I'm going home. Back to a new life.'

'What will you do?'

'Oh, options galore!' I said. 'The world is a big place. I can do anything, go anywhere.'

He shook his head, listening, agreeing with me.

'So! What happened to you?' I said, seeing he looked a bit under the weather.

'Oh, I am OK. I had some sickness. I was in bed rest for a time. But now I am OK,' he said, shrugging, dropping his mouth. 'What is happening with you?'

'Oh, I was the same. But now I'm back on me pins again. Fighting fit!' I said, half-laughing.

'Yes, I called to see you, but you slept, so I left.'

'You did! When?'

'I don't know. Some time, a week ago, maybe. It is not important.'

'How is Blondie? I was going to go up, see how she is, but I met the doctor.'

'The same. She is going to need time.'

'Maybe it would help if you gave her a little time,' I said, staring at him.

'What do you mean?'

'Well, it seems you are not helping by just dropping her, she doesn't understand why.'

He shrugged. 'It is part of the problem,' he said. 'I cannot allow her to become dependent on me. It would not be good for her recovery.'

'But surely you can at least talk to her. Show a little bit of interest?'

'No, now I must keep a distance. This is normal. I am used to this. She must find her own way.'

'Oh, I suppose you're right. But, by the way, how did you know I was going home?'

'Bah! I am part of the hospital. It is my job. So!' he said, wanting to say something but taking his time, thinking about it. 'Would you like to meet later, maybe for a coffee? We can go out, if you prefer?'

'Oh, I don't think so, thank you, Sergei! Not after the last time.'

'What do you mean?' he snapped.

'You pair of creeps got me drunk!' I hissed, remembering it all over again. Jaysus! Even me head is starting to remember. It feels like it should start up paining again.

'Don't be ridiculous!' he boomed. 'You drank. It is normal. But you disgraced yourself!'

'What?!' I screamed. 'The cheek of you. I've a good mind to give you a good kick up the arse! How dare you?' I rushed at him, snorting.

'Control! Take it easy!' he whispered, throwing his head back with a half-grin on his face, holding out his hands.

'Fuck off, Sergei! Before I do something you will regret!'

'Tut, tut! You will be escorted back upstairs. No, calm! Let us sit and talk. It is much more fun. I will meet you later. Don't be late!' he grinned.

'SERGEI! Go and piss in the wind!'

'I like a woman with passion! You remind me of my mother!' he said, blowing me a kiss. Then he smacked the door shut.

I snorted air in and out of me mouth. What an arrogant bastard. Hell will freeze over before he gets me to himself again!

'Are you ready, Martha?' Sister Eleanor puffed, hopping around the room, grabbing at big plastic bags stuffed with my things.

I looked at the long line of bags, suitcases and boxes. 'Bloody hell, Sister! I didn't know I owned so much stuff!'

'They must have thought you were going to take up permanent residence here,' she laughed, struggling with two heavy bags bigger than herself.

Katie breezed in the door and stood staring. 'Where's the pots we robbed from the kitchen?' she laughed, springing for the bulky-looking bags.

'What?' screamed Sister Eleanor.

'Shrrup, Katie! Ah, don't mind her! That's only her sense of humour!' I laughed, glaring at Katie.

'Ah, Martha! You wouldn't?' Sister Eleanor wailed, lifting her neck in the air, then screwing up her face at me like she was going to cry.

'Of course not! I wouldn't do any such thing.'

'Gangway!' Katie shouted, pushing past us, clanking pots and pans. My face reddened.

'Ah, what did you take?' Sister Eleanor cried, dropping the bags.

'Nothing, Sister Eleanor,' I sniffed, listening to Katie cackling down the corridor, banging the bleedin stuff, making enough noise to wake the dead.

'They will only come after you! For God's sake, put back whatever you took.'

I thought of the egg-poaching pan and the lovely big frying pan, reluctant to part with them. 'Who'll come after me?' I burst out.

'The Brothers! They know where you live!' she laughed, then looked pained, her face not knowing whether to cry or laugh. 'They have been very good to you,' she breathed. 'Think about it! You wouldn't be so well now if it wasn't for them,' she said, her face looking sanctified at the thought of the wonderful Brothers.

I thought of Sergei. 'Yeah!' I snorted. 'Well! They got well paid for me. They're not keeping me for charity, ye know,' I snorted, grabbing two heavy bags and dragging them out the door.

I could hear her muttering her disgust behind me. So I shuffled faster, wanting the distance. We landed down in the entrance hall, with Katie coming to meet us, pulling a big trolley to take my luggage.

'I'll load up with you, Katie,' Sister Eleanor said, springing down to heave the stuff onto the trolley.

'It's just as well we have the second car, Sister,' I said, eyeing her car sitting next to my Daisy, waiting to be loaded up for the big exodus home. A bit of a crowd was gathering at the front. People were stopping to see the back of me out the door.

'Bye, Rory! Bye, Maggie!' I hugged and kissed them, looking into their faces, feeling a little sad I wouldn't be around to torment them. 'Bye, Henry!'

'Now you be good and take care of yourself!' Esther warned, pointing her finger at me, giving me a big hug.

'I'll be very good, Esther. Thank you for everything!'

Jam-jar came over and shook my hand, then suddenly grabbed me, giving me a tight hug, then pushed me away, saying, 'I've done my penance in this world, thanks to you! Now off you go and give them hell out there! Don't ever set foot in this place again! We're already under way. Busy putting up an electric fence to keep you out.'

I screamed laughing. 'I knew it!' I said, thinking about the barbed wire. 'Ah, your bark is worse than your bite!' I shouted, giving him another hug.

'Are you right so?' Sister Eleanor asked, puffing back in, with her head already turning, rattling back out the door again.

'I'm on my way,' I shouted, making for the door.

'Ohhh! I'm going to miss you so much!' Katie said, wrapping herself around me.

'I'm not far. We can meet.'

'You have my home address?' Katie asked, eyes wide in case I lost it.

'Yeah! Course I have!'

'And my mother's telephone number? That's the place you'll get me. I spend more time there than at home.'

'We won't lose contact, Katie. I won't let it happen,' I said, hugging her tightly. 'Now, you make up your mind to go home next, Katie! Get yourself well.'

'I am!' Katie shook her head happily. 'I'm well on my way to going home.'

'Bye! I'm off!' I shot out through the door, seeing Sister Eleanor already driving off. I jumped into the car, fighting with a plastic bag wanting to sprawl itself over the steering wheel. Then I started the engine and took off slowly, waving and honking the horn at everyone standing and waving me off. I felt sad, and nervous, and happy, and looking forward to going home – independence and being my own person again.

'That's the lot,' Sister Eleanor puffed, putting the black plastic bag next to the long line of bags neatly lined against the wall in the hall.

'Thanks, Sister! I don't know what I would do without you,' I said, heading into the sitting room and looking around at my old familiar life. The fire had settled down to a rosy glow, with the goals glowing red-hot. The heat was lovely, giving me a warm feeling deep inside myself of security. I reached over, putting the plug into the socket in the alcove, and switched on the lamp. It gave out a warm cosy glow to the room.

'Goodbye now, darling! I'd better be off. They'll be wondering in the convent where I got to,' she said, reaching over and giving me a hug.

'Goodbye, Sister,' I said quietly, a momentary flutter of fear flapping in my chest.

'Will you be OK now?' she asked, staring at me for a minute.

'You go on, Sister. I'm perfectly all right. I'm home now,' I said, laughing and encouraging her towards the door. 'Don't you worry yourself about me! I'm perfectly fine.'

'You're looking very pale now,' she said, looking worried, staring at my face. 'Why don't you go on up to bed?'

'Yeah, I probably will,' I said, thinking it was a good idea. I am beginning to feel banjacksed.

I shut the door and looked around the hall, staring at the plastic bags. A testament to my having left the old life behind, and I'm now starting out on a new journey.

I woke up hearing an awful racket. Me eyes shot over to the window. Jaysus! I stared at two little birds having an almighty row over a piece of twig. They kept dropping off the windowsill, then flying back to steady themselves. One was trying to hold it, while the other kept making a run to grab it. I laughed, then stretched, feeling the heat from the early-morning sun. It flooded the bedroom, lighting it up in a blaze of golden sunlight. Ohh! First day home!

I looked around, seeing my old familiar surroundings, smelling the garden scents wafting in through the open window and hearing old and familiar sounds. Right! Breakfast!

I sat munching over toast and a soft-boiled egg, thinking, OK! What's first on the agenda? Open the post, see to the bills. Sort all that stuff out. Then collect Bonzo. Ahh! I can't wait to see him. Then catch up with people! Make a few phone calls. Ring Charlie! See what he's up to. Cook something nice for him.

I might take a run to the country. Stay a few days with Carol! Yeah, then maybe go off somewhere. Take a break on the Continent! Why not? I could even call in on Sarah! Make it up with her. Definitely! Make that head of the list.

54

I slammed the car door shut and started walking into the cats-and-dogs home, hoping Bonzo was still in one piece. A huge dog was rambling around the reception. I hesitated, terrified of big dogs.

'Excuse me!' I squeaked over to the big woman with the huge chest and grey hair. She was talking to a man with a water hose in his hand, wearing big dirty wellington boots. She didn't hear me.

I coughed to clear my throat. 'Eh, excuse me!' I shouted a little louder, not wanting to draw the attention of the bloody big Great Dane.

The dog and the woman both looked sharply over at me, my body bent in fear, ready to run for the door. She gave me a piercing stare, taking in the silly twisted grin on my terrified face and the buckling knees.

'Yes! What is it?'

The dog's ears flapped with interest, then he started making a move towards me.

'No! Please call him back!'

'What? HEEL, Samson!'

Samson stopped dead in his tracks, looking very disappointed, and collapsed on his arse, with the fat spreading around him to make a cushion. Then he dragged his huge mound of flesh up slowly, sitting himself upright, watching me like I am the most fascinating thing he ever clapped eyes on. His eyes stayed peeled on me, penetrating me, taking in every fibre that rattled in my body. I stayed perfectly still – the only way to deal with an animal that can sense fear.

'Are you looking for a dog?' she barked.

'Yeah!'

'Then come along. Stop being ridiculous! Samson is more gentle than most humans!'

I crept over to the desk, not really taking her word for it, keeping my eyes fastened on Samson. I walked the long way around, keeping one eye on him while the other looked for the nearest way out. The two of them watched my progress. The aul one's eyebrows sat rigidly in the air with the face stretched. The dog sat with his tongue flapping at the side of his mouth, looking like he was laughing at me.

I was still only halfway to the desk, but the silence was killing me. 'I'm here to collect me dog, Bonz . . .' then stopped, seeing Samson's ears flap with interest as he shifted the cheeks of his arse, tapping his feet. Fuck! He looks menacing. He's going to go for me! I got hysterical. I need to get outa here.

'I'm here for Bonzo! My dog, Bonzo! Bring him out! I'll be in the car.' I made to run, but me legs wouldn't move.

'Oh! Are you the owner?'

'Yes,' I said, creeping to the desk.

Samson stood up, raising himself to his full – what looks like – seven feet, and strode over towards me. I closed my eyes and held my breath, standing rigid, afraid to move a muscle. Samson stood beside me, so close I could feel the heat from his body, get the smell of Pedigree Chum off his breath and hear him sniffing. Any minute now I am going to be a juicy raw steak in his big jaws.

A little squeak slipped out from behind my throat, and I opened one eye to see what's happening. He was staring at me. Inspecting me, then walking around to sniff me. Noises started coming from somewhere deep inside me, sounding like someone who was on their last gasp. 'Please tell him to go away!' I whispered between the death rattles.

'Samson! Over here!' She pointed behind the desk, and I opened my eye to see if it was safe. He gave me a baffled look, then strode in behind the counter, slapping himself down on the floor with a big sigh and a grunt.

'Come along!' the aul one barked, grabbing a big bunch of keys off the desk and marching across a yard and down a long passage with a long line of cages on each side. Dogs of all sizes and breeds leapt over each other and stood on each other's necks to get a first look at us. I trailed behind the big woman with the huge arse and massive legs as she banged on cages, 'QUIET!'

I stopped to look in at a little black-and-white dog with huge sad eyes. He looked like he was hoping I had come to take him out. His leg was in a bandage and the light was on.

The big woman saw me stop. 'Knocked down by a car!' she boomed at me. 'No one has, as yet, come to claim him. No collar. He may be put down! Pity we can't put some of the owners down,' she said crisply.

'Yeah,' I said, thinking vaguely of Jackser and whoever was on me hit list.

'Bonzo has his own quarters, away from the rest. We allow him out to play with our own dogs. Samson is very fond of him. The visitors take to him too.'

I could hear him barking from here. She swung around a corner and bent down to open the cage door. Bonzo was throwing himself at the cage and belting down to the wall to have another go at trying to break his way out.

'Steady, boy!' She bent down to grab him, holding the gate half opened with her leg. She missed catching him and he came steaming out, sending her flying, big and all as she is. He sailed through the air, landing feet first at my chest, sending me flying to the ground, landing sideways.

'Ah, fuck!' I puffed, as I automatically turned myself into a ball and rolled – something I learned back in my childhood, when Jackser would send me flying with a kick. I wasn't quick enough, not managing to get the roll, and landed heavily on the right side of my arse. Ah! The pain shot through me. 'I think me hip's broken,' I gasped, staring in agony as he sat on top of me, licking the face off me. I turned away, hating the thought of what he had been licking last.

'Sit!' the big woman roared, pulling her skirt down over her massive hips and throwing the big clump of hair back over her head and trying to pin it back with a clip.

'THAT DOG is completely wild!' she roared, giving a vicious tug at her skirt to keep it down. She grabbed him by the collar and with a big massive pair of lungs roared straight into his face, 'BAD BOY!'

His long ears collapsed around his head, and he looked like he'd been hit by the *Titanic*.

'Take him!' she barked at me. 'Train him! Show him who is boss!' I got up, rubbing away the pain in my arse, and meekly took him while she grabbed the lead hanging on the wall inside the cage.

'Now heel!' she roared, while I took the lead, and he was off, dragging me down the passage.

'HEEL!' she screamed after us.

Bonzo's head swung on his shoulders, then he stopped dead, planking himself on his arse.

'I said you must lead!' she barked at me.

'Right!' I said, watching him watching the door, the two of us dying to get out.

We roared into the reception area at thirty miles an hour, with Bonzo barking his head off. Samson went mad with excitement and came thundering out, barking like he was going to tear me from limb to limb, and made straight for Bonzo, who tore at him. I let go of the lead, screaming, and the two of them jumped on me.

'Ah, I'm dead,' I moaned, collapsing against the counter, letting myself flop, feeling the blood rush from my face.

The big woman screamed, 'In the name of heavens! Why do you own a dog? You are not fit to be left with this animal.'

I opened my eyes and stared at her. That did it! Forgetting my fear, I rushed at Bonzo, banging Samson out of the way, and dragged Bonzo by the scruff of the neck. I took hold of the lead and tore at her, shouting, 'Someone mistook you for a woman but you are more like that overgrown bleedin donkey there,' I roared, pointing at Samson, 'than you are human!' I stood snorting at her, waiting to hear what she had to say about that.

'Wonderful!' she roared, clapping her hands.

I stopped, confused. What's she talking about?

'You have lost your fear! That's the way to treat 'em!'

I looked at Samson sitting beside me and Bonzo sitting the other side, and they were looking at me very intently. Suddenly I thought Samson looked like a pussycat, and I leaned over, patting him gingerly on the head. Bonzo barked his head off, jealous. 'Yes, and you too, Bonzo!' I said, petting him. Then I was off.

'Keep it up!' the big woman shouted. 'It's all in the voice!'

'Right! It's all in the voice,' I echoed, gasping out of breath.

We tore through the door, heading for the car. I held on desperately, fighting to hold him back. Puff! 'Bonzo! You are a bad boy!' I wheezed, trying to get my breath back, pointing my finger in his face the way she did. He shook his head and arse, looking like he was having a fit, then lowered his arse, not letting it rest on the ground. I threw my head back, letting out an unmerciful scream right into his face, sounding like I was singing soprano! He dropped his arse rapidly, planting it firmly on the ground.

'Good boy!' I said happily, thinking I'm getting the knack of it. But his feet kept tap dancing; he can't bloody sit still. Poor thing! He's suffering with his nerves. That woman must have put the fear of God into him!

I opened the door, pulling back the seat, and he sailed in, flicking himself around, landing in my seat. 'Out!' I roared. He likes to sit there, minding the car when I'm not in it, and sizes up the people walking past, deciding whether or not they're potential robbers. He hurled himself in the back seat, his tail flying around like a windmill.

'Sit!'

He sat for a second, then raced to the other side, looking out the window. I leaned around, opening it a little, then started the engine and we were off. 'The excitement is mighty, Bonzo,' I murmured. 'I know you are delighted to be going home.'

He immediately jumped up, giving me a big lick on the side of my neck.

'Ah, Jaysus! Sit down. Sit!' I roared.

He gave a big sigh, stretching himself on the back seat, and we were motoring again.

'Right! Here we are, Bonzo. Home again!'

He went bananas, his barking going straight through my head and out through my ears. I jumped out just as he threw himself at the door, getting locked in.

'NO! No gallivanting off for you!' I said, wagging my finger. Then I opened the garage door, drove in and locked it behind me.

'Come on, out you get,' I said, opening the car door.

He was a blur, squeezing himself so fast through the crack I barely got the door opened. Then he was free. He tore in through the side passage, flying to get his football, and headed it around the garden, making George Best weep with jealousy. The speed of him!

I side-stepped, not wanting to get the legs pulled out from under me as I opened the side gate into the front garden, and stood to one side as he shot past. I could feel the wind whipping around my legs as he skidded past. He was stopped by the end gate and hopped around waiting for me to open it.

He rubbed the back of my legs with his head to show me he loves me. 'Yes, Bonzo. I love you too,' I said, bending down to give him a tight hug.

The entrance gate opened, and I lifted me head, seeing Sergei appear. My mouth hung open. Good God! What's he doing here? He smiled, then settled his eyes on Bonzo, who was making a run for him with a deep growl in his throat.

'Bonzo! Stop!' I shouted.

Sergei stopped, giving him an evil stare, then rumbled in a quiet whisper, snapping his finger at the ground before waving the dog down. 'Sit!'

Bonzo stared in shock, then dropped his arse for a split second before wandering back, giving a dirty look behind him. He doesn't like yer man, I thought. But, then, he doesn't really like any man. Especially the postman, or drunks, or, in one case, a poor unfortunate on crutches! I gave him a wallop for that one. The hairy little coward.

'In, Bonzo,' I said, locking him in the side passage. He stuck his head out, barking like mad as he watched Sergei making his way up to me. For a split second me heart leapt, then I remembered. It doesn't matter any more. I have my old life back! Or, even better, my new start! I'm over twenty-one and fancy-free. No ties! I felt a jolt of happiness.

'What brings you here?' I said, wondering at his cheek to come waltzing up my path.

'Oh, sorry!' he said, waving his hands. 'I just thought, maybe, you might like to . . . You left without saying goodbye. We are friends, no? You did not agree to meet me for coffee! I am sorry, I will go,' he said, heading back out the gate.

I stared after him, trying to decide if I wanted him here or not. 'Ohh, wait a minute, please. It's OK. Yeah, sure, it's nice to see you. Come on in. I was just about to get something to eat,' I said, seeing him turn around slowly, not sure if he was interested after the insult.

He shrugged, looking a bit sulky, then let his eyes take in the height of the long grass. Jaysus! I better get moving and start cutting. That garden sure needs a bit of work. I want to have it looking lovely again.

'Would you like something to eat?' I said, whipping open the fridge. 'What have I got?' I muttered, half to myself. Ahh! Sister Eleanor is so good to me. Pork chops, a whole chicken, cheese, ham, eggs, rashers and sausages. I had some for my breakfast. Jaysus! The fridge is full. That will keep me going for a while. I opened the wall presses. Tea, sugar, coffee, cereals, porridge! Jaysus! No thanks. My eyes flew over the amount of stuff. Even fresh vegetables in the larder.

'What would you like?' I said, taking down the makings of a sandwich.

'No, nothing, thank you. But maybe just a small something,' he said, dropping his mouth and lifting his shoulder. 'Yes! I will join you for a little. I will have supper later, at home. Or maybe shortly I will go to see my friends,' he said, wandering out to the hall to get a look around.

I made a cheese-and-onion sandwich for myself and one with ham for him. I carried in the two plates to the dining room, hearing him wandering around outside.

'You must cut the grass. It is wild and will not be good,' he said, coming in looking lost about the state of the garden.

'Well! If you are so interested,' I laughed, 'the lawn mower is in the garage. A fine big strapping fella like you would have that done in no time!'

'OK, if you wish,' he said, not sounding bothered.

'You will?' I shouted.

'Of course! Why not? I will go now,' he said, taking off his Italian figured-in leather jacket before I could take the next breath.

'Ahh, no! First have the sandwich. I don't want them to go to waste,' I said, sitting meself down and pouring the tea.

I was on the phone, nattering away like mad, catching up with all me friends. Earlier I could hear the sound of the lawnmower getting heaved up and down the garden. But now it was just the odd sound of things banging, and even the dog was quiet. Occasionally he was thumping up and down the passage. Either Sergei is kicking the ball for him or he's heading it up and down himself. He gets into fits over that ball. Heading it against the wall and thumping it into the air, or chasing it around for hours. Everyone says he's mad! Yeah, suppose he is. Just like meself.

'OK!' Sergei said, coming into the hall and rolling down his shirt sleeves.

'Oh! Are you finished?' I said, hanging up the phone quickly and rushing out to get a look at the garden. Jaysus! Me breath caught. It's gorgeous. The grass is lovely and even, like it had been cut by one of them motor mowers. And even the hedge is cut! I looked at me apple tree looking nice and round. All the old branches were cut back.

Me eyes peeled to the lovely lavender tree, with all the lavender in full bloom, and the tree on the other side of the passage, forming an arch. It was hanging down with lovely branches covered in white heavy flowers. I never got around to asking someone what that tree was called. But it's lovely. The white one side and the purple on the other. Ohh! The smell! My very own paradise.

He watched me from behind.

'Ahh! You are so good! Thank you so much, Sergei! It really means a lot to me,' I said. 'You've done a marvellous job!'

He bowed at me, saying, 'It is my pleasure. I was happy to do it! Now, may I have something to drink? I am thirsty.'

'Oh, yeah, of course. What would you like? Jaysus! What have I got? Water? Oh! I think there's a big carton of orange juice.'

'It does not matter,' he said. 'Give me whatever you want. I can drink water.'

I reached up to the press, taking down a drinking glass. Then my eyes landed on the half bottle of vodka. 'Would you like a drink of this?' I said, holding up the bottle for him.

'Yes! Why not? Thank you.'

He finished the drink, then stood up, putting on his jacket. 'OK! Thank you. It is good to see you. That was nice.'

'Oh! Where are you off to?'

'I think maybe I will go home and do some things. I have to be up early in the morning.'

'Oh, are you not working tonight?'

'No, this afternoon I was free.'

'Would you like a cup of tea and something to eat before you go?'

He hesitated.

'Sit down. Do you want to watch the news?' I said, switching on the television.

'OK! Just for a little time,' he said, walking over to look out at the back garden and admire his lovely work.

I washed up, then rummaged through the black plastic bags sitting in the hall. First thing tomorrow, I must sort all this stuff out, I thought, digging through the bag full of biscuits and all sorts of stuff. Sister Eleanor brought me up this lot. She has a sweet tooth and thought I might enjoy them. I never touched a thing.

I grabbed a box of chocolates, saying, 'Here! Help yourself,' then sat down on the couch, letting him sit at the dining table, watching the telly. I dipped over, grabbing a chocolate, then flopped back down again, with the two of us companionably watching a Carry On film. I roared laughing, and he looked over, giving a big grin, seeing me get great enjoyment outa the fella trying to get blondie into the holiday nudist camp.

The farmer who owned the field where the caravans were stashed kept licking his lips, wrangling more and more money outa the desperate fella. 'One pound for breathing in the lovely fresh air!' he droned, holding out his hand, flicking his eyeballs to the air, trying to think up the next wheeze. The fella was sweating as he coughed up the money. But he was hoping, dying, for a bit of nookie! But yer woman had been told by the ma to wear her woolly vest and long knickers!

She sat looking shocked, buttoning her overcoat up to her neck. But when they got in, the only nudist was herself. She strutted around looking like an innocent schoolgirl wearing an itsy-bitsy bikini! Driving everyone, including the little Boy Scouts leader, mad! 'Ohh!' she panted, looking at his big beefy legs sticking out under the long brown shorts. 'Please! Can you fix my strap? Look!' she mewled, grabbing her huge chest, juggling the pair of them under his flaring nostrils. 'They are falling out!' Her boyfriend was nearly pole-vaulting out of his trousers with the want.

The film ended and Sergei stood up, making for his jacket. We both sighed happily, still smiling from all the laughs.

'OK! It is time. Thank you for a lovely evening.'

'Would you like a lift back?' I said, seeing the pair of us look at the time. 'It's nearly half past nine,' I said. 'Gawd! The day flew in!'

'Yes! Congratulations! You have a good life. This is an excellent home. Big enough for more people. It is a family home!'

'Yes, oh yes,' I said. 'But most people here are retired now. All their families are grown up. They have lived here for years.'

'Yes, yes,' he said slowly, shaking his head. 'You are fortunate. Enjoy!' Then he walked to the door and I followed him out.

'No, it is a nice night. I will walk to take the air. Thank you for your offer. Goodnight! Maybe some time we can meet again?'

'Oh, yeah, that's OK,' I said, happy with the idea.

'I will see. My time is busy,' he said, stopping and looking at me. Then he turned, heading for the gate, saying, 'Goodbye!'

'Bye, Sergei! Thanks for calling,' I shouted, seeing him wave, then shut the gate after him. It's a lovely night, I thought, staring up at the stars and drinking in the warm evening air that smelled of lavender and freshly cut grass. I stretched, feeling lovely and tired, then walked in, closing the door, locking it for the night.

'Bonzo! Bloody mutt is missing again,' I muttered, talking to meself. Right! Up the stairs. An early night is in order for you! Bed, book and candle! Maybe Radio Four might have a good play on? I will sleep tonight. That air is sure heavy with the weight of lovely warm garden scents.

55

I was dozing away with a book in my hand, lying sprawled out on a sunbed, enjoying the late summer sun. Nearly the end of August! I thought, turning over to have a snooze. Ahh! This is the life, I thought, giving me nose a quick scratch, then wriggling for more comfort. Bonzo started barking his head off, lunging at the side gate. That bleedin dog! I'm selling him to the zoo! They can use him for meat! Then he flew down, looking at me with his eyes bulging, staring, and his ears flapped up, then took off again. I lifted me head, stretching me back into the air. Wanting, but not willing, to get up! Then I heard the side gate opening. I grabbed me wrap, not wanting to show off me bikini. Tan or no tan! Well, mostly the front. As usual, the back of me nearly looks like a milk bottle. I hate lying on me belly!

'So! This is what you do!' said Sergei, standing at the passage, taking me in.

I looked at him and me breath caught. Jaysus! He looks gorgeous. His hair was glittering gold against the pale white underneath. It was thick and silky, slicked back off his forehead, just tipping the collar of his pale-blue striped shirt. His skin had gone a lovely golden tan.

'You're back!' I said, beaming with delight at the sight of him. I never know when to expect him. He nodded, then lowered his thick lashes, looking the length of me, taking in me legs with the bit of colour and the way they had filled out from all me eating. I could see a flash of interest, and a smile played around his mouth.

'So! You noticed I was gone!' he said, coming over and planting himself in the chair beside me. He put a plastic bag under the garden table, saying, 'Would you like to eat? Maybe I could prepare something in your kitchen? I have brought some food.'

'Yes, what did you get?'

'Steak! A man's food. Something to build you up! Tomatoes . . . Ohh, what we need . . .' he said, shaking his head and shoulders, drawing down his mouth.

'Do you know, I missed you, Sergei!'

'You did?'

'Yeah, I really did! Look at the grass. It's waiting there for you to come and cut it!'

'Oh, not today! Maybe when . . . soon!' he said. 'Now we relax. Take a look!' He pointed at the bag.

I dug me nose in the bag, seeing a big lump of foreign cheese, fancy crackers, a bottle of wine and a bottle of vodka wrapped in brown-paper bags. Celery, a fancy cake in a box, potatoes, fresh rolls, cream. All sorts of stuff.

'Can you cook?'

'Of course!' he shrugged.

'What else can you do?' I said, thinking I only learn bits about him at a time.

He took in a deep breath, saying, 'I have a lot of talents! Would you like to see some more?'

'What? Yeah!' I said, seeing a glint in his eye.

'Come here!' he said, taking my head on his arm, then lowered his head, landing his hot lips covering mine! A shiver went through me. They were so soft and warm and moist.

Then he pulled away from me, saying, 'OK! You looked very alluring. Sorry! I could not help myself. I am a red-blooded male!' Then he stooped down and picked up the bag. 'Is the kitchen door open?'

'Yeah, turn the handle.'

'OK, rest! I will feed you. We will eat in one, two hours. It is not important. The day is long.'

'Lovely!' I breathed, feeling very content, watching him walk off. Not able to take in he was here. My God! He looks like an Adonis! Wonder why he kissed me after all this time? He never did that before. I could have sworn he was not really thinking that way. Maybe he still isn't. Anyway! No harm! I'm happy just having the laughs with him, and sharing days out, going for drives, when he does show up.

I stared at the one mushroom left sitting on the plate, thinking, if I eat that, I will only burst. I want room for me chocolate cake and fresh cream with strawberries.

'Ohh! Indeed! You are a very talented man, Sergei,' I sighed, flopping back in the sunchair and stretching out me legs.

He grinned at me, saying, 'Yes! Almost as talented as you!'

'Me?'

'Of course! You are a very clever lady! But you like to hide it. I think you like to fool people, lull them into a false sense of security.'

'Oh, aren't you the astute one!' I said, thinking he is right about that one. I always prefer to play the fool. I shot up in the chair. 'Ohhh! Me foot! Me toe.' I grabbed it. 'Ohh! I've got a cramp.' I watched me toes curling over each other, gritting me teeth.

'Let me see!' He leaned across, taking my foot and picking the toes off each other very gently with his strong wide hands. Then he started to massage my foot, rubbing his thumbs and fingers up the length of it.

'Ohhh! That's lovely!' I sighed, closing me eyes and shoving me foot further into his lap, thinking, I have died and gone to heaven.

'You are looking well,' he murmured, stretching me ankle and rubbing the bottom of me leg. 'You have put some flesh on your bones.'

'Have I?' I said, opening my eyes, looking at him.

'Yes,' he said, looking at me, letting his eyes linger. I could see a glint in them. Then he lowered his lashes, looking down at my leg, massaging it, then back to my foot. 'It suits you.'

'Gawd! If Blondie could see us now,' I laughed, 'I bet she would be raging.' I must give her a ring when she gets back, I thought. See what's she's up to. Maybe get myself an invite to one of her house parties. The size of that house! It's a mansion. It must be nearly the same size as . . . something the Queen lives in, but, Gawd! She's a scream! Especially the way she gives poor Dick the runaround. That man worships the ground she walks on. But she leads him around by the nose. He loves it! 'Yes, my pet poodle,' he calls her, when she demands he run and get her handbag! Yet in business, he would chew you up and spit you out. One of her luncheon friends told me. That's what they're called. Now Blondie and himself are off in St Tropez at the minute. Then it's the Bahamas, if you wouldn't be minding! 'Dick's business,' she calls it, sounding fed up! I sniffed to meself. Gawd! She has a hard aul life. Now me! Well, I get excited just going down to the village. It's a great outing for myself.

Ah, but she's very good to me. Dragging me everywhere. Lunches with the pals. 'The girls,' she calls them. Aul ones dressed up like a dog's dinner. They spend more in a day than I would in a lifetime. All in the name of trying to stay 'young and beautiful', they call it. Sometimes Blondie an me get great enjoyment listening to the carry-on of them. Nah! You need something left to look forward to. Still, it's smashing if you can dip in and out of it. I get to stay overnight when Dick's away. Keep her company, she calls it.

'Oh, will we be sitting in watching the telly?'

'No!' Blondie explains down the phone. 'Be ready! Get the glad rags on. We're hitting the town. I'm picking you up!' she puffs, sorting me out for the weekend.

I couldn't afford to piss in some of those places, never mind eat and drink in them!

She's always giving me stuff. 'Here! Take that coat!' I look. It's a mink! I try it on. It wraps around me twice. But I look like a film star in it. 'Take it!' she says, giving it a dirty look. 'Dick has bought me a new sable! It's stored with the furrier's until I need it. I will get you a pair of boots to match for Christmas!' she says, eyeing me, then laughing her head off, seeing me strutting up and down, practising me new walk.

'Come up and see me some time! When I've nothing on! But the radio!' I drone, talking up through me nose.

Gawd! Will I ever forget the first time I dragged her up to my house for dinner, I called it! We had spaghetti bolognaise, garlic bread and a bottle of white-plonk wine. 'That was the best meal I had in a long while,' she sighs. 'I really enjoyed myself. You and me are going to make up for lost time,' she says, looking at me with a vengeance in her eyes, letting them glitter and harden, shaking her head thinking about them darker days. 'We have nothing to stop us!' she said, making it sound like the world had better watch out.

But then her eyes softened, letting a sadness creep in. 'A good friend is something very rare in my circle,' she said, shaking her head, thinking about it. Sounding very sad.

'Yeah! I know how lonely life can get, Hannah,' I said, putting my arms around her. 'But you and me, we're connected. We both ended up in the mad house! That's how bad it got us!' I puffed, staring at her with me eyes hanging out. Then we roared laughing.

We never stopped laughing the whole night, talking into the early hours about everything and anything. We talked about a lifetime, letting everything spill out as the hours slowly ticked away the night. The only things we didn't cover were my dark childhood secrets and just how rich her husband Dick was. He could afford to buy out my house with his lunch money and still have change over. Yeah, but our friendship is worth more than its weight in gold. Where would we have been without the mad house? I smiled to meself.

I looked up at Sergei, seeing him watching me with a serious look in his eyes, like he was thinking, not sure about something. I stared, trying to read him. He dropped his eyes, then landed them on me other foot, grabbing it.

'Oooh! You can give up the day job, Sergei! Just devote the rest of your life to keeping me happy! Ohhh! I never knew such pleasure existed until this minute,' I said.

'Hmm! You are very sensuous,' he murmured, landing his eyes lazily on me, giving me a slow grin.

'Ohh! A new discovery,' I moaned, getting lost in me world of pleasure. Then I suddenly screeched laughing, remembering something. 'To think I told Blondie you were gay!'

'What?' he boomed, shaking me foot.

'Ahhh! Go easy! You'll break me fucking toes,' I snapped, grabbing my foot.

He snatched it back. 'So, you told her I was only attracted to men! What an insult! Come here!' Then he grabbed me, lowering me down into his arms, and smothered my lips with his, opening my mouth and latching on to my tongue. My toes curled, and I melted into the seat, stroking his soft hair. Letting myself get lost in a world of even more pleasure.

Then he pulled his head back and stared at me, grinning. 'That is only for my mother!' he said. 'A chaste kiss!'

'Jaysus! I would call that criminal! It's positively incestuous if that's the kind of kisses yer ma gets,' I laughed, seeing him stare at me with his face grinning from ear to ear.

'Now! Enough! No more! My head needs calm,' he said, putting my feet and legs together, then lying back on his own chair.

'So does my heart,' I moaned, feeling it going like the clappers. But still wanting and wishing for more.

'Where were you for the last couple of weeks?' I said, after not hearing from him.

'I was in Rome.'

'You were! On holiday?'

'Yes.'

'Ahh, you never even sent me a card,' I said, feeling let down he hadn't thought about me.

'It was business,' he murmured, lifting his hand and resting it over his eyes, shielding them from the sun.

'Oh, well, it's not my affair. I won't ask what sort of business,' I said, taking in a big breath and closing my eyes to the sun.

He lifted himself onto his side, saying, 'I am to take up a new post.'

'Where?'

'Very remote. The other side of the earth,' he said, looking into himself, thinking about it.

'What will you be doing?'

'I will have my own hospital. That is what I am doing in Ireland. I have been here to observe. Now, soon, I think I will be leaving.'

'When? How soon?' I said, sitting bolt upright, getting a terrible land when I didn't even expect to feel that would happen to me. Gone! Jaysus! I'm only getting used to him.

'It will be very soon,' he said, standing himself up. 'Let us have a drink. I would like a vodka. Do you want the same?' he said, throwing the head at me as he made to walk off.

'OK, yeah, please.'

'I will bring it out,' he said, slowly walking to the kitchen.

'So! He's going?' I muttered to meself, trying to take it in as I reached for me smokes. Gawd! No more Sergei! These last few months, I really got to know him. I looked forward to seeing him. It even felt great having a man around. He would cut the grass and even fix something when it went wrong. We started to feel easy together. Fit ourselves into each other's ways as we got used to each other. Now, today, it got even better. More intimate. Like he really is attracted to me. I thought about that. I'm strongly attracted to him, too. It wouldn't take much for me to . . . No! Forget that. Don't start going down that road, Martha. Pull back, like you have up to now. Keep your independence. He has his life, you have yours.

He came out carrying the bottle of vodka in one hand and a bottle of tomato juice and a little bottle of red pepper for me in the other. He likes his vodka neat.

I watched him making his way towards me, throwing his eye over the lawn, not looking too impressed. Jaysus! He really is handsome, I thought, letting me heart take a little leap at the sight of him.

'Here, we will drink a toast,' he said, holding up his glass as he handed me my Bloody Mary. Blondie always laughs when she hears me ordering that.

'To the future, whatever it may bring,' he said, sounding very serious as he downed his vodka, then poured another one, sipping that slowly.

'So, you must not stay alone,' he said, staring at me with his eyes looking very stern, as if he was giving me an order.

I stared at him, thinking about what he just said.

'Don't keep yourself locked up. You have a big heart. Share it!' he said, snapping his hand wide open in the air.

'Fine! I'll come with you to Outer Mongolia, or wherever it is you're going, and help you to mop the brow of the blind, bothered and bewildered,' I laughed, trying to make light of the heavy feeling trying to strangle me heart.

'Bah! I will not be doing these things. My work will be administering the running of the hospital.'

'Is it in the bush?' I said, getting the picture of people running around with spears, trying to catch him for their dinner. Nah! No such thing. Some African princess with the latest fashions from Paris will probably drop herself into his lap, needing his help from all her exhausting high living! I felt a bit jealous with that thought, as I looked at him, seeing him watching me.

He seemed far away somehow. Like he was searching my face for something, then going off to think about something else.

'Are you delighted to be going?' I said. 'It's what you wanted, isn't it?'

'Of course,' he shrugged. 'But there are some things I must first think on.'

'Like what?'

'There are decisions for me,' he said, shrugging his shoulders, holding up his eyebrows. 'But first I think I will go to my homeland. I will go back to Moscow! Visit my family.' Then he whipped his head at me, really looking at me, getting a sudden thought in his head. I watched his eyes staring into mine, seeing the look of misery in my face. He said nothing. I waited.

'Do you want to come?' he said quietly, keeping his face still, but his eyes were soft.

'What! You want me to come with you?' I said, getting the shock of me life. Not able to take in the suddenness of what he just asked me.

'Martha, it is not impossible for you,' he said, reaching over to take my hand.

I watched as he examined my fingers, gently stroking them.

'Why not? You will like it. I will take you. You will stay with my family. My mother and sisters. They will be happy to see you. We are a big family. Very close!'

I sat rooted to me chair, feeling my whole world has suddenly changed. I didn't want to get the wrong idea, letting me hopes rise, opening myself up!

'Why, Sergei? Why would you want to invite me?'

'Why not? We can spend a little time together. Take a holiday. I need to prepare myself,' he said, letting go of my hand and examining his own. 'I must take this opportunity before I leave,' he said, sounding very mournful. 'It will be years before I see my family once again. Also, it would be good to have you share my world. I would like this. You must live your life, Martha. Do not be afraid to leave your village life.'

'When will you be going, Sergei?' I said, feeling me heart in me mouth, looking at him. I really wanted to get very close to him. But I'm afraid to think like that.

'September . . . I do not know yet. But it will be soon. I am thinking this way. But first, arrangements have to be made. OK! Now we must do some work. Please take away these dishes! You clean up the mess. I am afraid your kitchen is not as you left it,' he laughed, walking off to the garage, saying, 'I will take care of the garden. I must cut this grass.'

56

I put the book down, not able to concentrate on it. I looked around, sighing, wondering what to do with meself. It's only seven o'clock. I wonder what Sergei is doing? Pity I can't ring him, or, better still, go up and see him. Never! Not in a million years! What would I do? Wander around asking for him? He's probably over with the monks, doing whatever they're doing. Hmm! I wish I knew what's really on his mind. Visit his country, then come home, leaving him to go off into the wilderness. What would that get me? I wonder does he want an affair before he goes? No, not for me. It would most certainly be looking for trouble. Big trouble. No! I don't need that. Still, up to this he hasn't made any advances to me.

OK! Plain and simple, Martha. When he does finally show up – it's been two weeks since he mentioned Russia. I haven't clapped eyes on him since – Well! Just ask him straight out, does he want to sleep with me? If the answer is yes, then my answer is no! What good is an affair? I want someone around for a lifetime. A man who will value my worth. Someone I would give my love, my trust and total commitment to. Right! Get your bearings first, Martha. No point in wandering off down the wrong bleedin road. Time is precious. I have a whole lot of living to do. I sighed, letting out my breath, feeling better I had got that sorted.

Now! What about a bit of television? I hopped up, giving Bonzo a fright. His head shot up, looking at me with roaring-red bloodshot eyes. He stared for a few minutes, with the eyes looking shell-shocked, then gave up, seeing nothing much was happening.

'Ooooohhh!' he moaned, snorting like mad, then dropped back down again, giving a huge sigh of contentment.

I watched as he splattered himself right in front of the sofa, stretching himself for more comfort. Within seconds, he was back to snoring. 'Ohh! You've a dog's life!' I said, hearing me own voice.

The phone rang just as I sat down. Oh! Wonder who that is? Forget it, Martha. It's not Sergei. He doesn't ring.

'Hello!'

'Martha Long! Where have you been hiding yourself?'

I listened, then screeched, 'Kitty! Gawd! It's been ages!'

'What happened to you?' she said, making it sound like an accusation.

'Ahhh! Did ye not hear? I was locked up in the loony bin!'

There was a second's silence, then a scream came down the line. 'Oh, Jesus! Stop! So I heard. Oh, my God, I have missed you! Listen! Gotta go! Just a quick call. What are you doing tomorrow? Are you free for lunch?'

I thought, wondering if I had forgotten something. 'Nope! Free as a bird. Where will we meet?'

'What about Pink Lilly's? Just after the rush hour, say about two-ish?'

'Yeah, great, see you then.'

'Bye, darling! Can't wait!' she said.

'Yeah! Lovely! See you then. Cheers!'

I parked the car, looking to see if it was a double line. No! No tickets on the other cars. Great. Then I made it across Westmoreland Street, going down a side street and into the restaurant. I looked around, seeing the tables were occupied by mostly one person. Men reading the newspaper before they went back to the office.

I walked behind the cash desk and sat down in a little alcove with a window looking out into the street. No sign of Kitty yet! I picked up the menu, looking at the prices. Three-course special – four quid! No thanks. Give that a miss. Right! I'll just have the soup and a roll.

I opened my bag and rolled meself a cigarette, then sat back to wait. The waitress glanced at me, then decided I could wait, and went back to more serious stuff, talking to her friend sitting behind the cash desk with a wig on her that looked like a dead rat! It was black and went down to her shoulders. Jaysus! The state of the pair of them! The other one had her hair scraped back in a ponytail. It was very thin – that's from all the dyeing she gives it. Now it was mouldy black.

She looked over again at me, saying, 'Just let me finish this cigarette, love! Then I'll be wit yeh in a minute!'

I nodded, giving her a smile. But her head was already turned back to the friend, who was more interesting than serving me!

'It's OK, no hurry,' I said. 'But if you could bring me a glass of water, please. I'm waiting for someone.'

She flicked her head at me, giving a quick nod, saying, 'Yeah! Oh, yeah! Ye're great, thanks. I'll get tha!' Then she turned back to the wig, who was waiting to continue her conversation. But first she squinted, closing one eye with the smoke billowing around her, and said, 'I hate these early afternoon rushes! So go on! Ga sinta tell us! Did you go out with your man after all?'

I waited, listening to the conversation, knowing there was no point in complaining.

The wig one lifted her chin off her elbow and wrinkled her nose, letting her mouth curl up to meet it, then said, 'Do yeh mean the taxi fella?'

'Yeah, him!'

'Jaysus! Don't talk te me about him! All I got there was a bag a chips in the back of his taxi, then he was after a bit of the other!'

'Tsk, tsk! I thought ye were made up there!' Ponytail said. 'Him havin the taxi an all tha! Pity!' she said, turning back to me.

'He was a waste a space!' the wig one roared, getting herself all worked up when it slowly dawned on her just how much she had been insulted. 'I mean! The cheek a the fella! Thinkin he could a had me for the price of a bag a chips! I ask yeh! I should a bleedin brained him!' she snorted. 'Treatin me like a slag!'

'I know! Some fellas have the cheek a the devil!' Ponytail sniffed. 'It's not like he had any class! You'd expect tha from the likes a them. But still an all, Ga sinta! He had a taxi! Think a the money he'd bring home!'

'No! He was too common,' Ga sinta sniffed, getting an awful smell under her nose and shaking it away with her head.

'So, what can I get you, love?' she said, whipping out her notebook.

'Eh, just a glass of water, please. I'm waiting on someone.'

She sighed, stabbing the notebook back in her pocket, and made off, muttering to Ga sinta, 'Jaysus! Yer woman! The last a the big spenders! We're not goin te make much in tips today, Ga sinta.'

'No, certainly not outa me!' I snorted to meself.

She came slowly back, slapping the glass of water on the counter, giving me a sour look.

Jaysus! I wonder where Kitty is? This is not like her.

The phone at the cash desk rang. I heard Ga sinta talking, then she was looking around at me. 'Yeah! I see a woman of tha description all right. She's sittin here. Yeah, I'll tell her! Excuse me! Are you Martha?'

'Yes,' I said, getting worried.

'Well, a woman, she says her name is Kitty, she wants me to tell ye she's sorry but her car broke down at traffic lights on the way here. She's waitin for a mechanic te come an fix it. But she will ring ye this evening.'

Oh, bloody hell! Poor Kitty! She must still be going around in that old banger! I wonder if she will ever manage to get a few bob together and buy herself a decent one?

'Yes, OK. Thanks for telling me,' I said, smiling at her. Ahh! She's a decent girl, I thought to myself after all. They just want to make a few bob, like everyone does.

Right! What now? I rolled a cigarette, thinking about Kitty. I hope she's OK! She can be so bloody scattered. Jaysus! The pair of us go back a long way. I have known her for years.

Yeah, Kitty and her bright ideas. She's an artist. We have had some great laughs together. She even dragged me to a tea dance once in a hotel. Oh, Jaysus! That was a scream. The aul fellas, they were well past their prime, queued up to waltz us around the floor. We flew them off their feet, skating around to music from the First World War played by a geriatric band. Some of them were very lecherous and kept trying to squeeze my arse! One aul fella, he had one foot in the grave, actually pulled me into him so tight, my nose was pressing into his neck, then he whispered into my ear, 'Would ye like a dip a the wick? Ye're a lovely-lookin woman!' Then he stopped whirling me around and looked into me face. 'I'm not too far from here,' he said. 'Me place is in walkin distance.'

I stared in shock at his cheek, looking at his red rheumy eyes and purple lecherous face, and gave him a smack on the gob!

There was uproar. 'That's a shockin carry-on! Hittin that poor aul man, an he after dancin wit ye!' an aul one said, rushing over to poke me in the chest. 'Lookit him! Tha poor crature will never be the same after you molestin him!' she sniffed, pointing to the aul fella slinking off to hide in the men's toilet.

'He molested me!' I shouted, then told her through snorts from me nose, 'Excuse me, Missus! If you want to be groped on yer arse, then that's fine! You go and dance with him,' I shouted, getting all red in the face, seeing the whole place was turning against me.

'Get the manager!'

'Yeah, go on, somebody! Quick! Call that manager!' they all started screaming.

We had to leg it out the door before I got arrested! Fuck Kitty and her 'Ballroom of Romance' she called it. It was no such thing! She had the idea she might meet some old retired colonel type with a big stately home out in Wicklow or somewhere! She was already planning on turning the drawing room into a studio for herself, where she could get on with her painting, using the scenery for inspiration. Bleedin hell! That was something we definitely should have missed.

No, it was very sad, really. Just a load of retired, lonely old people. All sitting around staring, desperately hoping to meet someone. They were looking for companionship and hoping to find someone to curl up with on dark wintry nights. Jaysus! I pray I don't end up like that myself one day. It's too cruel.

Right! I'm not bothered about eating here. I think I'll get going. Do something more useful.

I walked out onto the street, seeing a taxi pull up with Kitty sitting in the back. She leaned across, paying the driver, then jumped out. 'Darling! Oh, am I glad to see you! What a bloody day! Here, where are you going?' she said, grabbing my arm. 'Have you eaten?'

'No, Kitty. What happened? Where's the car?'

'Oh, forget that! I've abandoned the bloody thing. I hope they tow it away to the scrapheap. Come on! Let's go back inside.'

'OK,' I said, letting her grab on to me arm.

'Ohh! I have so much to tell you. Wait until you hear! Oh, my God! What happened to you? Jesus! I nearly cracked up myself. That bloody awful agent of mine! Where will we sit?' she said, swiping the big hat off her head, tossing her long curly hair, then sweeping her eyes around the room, taking everything in. The place was nearly empty.

'Ohh, there's no atmosphere here. Come on! Let's go somewhere else. What about . . . Searson's? No! Let's walk up Grafton Street. We can go into that nice hotel on Wicklow Street.'

'Come on!' she said, linking her arm through mine. 'You look marvellous!' she gasped, stopping to look me up and down. 'You are simply bursting with rude health! Where did you get that tan?'

'In the back garden,' I said, managing to get a word in.

'Well! I could do with a bit of whatever it is that has put that glow back into your cheeks. My God! Everything has been so manic. My love life is a mess. My agent is a lush. That one spends her time getting groped under the tables by more London and New York galleries than she does trying to grope them to sell my paintings! Anyway! I fired her!'

'Again?' I said. 'Thelma Marsh?'

'Yes! Who else? Oh, did I tell you? I sold a painting.'

'You did?'

'Yes! Thirty thousand!'

'What? Oh, congratulations! I'm so delighted and excited for you, Kitty. Now don't go blowing it this time. You make huge money every now and then,' I said, looking at her sideways, 'then you are flat broke!'

'Oh, darling! This is not a rehearsal. We only live once!' she said, looking straight ahead. 'Oh, it was so lucky I didn't manage to burn that particular painting. Do you know,' she said, looking at me with her big sky-blue eyes under the thin eyebrows, 'I nearly joined you in the loony bin!'

'You did? When? What happened?'

'What do you think? I came home unexpectedly, found that fortune hunter, waster of a miserable wreck of a subhuman, Jason, in bed with an under-aged trollop! They were having it off in my studio! My inner sanctum! It was sacrilegious. I lost my mind completely. Picked up the nearest thing – a pot of paints and a painting. I fairly crowned him with it, I can tell you that. Once my fury was unleashed, there was no stopping it,' she sniffed. 'I kept going. Chasing the pair of them naked around the room. They managed to escape straight onto the street. By then I had a kitchen carving knife. They tore down the road in their pelt, both of them screaming in different directions. Oh, the spectacle. Naturally the police arrived in full force. I was arrested. Screaming he should be too – having it off with an under-aged Lolita! Here we are. Let's hope they're not having a wake. I need some live entertainment,' she said, pushing me ahead into the foyer.

'Oh, go on. Do have another drop, darling,' she said, pouring wine from the second bottle she had ordered.

'No, Kitty. No! Two glasses is more than enough for me,' I said, putting me hand over the half-full glass.

'I love dessert wine, Sauternes. Hmm! Delicious,' she said, slurping, then smacking her lips, wiping them with the linen serviette.

'Yeah, so do I, Kitty. Just as well you're in the money. Or we would be stuck washing up in that back kitchen for the rest of the night,' I said, taking a long sip of me tasty wine.

'Oh, money is no object, darling. Eat, drink and let's be merry. For tomorrow we die!'

'Yeah. Talking about graves, you seem to have a penchant for old geezers.'

'I do? Who?'

'Are you joking, Kitty? What about aul Kelly, Alan Kelly?'

'Oh, what a scream!'

'Yeah, you were mad about him. Jesus, Kitty, for the life of me I couldn't see what attracted you.'

'Oh, he, he was very glamorous! He used to take me to all these posh dos. He was a politician, you know. Hmm, until he dropped me for that tart from Ballsbridge. She was a fashion model. All eyes and no tits,' Kitty said, munching on a piece of limp lettuce, then slopping it onto the plate, looking sour and gloomy.

'We know. But the trouble started when you wouldn't give up!' I said, starting to laugh, feeling it hit me belly. 'You found out he went horse riding, then had the idea we could follow him. See what he's up to,' you said. I started roaring laughing, remembering us chasing him up and down the fields in Wicklow.

'Remember, Kitty? We used to hire out the nags at the stables where he kept his. Oh, my Gawd!' I said. 'Every Wednesday without fail we turned up. I even got a book on horse riding. I used to practise at home with the kitchen chair. Jaysus, Kitty! He was old enough to be your grandfather!' I shrieked.

'Oh, don't remind me!' she howled, laughing her head off. 'But you see,' she said, breathing in to explain to me.

I watched her lovely brown curly hair fall forward to land on the white linen table cloth. She gathered it up, throwing it behind her back, then leaned on her hand, showing her lovely manicured red-varnished nails. Mine never look like that. I just cut them, leaving well alone.

'He had that aura of power,' she breathed in a whisper, letting her eyes shine and stand out of her head. 'Waiters would walk backwards, grovelling, doing his bidding. I loved it! It is a wonderful aphrodisiac.'

'Yeah, until the day I had to take you up to the hospital for the tetanus injection.'

'Yes!' she snorted, fixing the big slide on her hair. 'I was in shock. But then you put the boot in by telling me I might lose the leg. I believed you!' she hissed, letting her mind wander off, getting a faraway, mournful look on her face, still feeling she had a close shave with death!

I screeched laughing.

'Gawd! Your sense of humour is wicked, Martha Long!' she roared, laughing and slapping the hand off me.

'Yes, and you were a spoilt wilful daughter who became a spoilt wilful wife, who inherited a fortune and lost it just as quick. Because you are crazy! Just like meself, Kitty Johnstone,' I said, lowering me head up and down, staring at her with a half-smile on me face.

'Hmm!' she said, thinking about it. 'So what do we do for an encore? You have done your stint in the loony bin. I have loved and lost. And will no doubt continue my track record. It is all written in the great tapestry of life. I am determined to live life to the full before I die,' she said, guzzling down the rest of her wine. 'What about you? What plans have you? Look for a job? A man? You could always pose nude for me and when they ask at one of my exhibitions to meet the demure nude, intrigued with the hidden depths behind those dark-blue eyes, I will recommend only the crème de la crème, telling them where to find you. What about it?'

'Kitty!' I shouted. 'Get stuffed. I had enough of you and your trying to fix me up with a man! Remember that gobshite Andy Simmonds, or whatever he was called. Arrived on my door with the bunch of daffodils! You bloody sent him without giving me a word of warning. I went crazy! The nutter stalked me day and night for months!'

I watched her getting red in the face, spluttering the wine all over me and herself.

'No! No more, Kitty! I mean it!'

'OK! OK!' she said, spitting and laughing, holding her dripping hands and mouth out, looking for the napkin.

'Right! Time to hit the road. I hope my car is still where I left it! Are you coming? The night-time crowd is starting to pile in!'

'Aww, darling. The night is young!'

'Yeah, but I'm going home, Kitty. I need to get me health back to full bloom. Remember, it wasn't too long ago I was a bloody invalid.'

'You?'

'Yes, me, Kitty!'

'Oh, all right! Come on. Where's the bill?'

'Oh, Jaysus, Kitty!' I said, feeling me nerves beginning to rattle. 'I hope you have enough money for this! How much is it? Twenty quid?'

'No, darling. Forty-two!'

'Oh, fuck! I knew it!' I looked around, seeing where the escape hatch was.

'Oh! No panic, darling! Take it easy,' she said, going cross-eyed looking at the bill. 'Honestly! We really do have enough. Let me check my wallet.'

'Oh, Kitty! I hope we're not in trouble. I swear, one of these days you are going to give me a heart attack!'

'Where's the notes?' she mumbled, pulling out a five-pound note.

Oh, sweet Jesus! I tore open me bag, taking out a five-pound note, looking at it longingly. Oh, well! No grub for a week.

'Here, take this, Kitty! How much have you got altogether?' I asked, feeling me face go red with the blood pressure flying to the roof.

'Ahh! Back of the wallet. Here we are. Look! Fifty-pound note!' she said, waving it at me. 'Now, that is class!'

'Oh!' I sighed, feeling the life coming back into me. 'What was I thinking, letting you drag me in here without first checking if one of us – you, Kitty – had the bleedin money?' I roared.

'Right! Let's get out of here. What about your car, Kitty? Will we go and see if it's OK?' I said, worrying it might really be taken.

She shook her head, not interested. 'Home! Forget the car. I am going to buy myself a little sports job.'

'What? That will take most of your money!'

'No! Don't be silly. A couple of thousand should do it. A runabout really. Something second-hand but good. Ohh, poppet, it really is great seeing you looking and sounding so well,' she said, wrapping her arm around me shoulder.

'Yeah, it sure is, Kitty. It sure is!' I mumbled to myself.

Thank you, God, for staying with me. It looks like I made it through, I thought, saying a silent prayer as I walked through Grafton Street, looking at the lights from the street lamps reflected in the shop windows, then seeing the light seep out, throwing their shadows back to us, two companionable friends, both lost in their own thoughts, walking along the dark side street. I could feel my face settle into a smile, enjoying the warm sultry air of an Indian-summer night. As it caressed my face, I gave a big sigh of contentment. Life is back to being a bowl of cherries. How long is it since I last thought that? A hundred years ago, it seems.

'Isn't life just great, Kitty?' I said, wrapping my arm around her waist. 'Come on, let's hope the car is still there.'

She shook her head, grinning at me. 'No problem, darling. We can always take a taxi!'

'Huh! You're incorrigible!' I laughed, feeling God is in his heaven and all is well with the world.

57

I finished drying up the dishes and put everything back in its place, then wiped down the sink. OK. What now? I wandered into the sitting room and switched on the lamp. The nights are drawing in very quickly now. I could see the leaves beginning to fall off the trees. Nearly another year over. Just over a week and we'll be into October!

Wonder whatever happened to Sergei? He never came back! Hmm! Just as well you didn't lose the run of yourself. Yeah, seems like he was just interested in a little interlude to fill in the gaps between his life here and moving on to his new one. Oh, well! Hope he finds what he's looking for. It certainly wasn't me! I thought, giving a little laugh. Blondie was convinced I had met the man of me dreams. No such thing. Happens only in schoolgirl dreams.

I wonder what's on the television? Or maybe take the mutt for a run? No! It's getting too dark out. Anyway, I'm feeling too lazy. He got his run today. Hope he's still in the garden. I don't hear him. Jaysus! That dog will be the death of me with his carry-on! I'm sick of walking the streets always searching for him. Good! Television it is.

I switched on the television and sat back to watch an old black-and-white film just starting. Lovely!

I leaned forward, munching on a chocolate biscuit, sipping me tea. Jaysus! He's going to kill her! I knew all along he was the neighbourhood strangler. Now he's run outa bodies, he's after the wife! I watched as the poor woman clucked around the kitchen getting his tea ready. She didn't hear him creep in the back kitchen door. Now he's silently making his way towards her with one of her nylon stockings stretched out, gripped between his two hands. The music got more haunting, and the tension was increasing. I held my breath, leaving me mouth open, still waiting for the next bit of me biscuit.

Suddenly, the doorbell rang. I screamed, letting me tea spill all over my skirt. Fuck! What happened? Then the bell rang again. I put the cup and biscuit down on the little table, and went out to see who it was. Bet it's someone dragging that bleedin dog home!

I whipped open the door and stood staring into the face of Sergei. My mouth dropped open. 'Oh! Hello! It's you!' was all I could get out.

He stood staring at me, trying to read my face. 'I have missed you,' he said, stepping into the hall.

'What?' I said, staring up at him, trying to figure out what's happening.

'I am sorry, very sorry. But I was not free to contact you.'

'No! What happened?'

'Please! Let us go inside. Here, take this,' he said, handing me a plastic bag that was heavy. 'Wait, I will put it on the kitchen table,' he said, going in and switching on the light.

I watched as he concentrated his attention on taking out a bottle of vodka and the biggest piece of white cheese I ever saw, wrapped in greaseproof paper. You only see that getting delivered to shops.

'Where did you get that?' was all I could say.

'From the monastery,' he mumbled, still keeping his attention on the bag. 'Here! Take these.' He handed me three boxes of tobacco.

Me eyes lit up. 'Where did you get them, Sergei?' I said, looking at him.

'From my friend, the captain who comes on the cargo ship. Also the vodka,' he said with a shake of his head and shoulder.

He unloaded all the stuff, sitting it on the table, then reached around, taking down two glasses.

I watched as he poured the drinks, then reached to the table, taking a full bottle of tomato juice he just brought.

'Come! We will talk inside,' he said, stepping back to let me go first.

I wandered into the sitting room, seeing the man and woman wrestling on the floor. She was screaming and desperately trying to claw away from him. Fighting for her life. I moved over and switched it off, turning back to look at Sergei.

He handed me the drink without saying a word, then gulped down his own. I watched as he poured another one and sat down.

'Come,' he said quietly, waving his hand for me to sit on the sofa.

I sat down, looking at him, then took a sip of my drink, then another bigger mouthful. It tasted cold, but then the heat hit me, and I sat back to hear what he had to say.

'I am leaving the order!'

I stared at him, seeing his face serious as he clamped his mouth, giving a shake of his head, meaning it's definite.

'You are leaving?' I whispered, taking nothing in but the shock.

'Yes!' he boomed. 'My decision is made. That is why I have not been here. I needed time. Also, a lot of things need to be arranged. I have spoken to my superiors at length. They have agreed to help me. They have offered me a job. I will work in their hospital. It does not matter to them where I go. They will help me. I am going abroad, Martha, and I want you with me!'

Me heart flew, rattling in me chest. I could feel the colour draining out of me. 'What do you mean, go with you, Sergei?'

'I would like to marry you,' he said quietly, staring at me, then letting his eyes drop, staring at his hands making a steeple.

I went into shock, then noticed the drink in me hand and took a huge gulp! I couldn't say a word. Questions flew across my mind, but there were so many, they vanished like the wind.

I reached out, grabbing my tobacco, rolling a cigarette. Then I took huge sucks and gulped on my drink. I felt it warming me, then a haze formed in my mind, relaxing my body, shifting out the shock. I still waited, letting myself drop back against the sofa, saying nothing. Then I heard myself whispering, leaning over to him, 'Why, Sergei? Why do you want to marry me?'

He stared at me, letting me see the gentleness and with it a pain that was coming from the fear of what I might say.

'I love you! You have captured my heart!' he said, sounding as if there was no other explanation.

'But why? When did this happen?'

'I don't know,' he said. 'I know you! You are different. You are crazy with life. It burns in your belly. But you hide it, like a sleeping volcano! I see the wisdom of an old woman in you. Yet your soul holds too many tears. It cries like the terror of a child in the night. I see this. I am drawn to you. I want to waken you! I want our passions joined. I need your softness. I need your fire, your passion! We will drive each other crazy! I am a Russian man. We are patriarchal. I do not want us crazy. So I will not try to tame you! I will lead you. You will lead me! I understand you must not be told. I will not do this! I will be gentle. This is how you listen. So!'

I looked at him, waiting for him to finish. My heart was flying. I wanted to throw my arms around him and sprawl next to him. But my head wouldn't let me do that. So I stared, seeing him look at me with exquisite gentleness. I stared at him, seeing all the vulnerability that was in his soul. He has left himself wide open to me, knowing I could hurt him. I could see it through his incredibly green eyes, and I wondered how someone who could have their pick of any woman with blood flowing through her veins, how is it he could have chosen me?

'I don't know what to say, Sergei,' I said, hearing it come out in a croak.

'No! Say nothing. Do nothing. Of course it is a shock! I could not make my feelings known to you. First, I had to be sure. Then, to be secure with the new direction my life must take. For that, I had to find a job. I do not want you to give me your answer now. Take time. I must return to Russia. I will live in a monastery there until this is all sorted. Then I will take up a new post in Canada. This is what I want. But if you do not like this, then we can choose. The order will help me to go where I decide.'

I lit up another cigarette, not wanting to make eye contact with him. I felt I needed to be on me own and absorb it slowly.

'Sergei,' I said, turning to look at him, then look at me drink, taking a big gulp. 'My feelings for you are very strong. But my mind has closed down.'

'Yes!' he said, standing up and reaching for me.

'Martha,' he whispered, holding my shoulders gently and looking into my eyes. 'I don't want you to feel pressure. I am holding out my heart, offering it to you on the palms of my two open hands. I want you to know this. Then it is you who will decide to take it or not. I can wait. We can speak on the telephone. If necessary, I will go to Canada. You can follow me if you wish. Or I can come back to you, and we can decide our future together.

'I am a patient man, Martha. I have waited this long for you. Now I have found you, I hope you have been waiting for me. We will see.

This is where my path has been taking me all along. You also, I believe. We were destined to meet in the hospital. This is where our paths finally crossed,' he said, lifting his crossed palms and slowly shaking them up and down. 'Now, all that is left for you is to heal. You are finally out of the darkness, Martha. You are safe. God has spared you for a purpose! He is revealing himself to you. You must get used to the bright light. It blinds you. Now you are afraid to believe. But you will slowly trust. Then you will see. Your destiny stares at you!'

Then he sighed, holding out his arms, saying, '*Dorogaya prihodyat ko mne moya lyubov*. Darling, come to me, my love,' as he wrapped his arms gently around me, squeezing me to him. I could feel the softness of his skin as his face brushed mine. Then he pulled away, kissing my hands, saying, 'OK, I must go.'

I walked after him, watching as he opened the door and then stepped out and walked down the path. He stopped at the gate and bowed, putting his open hand to his heart, then waved it at me. Then he was gone. Off into the night. Leaving me staring at the gate, wondering had I fallen asleep.

'No, you are not dreaming, Martha. You are wide awake,' I said, astonished.

58

I stood, staring out the window, seeing the robin pounce on the worm. He took off, heading for the garage roof, then landed, trying to wrestle the big fat worm that was nearly as big as himself. I watched, seeing him make mincemeat of it. Jaysus, what a tenacious little beggar, managing to dig him up even if the ground is frozen solid.

I sighed and turned away, gripping the hot mug of tea, letting it warm my hands. I wish Sergei was here! It would be great to sit here now, talking and having breakfast together. Still, as he said, everything takes time. I'm still not ready yet to take that jump into the unknown.

I heard the letter box rattle. Oh, that must be the postman. More bloody bills. Yeah! But maybe there's a letter from Sergei!

Me heart lifted. I put down the mug and hurried out. One letter. I picked it up and looked at the handwriting. No! Not Sergei! Wonder who this is? Someone writing to me?

I walked back inside and sat down at the dining-room table and lit up a cigarette, then opened the letter. My eyes flew down the page. I could feel me heart stopping, then flying, as my eyes opened wider as I read:

Dearest Martha,
I do hope, when you receive this letter, it will not come, dare I say, as an unpleasant surprise.

Earlier this year, while in Dublin on a short visit, whom should I meet but the sister from your convent. I had no idea of your whereabouts or way of knowing. I was on my way to the airport and actually sitting in the back of a taxi when there she was, walking across the road while I sat waiting for the traffic lights to change. On sudden impulse I told the driver to pull over and bounded after her. I gave the poor woman quite a shock. She was momentarily startled. I introduced myself, asking after you.

It was then I learned about your difficulties. You had poor health, she told me. I was terribly distressed on hearing this. I also learned you have a daughter. How lovely! But it saddened me to hear your marriage was not a success. Oh, but we knew, did we not, dearest one?

Martha, if you would care to contact me – perhaps not! But I would dearly love to hear from you. Do please write. Or you may even telephone me. I have enclosed my phone number. I have only quite recently returned from working abroad. I was a missionary doctor working in the Congo. Yes, medicine! Old loves do not die, my loved one. That, my dear one, is where I have spent the last sixteen years. The same age you were when we first met! Now, I am based in France. Not too far from home.

Do please take care of yourself. I have not forgotten you. You are always in my heart.

My dearest wishes to you.

Ralph Fitzgerald.

Sweet Jesus! Sweet divine Jesus! It's him! Ralph! Ralph Fitzgerald. The only man I have ever truly loved. Writing to me after all these years. The wheel has turned full circle. Now, here he is again. He wrote this letter, his hands were on this paper!

I read the letter again. Then put it down on the table and stared out at the garden, not seeing it. Then I picked up the letter and read it again, very slowly. Word by word, line by line. Trying to work out what each word meant.

Then I got up and walked out to the kitchen, putting the kettle on to get myself a fresh hot mug of tea. I carried it back and sat down, lighting up a cigarette. What does he mean, working as a missionary doctor? Has he left the Church? Maybe he could even be married, I thought, feeling me heart sink.

No! If he was, he wouldn't have written to me. He would never play with people like that. He must still be a priest. But then why is he writing to me? Obviously he knows I am not married. Sister Eleanor told him that. She said the marriage didn't last long. So he would know! Even understand I am vulnerable. I couldn't have him coming into my life just to open up old wounds.

No! I think he may want more from me, for him and me. I don't know. One thing is sure, I have never stopped loving him. Sergei and me, that is different. I could love him, even maybe marry him. I am sure we would be happy together. He is a good man. Very solid. But Ralph! Oh, my God! I would walk to the ends of the earth for him.

Jesus! Right this minute I could phone him. What's the number? I stared at it, seeing the long number. He has even put the access code from Ireland. Yes! He would have thought about that.

I smiled. Seeing the picture of him. Always so precise. So English. So aristocratic! A gentleman to his fingertips. But he is Irish. He will tell you that, quick enough. Ring him, Martha!

My heart flew with excitement. I leapt up and grabbed another cigarette, looking at me hands, seeing them shaking. Oh, my Jesus! I spend me whole life alone. Not one person, really, who cared whether I lived or died. No one to call me own. Except my lovely Sarah. Now, it's a feast! Jaysus! If you were here now, God, and I could get me hands on you, I would give you a kick up the arse, with your bleedin idea of a sense of humour!

Still! Time to think. Take it easy! Calm down. Ring him? What will I say? 'Hello! It's me, Martha.' Then what? He would ask how I am, I would tell him, then ask about him. Then the silence would kick in, leaving a nervous strain. It could end up a disaster, with one or both of us not saying what we really wanted to say.

The strain of the shock. Me hearing from him outa the blue. Then him getting a phone call from me, outa the blue. No! Forget that! Write? No! Same thing could happen. I can't read him. I don't know where he's coming from. He won't be able to read me!

Jesus! What will I do? I need to think about this. Go carefully. OK, I sighed, gathering up the breakfast dishes to start cleaning up.

What about Sergei? Where does this leave you and him? You could hurt him very, very badly. No! There's nothing to talk about. There may be nothing to it with Ralph. Anyway, I am losing the complete run of meself. Who says he's interested? Or, for that matter, it might not be even what I want. There are some things you can't make a decision about, not until you are actually faced with it. I could have changed without knowing it. Ralph and me are not the same people.

An awful lot of water has passed under the bridge since I last saw him. That was a whole lifetime ago!

Yeah, I thought. It might help decide me once and for all whether Sergei and I belong together. I need to think very carefully about this. I don't want to open a can of worms, a bleedin Pandora's box. No! Put it out of your mind for the minute. When in doubt, do nothing. That has always been your motto, Martha. It has served you well.

I fastened the suitcase and picked up my handbag, then looked around, making sure all the windows were locked. I checked the electric switches were off, then pulled the door shut behind me. I locked the porch doors, then headed down the path.

The taxi man jumped out, taking the suitcase off me and landed it in the boot. I sat in the back and he jumped into the driver's seat.

'You're going to the airport?' he said, looking at me through his rear-view mirror.

'Yes, the airport, please. Thanks.'

'Cold aul weather, isn't it?'

'Yes, freezing!' I said, pulling the fur coat around my neck, then stroking it. I felt myself giving a sudden shiver of pleasure. It was the comfort of being so snug and warm, and getting lost in all the lovely softness of it. I let out a big sigh of contentment, thinking, Blondie must have been mad to give this away! Still, she's not exactly depriving herself, not with that lovely new sable she's now floating around in! Gawd! She's a scream.

'Where are you heading off to?'

'France,' I said.

'Very nice!' he said, shaking his head, looking very impressed.

I hope so, I thought, thinking the only way to find out was to go and see Ralph face to face. We can stare at each other in surprise. But I will be there. We will have the time to say whatever it is we want to say to each other. Then I will know. But I am sure of one thing – it is time to have a man in my life.